I Am the Nigerian Nation
1914–2007

NIGERIA'S OWN STORY

I Am the Nigerian Nation: 1914–2007
Nigeria's Own Story

ISBN 978-978-931-966-4

Book and cover design and layout by
Martha Nichols/aMuse Productions®
Bellvue, Colorado, USA

I Am the Nigerian Nation
1914–2007

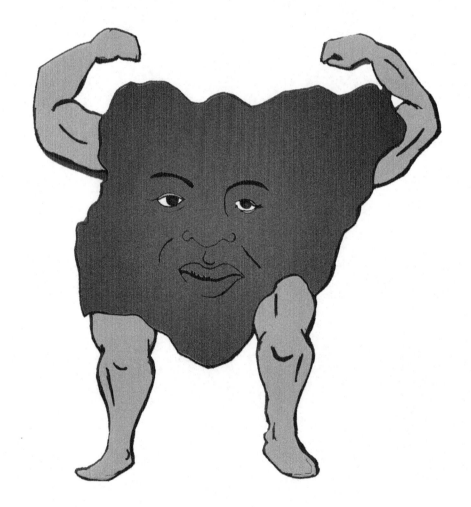

NIGERIA'S OWN STORY

OLUSIJI AWOSIKA

This book is dedicated
to the fond memory of my late brother,

Dr. (Chief) Victor Oloyede Awosika

He was an embodiment of generosity, hard work,
industry, painstaking initiatives, and progressive thinking.
He was a lover and promoter of worthy causes.
He was also a mentor to many and had shown keen interest
in my progress, welfare, and what he considered my 'flair
for writing' during our regular correspondence when
he was abroad and I was in Lagos—and more so
between 1966 and 1981, when I was in various
countries abroad and he was in Lagos.

ABOUT THE AUTHOR

Bankole Olusiji Awosika was born on November 7, 1939, in Ondo. Being the son of late Bishop and Mrs. D. O. Awosika, his growing up years were spent in those places where his father served as Reverend and Canon in Ondo; Archdeacon at Akure; and Bishop both at Benin and finally Ondo. These were in vicarages at Ondo and Akure and at Bishop's Courts in Benin and Ondo.

He was educated at St. Stephen's Primary School, Ondo; Christ's School, Ado Ekiti; Ibadan Grammar School; and the University College of Ibadan (UCI). At Christ's School, he was an all-round athlete, winning both the 'Victor Ludorum' in athletics and school colours and blazer in soccer. He was briefly a teacher and games master at Ise-Emure Grammar School, Ekiti, before joining the Ministry of External Affairs in 1965.

His first posting was to New York at the Nigerian Permanent Mission to the United Nations in 1966. From there he was posted to Cairo at the Nigerian Embassy in Egypt in 1968. He served briefly as Area Officer at the Area Office in Edinburgh in 1973. Posted back to Nigeria in 1975, he was temporarily seconded to the international secretariat of the World Festival of Arts and Culture (FESTAC), which ultimately took place in 1977. His last service posting was to the Nigerian Embassy in Tokyo, Japan in 1977 (1977–1980) as Minister/Counsellor and Head of Chancery. Thereafter, he returned to Nigeria and voluntarily retired into private business, consultancy, and writing in 1981.

ACKNOWLEDGEMENTS

I owe a debt of gratitude in many diverse ways and to a variety of people who have helped in my efforts to bring this exercise to a satisfactory conclusion. There was active collaboration between my children, Banji and Akinyinka, and their lovely wives, Tejumade and Adebomi, who spared no effort in ensuring effective and proactive liaison services between me and the book producer in Colorado, USA. Wole, Temi, and Ebun helped with proofreading, and Kemi 'Kemz' Wole's cheerful wife typed the initial manuscript when I visited them in London.

My nephews, Bayo and Sola Adepetun, facilitated my link up with the National Gallery of Art (NGA) in Abuja through Tolu Ighodalo and Biola Awotedu. The latter introduced me to Mr. Simon Ikpakronyin, who was magnanimous and cooperative in granting the necessary approvals. He was the editor of the National Gallery of Art-commissioned committee which produced the 50th Independence Anniversary Photo Exhibition. This became a veritable source of most of the pictures used in the book. With directives from the Director-General, the hard-working staff of NGA, particularly Mrs. Mma, ably set in motion the great efforts to collate and procure the required photographs. Mr. Jaiyeoba of the Center for African Art and Culture (CBAAC) and Mr. Tajudeen Adetoye of the Library Department of the National Council for Art and Culture rendered ready and helpful assistance with the facilities at their establishments.

My niece, Lola Kolawole, an artist with flair and imagination, produced the sketch of the muscular Nigerian Nation on page 6 with the inset sketch of the 'African Revolver' in which Nigeria sits precariously on the trigger point. She also tried to recapture the unforgettable picture of 'Ojola Ibinu' (the Irascible Python) as depicted by the highly imaginative D. O. Fagunwa, the inimitable Yoruba past master of gripping folklores, as mentioned in the book. My nephew, Mr. Kunle Awosika, who is the Director of Enterprise Business of the Microsoft Office in Nigeria, helped immensely in procuring the graphics according to required specifications.

Tunde Ayo-Vaughan not only introduced me to the book producer but also ably assisted in editing the manuscript. He also offered very useful advice and suggestions. Mr. Tunde Thompson's companionship and brilliant suggestions filled me with confidence and gave me good guidance.

I acknowledge and appreciate the brilliant in-depth analysis of events and ideas gathered from reading some of the much older Nigerian daily newspapers like the *Daily Times*, *West African Pilot and Tribune* and later, *The Punch*, *Vanguard*, *Guardian* and *The Nation*. They were replete with the well-informed contributions and analysis of notable critics and iconic journalists like Abiodun Aloba as 'Ebenezer Williams', Tai Solarin in his 'Thinking with You' column, Lateef Jakande as 'John West', Bisi Onabanjo as 'Aiyekoto' and Sam Amuka as 'Sad Sam'.

Apart from the brilliant analysis of the resourceful columnists, I also acknowledge the name and writing style of Kole Omotoso in his book *Just Before Dawn*. In the book, he adroitly blended fact with fiction to evolve an engrossing first 100 years history of Nigeria. This trend considerably influenced my writing of what is a fac simile of the autobiography of Nigeria in which 'I have made Nigeria to tell Nigeria's own story'. I also read the stimulating book of Nelson Ottah, *Rebels Against Rebels* in which he mentioned certain aspects of the earlier colonial history of Nigeria and described certain activities and trials inside 'Biafra' during the Nigerian Civil war.

I aver without hesitation that the two professors earlier mentioned and some unnamed authors, whose books I read and whose indulgence I sincerely crave for lack of referential details, have been a source of inspiration and information to me. Where some of such references were made, I endeavoured to refer to them with quotation marks in some places.

Finally, and by no means the least, I owe a debt of gratitude to my dear sister, Dr. Keziah Awosika. She continually expressed her interest in what she perceived as my narrative skills from what she saw in my regular correspondence with her, and she egged me on always to put my ideas and thoughts into writing. She literally ran errands for me in search of materials and equipment to ensure the logical and successful conclusion of this book.

TABLE OF CONTENTS

PROLOGUE

This is a conscious effort to make the land mass called Nigeria tell Nigeria's own story. It is a journey down memory lane. It dates back to the era of the Partition of Africa and the subsequent amalgamation of the Northern and Southern British Protectorates in 1914. It is the story of a notion conceived by the colonialists when the Protectorates were merged in 1914. This notion began to take form, aided by the antenatal care and attention of British colonial administrators, missionaries, and traders on the one hand and the existing traditional rulers, local journalists, freedom fighters, and activists on the other. The 'baby' arrived, and Flora Louisa Shaw, soon to be Lord Lugard's wife, gave it the name *Nigeria*.

Nigeria's growing up years witnessed all sorts of activities, trainings, initiations, and struggles, which attained consummation when Nigeria became an independent nation on October 1, 1960. In the overall presentation of this book, I have had to delve pleasantly and deeply into my invaluable experience and exposure to the global panorama at the Nigerian Foreign Service as a career diplomat from 1965 to 1981. I was temporarily seconded to the World Festival of Arts and Culture, known as FESTAC, as a Deputy Director of Protocol at the International Secretariat of the global festival scheduled to take place in 1975. At the inception of Murtala/Obasanjo's regime, the festival was wisely rescheduled to be held in 1977.

Most importantly, I learned about reading and writing post reports from the Ministry of External Affairs. I served in five different missions situated in all the designated major zones of the world where Nigeria had diplomatic missions: America (called the Americas), Africa, Europe, and Asia. I served at the Nigerian Permanent Mission to the United Nations in New York as private secretary to the redoubtable and highly respected Chief S. O. Adebo from 1966 to 1968. It was, at that time, the turn of Nigeria to occupy one of the two rotational African seats at the elitist and prestigious Security Council. That was a very busy and momentous period in U.N. annals. It featured debates on such topical issues as Rhodesia, apartheid South Africa, and the explosive and highly controversial Israeli/Arab Six-Day War in which Israel virtually destroyed all the Egyptian Air Force fighter planes on the ground. It was also during the civil war in Nigeria. Moreover, the divisive effect of the non-physically combatant but frostily ideological Cold War between the West and the East pervaded the atmosphere of the United Nations headquarters.

I was posted to Cairo, Egypt, where I served during the last seventeen months of the Nigerian Civil War (1967–1970). I was the Second Secretary (political). An appropriately designated liaison officer in the Embassy working with top Nigerian Air Force officers was responsible for the training of Nigerian Air Force pilots who came to get acquainted with the handling of Russian fighter jets. This was an exercise carried out under the covert tutorship of Russian-trained Egyptian experts. This was also in order to intensify the efforts to effectively prosecute the then on-going civil war at home. The idea was to ensure that at the peak of the Cold War, Nigeria should not be perceived by the West as procuring any form of assistance directly from the Kremlin, arrowhead of the Eastern Block. Hence, mercurial Abdul Nasser's then-United Arab Republic (UAR) Egypt, an Organization of African Unity (OAU) ally of Nigeria, which was also chummy with Russia, was selected as a neutral ground for the training exercise.

At the end of the war, the Embassy officer was posted back to Lagos in January 1970. On his trip back to Lagos, he had the harrowing experience of the aircraft in which he was travelling being diverted to Ivory Coast. That was one of the few African countries that recognized Biafra. That was also the country in which the Biafran leader, Odumegwu Ojukwu, had taken refuge after his flight from Uli Ihiala 'in search of peace' at the tail end of the war. The officer wondered why, under the circumstances, his plane should be diverted to, of all places, Ivory Coast, which showed sympathy for Biafra during the war and which was then harbouring Ojukwu. He feared that what might be perceived as his assigned role in Cairo might have been known to the other side and that he was being unwittingly lured into the 'lion's den'. Happily, it turned out to be a refuelling stop as he was later made to understand.

I was the political and students' desk officer at the Nigeria High Commission in London (1971–1975). I was temporarily seconded to Edinburgh, Scotland, as area officer in 1973. I returned to Lagos and got seconded as Deputy Director of Protocol for FESTAC (1975–1977).

Finally, I was posted to Tokyo, Japan, where I was the counsellor and Head of Chancery between 1977 and 1980. Part of my schedule of duties included liaison between the Chiyoda Chemical Company in Osaka, Japan and the Nigerian National Oil Corporation, or NNOC, now NNPC. The Japanese company was responsible for building and equipping the Kaduna Oil Refinery, which was the first of its type in Nigeria. About a dozen Nigerian chemical engineers were sent to the company to undergo training in handling the machineries and equipments and to get generally acquainted with the operations in the refinery. This assignment made me aware of the importance of turn-around maintenance of oil refineries as it affects the major revenue generating source for the Nigerian economy. It also underlined the forward-looking planning of the NNOC at the time to adequately train the staff to handle the refinery machineries. One wonders if this facility still exists now that there are four refineries and even more still being contemplated for erection.

When an officer gets posted to a country abroad, his first duty-imposed assignment is to go to the appropriate department of the Ministry or appropriate file in the mission which handles the affairs of the particular country to which he has been posted. This is for the purpose of reading the post report of the country in order to get himself acquainted with its geography, politics, culture, working conditions, cost of living, places of interests, recreational facilities, educational set-up for children, and available places for religious worship. A similar exercise also becomes necessary when an officer gets posted from one mission to another. Post reports of all countries where Nigeria has missions are made available to all our foreign missions. *I Am the Nigerian Nation (1914–2007)* can therefore be seen as a comprehensive 'post report' on Nigeria from the knowledge and experience of a former career diplomat and the Deputy Director of Protocol during the historic World Festival of Art and Culture—FESTAC '77.

FESTAC immeasurably afforded me the opportunity of seeing and knowing Nigeria more intimately. I was posted to the International Secretariat of FESTAC at Ikoyi, Lagos just before the festival was postponed from 1975 to 1977. Chief Anthony Enahoro was the outgoing president of the festival in his capacity as the Federal Commissioner for Information. With his characteristic gusto and panache, he had worked assiduously to lay the groundwork on which the framework of a very successful festival would evolve. I had the privilege of listening to the erudite explanation of his idea of what the cultural fiesta had set out to achieve.

I actively participated in the arrangements of hosting, accommodation, and the evolution of programmes and events encapsulated in the cultural event. The colloquium on black culture afforded me an eye opener and deep insight into various cultural aspects that would attract a lot of attention to African countries and other black countries in the diaspora in general and to Nigeria in particular. I traveled extensively through Africa with the gregarious naval music impresario, Naval Commander Oluwole Bucknor, to raise awareness and assess the state of readiness of participating countries for the international event.

I watched several brilliant dramatic and dance performances on stage or in film documentaries at the magnificent and well-appointed National Theatre at Iganmu, Lagos. Many of these people, places, and events have been mentioned and pictured in this book. I have deliberately created a platform for people to *see* Nigeria first hand. I have beckoned international tourists to come and visit Nigeria, learn about Nigeria, and get acquainted with her rich cultural heritage. The Nigerian Nation is eminently deserving of this type of recognition because of its superlative description as one of the culturally richest countries in the world. While other countries in Africa have between two and four languages, Nigeria has about 400 ethno-linguistic groupings. In terms of the culture of dress and costumes and the colourful nature of what Nigeria displays by way of modes and facilities, no African nation can be compared with it.

I visited several towns and locations in Nigeria which were relevant to the festival events. I saw places of cultural interest. I saw cultural and natural monuments, places, and events which are apparent wherever one goes. I visited some exotic places like the Shere Hills, consisting of the Shere Peak and the Shere Magog; the Idanre hills; Obudu Ranch; Igbo-Ukwu; and the Yankari game reserve. I witnessed the hilarious Ogun Festival in Ondo, the thrilling Eyo Festival in Lagos, the traditional Olojo Festival in Ile-Ife, the colourful Ojude Oba in Ijebu Ode, the Durbar staged in Kaduna during FESTAC, the fiercely competitive Argungu Fishing extravaganza, the all-comers Mmanwu Masquerade Festival, involving over 2,500 masquerades in Awka, and the historic Osun Osogbo Festival. This is therefore an open invitation to the United Nations Educational Scientific and Cultural Organization (UNESCO) to consider conferring appropriate status of World Heritage Site on more of Nigerian cultural events and places. It has already conferred such status on the Osun-Osogbo Grove, courtesy of the pioneering efforts of Susan Wenger, the revered Aduni Olorisa of Osun.

I have painstakingly created a platform for Nigeria to introduce herself briefly to Nigerians who would like to be familiar with their pedigree, heritage, and the builders of their nation. I have drawn the attention of students, researchers, lovers of culture, and tourists who would like to get acquainted with the people, places, music, and cultural events of the country. A much-needed impetus to travel to and within Nigeria has been given. It has given an invaluable tool for not just a traveller but for anyone interested in knowing Nigeria better. Descriptive photographs of what happens in different parts of the country, reflecting the cultures and ways of life have been featured. Using a bird's eye perspective on the issues pertinent to travellers and tourists, I have given succinct descriptions of what to expect as one journeys through the 920,000 square kilometres called Nigeria.

There is an aphorism that says, 'The child is father to the man'. So was it with the entity called Nigeria. Nigeria 'fathered' the children who have now become known as the founding fathers of the nation. Some of them, like the journalists who later became firebrand politicians, were there at the inception and at every juncture as chroniclers and *dramatis personae* at the nation's birth, through its infancy, its exuberant and almost impatient adolescence, and into its vigorous and determined adulthood. They stood on the podium at the juncture and venue of the attainment of independence.

The colonial administrators, in cohort with the Bible-wielding missionaries, were the midwives at birth. They were teachers, administrators, and lawgivers to the nation and her children in the growing-up years. The Colonialists left, and the relics of the Indirect Rule system of government metamorphosed into self-government, which in turn yielded initially to parliamentary democracy.

Thereafter, Nigeria became a Republic. A 30-month civil war ensued with the attendant consequences of military rule and its odious aberrations. States were created. Determined and conscious efforts have since been mounted, leading to the enthronement of Democracy in a civilian setting. The missionaries stayed behind, fanning the embers of religion and education. The vestiges of their efforts abound and are visible all over the terrain of the Nigerian nation.

Herein, Nigeria basks in the brilliant sunshine of achievements and awards garnered by her illustrious sons and daughters. Nigerians became high achievers in all areas of human endeavour. In matters of religion, Christianity and Islam flourished. But deeply ingrained tradition, undernourished by ignorance and illiteracy, still leaves room, however minuscule, for fetishism, voodoo, and animism to engage the interests of adherents and on-lookers.

Celebration participants, spectators, and local and international tourists will begin to see rituals and priests, gods and goddesses as mere dramas and *dramatis personae*. The spectacle will conjure the picture of the rumbustious exuberance of dancers in fancy dress at the famous annual Nottinghill Carnival in London. Nowhere else was this carnival atmosphere more pronounced, trivialised, and exhibited than at the hilarious display of fetishism and voodoo demonstrated by the Haitians during the all-participants closing parade at FESTAC '77 at the National Stadium in Lagos. The blood-curdling and unforgettable picture of some Haitians carrying smoke-filled pots on their heads and chanting gripping incantations assumed the specter of drama and carnival.

As a keen and ardent movie watcher, particularly on television and the African Magic series on DStv, I have watched over 250 'Nollywood' and Yoruba home video movies. This exciting and rewarding exercise has given me an intimate insight into the Nigerian movie industry with special emphasis on Nollywood and Yoruba home video movies. The prodigious and brilliant efforts of some actors, producers, and directors of these movies are highlighted. My interest in these video movies also includes Yoruba films pioneered by the legendary Hubert Ogunde. Other great pioneers of films and movies are Ola Balogun, Eddy Ugboma, and the Tunde Kelani, who is a popular movie and drama genius. I observe that the titles of these movies do not stick into one's memory. But names of actors and actresses are more easily remembered. This has enabled me to compile and mention the names of more than 90 actors and actresses who were featured in some of the video movies I watched and whom are immediately identifiable in any movie.

I also hope that ecumenism may in fact be realized sooner and faster among the various Christian sects in the country. This is because of the fervour and alacrity with which they all embrace the doctrines and the tolerant accommodation they exhibit in the Christian Association of Nigeria (CAN) and the Pentecostal Fellowship of Nigeria (PFN). The crossover mentality of worshipers from one sect to another, particularly the drift from the orthodox churches to the hand-clapping and praise-worshiping newer Pentecostal churches would seem to cement Christian unity in the clamour and adoration for the Almighty God. Modes of worship may differ and doctrines may be subjected to a variety of interpretations, but Jesus Christ is at the heart of Christianity.

CHAPTER ONE

I AM THE NIGERIAN NATION
(1914–2007)

I am the Nation—and I am big. I have been called the Giant in the Sun—the Giant of Africa. My territory sprawls from Lake Chad to the coasts in places like Lagos, Sapele, Warri, Calabar, Yenagoa, Brass, and Port Harcourt, where the Atlantic Ocean kisses the sandy beaches. River Niger flows into my territory from the northwest, while River Benue flows in from the northeast. The two rivers merge into a confluence at Lokoja, forming the letter 'Y', and stream southwards through my south-south areas into the Niger Delta. From there, it breaks into tributaries as the waters meander into the riverine areas of Brass, Bonny, Oron, Warri, and Opobo before emptying into the vast Atlantic Ocean.

I consist of about 924,000 square kilometres of arable land. I measure about 1,200 kilometres from east to west and about 1,050 kilometres from north to south. I am adorned with a mixture of rich farmlands, winding rivers and waterfalls, wooded sandy hills, rocky tors, and gigantic and solid rocks and boulders. My land mass ranges from lowlands along the coast and in the lower Niger valley to high plateaus in the north and mountains along the eastern border. Much of my land mass is also crossed by productive rivers.

I share a common border with the Republic of Benin to the west. The republics of Chad and Niger lie across my northern borders. All my borders are so porous that frequent incursions and infiltrations by unauthorized aliens and rampaging marauders into my northern villages are common occurrences. I once had to make the unilateral decision to close my shared border with the Republic of

Benin on the west to stem the tide of unfettered border-crossing brigands and car thieves. It was also meant to curb the excesses of some corrupt Customs officials on both sides of the border. Such is the proximity of these border states that I had to enter into a negotiated bilateral arrangement with each of them in the Chad Basin Agreement concerning the yet-undetermined natural wealth of Lake Chad.

The Republic of Cameroon is to my east with a proximity that is almost too tight for comfort despite our previous childhood cohabitation. The Atlantic Ocean is to the south, and the coastline, which extends across my base for about 853 kilometres, is marked by a series of sand bars backed by lagoons of brackish water and creeks that support the growth of mangroves and swampy forests.

The west is characterized by rugged Yoruba highlands. Orosun Rock of Idanre stands in perpendicular majesty, kissing the sky in misty ecstasy. Oke Idanre hills are a marvelous tourist attraction. Idanre is divided into an ancient town at the hilltop and the new settlement at the foot of the hills. The natural monument is steep-sided, smooth, and dome-shaped. Six hundred forty steps have been carved out to the top of the hill. Five resting posts are located along the steps where one can rest, relax, and view the spectacular scenery. At Oke-Idanre, one can also see other monumental attractions, including Arun River, the Wonderful Mat, the Aghagha Hill, Agbogun Foot Print, the Ancient Palace, and the Ark of Noah among others.

The historical Olumo Rock is a massive outcrop of granite rocks of pristine formation from which Abeokuta derives its name. Myth and mystery surround the rock and the tree, which has grown on top of it for over 200 years. Olumo Rock is a historic monument that served as a shelter and fortress for the Egba people during the Yoruba intercity wars. By 1830, the main body of my Egba people had already settled at the site of the Olumo and the refuge provided by the rock marked the end of their wanderings and struggles for existence. Since then, they regard Olumo Rock as their protection and shrine and a monument of faith in unity. They see it as a source of strength and unfailing protection and as sustenance from the Supreme Being who led their ancestors safely through the perplexities of life to Abeokuta.

The rocks roll down with soothing dignity as a haven and as an ennobling source of pride that inspires my Egba sons and daughters to sing thus in praise of the Olumo Rock:

> On the heights and in the valleys,
> Atop Olumo Rock,
> It was there I was born,
> In the land of freedom,
> I feel elated and full of praises,
> I will rejoice and be glad
> Atop Olumo Rock.

The Igele Hill is in the heart of Ikerre, Ekiti. It is made up of an undulating mass of rocks that concedes size and height to the gigantic Olosunta. The massive, concave, smooth Olosunta rock thrusts and reaches to the skies as if it is in an eternal commune with some heavenly bodies. Still in Ikerre is the Oroole, which is a cluster of four rocks, one of which looks like an inverted huge pot. 'O gb'ota l'ota' is the name of the place in which, as the Ondo dialectal meaning of the name implies, 'one big rock sits pert and precariously on top of another' in Ondo, where wooded forests grow on top of several hills that surround the town.

To the north of the Niger valley are the high plains of Hausa Land with relatively low topography with isolated granite outcroppings averaging 800 meters above sea level. The Mambilla plateau is a placid holiday resort that is a gently rising tableland covered with green grass. The vegetation is of luscious verdancy, and the climatic condition is very cool and temperate. The array of plateaus and the splendid background scenery is a photographer's delight in their spectacular beauty. The shapes and sizes of the houses there are unique. Chimneys jutting out on top of many houses attest to the presence and use of fireplaces in such homes. Temperatures often dip below zero degrees Celsius as if it were a European setting. Cattle and livestock here are some of the very best that could be found anywhere.

The enchanting size and beauty of the Rock in Song, along Yola-Muibi road in Adamawa area, is simply spectacular viewed against its rustic and virgin background. If as mentioned earlier, the rocks of Song are spectacular, the gigantic rocks between Bauchi and Yola, further away from Jos and Kuru, are sometime nondescript or grotesque and at the same time stately and majestic, tapering out in hideous and funny masks. To the northeast, the plains of Hausa Land grade into the basin of Lake Chad. The area is characterized by lower elevation, level terrain, and sandy soil. Then the high plains descend into the Sokoto lowlands in the northwest.

The Udi Hills, pregnant with coal, jut out menacingly to drivers who approach or descend reverently and with extra caution for fear of the risk of somersaulting into the yawning depths below. The Adamawa Mountain is very imposing and so are the northern central highlands and the woody western highlands. The Kukuruku Hills are a series of wooded rolling hills. The Zuma Rock stands boldly erect with visible presence, welcoming visitors into my new capital city, Abuja. It looks as if nature has permanently etched on it what looks like eyes and a mouth. Aso Rocks, also in the Asokoro area of Abuja, are a series of huge boulders which stand like sentinels guarding the presidential residence from which its name, Aso Rock Villa, was derived.

Major rivers, springs, brooks, and rivulets traverse my vast terrains. My name was formed around River Niger crossed symbolically by River Benue at their confluence at Lokoja where, when the intrepid explorer Mungo Park made a momentous rendezvous with history through the discovery, 'two rivers become confluent one with the other and the man met the hour'. The lagoon has made an island of Lagos from which that state derives its name. Rivers Ogun, Imo, Anambra, Oshun, Gongola, Yobe, Kaduna, Adamawa, Taraba, and Cross also became natural delineating boundaries to the ever-increasing number of states that were created within me.

These rivers were used in the olden days as waterways and canals for trips and for ferrying timber to the coast for exportation. Myriads of fishermen dotted the rivers and the lagoon in their fishing canoes. In the evenings, one heard the sound of pestles pounding yams in mortars for supper. One could also smell the aromas of fish broth and bush meat delicacies being prepared for farmers returning from their fields and fishermen home at sundown. My lands throbbed with farms and the rural dwellers who were dependent on the products of their farms for subsistence and livelihood. Excess products used to be carried on the head—or, later, in motor trucks—to nearby or distant market towns for sale.

The bloodlines of the black race run strong in my veins, because I hold one out of every five black persons on planet Earth. About 160 million souls live under my protection alongside the ghosts of millions who lived and died for me. A suggestive line that featured prominently in my previous national anthem kept reminding my citizenry that 'though tribes and tongues may differ, in brotherhood we stand'. The implication of this line is permanently relevant. After all, I am home to more than 250 tribes of distinctly different tongues. I am painfully aware that linguistic differences could become a roadblock to unity and cohesion. The Hausa language is as different from the Igbo language as both are different from the Swahili language in southern Africa. The Yoruba language is as different from the Ijaw language as both are different from each of the afore-mentioned tribes and tongues in all other countries south of the Sahara. In fact, there are even different dialects of the same language: for example, the Owo man and the Egba man, both Yorubas, speak the same Yoruba language but in distinctly different dialects, accents, and intonations. The same dialectal differ-ences are also noticeable among my Igbo-speaking peoples of the eastern and delta states.

My name is *Nigeria*. Flora Lugard mooted my name to the amorous listening ears of Lord Lugard as they both contemplated the serene beauty and signifi-cance of the area around the confluence of Rivers Niger and Benue. My name was thus spun around the Niger area. The name *Nigeria* appealed to Lugard. He recommended it to his home government to describe the territories under the control of the Royal Niger Company.

The Republic of Cameroon to the east was formerly closely interwoven with my territory when the Colonialists grouped us together. We soon broke apart as I carried along with me the Sardauna Province after a plebiscite. I recall that a Cameroonian, Solomon Tay, was in my pre-Independence cabinet of federal ministers. The colonial powers sat around a conference table at the Berlin Con-ference in 1865 and in their voracious and acquisitive wisdom, figuratively drew out their long knives and carved Africa into various areas of commercial and exploitative interests. My territory became the prize allotted to the British colonial power.

The ravages and vestiges of colonialism as manifested in the Partition of Af-rica still haunt and confront me. The disputed Bakasi Peninsula became a bone of contention over which Cameroon dragged me to the Court of Arbitration at the International Court of Justice (ICJ) at The Hague. The verdict was in favour of Cameroon. I have had to cede the territory to Cameroon, much to the displeasure and chagrin of my citizens who had lived in that area for ages and had become trapped in the web of international politics. They now claim, with touching persistence and nostalgia, that they and their forefathers before them have always been part of my territory.

When the map of Africa is turned sideways, it looks eerily similar to a cocked revolver, and I occupy the menacing position of its trigger. Indeed I *am* the trigger of the seeming 'African revolver'. I am filled with fear, trepidation, and apprehension, and yet poised to be pulled, because of the revolver's explosive contents of ethnic nationalities, diverse languages, and different cultures. As in the biblical Tower of Babel, the rather combustive equation between the adherents of the Christian and Islamic religions may become implosive. This explains the aversion of my National Population Census Authority to assign which religion has the larger number of adherents. The attendant claims and counter-claims in terms of numerical superiority might be triggered into an uncontrollable explosion.

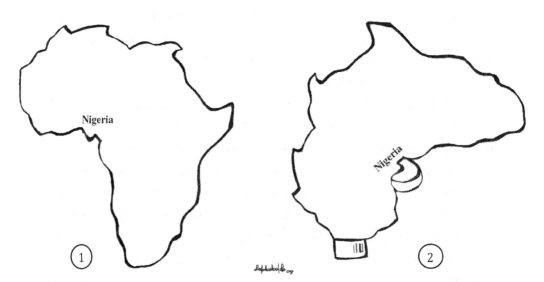

1—*The African Revolver, with Nigeria sitting pert and precariously on the "trigger position"—strategic, full of initiative, explosive; and* **2—raring to go off** *at the slightest pull by any of its handlers.*

As the strategic trigger point on this imaginary revolver, I would rather caution against firing or even what has been derisively referred to, in another milieu, as 'accidental discharge' or 'stray bullets'. I was afraid of being pulled from the way I had been handled and am still being handled by generations of nation builders—journalists, politicians, lawyers, soldiers, educationists and nouveau riche businessmen. I am sensitive, commanding authority and respect because of my vast size and abundant human and natural resources. I could become lethal and awesome because occasionally, when I am mishandled, I can give vent to a roar like that of a rampaging lion, making the smaller animals scamper for safety while the reverberations go round the world.

This would seem to explain the fear, alarm, caution, and reluctance with which the super powers viewed the possibility of my disintegration during my civil war that convulsed me from 1967 to 1970. These factors threatened rack and ruin to my internal peace and stability in the late 1960s. This may be in the form of genocide, famine, or refugee problems. Indeed, smaller countries, those dependent on my largesse and receivers of my financial aid or technical assistance, would have to take cover when I roar. I could squeeze them into submission through the withdrawal of aid and through economic strangulation by closing my borders. I could choose to look the other way when my requested and needed intervention might solve their internal problems. I may become choosey or selective in readily volunteering my military monitoring services to war-ravaged countries that may need my peace-seeking supervisory role. I could make my petroleum products unavailable even at prohibitive prices. Worse still, I could disrupt the services rendered by River Niger and the gigantic Niger Dam.

My vast terrain spans five types of vegetation zones. Some of these are the deciduous mangrove and evergreen forests where cash crops like cocoa, rubber, timber, and palm trees are cultivated. I am endowed with the low-lying, undulating fertile lands around Katsina-Ala River; the Savanna shrubs with the occasional lone baobab tree; the cocoa plantations of the old West; the yam farms of Abakaliki and Gboko environs; and the cassava plantations which grow all year round providing the staple food —gari. Indeed, cassava tubers are now heavily in demand as raw materials in the factories of some Far Eastern countries. There is the Mambila Plateau with tea ridges and verdant plains. I also have the Benue fertile lands that serve as the breadbasket to all, ensuring regular and abundant supply of food.

In some places, festering erosions have lacerated my features, exposing yawning gullies and deep ravines, leaving fissures into which, in a few cases, foamy waters splash in roaring torrents and furious winds whistle through. Erosions have become a bane to agriculture and a great promoter of urbanization, which causes families to relocate and makes able-bodied young people gravitate towards the cities in search of greener pastures and 'level ground'. The erosion has destroyed soil nutrients and rendered agriculture practically impossible. Every occurrence of erosion—an estimated 2,000 of them—hasbecome an ever-expanding monster that leaves tales of horror and devastation in its wake.

Indeed, disaster was providentially averted in 1983, when Shehu Shagari, one of my former Presidents, visited a site well known for incidents of erosions. The ground on which he had stood only a few minutes earlier to deliver his speech sank into a gully after he had walked away on his way back. He allegedly quivered with alarm when he was called over to see the fate that would have befallen him if he and his entourage had not left the scene when they did. To his credit, he instantly arranged the award of a contract for the construction of drainage parallel to the gully to minimize the surge and inflow of water. It was meant to be a provisional action, but it was denied a permanent solution as the military struck to terminate Shagari's regime.

In the north, my fringes and borders recede into the desert that encroaches at an alarming rate into my territory. This has forced me to resort to planting trees as windbreaks. The scorching heat of the sun has caked up the once sandy fringes of Lake Chad, which is fast drying up. It is only by the combined efforts of my neighbors and me that desert encroachment can be curtailed so that food and fodder may be provided for cattle which depend on grass that once grew for food in the area.

The drawing of a palm tree was once etched on the flip side to adorn my old 10 Kobo coin. Palm trees are a common feature of the rain forests. The palm tree from its roots to its leaves and fronds is a well-endowed tree. Palm leaves are used for roof thatching. Broomsticks are also made from the leaves. Palm oil is extracted from the oily red fruits. Vegetable oil and pomades are derived from its crushed kernels. Palm wine is tapped from its juicy top. The hard and dried kernel pods are used to stoke the blacksmith's furnace. The leaves and fronds are commemorative items of the triumphal entry of Jesus into Jerusalem as used by Christians on Palm Sundays. The leaves become 'swords' in the hands of the adherents of the Celestial Church of Christ sect. Worshippers of Ogun (god of iron) wear leaves in the form of knitted skirts during their festivals; the masqueraders habitually wear it as the paraphernalia of their cult.

The ubiquitous mango trees seasonally produce mouth-watering fruits. Groundnuts, also known as peanuts, used to be a dependable source of income for me before the advent of crude oil. In my ancient city of Kano, thousands of bags filled with groundnuts would be arranged in pyramidal shapes and prepared for shipment to distant lands. Latter-day agitators for equitable sharing of revenues derived from oil-producing areas are always quick to argue that previous revenues, generated from the sales of products like groundnuts, cocoa, and

1—Groundnut bags are built into pyramidal shapes in the North ready for exportation or for local use.
2—Palmnuts are harvested from the East.

Cocoa is harvested from the West for both exportation and local raw materials.

rubber, had been used to explore and tap the crude oil that literally gushed out then as it does even now from the entrails of the riverine soils of the Niger/Delta environs.

Cottons, soy beans, millet, and sorghum—which were useful foreign exchange earners—grow on the Savannah plains. In many places inside my leafy jungles are *trado*-medicinal (traditional) herbs that can be extracted from a variety of leaves, buds, flowers, barks, and roots of trees that abound on my vast terrain. Someday, somehow, it is hoped that with rapidly advancing technology, the fluids and balms extracted from roots, leaves, fruits, trees, and barks of trees will go a long way in facilitating the successful discovery for the cure of malignant ailments that have hitherto defied all attempts and researches in modern medicine.

A couple of years before I attained independence in 1960, the economy-sustaining crude oil, sometimes referred to as 'black gold', was discovered in large commercial quantities. In the oil fields—first at Oloibiri, then in places like Brass, Ogoni, Escravos, Calabar, and later in Ilaje Ese-Odo—substantial quantities were found. Prospecting for crude oil by multinationals could be traced as far back as 1937. Shell's lucky discovery was made on June 10, 1956, at Oloibiri and the first shipload of exportable crude oil took place in 1958. These discoveries have ensured my enviable position among the league of oil-producing nations, and I now produce about 2.8 million barrels of crude oil per day. Giant refineries interconnected by thousands of kilometres of pipelines link Port Harcourt and Warri with Kaduna. These pipelines feed refined petrol into large and cavernous depots located in several places to facilitate storage and equitable distribution to oil marketers. Oil exploration boosted my economy as I continued to earn billions of dollars in oil revenue.

Vigorous exploration activities by the foreign oil companies have undeniably left my Niger Delta areas denuded in sheer environmental degradation. Farming and fishing were the lifeline of my rural dwellers in that area but have now become practically impossible as a result of chemical pollution of both land and rivers. The place now looks ravaged, sucked dry, thrown away, and forgotten like sweet orange. The restless youths and displaced landowners of the Niger Delta areas have resorted, in protest, to the vandalisation of pipelines, brigandage, and kidnapping of foreign and local oil workers. People now wallow in abject poverty in those very places which provide the greatest revenue-earning item for me as a Nation.

I am literally bursting at my terrestrial seams with trillions of liters of gas. Such is the volume of excess gas being wasted in the process of exploration that

The site in Oloibiri where crude oil was discovered in 1956.

the sight of gas flaring is commonplace in the affected areas, particularly from an aerial view. This also constitutes, to a large extent, a grave occupational health hazard and avoidable environmental degradation. I am agog with excitement at the prospects and possibilities of the fulfillment and actualization of my dreams of financial gains and prosperity that would accrue from the Liquefied Natural Gas (LNG) project. This would be a valuable source of internally generated revenue for me.

Priceless mineral deposits lay buried within my subterranean entrails. Some of these minerals have been explored and tapped; some still remain hidden beneath the earth. The coal mines of Enugu; the tin mines of Jos; the gypsum deposits in Yobe, Sokoto, Adamawa, and Bauchi states; the Igbeti marble deposits; the iron ore deposits at Aladja and Ajaokuta; and the large deposits of gold in Ilesha and Zamfara State all combine to assure my steady march through the technological dreamland which the emerging twenty-first century portends and will open. Furthermore, bauxite, chalk, and manganese deposits have been discovered in large quantities in some areas.

It is common knowledge that uranium deposits in my northern parts have attracted the envy and belligerence of some countries near those areas. Some of these countries share geological bed structures with me. Their colonial masters egg them on to dispute the ownership of the areas concerned. Bitumen deposits literally ooze out of the earth, forming tiny tarry rings on the river at Loda (Tarry Town) in Ilaje near Okitipupa in Ondo State. Bitumen that jets out from my territorial stomach does so from yet untapped deposits that would rank me in the same league as Canada and Venezuela as major world producers of bitumen.

Nature is always generous in terms of my climate. In comparison with other lands, I do not suffer the extremities of weather conditions. Snow, with its attendant degree of cold and harshness, is almost completely alien to me. My nearness to the equator guarantees abundant sunshine all year round. Daytime is a little bit longer than nighttime. The latter is long enough to ensure long hours of healthy sleep-inducing hours of darkness. The two marked seasons are the dry and rainy seasons. Dwellers in cold climates in anticipation of sunshine and warmth would yearn for the season longingly by singing, 'When winter goes shall spring be far behind?' In my own climatic conditions, it is always 'tale under the moonlight' and sunshine all year round. When it rains, the song is,

'Rain, rain, go away, come again another day, little children want to play'. Rains quickly give way to invigorating sunshine, bringing life to both man and nature.

My warm climate makes the beaches and parks beckon throughout the year. Humidity is influenced by the surrounding rivers and airy spaces. In some places like the highlands of Jos, Sokoto, Maiduguri, Kano, Kaduna Katsina, and those cities that share proximity with the Sahara desert, cold and dust-carrying winds hang in the hazy harmattan air between October and February, causing the body to shiver and turn brownish white.

Rainfall is a soothing sound to the ears of farmers and people who live in the farming areas. It brings growth and sustenance to crops and makes drinking water available by swelling the springs and brooks, particularly in the rural areas. Sunshine brings smiles to the faces of cocoa farmers when the sun helps to dry their seeds ready for grading and transportation to designated depots for food manufacturers, and to the ports from where they are exported abroad to countries overseas. Lumber jacks relish sunshine as it makes firmer the marshy terrains on which they pulled felled timber logs during the rainy season. Furthermore, sunshine attracts holidaymakers and revelers to the beaches and lures tourists to various Holiday Resorts.

MERGER: SOUTHERN AND NORTHERN PROTECTORATES

I am the child of an amalgamation or, better still, of a negotiated marriage of convenience, contrived and brokered by the scheming indomitable brain of Lord Frederick Lugard, acting as the administrative emissary of Great Britain. The scramble for Africa had culminated in the Partition of Africa, and both sides of the River Niger became the prize allotted to Great Britain. Thus, the Protectorates on both sides, north and south, of River Niger were merged together to produce the geographical 'child' called the British Protectorate of Nigeria.

Incidentally, in one of his famous diatribes on this merger, one of my revered founding fathers, the sage Obafemi Awolowo—popularly referred to as 'Awo'—described it as a 'geographical expression'. Awo had in mind the heterogeneous nature and cultural diversity among my various tribes and tongues. Sagacious and forward-looking Awo had foreseen the emergence of a state that

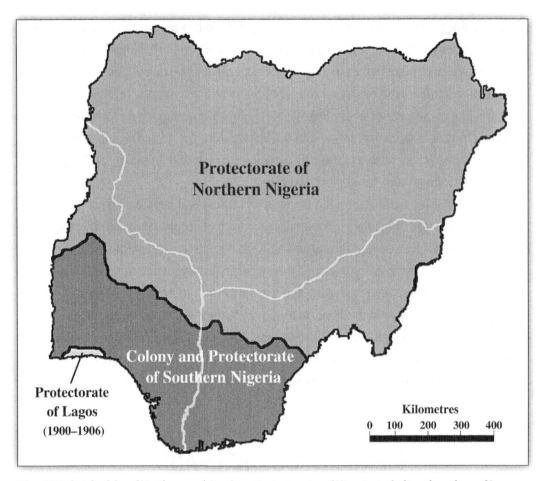

The 1914 sketch of the of Northern and Southern Protectorates of Nigeria, including the colony of Lagos..

would be difficult to classify. Would it be a Unitary System of government or a Confederation of States? Was it meant to be a permanent proposal or a transient arrangement? Time would surely tell, as this trend of thinking would engage the continuous and often acrimonious debates of scholars, historians, and a succession of seemingly interminable constitution drafting or amendment conferences.

When Britain arrived, it met separate tribes, cultural groups, and communities who had established their local authorities spanning centuries. The colonialists recognized the fact that they were bringing enemy tribes together into one union. Consequently, they opted for indirect rule in my northern territory

Frederick Lugard, the first Governor General (1900–1919), merged the two protectorates into an amalgam which became known as the Protectorate of Nigeria.

and left my southern territory to operate in the direct colonial governance. This misguided malformation would be seen to have come about by the force of conquest and domination. One of my former colonial governors, Hugh Clifford, said after my amalgamation that I was 'a mere collection of self-contained and mutually independent native states separated from one another by great distances, by differences of history and traditions and by ethnological, racial, tribal, political, social and religious barriers'. Indeed, the cerebral Zik, who later became my first indigenous Governor General, declared that he supported the views of American Justice Salmon P. Chase to the effect that nations 'grew out of common origin, mutual sympathies, kindred principles, similar interests, and geographical relations'. Zik averred with harrowing and telling finality that 'of the aforementioned factors, the only factor that is applicable to me as a territory is geo-political relations'.

Before the 1914 amalgamation, the colonial administration of my Northern Region was financed from the British treasury. My Southern Region was financially self-sufficient and viable; the north was poor and not economically viable. It became increasingly apparent that Britain was unwilling to educate or develop the north. Viewed from hindsight, it was clear that the British commercial and colonial interests influenced the conclusion that to educate the north might lead to the total loss of the two sides of the proposed amalgamation. This was a deliberate and retrogressive step that was selfishly contrived and myopic in execution.

Lugard was the greatest advocate of that policy. It became apparent that Britain was acting from a script written by Lugard. In his report to the British Parliament in 1901 and 1902, he stated that the Fulani people at that time were not good enough to govern 'having recently conquered the Hausas who did not like them'. But then he went ahead to mention that 'their sons and their sons' sons would be very good for roles if they would work with the British'. This was to presage the fact that the Hausas and the Fulanis would continue to rule me as a territorial unit.

It has been said that Lugard's policies in the north were disastrous. Instead of administering 'things' and developing 'service', he had been preoccupied with the widespread extension of rule over 'people'. It became apparent that the colonial authorities in Britain wanted to rectify the mistake they thought they had made in India. They believed that they mis-handled the Indian situation, which enabled Gandhi to emerge as the leader and sole voice for the whole of India. Lugard's first assignment was in India. Then his expertise was transferred, first to East Africa and then to my territory in 1888.

Thus, when I was being structured, Britain knew exactly what she wanted: the studious avoidance of the seeming 'Indian mistake'. Briefly put, the colonialists did not want me 'in one whole' as had happened in India. They strove to split me into three parts: north, west, and east. That was the trap into which my illustrious founding fathers—the indefatigable trio of Azikiwe, Sardauna, and Awolowo—fell. Thus, the singular voice of Ghandi in India contrasted sharply with the cacophony of discordant voices from three regional premiers within my territory.

The gestation period of the amalgamation lasted for almost half a century: between 1914 and 1960. It spanned the tenures of various colonial governors from Lugard through Richards to Robertson. To nurture the fetus, several energizing pills and soothing ointments in form of trade, spiritual balms, and tablets by way of evangelism and education were used in its antenatal care. Civil servants and merchants came in droves from their 'home country'. They met a system of administration that needed to be harnessed and coordinated. They also met a vast terrain of virgin land and myriads of people on whom they exercised their patronizing authority as a colonizing power.

They used their missionary zeal to introduce Christianity to my people. They found in my size an immense source of raw materials and farm products for the fledgling Industrial Revolution factories at 'home' and elsewhere overseas. They also met a large market full of prospects, in terms of size and population, as a consumer outlet for finished products from these factories. The dual roles of procuring raw materials and selling finished products became the responsibility of the versatile United African Company (UAC) that became a veritable commercial instrument in the hands of the colonial rulers.

The new amalgamation witnessed two types of administrations at inception. This led to the establishment of two legislative bodies and the enactment of two different laws. The southern provinces quickly imbibed Western education and culture. My northern provinces welcomed and embraced the Islamic and Middle Eastern education and cultures. This method of government made the south look westwards and the north look eastwards for orientation and emulation. This confusing and back-to-back growth was a classic example of what came about to be known as the 'divide and rule' system.

The colonialists met the Emirs in the north and the Obas in the west. They then called some of the rulers they met in the east across the Niger, the Obis. The concept of warrant chiefs originated from my Eastern Region, where the colonial administrators, exhibiting crass ignorance of the people's culture, hand-picked their surrogates as chiefs to administer the area in conformity with their indirect rule system. Predictably, the colonialists ran into a solid cultural brick wall as the people vehemently resented and agitated against such imposition. This culminated quite explicably into the tumultuous Aba women's riot of 1945. The success of the British colonialists in establishing the Indirect Rule system in East Africa and my Northern Region encouraged them to want to foist a similar system on my Yoruba Obas by making them to perform like my Sultan and Emirs of the North. But just like it happened in the East, they similarly met a brick wall in the indigenous political system rooted on the principle of checks and balances.

In the 1914 Amalgamation, I became known as the British Protectorate of Nigeria. It was a long period of experimentation in colonial administration. My latter generations of rulers were to call such an experiment a 'continuous learning process'. Through a curious interplay of the activities of administrators, missionaries, and merchants on the one hand and the existing traditional systems on the other, a variety of systems and regimes evolved. The returnee slaves landed on the coastal areas and were known as creoles (kiriyos). They formed the nucleus of the educated natives who worked as civil servants and teachers under the colonialists. They cloistered around the area that thus became known as the Aguda Quarters in Lagos where the Brazilian influence was predominant. This was reflected in their brand of architecture and culture and their heavy leaning towards the Roman Catholic religion. Their descendants attest to this in the names their sons and daughters still bear: Damazio, Domingo, Dorego, Fernandez, Gonzalo, Machado, Carena, Vera Cruz, Pereira, and Pedro. Some of the returnees also moved to Abeokuta, Calabar, and Port Harcourt.

Ajayi Crowther and Othman Dan Fodio had come earlier with two different types of missionaries. The first group of missionaries held the Bible as their weapon and evangelized my people from the coast to the hinterland. The other group had long held the Koran and threatened a Jihad from the caliphate to the coast. When the colonialists used the Christian missionaries to capture souls for their brand of religion, they also used the civil servants, teachers and merchants to administer, educate and teach the people and to tap their resources. The system of 'divide and rule' gave way to 'indirect rule' through token devolution of powers to the native authorities and finally through universal adult suffrage and electoral college systems into the larger regional houses of assembly. Earlier on, some eminent personalities among the people had been handpicked rather selectively to serve in the legislative assembly at the colonial headquarters in Lagos.

CONSTITUTIONAL CONFERENCES

My birth as a Nation was preceded and heralded by a spate of constitutional conferences which took place at the popular Lancaster House in London—the popular arena of most of such discussions in those days. It was a forum in which independence was bargained for between the colonial administrators and the colonized people from distant territories. Constitution-making process engaged the attention of my citizenry for more than three quarters of a century. It spanned the years between 1922 and 1999. The pre-Independence conferences were held in London and, of course, the post-independence ones were held within my territory. These repetitive exercises engaged their attention on about ten different occasions. This may be reflective of the atmosphere of instability and the insatiable yearning for change by all my peoples. This yearning can only be equally matched by their desire for true democracy, unrestrained and unfettered by military interventions.

The aberration of the 'half-man-half-beast centaur' type of government is known as *diarchy*. Under this system the military 'payers' invited the civilian 'pipers' and dictated the tunes the pipers would play and to which they would dance in the name of participatory administration. This mockery of a system, like in an unlikely symphony orchestral setting, was conducted, baton in hand, by the military using fiats, edicts, decrees, and authoritarian pronouncements. There would be no debates, no deliberations or consultations, and no questions asked by the people. Yet these orders and pronouncements were always to be carried out with 'immediate and automatic effect', which was the war cry and instantaneous order of one of the military regimes.

This was the very antithesis of the type of administration and ideology I craved for. Decrees and edicts gagged, stifled, and killed my peoples' initiative. My search, which led repeatedly to Lancaster House in London, was initially for discussions on how I would like to be governed along the lines of parliamentary democracy. After all, I had been spoon-fed and weaned on this menu and recipe for almost fifty years before my independence.

It was a different story altogether under the various military regimes that ruled me for about thirty years after I achieved independence. There was no doubt that the military rulers meant well. What was questionable was their ability to arrange such conferences in an atmosphere devoid of fear, suspicion, and coercion. It soon became apparent that they were inadequately prepared in terms of knowledge and background to manage affairs at such conferences. They fell into the mistakes of the past by hand-picking delegates who, in some cases, were their cronies and sycophants. They pronounced 'no-go' areas; they deliberated over the submissions of such committees in their superior military councils, expunging, keeping, and adding some details as suited their caprices. Of course, they controlled the purse strings.

Let me trace briefly from the beginning the course and the chequered saga of constitution-making from the time of the epochal 1914 Amalgamation. The first of such exercises was in 1922, when the Clifford Constitution made its debut and signaled the seemingly endless search for a solid and viable system of government. It had as its main feature a 46-member legislative council. Barely 10 of my people were selected to legislate and direct affairs, and then, only for Lagos and the southern provinces. This idea was very restrictive, and it was mere tokenism.

The Richards Constitution of 1946 came next. Provision was made for the creation of an executive council. Central Legislative Council was established, comprising nine from the north, six from the west and five from the east. This particular constitution brought the north for the first time within the ambit of the legislative council. One of the most significant provisions of this constitution was the establishment of regional councils consisting of a House of Chiefs and a House of Assembly without legislative powers.

The idea became mired in controversy because not only were the people *not* consulted but also the seed of discontent and perennial discord was sewn with four particularly obnoxious policies. These concerned mineral ordinance, public land acquisition, crown lands amendment ordinance, and the appointment and deposition of chiefs amendment ordinances. The people were made to look like eunuchs, shorn of their maturity and denied every opportunity to manage and control their wealth, their lands, and the choice of their leaders and rulers.

The Macpherson Constitution of 1951 was a landmark document for my political evolution and development. Eminent personalities from the individual regions were selected rather arbitrarily to participate in the drafting of the constitution. This particular constitution raised the bogey of the claims of numerical superiority between the north and the south. The north's fear of perceived southern domination reared its ugly head. There was no doubt that the colonialists precipitated the genesis of the numerical superiority of the north over the south. The contention still rages on almost uncontrollably, defying the prescriptive solutions of census after census. Of course, deliberate manipulations became the bane of such exercises.

The Macpherson Constitution also carved my terrain out into 22 provinces, with each being dependent on its Region of origin. This was the first time that my people would actively participate in their own governance. It was the first time that the issue of the status of Lagos as the Federal Capital became controversial in the consideration of revenue generation and revenue allocation. Quite remarkably also, there were no prior elections. The participants were handpicked and not representative of the people's interests.

The Lyttleton Constitutional Conference was held in London in 1954. Six representatives attended the Constitutional Conference from each of my three regions and Cameroon. The constitution, for the first time, adopted the Federal system of government. The police was brought under federal control. Lagos was separated from the west. In 1956, self-government was granted to deserving regions that earnestly asked for it. The constitution provided for a central council of 20 ministers made up of three from each region, one from Cameroon and the rest appointed by the Governor General. The post of the Prime Minister was not yet created at this point in time.

The Independence Constitution of 1960 was preceded by its initial deliberations which took place in London in 1957. It established a bicameral legislature of elected house of representatives and a nominated senate. The major drawback that rubbed the shine off the earlier exercises repeated itself in that it was drawn up by people who were not popularly elected. It was sheer tokenism again from a constituent body without adequate representation.

The Republican Constitution of 1963 was unique in many ways. It was the first of its type in my post-independent era. It signified the end and the severance of my old links with my colonial masters. The period between 1960 and 1963 had been characterized by the emergence of the incomparable Zik, first as the president of senate and later as the governor general, resplendently clad in the white English uniform during the annual Independence Day parade. This became a paradox, considering that Zik was well known in his native attire and black fez cap, which he habitually donned in those heady days of activist struggle during the clamour for Independence.

However, the Republican Constitution was the first badly handled and badly operated one in the series. The principle of federation was assailed and violated when the Federal Government intervened in my Western Region as a result of the fracas that broke out on the floor of the house of assembly at Ibadan. An administrator in the person of a medical doctor, M. O. Majekodunmi, was appointed to run the affairs of the region. The ensuing repercussions of this intervention were so grave as to precipitate the crisis that led directly or indirectly to the 1966 military coup.

The long and tortuous march towards democracy resumed, egged on by the military, who bungled and muddled up issues, coup after coup and one military regime after the other. This aberration haunted me from 1979 to the end of the twentieth century, during which I wobbled and reeled into the twenty-first century like a punch-drunk, dazed boxer. The 1979 Constitution adopted the presidential system of government. That was the first constitution-drafting exercise to be convened by the military.

In accordance with established precedence over the years, the 1979 Constitution was drawn up by a group of handpicked 'forty-nine wise men'. It was so called because Awolowo, the fiftieth member of the selected group, resented the idea of his nomination being announced on the radio without previous consultations with him. He demurred and protested that such an important event should be carried out with at least a modicum of propriety. However, when the final version of the constitution came out, Awo jubilated and warmly congratulated the 'forty-nine wise men'. The reason for his jubilation soon became apparent when he extended his felicitations to them and to himself by saying, 'I congratulate you, and I congratulate myself' on a job well done. There was no scintilla of doubt in some discerning minds when it was realized that the newly drafted constitution was virtually a rehash of a book Awo had authored, entitled *Path to Nigerian Constitution*. The constitution collapsed because of corruption and maladministration. It had retained federalism, but with an expanded number of states.

The 1989 constitution floundered on the same premise of not consulting the people before it was drawn up. Its major change was from the multi-party system to the two-party system. Every other facet of the 1979 Constitution was virtually retained. The military heads of state overplayed the old trick of getting the people to debate the way forward. The Murtala/Obasanjo/Yar'Adua regimes did it in the mid-1970s. They encouraged popular debates that culminated in the establishment of a Constitution Drafting Committee and the Constituent

Assembly. Much later, in 1986, Babangida characteristically elaborated on the performances of the previous military regimes by asking Samuel Cookey to collate the submissions on the way forward, which was being eagerly canvassed by my wary citizenry. Later, a Constituent Assembly was set up. All these debates produced the constitutions of 1979, 1989, 1995, and 1999.

MY BIRTH: INDEPENDENCE— MY NATIONHOOD STATUS

Some major political parties, which were active as participants in the struggle and debates that led to my independence, were present as midwives and witnesses at my birth. They were the Northern Peoples Congress (NPC), led by Ahmadu Bello; the National Council of Nigeria and Cameroon (NCNC), led by Nnamdi 'Zik' Azikiwe; and the Action Group (AG), led by Obafemi Awolowo. Other lesser parties were the Northern Elements Progressive Union (NEPU), led by Aminu Kano; the United Middle Belt Congress (UMBC), led by Ibrahim Imam; and the Rivers Congress, led by Harold Dappa Biriye.

A historic electoral battle was fought. Even though the elections were partially boycotted by the Action Group Party, a new word, 'bakodaya' (zero votes), was added to my political vocabulary when the votes were being counted. This came about as a result of zero votes recorded in the elections by some southern-based parties in certain northern constituencies because of the boycott. The radio announcer repeatedly mentioned the Hausa word 'bakodaya' in a sing-song manner as in the refrain to a song. For good measure, the popular highlife band leader, Victor Olaiya, composed a memorable song to celebrate the word *bakodaya*:

> December 12, 1959,
> Federal Elections Day
> In Nigeria:
> When we all learn to say
> Bakodaya.

NPC led at the polls. Subsequent coalition between the NPC and the NCNC enabled both parties to form the ruling government. That was how my first federal parliamentary government came into being. Some of the other parties teamed up with the AG to form the opposition. The Federal House of Representatives was modelled after the Westminster Parliament in England. Tafawa Balewa headed it as my first Prime Minister. Azikiwe became the Senate President and Awolowo became the Leader of Opposition.

The stage was set for my emergence as a full blown parliamentary government, complete with a ruling government and a formidable opposition. I was born as a Nation when I formally obtained my independence from Great Britain on October 1, 1960. My certificate of birth was handed 'down' to Nnamdi Azikiwe when the Union Jack was lowered ceremonially by the young Naval rating, Akano 'Jack', and my green-white-green flag was hoisted in the cool night sky. Performing the significant assignment of hoisting the flag earned Akano the adulation and admiration of his contemporaries and teeming friends who fondly nicknamed him 'Akano Jack'.

My eyes were misty with tears of mixed joy and sadness as my new flag was being raised. I had a feeling of sorrow when I recalled the long, often bitter, and daunting struggle and the souls of the fallen and heroic fellow-fighters. Joy welled up in me as I breathed the air of freedom. The prospects of self-rule could only be matched by the vista of opportunities that could open up for me if properly guided and judiciously managed.

My political firmament consisted of a galaxy of political superstars. The colourful careers of some of those political stars stood out in bold relief in an age when the colonialists held sway. There was Herbert Macaulay, dapper in his well-tailored suit and distinctly unique with his coiling moustache. He was the protagonist of my struggle for Independence. As a trained journalist and given the prevailing domineering influence of British administrators of the time, Macaulay could not be gagged. He wrote fiercely and was prepared to be damned either in the process or as a consequence. He became the legendary leader of many of my illustrious and committed sons and daughters. He was a firm believer in African freedom and human rights. His family background, his British education, and his fiery brand of journalism were factors that contributed to his rise to prominence in Lagos. He effectively loomed large, both feared and respected in my national political firmament.

1 Herbert Macaulay. *He could be rightly referred to as the motivator and father of Nigerian Nationalism.* **2 Nnamdi Azikiwe ('Zik').** *Frontline journalist and newspaper publisher; educationist; author; leader of the National Convention of Nigeria and Cameroon; first President of Senate 1959–1960; first and only indigenous Governor General of Nigeria, 1960–1963; first President of the Federal Republic of Nigeria, 1963–1966. He was adulated as 'Zik of Africa'.* **3 Ahmadu Bello**. *The Sardauna of Sokoto, a descendant of the Seventh Sultan of Sokoto. He was revered, respected, and seen as a reference point in his courageous and authoritative leadership style. He was the first and only Premier of the Northern Region.* **4 Tafawa Balewa**. *Teacher, politician, moderate and level-headed statesman who was very highly respected as the first and hitherto only Prime Minister of Nigeria, 1960–1966.* **5 Obafemi Awolowo ('Awo').** *Lawyer, newspaper publisher, author; leader of the Action Group party; first Premier of Western Region; protagonist of free primary education; first Leader of Opposition at the House of Representatives.*

1 Mbonu Ojike. *Frontline politician fully involved in the nationalist struggle for Independence. He was known as 'Master of the Platform' and 'Boycott King'; his battle cry was 'Boycott all boycottables'.* **2 K. O. Mbadiwe.** *Popularly known as 'KO'. Politician and nationalist in the forefront of the struggle for Independence. Known as a 'wordsmith' who famously coined such unforgettable phrases and expressions as 'Men of timber and caliber' and 'When the come comes to become' which have crept into Nigeria's lingo.* **3 J. S. Tarka.** *He was a teacher and political activist in the struggle for Nigeria's Independence and founding member of the United Middle Belt Congress of which he later became President. He was elected as a Member of the House of Representatives at the age of 22.* **4 Funmilayo Ransome-Kuti.** *Frontline political leader who led the agitation for equal representation and against women taxation. She was popularly known as the 'Lioness of Lisabi' because of her bold utterances and worthy agitations.*

1 Margaret Ekpo. *Popular leader, politician and nationalist who participated in some of the pre-Independence Constitutional Conferences* **2 Laila Dongoyaro** *and* **3 Gambo Sawaba.** *Laila Dongoyaro was a Popular women leader and politician from the North. She was the President of the ' National Council of Women Society (NCWS) (1993–1995). Gambo Sawaba was a fiery Amazon not only in the struggle for Independence but as a thorn in the flesh of the rigidly conservative ruling class.* **4 Florence Ita-Giwa.** *Astute politician; She was a member of the House of Representatives before she became a Senator. She was popularly known as 'Mama Bakassi' because of her committed leadership role in the affairs of displaced Nigerians in the disputed area between Nigeria and Cameroon.*

1 S. L. Akintola. *Journalist, politician, consummate campaigner and orator. Leader of the breakaway faction of Action Group; 2nd Premier of the Western Region.* *2 Tony Enahoro.* *Journalist who became the editor of a national newspaper,* The Southern Defender, *at the age of 21; youthful frontline nationalist in the struggle for Independence. He moved the first-ever motion for Independence in 1953. His political travails included imprisonment, and his sojourn in exile inspired him to write* The Fugitive Offender.

Nnamdi 'Zik' Azikiwe was my knight in the shining armor. By common consent, he was the acclaimed hero of the struggle that led to my Independence. Zik made an imprint on my people, on Africa, and on the world at large. Zik was very interested in the subject and importance of education. He brought glamour to the importance of education by quoting Thomas Jefferson on the issue: 'Enlighten the people generally, and tyranny and oppressions of the body and mind will vanish like evil spirits at the dawn of day'. To further the propagation of this noble concept, he established a chain of newspapers through which he attacked the status quo. He also used the newspapers to educate and enlighten the people against the twin evils of colonialism and racism.

A great believer in education, Zik was convinced that it was only through education that the theory, ideals, and practical problems of a free society could the people hear of the great patriots who worked for and wrote about freedom.

He believed that I needed freedom in order to promote and encourage growth and development. The motto of his popular newspaper, *The Pilot*, was 'Show the light and the people shall follow'. This motto was an eloquent testimony of Zik's belief in education. His battle song was

Freedom, freedom
Everywhere there must be freedom.
Freedom for you,
Freedom for me,
Everywhere there must be freedom.

Zik launched his virulent editorial attacks on the colonialists from the pages of the *Pilot* and dared them to join battle with him on that terrain. He did not believe in violence. He declared that all violent revolutions were bad and could be disastrous and counterproductive. He believed in the politics of compromise, which he called 'Surulere', which means in Yoruba language, 'Patience has its reward'. My oneness and unity as a nation was the object of his pursuit. Azikiwe's book *Renascent Africa* was based on the five concepts: spiritual balance, social regeneration, economic determination, mental emancipation, and political resurgence.

Zik was a man ahead of his time, and, like all early comers and pioneers, he was faced with tribulations from all quarters. He fired the imagination of young Africans with the nationalistic fervour that pervaded his utterances and writings. By so doing, he picked up and hoisted aloft the flag of Pan-Africanism that had earlier been raised by Marcus Garvey. Such eminent and legendary African personalities as Nkrumah of Ghana, Hastings Banda of Malawi, Leopold Senghor of Senegal, Nyerere of Tanzania, Kenneth Kaunda of Zambia, Jomo Kenyatta of Kenya, and Nelson Mandela of then-apartheid South Africa were inspired and motivated from the writings and utterances of Zik. That was how the inimitable Zik earned his quaint and fond sobriquet of 'Zik of Africa'.

When he advised against the Civil War that pitted me against my Igbo sons and daughters, he was labelled by some as a coward and a saboteur. However, the years have underlined his wisdom—events would combine to effect his vindication. He was a politician, a journalist, an administrator, a teacher, an educationist, and an industrialist. As a sportsman par excellence, he was to declare at his inauguration as my first President, 'I will not score an offside goal, I will not hit below the belt or punch after the bell and neither will I beat the gun in order to become the president of Nigeria'.

Zik was a polyglot in his own affable and admirable way. He astonished his audience with the ease he demonstrated in switching from one language to the other in mid-speech during campaigns. I recall once this facility came in handy when he virtually rescued a fellow-conferee at breakfast during one of the constitutional conferences in London. The steward repeatedly filled the man's tea-cup with several rounds of tea because he did not indicate his satisfaction, as required by old-fashioned table etiquette, by inverting his empty teacup on the saucer. When Zik noticed this, he advised the man in his native tongue, different from Zik's Igbo language, to invert his cup in order to avert the unfolding embarrassing comic relief.

My northern pearl was the very formidable and inspirational leader, Ahmadu Bello, the Sardauna of Sokoto. Blue blood runs in his family veins. He was the grandson of the seventh Sultan of Sokoto and a worthy descendant of the Islamic scholar and founder of the Sokoto caliphate, Usman Dan Fodio. His noble and impeccable ancestry enabled him to attain political limelight and rapidly ascend the socio-political ladder as a teacher, councilor, and regional minister of works. He virtually ruled me as a nation from his base in Kaduna where he was the premier of the Northern Region.

This happened because he was also the leader of the powerful NPC (Northern People's Congress) that won the federal elections, formed the government, and produced the first Prime Minister. He called the shots from Kaduna, and when he coughed from there, people in Lagos literally shivered with cold. He was an exemplary leader to whom the northerners were beholden. He combined his aristocratic upbringing with his Islamic background to stem the tide of haste and impatience, which he saw as characteristic of the people from the south. He felt that there was a yawning gap between northern and southern developments. He opined that, given all the apparent disadvantages, the north might be dominated and possibly overwhelmed by the south if Independence were hastily attained.

Arguably, it would seem as if the colonialists exploited or remotely encouraged this northern hesitancy and restraint. It became evident that my determined march towards self-government, freedom, and independence was somehow retarded, if not impeded. When Zik admonished Ahmadu Bello before independence by saying, 'Let us forget our differences and work together as a team in order to achieve our independence', the mercurial and sagacious Ahmadu wittily retorted, 'Let us talk about our differences, so that we can agree better to work together'.

These seemingly endless exchanges of repartee, political banter, and protracted constitutional conferences in London inevitably led to a delay in establishing a date for my independence. 'The wind of change blowing through Africa' had assisted a couple of other African states to overtake and surpass me in the race to breast the tape at the Independence post. 'The wind of change blowing through Africa' was the all-time historical and significant political weather forecast made by Harold Macmillan, the former Conservative Party British Prime Minister.

To his infinite glory and fragrant memory, Ahmadu Bello has become a reference point for all that is excellent in leadership style and qualities. He believed that an idle hand is the devil's workshop. He made this vividly clear to prospective graduates of northern origin when he gave an address at the Trenchard Hall of the University College of Ibadan in 1962. He had promised to absorb them into the region's nascent civil service. He ironically reassured them that they would be so preoccupied with the job at hand that they would have neither time, inclination, nor cause to agitate and protest. He was reputed to have said that he would divide my geographical territory in two and hand them over to his lieutenants. He bestrode the politics of the north like a Colossus. History will continue inevitably to bear testimony to the fact that he ruled me by proxy as a nation. His adherents as well as his opposition continue to refer to him with awe and respect.

Obafemi 'Awo' Awolowo captivated the admiration and imagination of both the leaders and followers of his age by sheer dynamism. He had a reputation for achieving all his stated objectives. He was a consummate planner and a determined achiever once he got to the terminal of execution. He bestowed a legacy of education on the Western Region, the like of which has never been rivalled before or even replicated since.

During his high-profile tenure of administrative achievements and initiatives, 'Awo', as he was fondly called, garnered a plethora of 'firsts' in terms of

record-making and ground-breaking ventures and achievements. The Western Region, under his imaginative plans and moves, pioneered the first free primary education scheme aided by such lights as Ajasin and Awokoya. The first television
sion
station in Africa was established in 1959, and this was a monumental and epoch-making achievement. My first modern stadium, Liberty Stadium, was built in Ibadan. His was the first of the initial three regional governments to introduce minimum wages for workers. The first planned and massively industrialized zone was sited and built in Ikeja. He created the first state-owned agricultural settlement, fashioned after the Israeli kibbutz system. He set up the Pilgrims Welfare Board, which was the first of its kind and a forerunner of many more to come.

Awo was an avid and persistent advocate for the creation of more states. He was an avowed and dedicated pioneer and protagonist in the vanguard of the quest for true Federalism. He never hid his abhorrence and disdain for the military in government. Like a good and calculating Army General who knows when is best to retreat, he quickly beat a retreat by resigning from Gowon's cabinet soon after the Civil War was over. He considered his mission accomplished, and immediately thereafter, demonstrated his aversion for military rule by withdrawing his services. In his capacity as the Federal Commissioner for Finance, he ensured that the war was prosecuted without borrowing money from anywhere.

Such was his outstanding success in the method of his administration that Harold Wilson, the British Prime Minister of that era, assessed him as the only person he knew to be capable enough to rule any of the western democracies. During his lifetime, Awolowo was seen as the barometer by which other governments measured the acceptability of their policies. Babangida, one of my former military presidents, once described him as 'the main issue in Nigeria's (my) politics'. The former Biafran leader, Odumegwu Ojukwu lamented at Awo's death, 'He was the best president that Nigeria [I] *never had*'. His administrative acumen was unparalleled and the aides and top government functionaries under him were always at alert to measure up to his high expectations and requirements.

Furthermore, Awo was the first politician in Africa to use a helicopter to conduct his electioneering campaigns. It was always a spectacular aerial display, during which tracts and leaflets of political manifestos were scattered from the skies to reach all nooks and corners of the targeted areas. This exercise boomeranged under clandestine circumstances when some of his political opponents in some predominantly Moslem areas deliberately defiled some pages of an old disused Koran by sacrilegiously tearing them into pieces and maliciously scattering the shreds over conspicuous public places at night. This naturally offended the religious sensitivities of rural and unwary Moslems who believed (incorrectly) that the shreds from their torn holy book were those that had been sacrilegiously scattered from Awo's helicopter. Of course, their revenge was to promptly return 'bakodaya' (zero) votes for him for daring to assail their personal, highly esteemed religious values.

He travelled throughout the length and breadth of the north, preaching the gospel of 'freedom for all and life more abundant'. So purposeful and successful was his mission that he bestirred my over-confident leaders of that region from their smug complacency. Confronted literally at their backyard by the audacious hordes of political invaders from the south, my northern leaders had to climb down from their high horses to contain the aggressive incursion of Awo's team of intrepid campaigners with their novel vote-catching tactics.

The evolution of a virile and excellent civil service structure was the excellent brainchild and handiwork of Awolowo. He had the admirable instinct to select or appoint persons into appropriate places. His discovery and appointment of Simeon Adebo, in particular, as the Head of the Civil Service of the old Western Region, initiated an excellent structure which became the sample and reference point to all other regions. Adebo was to carve a niche for himself at the United Nations (UN), where he served as my Ambassador and Permanent Representative.

At the UN, Adebo exhibited the traits of an astute and consummate diplomat and a lively and much-sought-after speechmaker and circuit lecturer. He was easily recognized as a traditionalist, always dressed in his native Yoruba 'gbariye' attire. His colleagues and admirers affectionately and respectfully referred to him variously as 'the chief' and 'our chief'. He retired at the end of a brilliant and successful tenure as my UN Permanent Representative. My loss of his services was the gain for the UN, which retained his services as the director of an influential arm of the UN, called the United Nations Institute for Training and Research, or UNITAR.

I pride myself in the quality and leadership style of Tafawa Balewa. He became the first prime minister of my elected Federal Government. He possessed a deep resonant voice and a very gentle and amiable disposition that endeared him to all. Throughout his reign as the prime minster, he was a stabilizing factor. He was a voice of moderation between the deliberate and rather patient conservatives and the firebrand and fast-paced liberals. More than a few tears were shed after his assassination at the hands of the coup plotters in 1966. He was mourned by all.

I applaud Michael Okpara—'M. I. Power', as he was popularly hailed by his followers. He lit the political rostrum with his vigorous voice and fire-spitting oratory. At my Independence, he became the third leg of the regional triumvirate of power, replacing the great Zik as the premier of the defunct Eastern Region when the latter moved over to the federal capital to become the first Governor General. Michael Okpara's quest was for pragmatic socialism of the NCNC in answer to the battle cry of democratic socialism as orchestrated from across the Niger in the west by the Action Group government.

The political annals of those early years of my Independence would not be complete if I did not recognize the personalities and exploits of some other memorable stars that made the era unique. Akanu Ibiam was a mild mannered and benevolent physician who became the governor of my now-defunct Eastern Region. During that same period in my history, and operating at the same level of service, were both Oba Adesoji Aderemi, the Ooni of Ile-Ife, as governor of the defunct Western Region, and Kashim Ibrahim who was also governor of the defunct Northern Region. The mid-west region was carved out of the old Western Region, and the poet–statesman, Osadebey, became its first Premier while Jereton Mariere was appointed Governor.

Apart from the premiers and governors of the various regions, many other political actors appeared at that stage of my history. They played significant roles in their various capacities, either in reigning government or in the opposition. The stars of charismatic leaders and flamboyant politicians often flickered and glittered in my political firmament from their utterances, performances, and personalities. From the north, I had the youthful and politically adroit Waziri

Ibrahim. He was a federal minister in my First Republic and became the apostle of 'politics without bitterness' when aspiring to the presidency in my Second Republic. He advised that politics should not be a matter of life and death or 'fight to the finish'. Little did he know that another leader would come who would flex his political muscle by declaring a 'do-or-die' contest for power at my highest level of governance. Ibrahim warned that election campaigns should be devoid of bitterness, recriminations, thuggery, and wanton vandalism. Character assassination, vendetta, and unfounded allegations used to score cheap political points against opponents were alien to Ibrahim's brand of politics. All the aforementioned evils continued to characterize elections even into the twenty-first century.

Shehu Shagari wore his caps long and cylindrical on his head. It became his trademark, complete with his heavily embroidered 'babariga' flowing robes. He was an unwilling and reluctant candidate for the presidential diadem. His ambition was merely to be a senator. The honour of ruling me as a nation was literally thrust on him. Mediocre advisers surrounded him. Wily and foxy Adisa Akinloye was the chairman of his ruling National Party of Nigeria (NPN). The economy was badly managed. Ministers doubled in number from 'minister in the ministry of' to 'minister in the ministry for' in blatant replication. It was a wasteful exercise that drained the treasury in an attempt to create 'jobs for the boys'.

Shagari was said to have dutifully sought permission to say his prayers (and, perhaps, smoke one or two of his favourite cigarettes) when his right-hand men were busy shoring up the NPN campaign war treasury without regard for due process, accountability, or the need to award and ensure the worthy execution of contracts. It was during Shagari's regime that Shugaba, a northerner, was forcibly supplanted from his home inside my territory and deported to a neighbouring country. This was a charade that had no place in justice and morality. Voices in protest and opposition prevailed, and Shugaba was quickly returned to his fatherland. To his credit, Shagari continued with the 'Operation Feed the Nation', which was an agrarian revolution that encouraged everybody to be involved in farming and food production, even at the most minimal level.

Aminu Kano was fondly called 'Malam' (the Teacher) by all. He was the acknowledged champion of the lowly and down-trodden, the so-called 'Talakawas' of the north. He began to preach a new concept of social welfare in my ancient city of Kano. Aminu Kano's movement that started around 1950 ignited Kano with the policy of emancipating the Talakawas by reforming the autocratic political institutions. He fought for their cause till he died. His conviction in the dignity of man made him hold tight to the principle of his own fight with aristocratic ethos. This has accorded him an enviable mention in my history. It has been said that Aminu loved to protest—so much so that he could, if the need arose in the interest of justice and fairness, carry a placard against his own office, even when he became the Federal Minister of Communications. He also ran for the presidency in my Second Republic on the platform of his Northern Elements Progressive Union (NEPU).

Ibrahim Dimis was a pain in the neck to the aristocratic setup in the north. He was known to have carried his mat and arm chair in protest and to go and relax in an area that was out of bounds to his teeming fellow 'talakawas'. He was sentenced to a jail term of a few months for his temerity. He was a human rights activist before it became the trend. Joseph Tarka was the political stormy petrel of the north. He was champion and leader of the Tivs of Benue area of the north. He cut a fierce image during his struggle, along with his fellow Tivs, to create an identity of their own, different from the northern establishment. He found a fellow traveller in the same cause in Ibrahim Imam, leader of the United Middle Belt Congress or (UMBC).

Ladoke 'S. L. A.' Akintola became the premier of the Western Region when Awolowo, in his quest for power and the opportunity to serve and make his talents available at the center, ventured into Lagos as the leader of the opposition at the federal House of Representatives. This move by Awolowo is still being perceived as regrettable and ill-conceived, as it would inevitably change my political trend and landscape. Maybe he could have stayed behind to further hasten the pace of development he had initiated in the west. Some are of the opinion that he could have left Akintola behind in the center, just like Ahmadu left Balewa in the center, and stayed at home to rule the roost and, perhaps, eventually call the shots from Ibadan as Ahmadu did from Kaduna.

However, Akintola was a very formidable politician. He had a reputation for stinging, vituperative, sarcastic anecdotes and repartee which he employed against his opponents. He had the gift of gab and usually delivered his harangues in his high-pitched voice. His tremendous skill in playing upon words employing caustic and scathing idioms and expressions in his Ogbomosho dialect, delivered with bristling intellect on the meanings and pronunciations of other people's names, made him a fearsome debater and a rabble-rousing campaigner. The colonial Governor McPherson described him as 'master of ambiguity'. He was uncharitably described in another verbal encounter by Zik as the 'Ogbomosho zebra' on account of the prominent tribal marks on his otherwise handsome face.

I like to reminisce with sheer delight on the ebullience of Adegoke Adelabu 'penkelemesi' (peculiar mess), the author of *Africa in Ebullition*. He was a radical socialist, a fanatical nationalist, and a populist with extraordinary mass appeal. He was essentially a grass-roots politician who was always most at home with his Ibadan kinsmen. Adelabu brought drama, flair, and native intelligence into politics. He customarily brought the Ibadan native drums, complete with 'sekere and gangan' drummers, to shatter the hallowed peace of the exclusive Ikoyi government reservation area (GRA). This practise usually provoked the ire and offensive criticism from the high-browed residents of the neighborhood. He invoked the fabled Malthusian theory and practise, which invited the disdain and wrath of the affluent in the neighbourhood in order to chase them away from their haven of opulence.

Adelabu's kinsmen erected makeshift hearths and tripods on the mown lawns of the large compound of the quarters allocated to him at Ikoyi. There, they set out to cook their favourite Ibadan 'amala and ewedu' dish. His all-embracing populism defied all religious barriers. He confessed that he was a Moslem by birth, a Christian for convenience, and an Agnostic by conviction. Adelabu proclaimed that education was the foundation of wisdom, and ignorance was the basis of slavery. He opined that the illiterate man is only half a man, shackled to his unfounded fears and submissive to his uncurbed passions and animal instincts. He preached that career should be open to talent and that opportunity should be based on merit. He inveighed against all the ills and negative results of tribalism, disunity, and class-consciousness. He maintained that no sacrifice could be too great for national unity and cohesion. His death in a road accident on his way to Ibadan in 1958 led to an orgy of uncontrollable mourning and riots.

Remi Fani Kayode ('Fani Power') was the youthful and assertive deputy premier to Ladoke Akintola in the defunct western region. He was a brilliant Cambridge University-trained lawyer. He brought flair and colour into politics by cocking his cap at a frontal jaunty angle on his head and raising his clenched right fist in acknowledgement of the cheery shout of 'Fani Power' from his teeming fans. A dance step was created, imitating his raised clenched fist pose and with cap worn at a similar frontal curve. He baffled observers, critics, political analysts, historians, and, indeed, the electorate (including all his opponents) when he asserted, during the heady days of 'the wild, wild West' imbroglio that, with or without their votes, his rather unpopular party, the NNDP, would win the elections because 'angels would vote'. Quite understandably, that was interpreted as an overt threat to rig the elections. That would amount to sheer mockery, travesty, and rape of the type of Democracy to which I aspire as a nation. It also signified the beginning of the game of election rigging.

T. O. S. Benson, called 'Tos' Benson, was a highly principled politician. He made his mark as a steadfast supporter of Zik and loyalist to the NCNC. He was born in Ikorodu but lived virtually all his life in Lagos. He came into prominence when, as a young lawyer in 1948, he teamed up with other NCNC lawyers and descended on Enugu to defend the coal miners who had gone on strike to protest their inhumane treatment in the hands of the colonial masters. From there, he never looked back. He became my pioneer Federal Minister of Information. He also became a lifetime bencher and a senior advocate. He also married a beautiful Liberian lady who became a socially and eminently recognizable figure in the areas of culture and fashion. For this, she became the *Iya Oge* (Matron of Fashion) of Lagos.

Abraham Adesanya could best be remembered as a leader of Afenifere and my Yoruba ethnic group. As leader of the pan-Yoruba socio-cultural, political, and economic organization, he loomed larger than life. He successfully carried the flag first hoisted by Awolowo and Ajasin. He was a prominent member of the House of Senate in my Second Republic from 1979 to 1983. His role as the national chairman of the National Democratic Coalition (NADECO) was a high point in his political career. He saw politics purely as an altruistic endeavour to serve the people. It was in demonstration of this principle that he never consented to serve in the executive arm of any government as an unelected leader.

He was an avowed and faithful follower of Awolowo, particularly at the height of the Western Region crisis of 1962–1966. Adesanya was to suffer persecution at the hands of the Sani Abacha regime. His miraculous escape from attempted assassination mesmerized and befuddled observers as he emerged unscathed from his bullet-riddled car—which was *not* an armored car.

Richard Akinjide was the Attorney General and Minister of Justice in my Second Republic government under Shehu Shagari. At every stage of governance in my old Western Region, particularly among the Yorubas, he had always taken a unique and principled stand. He pitched his tent firmly with the NCNC when cross-carpeting was the vogue. Then he went along with people of his political leanings to the National Democratic party and then almost predictably to the National Party of Nigeria (NPN) and the Peoples Democratic Party. He was elected as a member of the House of Representatives in my First Republic when he was barely 24 years old.

Akinjide was the protagonist and theorist who cleverly argued the '12$2/3$' calculation, which enabled Shagari to win the Supreme Court verdict that confirmed his victory at the polls. Akinjide opined that a change in my system of government had become necessary. He was referring to the successive failures of my parliamentary, military, and presidential governments. He was of the view that it would be worthwhile for my politicians and planners to go back to the drawing board and look for a system that is indigenous, original, and suitable for my people and environment.

Mbonu Ojike vigorously participated in the struggle for my Independence in words and deeds. He demonstrated his abhorrence of all the vestiges of colonialism and all the reminders of its shackling and stereotype styles and practises. He became known as 'master of the platform' and the 'boycott king'. His battle cry was 'boycott all boycottables'. He led by example and by precept when he dropped his foreign name and answered to 'Mazi' instead of 'Mr.' He urged the people to renounce all foreign names, appellations, and apparels and to adopt the meaningful names and suitable dresses available in my culture, tradition, and climate. He was always dressed in simple 'agbada' and 'sokoto'. He never dressed in western suits. In his consuming passion for an unadulterated yearning for freedom and liberty, he carried along with him, in Zik's campaign train, his invariable message of boycott. For him, whisky was out of the question. He always opted for good old home-brewed palm wine, akara (bean) balls, and ritual kolanuts rather than cakes and biscuits. One of his most memorable declarations was his grandiloquent description of politics as 'the art of creating problems and offering unsuitable solutions'.

Kingsley Ozurumba Mbadiwe—popularly known as 'KO'—was another firebrand politician. He was famous for his oratory, usually laced with flowery and bombastic expressions. He coined such an unforgettable phrase as 'men of timber and calibre' to describe eminent personalities. He would also say, 'When the *come* comes to *become*' as a synonym for 'ultimately' or 'in the nick of time'. He was a prominent member of Zik's political entourage until they fell out over issues that emphasized their incompatibility. The irrepressible E. O. Eyo played a role in trying to demystify the great Zik. His allegations and accusations were parts of the reasons that led to the setting up of the Foster Sutton tribunal of enquiry.

In the midwest, the name of the flamboyant Festus Okotie-Eboh, or 'Omimi Ejoh', would invariably crop up. He was the Federal Minister of Finance in my First Republic. His most visible presence was usually on the days in which he would present the budget at the Federal House of Representatives. On such days, he would come dressed in his flowing Itsekiri attire, which had a long trail tied round the necks of three able-bodied men. He would then top this up with a felt hat bedecked with a long and colourful feather. Unfortunately, and to the shock of his many friends and admirers, Okotie-Eboh became one of the victims of the 1966 coup that ushered the military in to my governance.

Other players worthy of mention in the mid-west included Humphrey Osaghie. He was a leader of thoughts in the region. He was a Federal Minister, and he commanded a lot of respect among his Edo people. Okorodudu was another mid-westerner who rose through politics to become the Western Region's agent general in the United Kingdom when the mid-west was still part of the Western Region.

Tony Enahoro, from Uromi in the Ishan area of the mid-west, was the icon and quintessence of my struggling image on the long and tortuous journey along the route to the terminal of independence. He was one of the foremost anti-colonial and pro-democracy activists. He had an extensive and distinguished career in the press, politics, the civil service, and the pro-democracy movement. He led great protest marches and was once hailed and adulated as he rode on horseback from Yaba to Tinubu Square on Lagos Island on his return, in a triumphant entry from one of his political forays in Kaduna. He became a member of my Federal House of Representatives in 1951 and was the opposition's spokesman on foreign affairs and legislative affairs. He was the point of the arrowhead, along with other patriots in the struggle culminating in the attainment of independence on October 1, 1960.

It is also an irony of history that what the colonialists did to Enahoro by imprisoning him as a young activist fresh from Kings College paled to insignificance compared with what he suffered in the hands of compatriots in my First Republic and the indignity to which he was subjected under the tyrannical rule of a later generation of much younger military rulers. Quite significantly, most of his military adversaries and tormentors were barely over ten years old when Enahoro first proposed the motion for my independence on March 31, 1953. Even though the motion was at that time defeated, it was considered revolutionary when he made it. This led to the collapse of the Macpherson government and hastened the move towards my independence as a free nation. He stood out as a conscientious nation-builder who strenuously led key political platforms and pressure groups to chart a democratic road map throughout my chequered history.

A hounded but determined and imperturbable victim of the colonialist repression, Enahoro was imprisoned on three different occasions, only to emerge again and again to join the struggle. He was nurtured in the anti-colonialist struggle and the torrid brutality of the era. He was first convicted for seditious libel and jailed for insinuating that Bernard Bourdillon was always travelling north to receive 'KOLA'. He was again convicted for making a speech in Warri, advising African policemen not to shoot at Africans on strike. On the third occasion, he was convicted for being the chairman at a Zikist movement rally in which Osita Agwuna made an inciting speech at the Glover Memorial Hall.

For the same reason, eight other Zikists, present when Agwuna made his rousing speech, were also jailed. The ultranationalists included Raji Abdallah, Nduka Eze, Oged Macaulay, Sa'adu Zungur, and others. I recall with pride and nostalgia the spirit of nationalism that formed the main theme and focus of Abdullah's statement when he refused to enter a plea before the (white) judge. He stated, 'I hate the crown of Britain with all my heart, because to me and my countrymen, it represents a symbol of oppression, a symbol of persecution, and in short, a material manifestation of iniquity'.

Enahoro was a fearless but refreshingly brilliant journalist who became the youngest editor of a national newspaper—*The Southern Defender*—at the age of 21. He later became 'the fugitive offender' after prophetically making his speech on the floor of the House of Representatives about 'the chain of events, the end of which no one can foretell,' which ominously heralded and provided a setting for the civil war that began in 1967. It is pertinent to observe at this juncture that the British government did not grant him asylum, because the Balewa government invoked an existing extradition agreement to bring him back home to face the treasonable felony trial with Awolowo. The circumstances surrounding this episode led to his writing the popular book, *Fugitive Offender*.

Enahoro spent many years along with others for the promotion and defense of democratic governance, protection and defense of civil liberty, and sustenance of equitable distribution of my natural resources and government offices. He was always a dogged fighter who spent his entire life being involved in one political landmark event or another. His political philosophy consistently tackled my distorted federal structure. He consistently recommended scientific and true federalism along the geopolitical spread existing within my territory. He maintained that true federalism would bring peace, unity, and progress to my people. He cautioned that the ethnic nationalities should be allowed to federate on the basis of their historical and cultural affinities and geographical contiguities. He postulated that all the nationalities are allowed to retain some fundamental degree of autonomy in virtually all spheres of national life *except* in the spheres of national defense, foreign affairs, currency, immigration, and other areas not unfriendly to my national sovereignty.

He will always be remembered—not for his inexplicable dalliance with the conservative NPN during my Second Republic but also as one who was the first to put forward the formal motion for independence in 1953. He was the man who oversaw the Western Region Home Affairs Ministry, which brought the first television station to Africa. He was also the man who effectively packaged the propaganda portfolio during the turbulent days of the civil war.

He was appointed as the president of the World Festival of Arts and Culture, known as FESTAC. As the chairman of the National Democratic Coalition, he was the man who propelled and guided the pro-democracy struggle into higher and faster terrain. His contributions—mentally, physically, and emotionally—to the struggle to hasten the end of the military cannot be overstated. His actions and pronouncements evidently helped to amplify the struggle for the actualization of the June 12, 1993, election debacle. In 1994, he spent 134 days in detention without any reason adduced. After his release from detention, he eventually became targeted for his pivotal role in the National Democratic Coalition (NADECO). He went into exile, where he along with other eminent NADECO chieftains directed the affairs of the alliance.

Alfred Rewane was a loyal supporter of Awolowo during the glorious era of AG. He was known as a selfless and wealthy philanthropist. He was also arrested and tried during the treasonable felony trials. When he was at the Broad street prison, he comforted his fellow *ATs* (awaiting trial) as he recalled his favourite Boy Scout song:

> Pack up your troubles in your old kit bag,
> And smile, smile, smile,
> While you've a Lucifer to light your fag,
> Smile, boys, that's the style.
> What's the use of worrying?
> It never was worth while, so
> Pack up your troubles in your old kit bag,
> And smile, smile, smile.

Assassin's bullets mowed down Rewane after his illustrious and illuminating career. The rampaging goons and security thugs who operated under the Abacha protective umbrella were suspected to have been responsible for the dastardly assassination. He was a stickler for Awolowo's ideals of honesty, integrity, and selfless service to my national cause. He preached accountability and questioned the stupendous wealth of the military.

I remember with cold shudder the treasonable felony trials in which Awo and his close aides were jailed. The judge had ominously claimed that 'his hands were tied'. As if his biblical Job-like ordeals were not enough, Awo lost his eldest son, Segun, a Cambridge University-trained lawyer, in a gruesome motor accident. Awo received the tragic news during this trying period with an unusual display of courage and equanimity. He stepped into prison with prophecy on his lips. He assuaged the bitter and sorrowful feelings of his followers and posterity by saying that he could 'see some light at the end of the tunnel and after the darkness shall come a glorious morn'.

Coincidentally, two great mathematicians of that era made their marks on the political sands of time. Both of them were professors at some of my foremost Universities. Chike Obi was there at the beginning during the First Republic. He was a nationalist and patriot who took part in politics as the secretary general of the Dynamic Party of Nigeria and member of Federal Parliament, representing Onitsha (1960-61). He was also a member of the eastern House of Assembly (1961-66). I recall that the party symbol was the ram. He did not make much of an impact, but he had the pleasant aura of an extrovert and was very much liked by students and undergraduates, more for his mathematics genius and his genial eccentricity than for his political clout.

His venture into the politics of his era was not without its own share of peculiarities. He woke up one morning to hear on the radio that he had resigned his seat from my Federal House of Representatives. He went to court to contest and deny the fictitious claim, and he won. To demonstrate his patriotism and his love for my unity and oneness as a Nation, he bestowed names that defied ethnicity and religion to his two male children. Even as an Igbo man, he called one Mustafa, which is definitely Arabic in culture and decidedly Muslim and northern in orientation. The other son he named Balogun. The name is deeply rooted in the Yoruba cultural history of heroism and warfare.

Victor Omololu Olunloyo made his entry into politics during the turbulent days of the tumult that engulfed the Western Region. He pitched his tent with the recalcitrant Akintola and actually joined the band that broke down the barricaded door of the western House of Assembly in order to oust the 'regularly and popularly elected' Soroye Adegbenro. The fracas that ensued led to the breakdown of law and order, and a battle was literally fought on the floor of the House.

Olunloyo's stand was always clear on all issues. His fixation with the conservative civilians and the aberrant military regime earned him gratuitous respect, favours, and status as a trusted adviser to the powers that be. He sounded very much like an apologist for the military in his weekly column 'Think Tank' in the *Tribune*. He was well known for his thoroughness, even when the odds were stacked against his mentors. Lastly, he allegedly won the Oyo State gubernatorial contest against Bola Ige in the massively rigged 'moon slide' elections of 1983.

Tunji Braithwaite, scion of a wealthy and noble lineage in Lagos, pranced across the stage to participate in the politics of my Second Republic. He came as an intellectual threatening to rid the 'Augean Stables' of mosquitoes and cockroaches if he won the presidential election in which he was a young and fresh contestant. *Mosquitoes* and *cockroaches* were his euphemisms for the parasitical genre of politicians and sycophants whom he alleged had been parading the corridors of power and sucking dry the economic well-being of my First Republic.

Mokwugo Okoye represented different personalities to different people. He tried to leave his footprints in the sands of time in any area of human endeavour he explored. He was a prominent actor in the heady days of the nationalist struggles, which eventually—in 1960—ushered in Independence. He learned the political ropes under the tutelage of the fiery Zikist movement, cutting his political teeth on the movement as a young member. He injected radical and socialist ideology into his fiery political agitation for self-government by prevailing on his fellow agitators not to pay tax to the colonial British government. He was a firm believer in improved welfare for the masses. This was amply demonstrated when he co-founded the United Peoples Grand Alliance (UPGA). He preached these ideas as he indefatigably traversed my political terrain of the time. Till his death in 1998, he maintained an unwavering position on the need for me as a Nation to evolve a progressive ideology that will enthrone symbolic expression to fundamental unity.

The activities and performances of my daughters, who operated in a milieu that was preponderantly male oriented, promoted and fought for my emergence as an independent nation and the tremendous struggle that preceded it. It was one thing to use the feminine touch in tending homes on behalf of their menfolk and encouraging them in the struggle against the colonialists; it was quite another thing entirely to gain their own emancipation from their male compatriots. I recall the picture of Aduni Oluwole, dressed in a robe made of sack, riding on a white charger, and joining the political fray. She was imbued with a keen sense of justice and was always present at campaign meetings whipping feminine emotions to a state of frenzy. She played the role of a mother to the workers during the Imodou-led 44-day strike of 1945, feeding and tending them during those turbulent days of struggle, travail, and sorrow.

Funmilayo Ransome-Kuti was a 'one-woman riot' from her Abeokuta enclave. She founded the first Pan-Nigerian women's body, the Nigerian Women's Union, and had it linked with women in various parts of Africa and also affiliated it with the Women's International Democratic Federation. Her inspired and bold leadership of the women in their agitation against the sole native authority—the then-Alake of Abeokuta, Oba Ademola himself—and against the payment of tax by women earned her the nickname 'Lioness of Lisabi Land'. Her determined leadership and courageous activism caused the Alake to flee into temporary exile in Osogbo. She was selected as representative for women in the NCNC to attend the Richards Constitution in London. At one point, before my independence, she was denied an entry visa into the United States of America because of her supposed 'communist' leanings.

Oyinkan Abayomi fought for women to be represented in both the Lagos town council and the legislative council. She agitated over the long and deliberate neglect of women in the scheme of things socially, economically, and politically. She and the Nigerian Women's Party (NWP) vociferously supported the enfranchisement of women and their representation in political committees. As a specially appointed member, she also represented women in the western House of Assembly.

Many of my daughters have been known to act creditably in various ways to nurture me into full-blown Nationhood. Margaret Ekpo combined beauty, brains, and elegance with her involvement over several decades of political activism. At a stage when women dreaded political agitation and the unpalatable repercussions, Margaret Ekpo travelled with Funmilayo Ransome Kuti to Enugu to lead protests. She had, on one occasion during the Independence struggle, threatened to shoot down a white person in retribution if she found out that a black person had been killed in a colonial conflict. This was her reaction to the shooting by the so-called colonial police of the Enugu coal miners in Iva Valley in 1949. She was also known to have mobilized Aba women in a massive protest over taxation of women. In the twilight of her career, she lent support to the prolongation of the military dictatorship of Babangida. She found herself in the unlikely group of other elder statesmen and women canvassing support for Babangida to continue, one way or the other, in office.

Aduke Moore exhibited charm, elegance, and brilliance in her legal profession. Oyibo Odinamadu was an icon of politics, civil rights, and the women's movement. She made a name for herself as a leader of various organizations and as a public servant. She was especially active in the founding of the National Council of Women's Societies (NWCS) and was president of my eastern wing of the council until she joined active partisan politics. She became the first national vice president of the Unity Party of Nigeria.

Grace Alele-Williams, the mathematician, acquitted herself brilliantly when she became my first woman Vice Chancellor at the University of Benin. This feat was followed by that of the brilliant professor of law and renowned scholar, Jadesola Akande, daughter of a great political-activist mother, Wuraola Esan. The latter was the first woman to become a senator in the First Republic and also became the formidable Iyalode of Ibadan. Jadesola was also in the saddle as a vice chancellor at Lagos State University and later as the pro-chancellor of the Federal University of Technology (FUTA) at Akure. Bolanle Awe, a distinguished scholar and a brilliant professor of history, successfully led the National Commission for Women in Nigeria.

The trio of Janet Akinrinade, Simi Johnson, and Ebun Oyagbola rose to the enviable ranks of honourable federal ministers. Suliat Adedeji, known as the Ibadan iron lady of politics, was also known as an astute and successful business woman, who, as a go-getter, would never take no for an answer. Franka Afegbua was an active participant in the politics of the Second Republic as the only female senator. Florence Ita-Giwa became an active and high-profile member of the House of Representatives in the failed Third Republic. She was well known for her social, motherly, and philanthropic role in aid of my beleaguered sons and daughters in the disputed Bakasi area, for which she earned her nickname of 'Mama Bakassi'. Ita-Giwa was a one-term senator when she was appointed as a senior special assistant and a liaison between the presidency and the national assembly during the first term of Obasanjo's administration.

Gambo Sawaba was a fearless and loyal follower of Malam Aminu Kano. Her voice was heard distinctly in an era and in an environment that was male dominated. She was the leader of the women's wing of NEPU, in which role she insisted on a place of pride for women in the scheme of things. She was a thorn in the flesh of the colonialists, who saw her as a troublemaker. She made the first of her 15 trips to prison in 1952. What the colonial administrators did to her was resumed by the new local dispensation that consigned womanhood perpetually to a state of docility. She was truly the Amazon of that era.

Laila Dongoyaro, the Garkuwa Garki, was a vibrant spokesperson for womanhood. She was also the president of the National Council of Women's Societies (NCWS). In that capacity, she occupied a chair that had been at various times graced with distinction by such eminent women as Lady Ademola, Dr. Abimbola Awoliyi, and Justice I. C. Nzeako.

CHAPTER TWO

SOME JOURNALISTS AS MY FOUNDING FATHERS

My story as a Nation will sound or look abridged and incomplete without mentioning the significant roles played by the press and journalists in building me into a Nation. Oral information about events, as witnessed and attested to by those who were there at the beginning, would still have to be documented for posterity. That, exactly, is why the roles of the journalists and the press can hardly be overemphasized. I am going to show therefore how indisputable it is that my history is a tale told by journalists about journalists and their continuous struggle to nurse and nurture me, as a Nation, from cradle to vigorous and vibrant adulthood.

The intrepid and industrious journalists, who were present at my birth, ably assisted the process of my birth and upbringing. It became apparent that the ubiquitous pressmen, their diligent and excellent reportage, and their palliative editorials chronicled my growth through crawling and teething infancy and boisterous and exuberant adolescence into the full-grown adult I am today. I am still growing in all ways, and the ever-present journalists are forever keeping watch over me and observing every step of my journey through life.

The roles of journalists in my life have been so consistent as to be predictable. They are the disseminators of information. They are the product of good education, and they continually project the beauty and essence of sound education. They identify and promote places and practitioners of amusement; they are the watchdogs of ordered society, keeping all strata of society on their toes

1 Abiodun Aloba. *His pen name was Ebenezer Williams. He displayed masterful use of English language. He was versed in biblical quotations and witticisms. His 'must-read' column in the* Sunday Times *was full of exposé and criticisms.* **2 Bisi Onabanjo.** *His pen name was 'Aiye koto'. He wielded a mighty pen and was a vigorous and hard hitting writer in the* Tribune. *He was a past master in the 'carrot and stick' journalism by identifying problems and proffering solutions. He was a 'coiner' of aliases as he bestowed the nickname 'Maradona' on Babangida. He became the Governor of Ogun State (1979–1983).* **3 Lateef Jakande.** *His pen name was John West. He was a forceful writer of compelling and telling articles in the* Tribune *where he became the General Manager and Editor-in-Chief. He was an excellent administrator, for which he was given the sobriquet 'Action Governor' as the Governovr of Lagos State (1979–1983).* **4 Sam Amuka.** *He is a witty and experienced journalist who initially cofounded the* Punch Newspaper *with Moyo Aboderin before opting out to found the very popular* Vanguard Newspaper. *He wrote under the pen name 'Sad Sam'. He has brought creativity and administrative flair into the journalistic profession.*

1 Dele Giwa. *Journalist and an inveterate news hound. His specialty was investigative journalism. His unique style and flair became apparent in his 'Parallax Snap' column in some newspapers. He met his gruesome and suspicious death through a letter bomb.* **2 Segun Osoba.** *A dynamic journalist and Managing Director of the Daily Sketch and also the Daily Times. He later became the Governor of Ogun State (1999-2003).* **3 Lamidi Adesina.** *He exhibited wit, political sagacity and dynamism in his Lam Adesina column in the Tribune. He was first a member of the House of Representatives before he became the Governor of Oyo State ((1999-2003).* **4 Ray Ekpu.** *A brilliant journalist whose narrative and analytical skills are reflected in the 'Newswatch' magazine, which he co-founded with Dele Giwa.* **5 Reuben Abati.** *Brilliant and academically sound journalist, critical analyst of political events and a celebrated book reviewer.*

through copious and effusive expressions of appreciation or biting criticism. They are consummate salesmen propagating ideas and promoting the sales of theories, practises, and products through advertisements and publications.

My history has been inseparably intertwined with the history of my press. The history of the press has formed the basis for compiling data for my biography. In the interest of historians and in honour of my forebears, the institution now known as the Nigerian Press predated me as the Nigerian Nation, which I have now become known. I would be echoing the causes and courses of the journalists' performances and activities by telling the story of my birth all over again.

The journalists were there at my inception not only so they could testify that they knew how it all happened but also to proclaim to the waiting world that a new child was born whose star portended greatness—a bouncing baby that would grow into a giant in the sun. The baby would have potential in terms of human and material resources which could ensure an inexorable march to the pinnacle of leadership in Africa and for all black people in the diaspora.

My illustrious sons and daughters of the pen are still holding high the beacon and bearing the standard of African journalism. Freedom of expression is the shining object of their adoration, adulation, and infinite search. They hold tenaciously to this ideal and continue to jealously guard and protect their victories and achievements every inch of the way. They were there at the vanguard of my struggle for Independence. They supplied the tools mentally, physically, and materially and kept the colonial administrators on the alert. No shot was fired and no blood was shed, yet salvos of thundering editorials were let loose, many biting, hard-hitting articles were scripted, and verbal combat was pitched on the pages of many newspapers. Sarcastic and meaningful cartoons were sketched with telling satirical captions and innuendos. They all heralded and hastened my birth as a nation.

The work of the pioneers was not all cut and dried; neither was it all social gathering or merrymaking tea party. The road to attainment of the measure of freedom now being enjoyed has been long, arduous, tortuous, and splashed with the ink of bitterness and acrimony. Ultimately, success re-echoed. Every so often, the road led straight into the colonialists' courts, jails, and painful proscriptions, particularly by the military rulers. Sadly enough for the journalists, the road is still wide open, as even those politicians whose births the journalists 'midwived' and later 'circumcised' have now become so mature and bold as to 'make passes at the journalists' wives', so to speak, sending those who liberated them into civilian or military jails.

It is a verifiable fact that the media, particularly the press, has gone beyond chronicling my political history. It has gone ahead to provide the leadership. The story of the press followed a consistent and identifiable pattern. The pattern evolved as the British colonialists expanded their hold on my territory. My citizenry thus acquired western values and critical heritage, boldly reflected in print. By the time my indigenous and foreign-trained journalists arrived on my scene towards the end of the nineteenth century, the colonialists were already getting entrenched through their missionary propagation, 'enlightenment through education', and vigorous commercial activities.

Trouble loomed large for risk-taking and bold indigenous journalists who would dare to challenge the overbearing colonial masters. The colonial overlords would usually introduce trap laws that would send erring indigenous journalists to jail. During this pioneering era, Lugard found the Lagos press so unflattering that he once contemplated moving the central capital of the protectorate to Kaduna. He had 'nothing but disdain for journalists based in Lagos' because of what he described as 'their scurrilous yellow press', and he continually sought a way of curbing their excesses, which he called the 'monstrous freedom of the press'. Apparently, the colonialists had begun to feel the niggling and pestering effects of the wake-up calls of the indigenous journalists. The people had begun to listen to the clamour and call from local journalists for freedom and independence.

It would be anachronistic and archaic now to start to recount the valiant albeit pristine efforts and resourcefulness of the succeeding generations of journalists who were the very personification of my growth and industry. However, it will not be out of place to mention the names of some of the journalists and the newspapers which were established before I was conceived as a Nation in 1914. Henry Townsend, a missionary, founded the first newspaper, *Iwe Irohin*, in 1859. Adeoye Adeyiga laboriously compiled and scribbled by hand an appealing newspaper in 1909. Coulson Labor displayed a prodigious effort when he printed *The Dawn*. It was a one-man affair in which he gathered the information, processed it and set the type. He would then print the paper and go into the street to sell it.

John Payne Jackson and his son Horatio became very influential as they dominated the scene as the uncompromising Tribune of the people, great evangelists of social reform, matchless propagandists and acknowledged patriots. Christopher Kumolu Johnson first brought indigenization into newspaper management when he published *The Nigerian Chronicle* just before my birth. The paper was noted for its candour. John Davies was a prolific writer with an appreciable command of English language. He threw the floodgates open for the market of ideas from the fiery pens of Habert Macaulay, Pastor Agbebi, and author Laotan. Akinwande became rather too rash and abusive in his *Weekly Spectator.*

When the *Daily Times* was founded in the 1920s with Earnest Ikoli as the first editor and Adeyemo Alakija as the chairman of the Board of Directors, the paper was virtually being spoon-fed on foreign news from belated telegraphic transmissions from Reuters and with local news and comments from writers like Herbert Macaulay. The fire in Ikoli was rather mellow, coming as he did from *The African Messenger* to the pro-establishment *Daily Times*, which brought him into direct confrontation with Macaulay, whose patently libelous articles were rejected by the middle-of-the-road stance of Ikoli.

Macaulay was soon afforded the opportunity to parade his skill and journalistic flair in *The Lagos Daily News*. As a staunch believer in African human rights and freedom, he loosed his journalistic salvo, and his pen blazed away with fire and menace against the British rulers. Having now put on the political mantle of leadership, he became increasingly inflammatory in his writings and so virulent in his sarcasms, lampoons, and publications that the British administrators began to fret and fidget with each issue containing his articles.

The colonialist administration could almost feel Macaulay breathing down their necks whenever they embarked on any untoward or oppressive project. They invariably had him in the back of their minds when they made plans and evolved policy decisions. He loved to publish and be damned in the process, if need be. Through his various journalistic and political activities, he became known as the father of Nigerian nationalism. He garnered several titles and appellations from friends and foes alike throughout his colourful career and was variously called 'the wizard of Kristen Hall', 'the Gandhi of West Africa', 'the Defender of Native Rights and Liberties', and 'Minister Plenipotentiary of the House of Docemo'.

The *Comet* momentarily made a brief appearance in the early 1930s and had some regular writers serving their journalistic apprenticeship. These included Dennis Osadebey, Obafemi Awolowo, and Fred Anyiam. The paper dealt more with the activities on the west coast of Africa at large rather than immediate local affairs. However, it gave adequate coverage to the youth movement's activities until it was taken over by Zik's press. Let's look at the names of the journalists being thrown up. They later became big players and dedicated activists during the era of protests and struggle for my independence. *The Eastern Mail* dominated the newspaper scene in the Eastern Region in the mid 1930s. It was conservative, pro-Establishment, and timid, and it read with alarm and trepidation the fiery and belligerent language emanating from the *Lagos Daily News*. The paper soon lost readership and revenue and finally succumbed to the anti-British sentiments of the day.

A different brand of journalism spitting fire, hell, and brimstone came alive with the arrival of cerebral Zik on the scene with his *West African Pilot* in the late 1930s. The role that the *Pilot* played can hardly be overestimated. Being the brainchild of Zik, it was there long before Independence. The message it carried was the battle cry of the front line nationalists and die-hard freedom fighters of those glorious yesteryears. The *Pilot* admonished 'show the light and the people will follow'. The paper preached with menace, like a demonized prophet of doom, that 'the tree of liberty shall be watered with the blood of tyrants'. It extolled the redemptive influence of education and hailed the inestimable virtues of good leadership.

The *Pilot* harped on all those deeds and virtues that could only make me great as a Nation. It reported the successes and achievements of my citizens who had graduated in distant lands. Such achievers were invited to come back home with their accolades and golden fleece to man the cockpits and the pinnacles of administration that would soon be vacated by the itinerant and patronizing British administrators. Their time—'the tormentors' time'—was up.

As an American-trained journalist and a graduate in political science and anthropology, Zik was eminently suited for the job at hand. *The Pilot*'s mass appeal and strictly indigenous orientation made it extremely popular. John

Okwesa worked hard in trying to ensure its popularity and retain its wide readership. Zik also founded the *Eastern Nigerian Guardian*, the *Southern Defender* at Warri, the *Nigerian Spokesman* at Onitsha, and *The Comet* at Kano. He thus spread his tentacles to all the nooks and crannies of my vast territory.

A colonialist secretary once ventured out of his imperial heights to exchange tirades and abusive banter with the young and bold 'Zik of Africa'. Youthful and vigorous, Zik relished the opportunity and entered into the heated argument with the characteristic sting and brashness which only vintage Zik could muster. He warned that if the secretary could climb down from his high horse to accost him in his milieu, he, Zik, would oblige by splattering mud on the secretary from the muddy environment from which he operated. The struggle was desperate and daring, calling for occasional bravado. Zik was to make an oblique reference to this penchant for injustice and arrogance on the part of the colonialists when he wrote a scathing article saying 'Since correction lies in those hands that made the faults we can not correct, but put we our trust before God who, when the hour is ripe shall rain hot vengeance upon the offender's head'.

Through it all, the clever and slippery Zik—ever compromising, always smart and calculating—was never arrested or jailed. It might be that he was lucky, or wise, or calculating, or that he had all three assets combined. But it was always his followers who bore the brunt of the colonialist yoke of oppression, harassment, and deprivation. Zik probably explained this uncanny factor in the twilight of his life. He had decamped from the Biafran enclave, having written the Biafran national anthem. He first supported Biafra during the civil war but soon defected to my federal side for reasons of political expediency. He later offered an anecdote to explain his decision to decamp. He said, 'A wise and discerning elder does not wait, nose-up, under a tree that is being felled'. Furthermore, there is an adage that says when the young ones are felling a tree in the forest, it is only the elders that would know in which direction it would land. In fairness to good old Zik, the war was weighing heavily against Biafra. More importantly, it would be an irony of history for anyone to expect Zik to preside over my dismemberment, which would result in the liquidation of an entity he had fought so relentlessly to liberate and nurture most of his lifetime.

The great Zik himself gave testimony to the virility and the kind of press that existed in those days when he said, 'The pioneers of the Nigerian press held their own in establishing a virile press at a time when, in the colonial territory, freedom of expression was not respected as a right but as a privilege'. Zik often pitted himself against the British imperial system and its personnel, subjecting both to fierce criticisms. *The Pilot* was the medium through which the yearnings and aspirations of the people were conveyed. Even when acting as an irritant, the paper gave insinuating slants to annoy the colonialists. This was in spite of the fact that the freedom fighters were contending with the superior and seemingly invincible machineries and publishing equipment and facilities at the disposal of the colonial administrators.

The war was fought in the language and tongue of the colonial masters, and it became apparent that the freedom fighters and their collaborators were not operating on a level playing ground. There were obvious advantages for the colonial masters and obvious disadvantages and impediments for the freedom fighters. *The Pilot* marched on to greater glories, introducing cartoons and other readable and amusing items that would attract the masses. It created new avenues and launching pads from where the budding nationalists exploded fusillades of attacks and criticisms on the prevalent colonialist system.

The Pilot was outspoken, uncompromising and fervent on the twin issues of Nationalism and African unity. It had editorial depth and incisive and analytical reportage on the burning issues of the day. It constantly alerted the colonialists on the prospects of my birth as a nation, painting a vivid picture of my greatness and my unquantifiable potentialities. It was like John the Baptist, heralding, forecasting, presaging and generally preparing the way for the myriads of newspapers and magazines, which would emerge in the latter half of the twentieth century and blossom into the twenty-first century.

At that stage, *The Pilot* began to totter with old age. It had dutifully performed its initially projected assignments: My Independence was a reality in 1960. The end had justified the means as *The Pilot* became jaded and bereft of the power that gave it venom and acceptability at inception. It made a feeble reappearance in mid-1960s, but its once vigorous voice was muffled amidst a maze and cacophony of voices emanating from an avalanche of newspapers and magazines that were emerging in the 1990s to continue to write my story as a Nation.

Tony Enahoro, impressionable and prodigiously intelligent, began to vent his spleen about the ways and imperious attitudes of the colonialists during the

1945 General Strike. He had served his tutelage at the *West African Pilot* two months after leaving Kings College. Then he moved to *The Comet*, whose full weight and support he was able to place at the disposal of the workers. For his temerity, he was arraigned before the courts and marched to jail several times for criminal libel and sedition. He later moved on to become, at 21, the youngest-ever editor of the *Southern Nigerian Defender* and the *Weekly Comet* from Zik's stable of newspapers. He was also the associate editor of *West African Pilot* and finally the editor–in-chief of the *Morning Star*. He combined his pungent and hard-hitting comments on the pages of newspapers with vigorous political activism. As mentioned earlier on, Enahoro was the first to make the motion for my Independence on the floor of the Federal House of Representatives in 1953. However, it was defeated in 1956. He lost that battle but not the war, as Independence was just four years around the corner. The unalterable fact remains that he was the first to propose the motion.

Abiodun Aloba, popularly known by his pen name 'Ebenezer Williams', kept everyone waiting and agog with expectation for his Sunday morning 'must read' column in the *Sunday Times*. He was versed in biblical quotations and witticisms. He was also apt and adept in the use of figurative expressions. By his style of writing, he fired the imagination of the youths, attracting them into the profession of journalism and giving impetus to their aspirations and ambitions to aim higher in order to acquire more knowledge. He kept errant and undisciplined politicians on their toes and brought out the best from their great and constructive minds. He prompted debates on great national issues, often highlighting problems and proffering solutions in his brilliantly expressed comments and criticisms.

As the irrepressible political satirist 'Aiyekoto', Bisi Onabanjo wielded a mighty pen, displaying a catchy and masterful use of English language. Like an irritant bedbug, he would bite his quarry and immediately apply a soothing balm on the bitten spot by blowing cold air on it. He was a past master in carrot-and-stick journalism. He would identify a defect and would quickly weigh in with criticisms, constructive comments, and ultimately, soothing palliatives when the need arose. He did not use his real portrait to identify himself when writing his column, but instead, he peers dolefully and pitifully from an artist's impression of a parrot ('Aiyekoto'), perching cagily but alert on a tree branch. By this and the Yoruba meaning of his pen name 'Aiyekoto', he proclaimed that 'Human beings shun the truth'.

He watched with amusement and pent-up indignation the antics, swearing, and prevarications of crafty Ibrahim Babangida (IBB) and bestowed on him the nickname 'Maradona', after the legendary Argentine footballer who dazzled the world with his mesmerizing dribbling runs at the Mexico World Cup Finals. Diego Maradona later stunned astonished spectators and global television viewers with a fraudulently contrived goal. He had cleverly punched the ball into the net manned by the agile English goalkeeper Shilton. Cornered by inquisitive sports journalists, Maradona was to claim that it was the 'hand of God' that scored the goal.

Babangida seemed to have played out this rather apt and eerie description of Maradona's style and performances. He had dribbled and outsmarted the people, swearing 'Insha Allah' each time he repeatedly postponed his handing-over date until he at last stepped aside in 1993. The Argentine Diego Maradona overdramatized *his* own instinctive script when he got involved with cocaine and had to flee from Milan to Buenos Aires, but Aiyekoto's 'Maradona' simply stepped aside from Aso Rock Villa and departed to his hilltop mansion in Minna.

The new decade of the 1950s witnessed the birth of new political parties. These parties fought for and won not only regional self-government in the mid-1960s, but also National Independence at my birth in 1960. It is therefore conclusive that the thriving and popular newspapers, like the *Pilot*, the *Tribune*, and the *Service*, played vital roles in selling ideas, disseminating news, and generally commenting on topical issues of the day. It is also to be assumed that the privately owned newspapers would serve the immediate needs of their owners, particularly from the political angle.

Three major political parties held sway in the three different regions. It was the Northern Peoples Congress (NPC) in the north, the National Convention of Nigeria and the Cameroon (NCNC) in the east, and the Action Group (AG) in the west. These three major political parties plus the smaller ones drew the battle lines at the centre in Lagos to vie for control at the all-important Federal House of Representatives.

The political rumpus that arose between Zik and Mbadiwe prompted the latter to establish the *Telegraph* in order to counteract the effect of the propaganda mounted against him by Zik's *West African Pilot*. *The Daily Service* was reinvented as a new and improved-quality paper going by the name *Daily Express*. Alade Odunewu (also known as 'Allahde') made remarkable inroads in journalism as editor, managing editor and editor-in-chief of several newspapers including the *Daily Service*, *African Press Limited*, *Allied* newspapers of Nigeria, and the *Times* publications. The combination of the newly created newspapers like the *Tribune's Iwe Irohin* in Ibadan, the Calabar–Ogoja–River *COR Advocate* in Uyo, the *Mid West Echo* in Benin, the *Middle Belt Herald* in Jos, and the *Northern Star* in Kano all led to very effective and formidable propaganda weapons and megaphones of the AG.

The *Tribune* became an addictive, compelling, and very dependable source of information and political guidance to its fiercely loyal readers. The paper appeared to wax stronger in crisis, eliciting dogged and devoted loyalty and sympathy from its army of readers. It was vocal in nationalist politics, and it became a great disseminator of news and current affairs. It drove the fear of exposure and sarcasm into the minds of political fair-weather friends and the groveling sycophants of the British administration. It has stood the test of time as the darling of the masses.

During the internal crisis of the Action Group in the early 1960s, the *Tribune* suffered tribulations and persecution at the hands of the powers of the day at the centre. The latter had understandably taken sides with the opponents of Awolowo inside the Action Group. The *Tribune* was banned, sealed, and put under police surveillance. Yet it came out every morning as surely as the sun rises. The paper reflected the tenacity, fixity of purpose, and doggedness of its meticulous proprietor, Awolowo, who inveighed that 'Democracy demands that charlatans and saints should be called by their proper names.'

Lateef Jakande wrote under the pen name of John West. As a practising journalist, he was a vigorous and forceful writer who packed lethal and hard-hitting weaponry into his journalistic arsenal. He played a vital role in the life of the *Tribune* when he was the chief executive for over a decade till the late 1960s. He was a fervent and diligent disciple of Awo, whose principles and teachings he espoused in his writings and during his management of the *Tribune* newspapers. When he later became the 'Action Governor' of Lagos State, he epitomized the perfect imagery of a leader cast in the mould of Awolowo, Spartan life and all.

Jakande was able to concisely demonstrate the theory and practise of good governance which Awolowo preached. He was even euphemistically referred to as 'Baba Kekere', which means 'Mini Awo'. When Awo was released from prison to participate in Yakubu Gowon's government in 1966, he assumed duties, ready to work always in his spartan native dress of 'buba' and indigenous trousers 'sokoto'. Jakande adopted this type of attire, which he inevitably wore, plus the popular Awo fez cap.

Jakande possessed the acumen to survive all odds. He experienced the tribulations and occupational hazards of journalism by going to jail and by being restricted during the turbulent days. The period witnessed the state of emergency declared by Balewa to smooth the way for the sole administrator—Majekodunmi—to be in charge and administer the old 'wild, wild West'. Jakande's vitriolic writings and criticisms in the *Tribune* became so persistently worrisome and unbearable to the usually unflappable Balewa that the latter declared in sheer exasperation, 'If I had my way I would tuck away this John West.'

He was to suffer that specific fate not only under the yoke of Buhari–Idiagbon regime but also during Babangida's regime when he, along with some other political 'eggheads', was incarcerated at Epe for violating the political ban placed on them during the time. It was a great pity that Jakande became a strange bedfellow and an unrepentant apologist for the aberrant military regime of Abacha, because Jakande seemed to have turned his back on the popularly acclaimed victory of Abiola at the polls.

This gratuitous alliance with Abacha during the prolonged incarceration of Abiola had several implications on Jakande's political future. He eventually broke off his links and long association with both Afenifere and the other Awoists. He was known to have joined forces with the rival All Nigeria Peoples Party (ANPP). In fairness to Jakande and also in extenuation, it should be presumed that he was acting true to type as a man of principle and courage. He was said to have argued that he was carrying out on principle a collective decision purportedly agreed upon with the tacit understanding and acquiescence of Abiola himself. He and some of the others in Abacha's cabinet like Kingibe and Ebenezer Bababatope claimed to have remained behind on principle. History will surely pronounce their vindication or vilification, condemnation or commendation, one way or the other.

The Morning Post was established in the early years of Independence. Its first executive boss was H. O. Davies, and the paper was in fact the mouthpiece of the Tafawa Balewa Federal Government. This was because the older established papers like the *Times* and the *Express* could not—or would not—give adequate and much-needed publicity to the government's actions and programmes. In a similar vein, the self-government status granted to the Eastern and Western Regions made the *Tribune* become pro-Awo and automatically pro-AG. The *West African Pilot* was understandably pro-Zik and therefore the mouthpiece and supporter of the NCNC. The partnership and interwoven history of the press and journalists on the one hand and politics and politicians on the other began to evolve in my growth as a Nation.

The Express did not recover from the shock defeat its proprietors suffered at the 1959 federal elections. Riddled with the internal dissension that vigorously shook the Action Group and the attendant crisis and carpet-crossings that broke its rank and file, the *Express* folded up unsung, unapplauded, and with its owners in disarray. The *Gasikiya Tafi Kwobo* was arguably the leading propaganda medium of the northern press. It readily committed its services and support to the ruling NPC. This, of course, was in return for patronage and advertisement that guaranteed regular and stable income, expanded readership, and more authority and confidence in its pronouncements.

The *Sketch* newspaper and other state-owned newspapers like it operated in utter disregard of the journalists' code of conduct: that the journalist's total responsibility is to his audience rather than to his proprietor. But it began to seem more and more that the proprietors, who paid the journalists, dictated the lines along which the journalists could write. They dictated the tunes and rendered the full-throated solos which the journalist accompanied in loud chorus. Hence, the various governments expected their favoured clients or protégées to propagate their ideas—to slant the news and manipulate public views in their favour. This was what led Akintola to found the *Sketch*—to counter the overwhelming influence of Awo's *Tribune*.

This also heralded a vogue for the individual states that sprang up later: to establish their own state-owned newspaper for the same self-serving reasons. *The Herald* was established by the Kwara State government in Ilorin. The Rivers State government published the *Tide* in Port Harcourt. Bendel State published the *Observer* in Benin. Niger State government published the *Newsline* in Minna. The Cross River State government came out with the *Chronicle* in Calabar. The *Star* was the brainchild of the Anambra State government in Onitsha. *The States-man* was established in Owerri by the Imo State government and the *Standard* was sited in Jos by the Plateau State government.

The Daily Times and the *New Nigeria* were taken over by the Federal Government by a decree early in the 1970s. Even though the *Daily Times* essentially propagated positively for the Federal Government without making any pretenses at being critical or offensive, the *New Nigeria* never felt it was under a similar obligation. It became the mouthpiece and defender of northern interests. This was not surprising, as the paper enjoyed much greater circulation and readership in the north than in the south.

Over the years, before and after my birth as a Nation, the proliferation of newspaper houses and publishing outfits became a phenomenon. Ownership of the printed media has never been the exclusive preserve or prerogative of governments. It was well known that some of the privately owned papers always enjoyed wider circulation and readership than the government-owned ones. But the government-owned papers were merely government megaphones in disseminating information and touting government's stand on vital issues. The privately owned papers were more popular for their display of greater flair and their penchant for criticizing more freely and, inevitably, for reflecting the views of their publishers who, in almost all cases, were politicians.

At this point, a sober reflection on the activities of journalists as chroniclers and historians of my birth, growth, and adulthood is necessary. Before resuming my narration about the proliferation of additional newspaper establishments, I will comment on the emergence of a brilliant array of journalists and writers who learned the ropes from older newspapers and their founders. This new breed of journalists paraded brilliant writing skills. They were also well known as columnists and critics. Their views covered the gamut of politics, finance, economics, labour, culture, International Relations, sports, and general documentaries.

The fact still remains that the older journalists who were the main actors and dramatis personae before and during my birth as a nation had then become veterans and fully involved politicians. In the mid-1950s, their newspapers were their power bases and very effective propaganda media to proclaim and propagate their political ideas. They invited their followers to join the struggle to attain first, regional self-government, then national independence. Therefore, the involvement of such established proprietors as Azikiwe and Awolowo in full-time politics marked them as the recognized political leaders.

Tested and experienced journalists and writers like Akintola and Enahoro began to exude greater interest in politics. It would therefore be seen that no vacuum was created when known publishers and veteran journalists moved on to total involvement in politics. A new army of journalists, writers, and critics who mostly trained and operated in the old newspaper houses easily stepped into the shoes of their idols, mentors, or employers. They assumed the positions of my chroniclers and historians. Their roles were soon defined, and many continued in the footsteps of their mentors as critics and disseminators of their employers' ideas and ideals. They trumpeted in writing the clarion call to arms against colonialists' rule and the forces of retardation and ignorance.

Such was the setting and the background when Olu Aboderin established the *Punch* newspapers in 1973. In the process, he evolved a unique press technological breakthrough that lent greater status to the *Punch* in modern typography, printing process, and publishing technology. The story of the *Punch* would not be complete unless an honorable mention is adequately accorded to the inimitable Sam Amuka, popularly known as 'Sad Sam' or 'Offbeat Sam'. He had seen service at the *Daily Times* where he rose to the position of editor. He was at the inception of the *Punch* as its co-founding director when he brought his expertise in journalism to complement the managing and accounting background of Olu Aboderin. However, things soon fell apart between the two when their inability to work harmoniously together degenerated into a well-publicized court case as they parted ways. Aboderin held on to the *Punch*, and Sam Amuka figuratively 'punched' his way out of the *Punch* to resurface with his own formidable *Vanguard* newspaper.

The Vanguard came into being in 1984 with a bang as a Sunday paper. Sam Amuka, the publisher, brought with him the aggregation of his invaluable experience and considerable writing ability from the *Times* and *Punch*. He was imbued with a unique sense of humour, which permeated his writing even though his portrait depicted a spiteful, mournful, and sad face—thus his descriptive sobriquet 'Sad Sam'. He exuded wit and charm and possessed a vast repertoire of jokes, sarcasms, and anecdotes. His writings were often laced with a combination of all these journalistic weapons.

The Vanguard paraded a brilliant array of writers and journalists whose versatility covered the whole gamut of topics that added glamour, amusement, and knowledge to the evolution and growth of a nation. These included politics, culture, dissemination of ideas and ideals, international affairs, and sports. Therefore, it would be seen that such writers constituted a veritable source of information and guidance in compiling my history. This was a commonplace fact among the myriads of newspapers and magazines that sprang up from the 1980s, particularly with the first departure of the military and the emergence of the Second Republic.

The Vanguard bubbled with the effervescent column of Bisi Lawrence, or 'Biz Law'. He was at home with searching serialized interviews, analytical current affairs, and in-depth sports reports and comments. He was very versatile and expressive with a wide repertoire of choice journalese. He had been a brilliant broadcaster with the erstwhile Nigerian Broadcasting Service (NBS), where he had the cliff-hanging encounter and not-too-winsome privilege of meeting face to face with the rather confused and inebriated coup plotter, Dimka. The latter had sauntered into the studio and seized it to, as customary, hail his 'fellow Nigerians' to 'declare the good tidings'. He had ended his broadcast by declaring a puerile and confusing curfew 'from dawn to dusk'.

That was history in the making, and Biz Law was there, albeit as an unwilling observer. However, he lived to narrate his weird and bizarre experience. Some of the other writers at the *Vanguard* included Kunle Animashaun and Shobowale, whose columns are always filled with incisive comments, constructive criticisms, and palliative measures. Others are Ikkedy Isizugo, Mideno Bayagbon, Pini Jason, Owei Lakemfa, Ochereome Nnanna, Ladipo Adamolekun, Helen Ovbiagele, and the ubiquitous sportswriter Anochie Anibeze, who jetted to wherever Nigeria was involved in any sporting action and recorded all the blow-by-blow action as it happened. *Vanguard*'s absorbing and brain-wracking crossword puzzle appearing on its back page made the paper the darling of many crossword puzzle enthusiasts.

In 1980, M. K. O. Abiola, a highly successful accountant, vice-president of the ITT, and a high-profile multi-millionaire, applied his Midas touch to the newspaper industry as the proprietor of the *National Concord* and the *Sunday Concord*. The *Concord* could be called a child of political circumstances. When the ban on politics was lifted, Abiola entered the political arena with a bang to flag on the race for leadership in my Second Republic. He pitched his tent with the conservative National Party of Nigeria (NPN) as a founding member. He soon discovered that the fledgling party had to contend with the well-oiled machinery of the giant octopus—*The Tribune* and the *Sketch*. Both papers articulated the views and propagated the ideas of the vastly experienced group in Awolowo's Unity Party of Nigeria (UPN).

The Concord made its debut with a confrontational and highly provocative personal attack on Awolowo. The paper had blared a screamer about 'Papa's Land'. It portrayed Awolowo as obtaining land in lieu of payment for services rendered to the Oniru family of Lagos. The perceived motive for the story was to portray Awolowo as a hypocrite who professed to be a socialist while actually being an acquisitive, wealthy man. *Concord* also sneeringly echoed the alarm that Awolowo raised, about the 'economic ship of State' heading rudderless for the rocks with NPN's Shagari at the helm. The *Concord* then went ahead to scream out the pugnacious and unrealistic reply of NPN's chairman, Akinloye, and Emma Edozien, special adviser in Shagari's government. The duo had lied to the world press that the economy was as buoyant as ever. But then the handwriting concerning my imminent economic collapse became legible to everyone on the wall of reality. Thereafter, Shagari paradoxically warned that 'Those who sowed the storm shall reap the whirlwind'. Such was the war of words fought on the pages of the newspapers by politicians who were steeped and rooted in journalism as proprietors and writers. These indefatigable journalists were preparing me, deliberately or unwittingly, to be able to emerge as a strong and virile nation. The vibrant press entrenched me on a very strong foundation.

Unfortunately, at this early stage of his political career, Abiola's aspiring to leadership at the national convention of the party was severely jolted, summarily thwarted by the party's strongman, Umaru Dikko. Abiola's ambitious challenge was roundly rebuffed. Dikko's foreboding that 'the Presidency is not for sale' amounted to what was seen as a wicked and malicious inference that Abiola was trying to impose himself on the party by scheming to buy his way to the apex of power with his tremendous wealth.

Abiola quit the party when it became clear to him that power seemed perpetually zoned into the hands of only a privileged few and to a particular section of my vast territory. Indeed, zoning was seen as a truce with mediocrity, incompetence, and the idiocy of false stability at the expense of genuine progress and true Nation-building. Abiola soon concentrated more attention on his newspapers with fruitful results. He enlarged his stable of newspapers by adding a weekly magazine, *The African Concord*, and a variety of vernacular newspapers like *Udoka*, *Amana*, and *Isokan*. He capped it all by establishing the *Community Concord*.

A team of versatile and intrepid journalists joined the *Concord*. The pioneering group included Henry Odukomaya, S. L. Bolaji, Dayo Duyile, and Doyin Aboaba (who was later to become Mrs. Abiola and eventually the paper's managing director). *Concord*'s planning and progress chart bore all the attributes of Abiola's meticulous entrepreneurship and brilliant execution. It attracted professional journalists who were worthy of the stupendous salaries offered by the proprietor. The telling declaration of the publisher at its inception was that the paper was 'out for harmony, unity, peace, friendship, understanding, and cooperation'.

Abiola eventually decided to run for president at the next presidential elections when Babangida declared the race open. His newspapers inevitably became a tool he used to garner support and votes until Babangida strangely snatched victory from his grasp by annulling the 1993 federal presidential elections. The elections had been universally adjudged as the freest and fairest ever held in the annals of my evolving history. The *Concord Printing Press* was shut down and later proscribed under the pretext that guns and ammunitions were being stored inside the *Concord Press* compound.

Alex Ibru brought the name, industry, and vast business entrepreneurship of his family to bear in the founding of one of the most prestigious newspaper establishments ever. It was called the *Guardian*, and its motto was 'Conscience nurtured by truth'. The paper's layout and pagination were very impressive and easy to follow. It dwelled on news of my affairs as a Nation as well as on Africa and world events. The participants, who in this case were some of the most brilliant names in journalism, could report all events and activities pertaining to a nation's history. Tunji Dare, Eskor Toyo, Odia Ofeimum, Joe Igbokwe, and the profound thinker, prolific writer, and discerning critic Reuben Abati were only a part of a galaxy of professionals who gave character and depth to the *Guardian*. They wrote on a variety of topical issues and established for the newspaper a reputation for fearlessness and incisive investigative journalism.

The paper also enjoyed the services of brilliant Stanley Macebuh and the scholarly Yemi Ogunbiyi, both of who were very knowledgeable and a pride to the publishing industry. Its logo proclaimed it 'the Flagship of the Nation', and its editorials were a mirror of the Nation's conscience—enlightening, invigorating, refreshing, candid, and ennobling. Even when the daring and historical duo of Tunde Thompson and Nduka Irabor was tried and sentenced under the draconian Decree #4 of Buhari–Idiagbon's regime and the paper itself was penalized with a sum of N50,000, the paper marched on, relentless and undaunted in nurturing the truth.

The paper was not given to sensationalism. It throve on candour and fearless criticism. This trend peaked when Alex Ibru, the publisher, became the Federal Minister of Internal Affairs and a member of the elite Provisional Ruling Council under Abacha. The new Minister was greeted with a warning editorial when the *Guardian* left no one in doubt that Alex Ibru, the paper's publisher, would be constantly under the searchlight of the *Guardian*. He was tacitly reminded that rules would neither be bent nor news unduly slanted to please or to protect anyone, regardless of who it was. To the consternation of all and particularly to the calm dismay of Ibru himself, Abacha proscribed the *Guardian* on the suspicion of Ibru being the source of news leaks emanating from Aso Rock Villa.

Even though he was Federal Minister of Internal Affairs and a civilian member of the Provisional Ruling Council, Ibru refused to raise a finger to protest the proscription, discretion being the better part of valour. If he protested rather petulantly or insistently, overtly or loudly, the vast Ibru business and commercial empire would have been consigned to the same fate of looming collapse and, ultimately, total eclipse planned for Abiola's conglomerate. This clearly depicts the power that publishers and journalists wielded and the role they were able to play in the course of Nation building. Alex Ibru paid dearly for the outspokenness and brazen temerity of his paper. The goons and thugs of Abacha were let loose on him. He survived by sheer miracle a vicious attack in an assassination attempt to eliminate him. He left government and retired to temporary seclusion whilst allowing his newspaper to march on.

Proprietorship of a solid and vibrant newspaper had come to be identifiable with the political ambitions and aspirations of people who were interested in participating in my growth, development, and governance. To this extent, an astute and forward-looking businessman, Maurice Iwuanyawu, founded the *Champion* newspaper in the early 1990s. Wealthy and imbued with plenty of foresight, drive, and tenacity, he first used the formation of a popular football team—Iwuanyawu Nationale Football Club—and then the establishment of the *Champion* newspaper to project himself into the limelight and into my people's psyche. The team quickly rose to the top of the First Division table of my football league bearing Iwuanyawu's name. His *Champion* newspaper establishment similarly flourished and waxed popular.

This combination became Iwuanyawu's launching pad into political stardom. It afforded him the vehicle on which he drove his Presidential aspirations via the Nigerian Republican Convention (NRC) into the people's collective psyche. The first managing director of the paper was Henry Odukomaya. The paper commanded wide readership, particularly among the Igbo community. When the big 'cats' like the *Guardian*, *Punch*, and *Concord* were away, courtesy of ban, harassment, and proscription, the 'mice' like the new comer *Champion* could play. The *Champion* did play along with other lucky newspapers that dotted an era when proscription of papers belonging to perceived opponents and critics of government was the vogue.

There are some newspapers that are not mentioned here. It is not because of their lesser significance, but because of their lack of relevance to the issue of chronicling my history. Moreover, their publishers did not show any interest in competitive politics. Suffice it to say that the indefatigable Jakande made a solo comeback effort with *The News*, which always came out around mid-day. This was soon after he ceased being the acclaimed 'Action Governor' of Lagos State and his eventual release from detention. As should be expected, the paper's scoops and exposés soon landed it in trouble; so much so that it was once sealed and kept under police surveillance. Soon, the paper disappeared from circulation. It could easily be remembered for saying it all in catchy, screaming headlines spread right across three quarters of its front page. It was the gimmick of a political past master using eye-catching screaming headlines, political stunts, and propaganda tactics.

'In essence it is a veritable and unalterable fact that journalists and the press supplied the bricks and mortars that went into my foundation and construction as a national edifice named Nigeria at my birth. The solid rock and steady ladder on which they ensured my birth and growth have stood the test of time. The involvement of journalists at every stage of my evolution has led progressively to my present status. They used their professional clout and ingenuity to set up formidable newspaper establishments through which they were enabled to air their views and give voice to the indigenous views and feelings of discontent.

It is not mere coincidence that the emergent politicians who, even before and after my independence, were mostly the same journalists who formed the political parties that held sway as President Nnamdi Azikiwe in the 1st Republic, Premiers Obafemi Awolowo, Ladoke Akintola and others. Their followers were of the ilk of Tony Enahoro, S.G Ikoku, Lateef Jakande, Mbazulike Amechi, Bisi Onabanjo, Lam Adesina, Segun Osoba and others who in their various capacities are still sustaining me as a nation.

CHAPTER THREE

MILITARY GOVERNMENTS: FIRST SET

AGUIYI IRONSI AND 'UNITARY GOVERNMENT'— JANUARY–JULY 1966

My Armed Forces had always had both their 'say' and their 'way' at the same time.

That attitude was in direct contradiction to the tenets of Democracy that I always strove to adopt and yearned to imbibe. In the greater scheme of things, I would rather both the minority and the majority have their 'say', but the majority should have the 'way'. In actual fact, the military kept winning in the toss-up for who controlled my government. Succeeding soldier-politicians liked to eat their cake and have it. However, when the chips were down and political exigencies cropped up, they did not care about the electorate. They were neither voted for nor trained to govern in the first place, and they were not answerable to anyone. Hence, they would not lie awake at night at election time worrying about the results. For them, there could be only one exit—one directed by superior force. A coup either succeeds or fails, with attendant consequences and repercussions: trials by military tribunals, execution by firing squad or by hanging, long jail sentences, and punitive demotions.

Coup planners, unlike elected governments, worry little about unemployment figures, mass transportation systems, technologies in power generation

71

and water distribution, inflation and price indices, foreign exchange rates (the weaker my naira, the better for them), or human rights and the environment. Failure to attend to these vital needs by a civilian government may create problems that could lead to it being toppled. But such mundane matters of popularity or acceptability would not bother the military. After all, did the legendary Chinese Chairman Mao Zedong not say, 'Power emanates from the barrel of the gun'? When Oliver Cromwell, the Protector, was confronted with a similar situation during the monarchical interregnum in British history between 1629 and 1641, it was brought to his attention that nine out of every ten men were against his reign, he promptly dead-panned, 'I will disarm the nine and arm the one'. A desperate and beleaguered armed man in the midst of nine aggrieved unarmed men would be like a bull in a China shop.

Too often—in fact, more often than not in my chequered history—military incursions into my governance revealed many characters. Some were fascinating and others nauseating. Hardy's 'The Convergence of the Twain'—my fiercely individualistic and republican middle-ranking Igbo military officers and my few university-educated Yoruba officers—made an almighty bang when it came into conflict with the stonewall bastion of my rigidly conservative northern military hierarchy. This led to murderous mayhem when, in the early hours of January 15, 1966, some Army officers cited a list of complaints against the political class. They were propelled by the urge for change and motivated by idealism and a desire to tackle corruption.

Chukwuma Kaduna Nzeogwu was brave, charismatic, and calculating. He coordinated affairs from the north and became the protagonist of all coups in the 'Coup of the Five Majors'. It was his assignment to handle the north, and he executed affairs with ruthless efficiency. This military uprising left a trail of bloodshed in its wake. Nzeogwu dispatched Ahmadu Bello. In his broadcast on Radio Kaduna on that 'red-letter' day, Nzeogwu had said, inter alia, that 'The aim of the Revolutionary Council is to establish a strong, united, and prosperous nation, free from corruption and internal strife....Our enemies are the political profiteers, swindlers, the men in the high and low places that seek bribes and demand ten percent, those that seek to keep the country divided permanently so that they can remain in office as ministers and VIPs of waste...we do promise freedom from fear, freedom from general inefficiency. We promise that you will no more be ashamed to say that you are a Nigerian'.

The majors were predominantly of Eastern extraction. They included Don Okafor, Chris Anuforo, Humphrey Chukwuka, Ademoyega (a Yoruba man from the west), and Emmanuel Ifeajuna. The politicians who were killed as a result of the coup were mostly northerners in addition to some westerners and a couple of mid-westerners. The army lost Ademulegun, Maimalari, Unegbe, Largema, Kuru Mohammed, Pam, Sodeinde, Adegoke, Odu, and others who were killed to make way for Johnson Umunnakwe Ironsi's 'Unitary Government'.

Quite significantly and rather ominously, it was a paradox that no easterner lost his or her life at that stage of the looming conflict. Major Don Okafor was supposed to execute Major-General Aguiyi-Ironsi, head of the army. But he failed dismally. Those who averred that the mutiny was propelled by nationalistic fervor rather than narrow tribal inclinations explained that Ironsi, a well known party crawler, escaped being killed because he was attending a party on a boat moored on the lagoon along the marina in Lagos. He was not, therefore, at home when the mutineers called. This claim seemed to have fallen flat when tenuous explanations were offered for why the lives of some Igbo-speaking politicians and officers were spared.

Among the civilians, the north lost popular and much-loved leaders in both Ahmadu Bello and Tafawa Balewa. Captain Nwobosi riddled the body of Akintola with bullets in the west, and in the mid-west, Okotie-Eboh was also killed. By an inexplicable and at times suspicious quirk of fate, the lives of top-notch Igbo leaders were spared. These dastardly killings assumed the coloration of selective elimination and a corrosive ethnic agenda. The great Zik was away in Haiti on vacation. Lieutenant Oguchi was detailed to handle affairs in the east and eliminate Okpara. But Okpara was supposedly placed under house arrest. Was it, instead, protective custody? It was alleged that he was then playing host to Archbishop Makarios of Cyprus, who was visiting the east after the recently concluded Commonwealth Conference in Lagos. Providentially, the legendary Awo was at that time languishing in Calabar Prison, where he was incarcerated on charges of treasonable felony.

Given the balance of forces, it was quite obvious that the majors needed more than ardent idealism and sheer courage, which formed the propelling force behind their action. They exhibited their lack of political sagacity and were wanting in comprehension of the prevalent forces at play. They succeeded only in temporarily whittling down the number of the people at the helm of affairs, without decapitating the leaders of thought in the bastion of the conservative northern military and political hierarchy. For the coup planners, this was a very careless, costly, and presumptuous mistake. For my Federal Government, it was the case of 'time out' like the ram in folklore that deliberately retreats in order to come back to re-execute a more ferocious and devastating series of head butts.

Ironsi miraculously survived the carnage after allegedly browbeating the young Igbo officer who was detailed to kill him. He succeeded in arresting some of the ringleaders. Having aborted the coup, he failed to apply the redoubtable military law against failed coup plotters. In subsequent coups, certain death by firing squad became the lot of failed plotters. Such executions were carried out after the usual military tribunal trials. The northern political establishment withdrew to lick its wounds. They later quietly regrouped to plan the craziest of all revenges.

It was obvious from the beginning that Ironsi was living on borrowed time. In an attempt to sweep the issue of the coup under the rug, Ironsi dabbled into a more critical and complex condition. He was immediately confronted by a crippling dilemma. He owed his ascendancy to the majors' uprising, which in turn had been routed by forces antagonistic to *their* vision, and they were consequently branded as villainous murderers who were to be visited with swift justice. Swamped and confused by the new effect of ethnic regrouping, Ironsi seemed to be enthroning a new ethnic power by embracing and promoting the Unitary System of government, which was not suitable for the existing situation at that time.

When he promoted the controversial Unification Decree Number 34 on May 24, 1966, Ironsi appeared to have unwittingly played into the hands of his opponents. This military law banished political parties and transferred the legislative powers of the regions to the center. This instant transformation from a federal to a unitary system was interpreted as a further ploy to weaken my Northern Region, which was so powerful, given its official population and geopolitical size granted by my erstwhile British colonialist masters, that it was able to unilaterally produce for me a leader. This inevitably helped to fuel the passion that resulted in a conflagration in form of the pogroms of 1966.

Ironsi, using a stuffed crocodile as a mascot—which he carried about on his mission to expatiate on the tenets of 'Unitary government'—met his gruesome death in a counter-coup staged at Ibadan. As a result of this coup, the morally upright Colonel Adekunle Fajuyi played the role of a soldierly 'tragic hero' of a host till the end. Rather than release his august guest to the bloodthirsty vengeance seekers, Fajuyi opted to do what only a soldierly, hospitable, and sincere host would: He literally accompanied his guest into eternity. But he had paved his way into the warm affection of history, because his admirers and foes remembered him as a soldier and a gentleman. His fellow Ekiti people are very proud of him as a soldier of distinction and impeccable integrity.

The pyrrhic victory of the five majors was to prove illusory as it did not take long for the political and military authority of the north to reassert itself. Blood literally flowed in the cantonments at Ikeja, Abeokuta, and Ibadan, when about 300 officers of eastern origin were killed and 50,000 Igbos were massacred in the north. This horrendous bloodbath was the closest I ever came as a nation to the throes of that modern-day expression of 'ethnic cleansing'.

While this wanton carnage went on, a northern soldier who was a sergeant rudely rebuffed the top-ranking military officer, Ogundipe. The sergeant had insolently told him that he would only take orders from his captain, who happened then to be none other than Joseph Garba, later a retired general. Ogundipe saw this as a contemptuous and ominous signal that ran counter to the prevalent military decorum, protocol, and pecking order to which he was accustomed. He therefore opted to flee with the assistance of the British High Commission to the safety of a British frigate moored off the marina in Lagos. This took him to the safe haven of London, where he was when Gowon appointed him as my High Commissioner and the Ambassador Extraordinary and Plenipotentiary to the Court of St. James.

Ironsi's arguably enduring contribution to the structure of my political landscape was that he set up the centralized system of government in which my Federal Government assumed vastly superior powers over my other units. The section that produced the leader at the center remained the dominant political force.

YAKUBU GOWON: THE CIVIL WAR AND THE '3 RS' —JULY 1966–JULY 1975

The military relay race for my governance thus resumed when the young, handsome, 32-year-old Christian, Yakubu Gowon, was handed the baton of leadership. From then on, there was an apparent convergence of interests between the agenda of the military and the political agenda of the dominant power group of that era. That signaled the beginning of a new dawn for my young military, which began to lose much of its widespread prestige and to assume, in the eyes of observers, the shape of sectional and regional interests. It would later metamorphose into what the foxy Akinloye was to call the other National party—parallel to the National Party of Nigeria, over which he was chairman.

From this moment in my history, I began to lurch and stumble like a drunken sailor from one crisis to another. My chequered history was to accommodate a 30-month civil war fought on land, in the air, and at sea. There were several abortive military uprisings, occasionally successful military coups, sporadic political insurrections, crippling and widespread strikes, and several religious and ethnic conflagrations. The period would witness the macabre succession in the absurd and bizarre military leadership relay race.

Gowon's reign over my people spanned nine years. The coup and the ensuing counter-coup had left me high and dry. If that coup was bloody and lopsided in favour of my eastern military personnel, the subsequent counter-coup was unleashed with ferocious vengeance, culminating in a series of genocidal attacks in my Northern Region on people from the south, particularly from the east. The resultant mass movement of peoples, predominantly of the eastern parts, was spontaneous.

They converged in Onitsha across the bridge from the old mid-west and also across the Jebba Bridge. They trooped by rail and by road down into the heartland of the mortally aggrieved Igbos, who brought with them all the vital household items they could hurriedly lay hands upon. When the Oxford-educated Ojukwu made the clarion call, the willing people of my Eastern Region were galvanized into a mood in which they were determined to protect themselves and, if necessary, seek revenge. The movement soon became an avalanche. The Igbos felt push was coming to shove, and all roads therefore led towards my Eastern Region.

Well protected and smug in the safety of a solidly built bunker, Ojukwu orchestrated and directed the war efforts. His propagandist, Okokon Ndem, who raved and ranted like a latter-day Goebbels, indefatigably assisted him. Like a warped gramophone record, Okonkon Ndem blared with fury and malice the threats and vituperation of the war council. This type of alarmist and malicious propaganda was to be re-enacted in an even more reprehensible fashion early in the regime of Abacha. In an orgy of unabashed disinformation, Uche Chukwumerije had alleged that Lagos, Kaduna, and Enugu were to be bombed by M. K. O. Abiola. He alleged that Abiola had fled abroad to invite foreign intervention to attack his fatherland in an attempt to reclaim the popular victory that had been wickedly snatched from him on his way to Aso Rock Villa. Hence, just before the outbreak of the civil war, the stampede that ensued was encouraged by the loud, insistent, and tremendous propaganda. The mass movement of people was the order of the day.

It became obvious that Gowon and his team were oblivious of one solid fact: Oil politics and the plan to corner the oil resources for the Biafra of their dreams had become paramount in Ojukwu's agenda. Gowon was smug in his belief that 'after all, the Igbo domination has been broken by the pogrom, and Nigeria can move forward without the Igbos'. He was reckoning without the indomitable spirit of the Igbos and their ability to bounce back from the brink. 'On Aburi we stand' became the watchword and battle cry of Ojukwu and the secessionists.

This outcry arose because Gowon was advised to repudiate the Aburi Accord when he and the civil servants who were not present at Aburi sat down to take a closer look at the accord. The idea of accepting separate military commands, separate police, and separate civil service was repugnant to them. It was therefore recommended that the entire arrangement should be repudiated or even jettisoned. Ojukwu and his advisers demurred and began to perceive that the Gowon government honoured the Aburi Agreement 'more in the sheer arbitrariness with which its terms were breached than in their observance'.

To pre-empt the looming revolt, Gowon carved out my geographical terrain into 12 states 'for ease of administration' on May 27, 1967. Creation of states became the graveyard of Regionalism even in the north. It suddenly dawned on all that the Kanuris are different from the Tivs, just like Hausa/Fulani are different from Langtans and Ebiras. The monolithic North has since persistently striven to establish its oneness. But then, it was even more cataclysmic and significant under the prevalent circumstances in the Eastern Region where my citizens came from distinctive ethnic groups. Additionally, and most importantly, the newly created states occupied the vast areas in which abundant crude oil could be found. It was educative to observe that the newly created states were outside the Igbo heartland. Ojukwu's reaction—concerning the creation of states by excising the entire land mass and riverine areas of the old Eastern Region and declaring it as the Republic of Biafra—was pregnant with acquisitive and selfishly exploitative implications.

Parts of the excised enclaves were towns and villages of my sons and daughters whose only thin uniting cord with the Igbos was proximity. But their cultures and inclinations were intrinsically different. In that heterogeneous collective, the Igbos were preponderant, with the minority groups being the Ibibios, the Efiks, the Ijaws, and the Ogojas. This conspiratorial declaration elicited a negative reaction from both the Federalists and my eastern minorities, who braced to meet the bogey of Ibo domination.

Ukpabi Asika was appointed the Administrator of the East Central State. He creditably managed the affairs of the new state in a period of war; Ken Saro-Wiwa became the administrator of Rivers State. A memorable verbal exchange that arose between Asika and Zik is worthy of mention. Asika had wanted to assert and flaunt his newly acquired authority in the face of the vastly experienced, formidable, and cerebral Zik, by proclaiming 'enough is enough' and referring to Zik as the 'nattering nabob of negativism, ex-this, ex-that and ex-everything else'. Zik, the old maestro, fired back, reminding 'the son of an ex-postmaster' that 'no condition is permanent'.

Jacob Esuene was appointed governor of South-Eastern State and at the same time, Alfred Diete-Spiff was assigned as the Governor of Rivers State. The implication was clear and unambiguous, and Ojukwu, along with the advisory committee of the Eastern Region, would have none of that. They had their own agenda to which they adamantly planned to adhere.

The advisory committee handed Ojukwu the mandate to declare and proclaim Eastern Nigeria as a free, sovereign, and independent state to be known as the Republic of Biafra. Ojukwu consequently complied on May 30, 1967. This was in accordance to the mandate of the committee and in response to the creation of the 12 states announced three days earlier by Gowon. Because of this act of defiance, the Federal Government, headed by Gowon, reacted by ordering a naval blockade of the Bight of Benin and Biafra and mapped out a six-point programme for Ojukwu to retrace his steps:

1. Revocation of the Biafran Independence Edict;
2. Acceptance and recognition of Federal authority over Eastern Nigeria;
3. Acceptance of the newly created 12-state structure;
4. Acceptance of the participation of civilians in the Federal and States Executive Council;
5. Revocation of the Revenue Collection Edict, which stopped taxes and revenue originating in the east from going to the Federal Government purse; and
6. Accepting that future constitution talks would be duly accredited and equally representative of the 12 states.

The war was joined. Biafra launched a vigorous propaganda machine. I thought that, as declared by Gowon's government, it was going to be a short-lived 'police action'. Days turned into weeks, and my loyal forces struck at Gakem, which later became the theater of some of the fiercest battles. Ojukwu had boasted, and his sabre-rattlers had proclaimed, that 'no country in black Africa' could subdue Biafra. This was reminiscent of Winston Churchill's clarion call to arms at a stage during the Second World War in which he proclaimed that Great Britain would 'fight on land, on the seas and in the air'. Daredevil men and women on the Biafran side with Igbo nationalistic fervour formed themselves into militia bands and voluntarily joined the fray.

Inevitably, the influence of external forces was brought to bear on the direction and stand on which both sides decided to pursue the war. It became apparent that Britain initially could not openly and unequivocally declare a stand that could be instrumental in hastening my collapse as a Nation, considering that it had just granted me Independence barely seven years earlier. Neither Britain nor America, France, and their allies, indicated a willingness to tolerate, witness, or participate in my looming disintegration. They had all taken into consideration the reverberations and ripple effects such disintegration might unleash throughout Africa.

The ensuing war raged on simultaneously on the battlefield of diplomacy. A peace mission dispatched by my Federal Government to the Organization of African Unity (OAU) in Addis Ababa achieved its desired positive results. OAU, under the chairmanship of Ethiopia's Emperor Haile Selassie, acceded to my quest for the recognition of 'one Nigeria' when it condemned the secession of Biafra. Not only did Britain choose to back the stand of the OAU, but also any talk about my Civil War was effectively shut out of discussions on the floor of the General Assembly at the United Nations. S. O. Adebo, my Permanent Representative at the United Nations, was at his diplomatic best in presenting my case to the world press and to inquisitive envoys. They always wanted to be fully briefed about my on-going civil war. France offered support to Biafra. Some African countries like Gabon, Ivory Coast, Tanzania, and Zambia were sympathetic to Biafra. These African countries joined France and some non-state supporters like Joint Church Aid, Caritas International, and the Holy Ghost Fathers of Ireland in supporting Biafra in many humanitarian ways.

Both sides endeavoured to obtain international support from wherever they could get it. Biafra collected huge consignments of ammunition of French weapons at night at Uli Airstrip. Gabon, Ivory Coast, and Sao Tome were also used as bases for gun-running to Biafra. My neighbours like Equatorial Guinea, Benin, Chad, Niger, and Cameroon demurred and refused to support the secessionists. My Federal Government did not totally lack support from abroad. Britain provided minesweepers and a frigate; a submarine chaser was obtained from the Netherlands. Russia also made available torpedo boats and several radar-equipped seaward-defense vessels at the beginning of the war.

A skirmish around Nsukka soon escalated into full-blown war. Action emanated from air, land, and sea. Various segments of the armed forces were fully involved. War raged relentlessly like fire on the prairies for 30 solid months. It was as if my anatomy had developed a serious disorder in which one of my vital organs was rebelling. I spilled my guts in the trenches at Owerri and during the urban guerilla warfare at Abagana, where a Biafran ambuscade turned a convoy of vehicles carrying my Federal troops and ammunitions into a raging inferno. The waters of River Niger took on the colour of blood at Asaba, where my soldiers, in mid-stream, ran into a hail of bullets rained on them by my other, rebellious soldiers lurking undetected on the Onitsha shore. It was a horrendous blood bath. It also served as a great morale booster for my seceding part.

At Azumiri, near Opobo, a pitched battle was fought in which several lives were lost and the rebel troops broken into two sectors. My Mid-West Region was invaded in one fell swoop, and Biafra planted its flag there for five weeks. The suddenness of the incursion was such that Ejoor, the military governor, was caught unawares and allegedly fled on a cycle, riding night and day in the jungle to freedom. Nwawo led the incursion. The seeming lightning victory was illusory, as Biafra's invulnerability soon became a myth rather than reality and its overblown ego was deflated. They had moved towards Lagos and the prevarication of Banjo, fighting on the Biafran side, enabled my Federal troops to nip the march towards Lagos in the bud at Ore, where Major Oyin Iluyomade, an Ondo town indigene, led the troops that fought my rebelling member to a standstill. The ferocity with which this battle was fought was such that it has gone into the people's lingo as 'Ija Ore O le ku' (the battle of Ore was fight to finish).

The Civil War took its toll in terms of human suffering. My troops took to the skies in the MIG bombers and strafed major cities and densely populated areas in the war zone. My rebelling forces retaliated by swooping low in B52 bombers and wreaking havoc and vengeance on Federal positions. Then the 'Ikenne sage', Awo, freshly released from Calabar Prison, made a memorable pronouncement to the effect that 'all was fair in war' and that 'hunger was a weapon of war'. Awolowo's pronouncement sounded like a fresh clarion call to resume all-conquering hostilities with no holds barred. All hell literally broke loose by way of blockades and hunger when all routes to food and succour were rendered inaccessible. I shudder to think of how malnourished infants and orphans were sent to their early graves as victims of kwashiorkor. Families broken asunder and dislocated roamed about in the bush, seeking food, succour, and refuge. Lizards, frogs, roots, and fruits were eaten where and when available. Occasionally, some hitherto forbidden food items freshly laid waste in the forest became acceptable food substitutes to the fleeing victims of that needless war.

My last operation to remove the ulcer that was getting bloodier was at Uli-Ihiala, where Ojukwu turned tail under the pretext of going 'in search of peace'. Such inane posturing, saber rattling, and shadow boxing had virtually become

*1 **Aguiyi Ironsi.*** *First Military Head of State and Commander-in-Chief of the Armed Forces January–July 1966.*
*2 **Yakubu Gowon.*** *He became the Military Head of State at the age of 32. He successfully prosecuted the 30-month Civil War. In victory, he declared 'No victor, no vanquished'. He proclaimed and implemented the celebrated agenda of the '3Rs'—Reconciliation, Rehabilitation, and Reconstruction. A meaningfully suggestive acronym was formed around his name: **G**o-**O**n-**W**ith-**O**ne-**N**igeria (GOWON). **3 The 12-state structure of Nigeria** created by Gowon. This came after Biafra's Advisory Committee on the composition of Eastern Regional proposed boundary.*

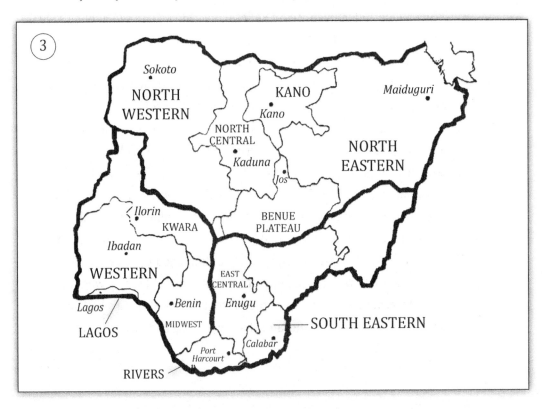

1 Odumegwu Ojukwu. *Oxford-educated scion of the Ojukwu family who willfully joined the Nigerian Army as a private. He became the secessionist leader of the breakaway Biafra, which fought a 30-month war against Nigeria.* **2 The creative** *genius of the beleaguered Biafrans and the Army produced and used the 'Ogbunigwe', also known as 'leg cutter', during the civil war.* **3 Minicons** *of Biafra Air Force.* **4 MIG17F** *of Nigerian Air Force.*

*1 **Murtala Muhammed.** He toppled Gowon and turned around the governance of Nigeria in 200 spell-binding days. He ruled by decrees and fiats in a reign characterized by purposeful and resourceful leadership. His orders and decrees were to be carried out 'with immediate effect'. 2 **Olusegun Obasanjo.** Military Head of State after the assassination of Murtala Muhammed. He applied the coup de grace on the beleaguered Biafran Forces to end the war. He won the war and sustained the peace and later, as Head of State, he ceded power to the democratically elected civilian government of Shehu Shagari. 3 **Obasanjo obtained the surrender documents** of Biafra as military leader of the 3rd Marine Commando at Dodan Barracks in January 1970.*

1 Muhammadu Buhari and *2 Tunde Idiagbon. January 1984–August 1985. **Muhammadu Buhari** was Head of State and Commander-in-Chief, and **Tunde Idiagbon** was the Second-in-Command as the Chief of Staff at the Supreme Military Headquarters. They instituted the operation of War Against Indiscipline, WAI to instil discipline into the polity. **3 Ibrahim Babangida** 'IBB', August 1985-August 1993. Soldier and willy politician. He banned and unbanned politicians; foisted first the Zero Party option and later two-party system on the people. He annulled M. K. O. Abiola's popular election; imposed Interim National Government, ING; and retired himself by 'stepping aside'. **4 Ernest Shonekan.** August 27-November 17 1993. Private sector consummate boardroom technocrat as United Africa Company, UAC chairman turned government bureaucrat as the virtually hand-picked Head of the Interim National Goverment.*

*1 Sani Abacha. November 17, 1993–1998. Maximum dictator; he summarily ousted Shonekan and his ING from power. He unleashed a reign of terror and suppressed the press and human rights activists. His security goons killed by assassination and bombings. People like Abiola, Shehu Ya'radua, and Obasanjo were either arrested, detained, or imprisoned. He stashed away more than $3 billion in foreign banks. **2 MKO Abiola.** Billionaire industrialist, philanthropist, newspaper publisher, and politician. He comprehensively won the Presidential Election of June 12, 1993. The election was annulled by Babangida. **3 Abubakar Abdulsalaam.** Soldier and gentleman. He deliberately set out to amend the past errors of his predecessors. He presided over the smooth and orderly transfer of power to a civilian government. **4 Bola Tinubu.** An astute politician and former Senator before he became the Governor of Lagos State. He boldly and successfully resisted the aggressive incursion of Peoples' Democratic Party into Lagos State when, under the presidency of Obasanjo, the state's budgetary allocation was withheld. He is well respected for his clout and political savvy particularly, more so in the South-West zone. He became the acknowledged leader of the Action Congress of Nigeria.*

the trademark of Ojukwu as he sought to 'gain his pound of flesh' from the Yorubas, whom he perceived as the stumbling block of the rise to power by the Igbos.

Awo was indeed chided and maligned for supposedly reneging on his misinterpreted pledge to pull out the West in tandem with Biafra, whereas, in fact, Awo had laid emphasis on the 'oneness and nationalistic fervour' of my Federal military establishment by warning them to be wary of any conscious effort aimed at the disintegration of my national status through any 'error of commission or omission'. After the flight of Ojukwu to Ivory Coast 'in search of peace', it became the lot of Philip Effiong and Justice Louis Mbanefo to surrender Biafra to the Obasanjo-led Third Marine Commando and into the waiting, welcoming embrace of Gowon.

At the end of the internecine war, Gowon tellingly pronounced a magnanimous verdict of 'No Victor—No Vanquished'. It was a reconciliatory proclamation, because it was all too obvious that it was the vanquished that surrendered to the victorious. The leader of the rebellion had fled into exile. His deputy wisely surrendered on the lawns of Dodan Barracks in Lagos, far from the theatre of war and inside the winners' territory.

As a great nation builder and forward-looking Reconstructionist, Gowon immediately embarked on the much-vaunted policy of 'the triple Rs—Reconciliation, Rehabilitation, and Reconstruction'. He used the proceeds of my first-ever crude oil boom to lay the infrastructural foundation, which remains the mainstay of my economy. This proclaimed policy earned him praise and honour on both sides. An anagram was formed round his name G-O-W-O-N: 'Go on with one Nigeria'. The popular chant that rent the air then was 'To keep Nigeria one is a task that must be done'. Ironically, people had quickly forgotten that Gowon had said three years earlier that the basis for unity was no longer there. This was because the cream of my Northern civilian and military leaders had just then been decimated in the January 15, 1966 coup.

Luck smiled on Gowon. A dashing bachelor at 32, he became my youngest-ever ruler. He took a lovely bride, Victoria, and married her with pomp and pageantry while the war was still on. He had thereby offended the sensibilities of my rebelling part with the timing of the marriage. He led my people during a war and finished the war at that moment in my history when there was an oil boom (1969). Awash with the revenue from petroleum resources and flush with the excitement of victory, Gowon was to embark on a spending spree. He was alleged to have said rather effusively and matter-of-factly, 'Money is not our problem...but how to spend it'.

Eko Bridge was built in Lagos. The rickety and old Carter Bridge was dismantled to make room for a more solid and enduring structure. Kainji Dam was constructed to generate more electrical power. A solid concrete bridge linked Asaba and Onitsha. Another one, Jebba Bridge, was built to link Lokoja with Talata Mafara. A bridge linking Maiduguri with Chad and Cameroon was built to facilitate access for people, goods, and cattle to the neighbouring countries. The foundation was laid for a durable and fantastic network of roads across my terrain.

To his eternal and enduring credit, Gowon established the National Youth Service Corps (NYSC). Thus evolved a laudable project in which fresh graduates from the universities began a compulsory national service for which they were paid allowances. Such fresh graduates were posted to various states and locations different from their states of origin and away from their accustomed environments. There is no doubt that the NYSC has become very useful in forging unity, exposing my youth to the need to serve their fatherland, and gaining useful employment that will prepare them for the future.

'Super-permsecs' emerged from my coterie of top civil servants. This was a title acquired because of their tremendous leverage and power, which they acquired before and during the reconciliatory and reconstruction period. The Indigenization Decree was promulgated, making my indigenes more profitably involved in the economy. The Udoji Salary Review Panel brought more money into the pockets of workers but sent prices skyrocketing. It was the era of the acquisition of electronic gadgets and motorcycles by workers who found that they suddenly had enough money for those imported gadgets.

Gowon began to misread the handwriting on the wall. He mistook the jeers for cheers and the unusual shouts of disapproval for ovation and applause. The army began to enjoy the spoils of occupation, and this was when Gowon started prevaricating about an exit date for the military. He presumptuously declared that his set departure date was no longer realistic. He refused to take an honourable parting bow from the stage when the ovation was loudest. He thus became my first Head of State to attempt tenure elongation, which was to bedevil the regimes of most subsequent rulers, whether military or civilian. To worsen matters, corruption was prevalent in high places. The notorious '10 per centers' overtly paraded themselves in the corridors of power.

The 'war of affidavits', which exposed ugly skeletons in some dirty cupboards, became endemic, followed by mudslinging in the newspapers. Godwin Daboh, a daring Gboko businessman, had sworn to an affidavit leveling corruption charges against Joseph Tarka, a Federal commissioner in Gowon's cabinet. It became the language of revenge and reprisal to say, 'If you Tarka me, I will Daboh you'. The allegations, counter-allegations, and investigations led to the removal of Tarka from my Federal Military government Executive Council. Tarka fought back with calculated vengeance. He retaliated by raking up charges of graft and manipulation of insurance claims against Daboh. This got the latter sent to jail. Aire Iyare exposed the sharp practises of some top figures in the old Bendel State, and the wide-ranging repercussions of his action heralded the activities of anti-corruption crusaders, social critics, and activists who later featured prominently in subsequent regimes.

Flush with the glow of peace engendered by undeclared but perceptible victory in war, Gowon started globe-trotting with profligate abandon. His entourage was always a list of who was who of the day. He visited the major capitals of the world, including London, Moscow, Peking, and Bonn, in breathtaking grandeur. The plane that brought him and his retinue from Hong Kong had to return to Hong Kong to retrieve excess luggage left behind by his overprivileged entourage of favoured civil servants and eminent co-travellers who went on shopping spree in the Orient with their pockets loaded with generous but often questionable 'Estacodes'.

Despite the civil war, Gowon ruled me as a Nation at a time of relative political innocence. I would assess the regime of Gowon as that of a war hero who could rightly be forgiven for thinking that he had been destined to lay my foundation as a modern State from the ruins of the toppled Republic. Even though it was the era of sit-tight rulers all over Africa, he seemed to have forgotten how he himself came to power. Subsequent events would see him removed by the same set of officers responsible for his ascendancy in the first instance.

It was not surprising that during one of his tours—this time to the OAU conference at Kampala, Uganda—a palace coup was bloodlessly carried out to unseat him. Joe Garba, tall and gangling head of the Brigade of Guards, announced the coup with what became the increasingly familiar refrain that usually came after the national anthem: 'Fellow Nigerians, I, Joseph Nanvem Garba...'. He was to become the next Foreign Minister, in which post he acquitted himself with aplomb. He became the Permanent Representative to the United Nations, where he also was elected as the President of the General Assembly when it was my turn on the agreed zonal rotational basis.

Gowon went from Kampala into exile in England, where he enrolled to study political science at the University of Warwick. When asked by inquisitive journalists about his ouster, he replied by quoting Shakespeare: 'All the world's a stage, and all the men and women merely players: they have their exits and their entrances'. He obtained a doctorate. Stripped of his rank in the army, he was to be fully rehabilitated by the benign Shagari administration—enough to embolden him to become a presidential aspirant in the aborted Third Republic. He was beaten at the ward level of the Option A4 of the new and popular electoral guidelines by an outsider, one Dr. Tafida, who was best known until then as Shagari's personal physician and later as a secretary of health in Shonekan's Interim National Government. Shagari reinstated Gowon to his rank of general with full payment of his salary in arrears.

The Civil War had its heroes and its villains. It also had its victims and survivors. The theatres of war were full of drama, sometimes heroic, but often tragic. We had the Ojukwus, father and son, and money was not their problem. The desire to reacquire his father's property in Lagos made Ojukwu sing new songs to both Babangida and Shonekan. There were also Ifeajuna, a handsome UCI graduate turned soldier and Commonwealth gold medalist high jumper; Samuel Agbam, a suave and urbane career diplomat turned rebel; Banjo, Yoruba-born graduate engineer turned soldier, with ambition different from Ojukwu's; and Alale, an economist and trade unionist with communist inclinations. These were four Biafran soldiers who were made to pay the supreme price for espousing the cause of my people's unity and oneness as a Nation. They tried to sing the song of freedom in a strange land at the same time those who held them hostage requested them to over-run their fatherland.

Swashbuckling Benjamin 'Benjy' Adekunle was arguably the most colourful of the war heroes. He was pint-sized and as brave as a lion. He acquired the sobriquet 'Black Scorpion' because of his heroic exploits as the commander of the elite Third Marine Commando. The forceful and commanding character encased in the fragile bantam-weight frame of Benjy, as he was fondly called, could only be ignored at the risk of incurring an explosive and expletive reaction. He usually bawled out his orders, and woe betide the subordinate soldier who flouted Adekunle's orders or countermanded his instructions. There is no way the history of the war could be adequately recorded without according a special place of honour and reference to the exploits and style of Benjy Adekunle.

Joe Akahan of the Air Force died in active service. Shittu Alao also of the Air Force, and with the prominent facial tribal marks, died in circumstances that were rather mysterious in a seemingly hapless plane crash. A famous medical doctor performed an autopsy on Shittu Alao's 'bullet-riddled' body. Dr. Gboyega Ademola's incriminating knowledge of the ulterior motives of Alao's killers and the tell-tale bullets he found in Alao's body led to his own (Ademola's) death. Those even closer to Gboyega Ademola by blood, who knew how and why Gboyega died, refused to tell. That knowledge and that awareness also died with them when death came calling years later.

Wole Soyinka was then a university lecturer and the voice of dissent against the pogrom unleashed on the Igbos in the north. He was put in detention on the false assumption that he was with Ojukwu in Benin on the day Biafran soldiers infiltrated the Mid-Western Region. Bola Ige nearly suffered the same fate. In the interest of peace, Tai Solarin went all the way to the east to meet with and talk to Ojukwu.

Isaac Adaka Boro, who called for state creation before it was the vogue, met his death in a land mine planted by my retreating rebel soldiers. Murtala Mohammed strove to wipe away the memory of his troops' misadventure in my old Mid-West while attempting to cross the Niger. Mohammed Shuwa did his best in the 'Loss–recovery–loss' of Owerri. There were many stories of Federal soldiers whose self-inflicted gunshot wounds to their legs qualified them for evacuation from the war zone or to go AWOL (absent without official leave).

Mercenaries had a field day as soldiers of fortune got actively involved. Some do-gooders flew in guns and ammunition under the guise of bringing food for the war-beleaguered and starving children in the rebel enclave. The Red Cross flew mercy missions, carrying food for the same victims. But it was alleged that rebel soldiers grew fat on the food while the masses stayed famished. Egyptians flew missions for me and were handsomely rewarded, even after death, through negotiated insurance agreements. The Egyptian government of Abdel Nasser harboured student pilots from my Air Force under the able leadership of Bob Alayideino. They were there in Cairo to learn how to fly the Ilyushin jets, with which the Biafrans were eventually bombarded. Dan Suleiman ably coordinated this military aid programme. He exhibited tact and consummate military diplomacy in covertly handling the involvement of the USSR in the training of my Air Force personnel in the prosecution of the war.

'Bebeye Aloma' Ndiomu, who later headed the tribunal that sent my 'western' UPN governors to long jail sentences, talked and dreamed of war even as a university student. He saw action in Onitsha, and he lamented the death of Osuolale Aremu at Abagana, where I am told another soldier from my premier University College of Ibadan (UCI), Ngozi Alana, could not raise a finger to help Aremu, his erstwhile antebellum friend. It was as bad as that—old friends and mates found one another in opposing camps. That was tragic.

They say, 'Necessity is the mother of invention'. My beleaguered sons in the rebel enclave fashioned their own tanks, armoured vehicles, and guns. Professor Gordian Ezekwe manufactured the *ogbunigwe*, a bomb which, when detonated, echoed in deafening staccato booms. When it exploded, it discharged hundreds of high-velocity pellets to a range of about 50 yards, killing, maiming, and dazing human targets. This ingenious contraption was essentially a defensive weapon built like a mine but was remotely detonated through electricity or drumbeats. It could kill scores of troops in one fusillade. The uninterrupted loud booming noises were enough to send my Federal troops scurrying away in disarray. Ogbunigwes were of various sizes and capacities, depending on the purpose for which each calibre was meant.

The smallest ogbunigwe was used as a booby trap along unmanned tracks at the war fronts. It was also called the 'foot cutter', a name derived from the type of damage it inflicted on the victims. The medium-calibre ogbunigwe was used for both attack and defense. When operated from an advantageous terrain, ten of them can lay waste a company of advancing troops. But the mother of all ogbunigwe was the flying variety, which was both anti-tank and anti-troops.

The Niger Bridge was attacked and threatened with demolition by the 'local Hannibal', 'Air Raid' Achuzia, in his attempt to stop my advancing Federal troops. 'Air Raid' Achuzia was a warrior of steel in his set purpose. Implacable and swashbuckling, he was alleged to have been singly responsible for the prolongation of the war. This likely explained the fact that he was in one of the last sets of war prisoners to be set free, years after the war was over.

Madiebo was generally regarded as a mild leader. Onwuategwu was seen as a magnificent commander and motivator. Major Chukwuma Nzeogwu saw action at the fiercest and deadliest war zone where he was allegedly sent by design. It was like the biblical version of King David, sending the patriotic Uriah to the hottest war front in order to have him eliminated. Apparently King David had lusted after Uriah's wife, Bathsheba. Nzeogwu met his gruesome death when a vengeful and vindictive soldier virtually sliced him up with a bayonet. There seemed to have been a singularity of purpose to kill him exactly as he was known to have executed Ahmadu Bello, the Sardauna of Sokoto, a few years earlier. Recognized by the leader of a Federal troop, his body was picked up and accorded a decent burial, fit for an arguably popular hero.

Let it be said that Olusegun Obasanjo, years later, authored a book on his friend Nzeogwu. This was to earn Obasanjo condemnation and castigation from those who thought the book was a glorification of a murderer. Obasanjo's accusers could not easily forget that it was the same Nzeogwu who killed the popular and unforgettable Ahmadu Bello in cold blood and signalled the beginning of all the coups in 1966 and beyond.

Scientists in the secessionist enclave dug deep into their scientific books and arsenals and were able to give free rein to their creative ingenuity at the Amandugba Oil Refinery. They tinkered and improvised experimentally in such a way that essential commodities like fuel, kerosene, brake fluid, and engine oil were made to evolve. These were items that were indispensable for the prosecution of the war. When it became increasingly difficult to procure these items owing to embargoes and blockades, ingenious technological inventions and daredevil acts of desperation kept the war machine going. The first-ever plane hijack in my history took place in Benin, when desperate secessionists seized and diverted a commercial aircraft to Enugu.

In my foreign missions abroad, chancery budgetary allocations were virtually stolen by privileged career diplomats in some parts of Europe and West Africa. It was alleged that such money was used to buy arms and equipment for onward transmission to the cash-strapped rebel enclave. Bomb blasts suicidally detonated by Agwu ripped him and entire buildings open in Ikoyi. Kamikaze (a Japanese suicide style) pilots' planes were shot down around Carter Bridge in Lagos, and Lagosians saw human limbs and other parts of the human anatomy jettisoned from exploding planes.

Then the war ended, and once again, I started my journey towards adolescence.

MURTALA MOHAMMED— JULY 1975–FEBRUARY 1976

'Those whom the gods love die young'; so the saying goes, and so it was with my illustrious son, Murtala Mohammed. I have never been governed so well, so fast, so furious, and so surgically. He came on to the scene like a whirlwind, and he raged and stormed like a hurricane. Murtala thundered on television with soldierly firmness and emphasis, his two eyes popping like balls of fire, 'We shall not tolerate indiscipline [pronounced as 'indispline'], we shall eradicate corruption' (with the 'r's' rolled for emphasis). Deadwood, sycophants, and public servants with declining productivity were dismissed 'with immediate effect' (the phrase has crept into my everyday usage to denote automatic and affirmative action). I got moving like a Nation once again as Murtala matched affirmative actions with his authoritative pronouncements.

For a spellbinding seven months (only 200 days), I knew what it was to have an accepted and acceptable leader. Within a short time, his policies won him broad popular support and his decisiveness elevated him to the status of a national hero. Murtala led by example and by precept. He went headlong into the job at hand by first declaring his assets and allegedly surrendering his estate in Kano to the State. This was later to be denied by his wife, Ajoke, who claimed that Murtala had only one house to his name in Kano.

It was therefore with anger and indignation that Murtala reacted when Dr. Obarogie Ohonbamu, a law lecturer at the University of Lagos, made a libellous allegation through an affidavit against him. Mohammed did not harass his accuser. He did not do what his successors were going to blatantly do later—send an army of overzealous security agents to harass a person like Ohonbamu, who had had the temerity to challenge him. He sought to defend himself by physically appearing in court. He had thus acquiesced that the courts are the undisputable arbiter and last hope of the masses in their search for justice. By so doing, he had confirmed the precept that no one is above the law. Death by assassination was to deny him this exemplary initiative of appearing in court, which would have accorded more dignity, reverence, and honour to the Judiciary and the rule of law.

Various machineries were set in motion, and orders were effectively carried out. A man of great courage and unparalleled decisiveness, Murtala's populist acts came in rapid-fire succession with a dizzying effect on the public. He executed policies which permanently transformed my socio-political roadmap. By government fiat, Murtala created seven states to add to the existing twelve. He established a commission to search for a new, well-appointed virgin land where the Federal capital could be relocated. He cancelled the controversial and disputed census figures of 1973, which had generated acrimonious debates because many considered the numbers weighted in favour of my northern region. He decreed that all official transactions immediately revert to the 1963 figures. This decision was rapturously applauded and highly acclaimed, particularly by my southern states that felt shortchanged by the outcome of the 1973 census.

He postponed FESTAC from 1975 until 1977 because of inadequate preparations. By so doing, he warded off a situation that would have brought shame and embarrassment to his regime and to me as a Nation. He re-engaged the services of retired Benjy Adekunle to decongest the ports of the 'Cement Armada', which clogged the ocean gateway to Lagos. The 'armada' consisted of several shiploads of imported cement, ordered to solve the scarcity of cement in the construction and building industries. Adekunle embarked on this decongestion exercise with his characteristic gusto, achieving maximum success in minimum time.

Without time-consuming elections and the luxury of procedural consultations, Murtala selected 50 people to review and redraft my constitution. Ever-punctilious Awolowo demurred and opted out, taking umbrage over the fact that such an important appointment was conveyed to him via general news items on the radio. Awo could not know that Murtala had a covenant with destiny to compact so much into so short a time. Commissions of enquiry were appointed to probe the corrosive corruption that blighted the last years of Gowon's regime. It was symptomatic of the times that only two governors—Mobolaji Johnson and Oluwole Rotimi—were alleged to have come out of the revealing enquires unscathed. Some top civil servants were besmeared with filthy lucre.

My voice was once again heard in the comity of Nations. A clear foreign policy was defined for me. A 'Nigeria first' orientation was evident in all my transactions under Murtala. I became active with righteous indignation rather than non-aligned in international affairs. When others were fence sitting or kowtowing to the powers of the time, Murtala Mohammed took a resolute stand, pitching his tent behind Soviet-backed People's Movement for the Liberation of Angola (MPLA) on the Angola question. He had cited apartheid South African intervention on the side of the rival National Union for the Total Independence of Angola (UNITA). He delivered his shots straight from the hip when he thundered, 'Africa has come of age; it is no longer under the orbit of any extra-continental power; the fortunes of Africa are in our hands to make or mar'. Some other African countries that had been prevaricating fence sitters followed suit, jumping down from their precarious roosts on the fence to join the bold and noble cause that Murtala had articulated.

Murtala and others opined that African solutions must be sought to tackle African problems. It was apparent that the powerful USA stood solidly behind the spoiler Savimbi to thwart African efforts for a whole generation. The USA used unscrupulous surrogates like Zaire's Mobutu, the (understandably) pro-West monarchy of Saudi Arabia, and the former leprous apartheid exponents in South Africa to support Savimbi by providing him with arms and funds. Murtala Mohammed showed the way, and other discerning African countries followed suit.

It was the combination of the $20 million—which my government under the bold leadership of Murtala gave to the MPLA government in Angola—and the injection of 8,000 Cuban soldiers into the country's defense mechanism that tilted the pendulum of success in favour of the government of Augustino Neto. The USA was unimpressed when Murtala resented dictation from her and refused to receive in sanctimonious and patronizing audience the ubiquitous Henry Kissinger, President Ford's roving Secretary of State and universally acclaimed troubleshooter.

CHAPTER FOUR

OLUSEGUN OBASANJO: THE FIRST COMING— FEBRUARY 1976–OCTOBER 1979

To succeed Murtala would not be an easy affair. Several hurdles were in the way of anyone considered as successor or even aspirant. Apart from the fact that Murtala was a tough act to follow, Dimka, the coup maker who assassinated the Muslim Murtala, was a Christian from the Middle Belt. Ramrod-straight and bespectacled Danjuma, easily the next automatic choice by virtue of his extraction, was also paradoxically a Christian from the Middle Belt. Possibly to avoid the appearance of a Christian–Middle Belt ethnic conspiracy, the searchlight beamed at Obasanjo. The latter must have recalled how his fellow Yoruba clansman, Brigadier Ogundipe, had had to flee for his life to London a decade earlier when a rebellious and rather junior army sergeant of northern extraction refused to take orders from him (a Yoruba). Obasanjo was in fact alleged to have demurred, and in seeming confusion, disappeared into the washroom saying, 'You want them to kill me as they killed Murtala?' It had become apparent that the mantle of leadership was about to be wrapped around Obasanjo by his peers.

Courage and the resolve to assume power and responsibility welled up in him. Obasanjo had position and authority virtually thrust on him when he emerged as the successor to the eminent Murtala Mohammed. He accepted the proffered leadership, and my history was the better for it. Having won the war,

Fate now placed the battle for peace in the hands of Obasanjo. He made the brightest moves by remaining faithful to the transition programme and brilliantly navigating the course assiduously charted out by his assassinated predecessor. His first move was to appoint the young and relatively junior Shehu Yar'Adua as his Chief of Army Staff and second in command in the military pecking order.

It was a deliberate ploy to bypass senior officers like Danjuma, Haruna, and the others. Obasanjo went the proverbial extra mile by 'awarding' Shehu an accelerated promotion to the rank of brigadier from that of lieutenant colonel. This was to fortify Shehu's power base and enhance his standing and authority as second in command. Shehu's credentials included being a Hausa/Fulani officer and one of the brains behind the ouster of Gowon. He was also one of the king makers who enthroned Mohammed. It was a very tactical and bold choice that would eventually pay off, and the end would be seen to have justified the means.

Olusegun Obasanjo carried out, in every material particular, the programme of actions enunciated by his legendary predecessor. The new states launched amidst 'automatic-driven' orders; the new Federal capital territory was sited in Abuja, and work began in earnest with the establishment of a Federal Capital Development Authority. A new team took over the FESTAC committee, which postponed and successfully celebrated the event two years later, as proposed by Mohammed. The Constituent Assembly deliberated on the new constitution and came out with a blue print over which the unofficial '50th' (non-participating) member, Awo congratulated 'the framers and... myself' (Awo) because they came out with what appeared to him a facsimile of his book, *Thoughts on the Nigerian Constitution*.

Obasanjo carried on with the newly adopted system started under Murtala, which specifically precluded Permanent Secretaries from participating in Executive Council meetings. This was designed to clip the overbearing wings of so-called 'super perm-secs', who emerged during the Gowon era and were so ubiquitous and self-assertive as to have practically overshadowed the Ministers. It was noteworthy that only Festus Adesanoye continued to attend these meetings by virtue of his stand-in representative status for the executed Bisalla. For tactical reasons, Obasanjo refused to appoint another Minister of Defense after the perfidy perpetrated by the overly ambitious and at times disgruntled Bisalla. He had been fully involved in the very unpopular, ill-contrived, and abysmally unsuccessful coup that led to the death of Murtala Mohammed. Adesanoye was to wield immense power in the Ministry of Defense. He later became the Oba Osemawe of Ondo and continued to enjoy the adulation and respect of some top military brass, who endearingly referred to him as 'Oga' until he joined his ancestors.

Obasanjo saw the importance of agriculture and fully supported the 'Operation Feed the Nation' (OFN) programme. This national hobby was to stand him in good stead as he retired into full-scale farming at Ota, near Lagos.

He lifted the ban on politics, which had been in the doldrums for 13 long years. Guidelines were given for the formation of political parties, and expectedly, when the battle line was drawn, old alignments resurfaced. The banned NPC was resurrected as the National Party of Nigeria (NPN) with its bases in the hard-core north. The erstwhile Action Group was reinvented as the Unity Party of Nigeria (UPN) on its former bedrock in the west and in Lagos. The former NCNC resurfaced as the Nigerian People's Party (NPP) and held sway from the east. A disagreement among topmost members of the NPP led to the addition of letter 'G' to 'NPP' to become the GNPP: Great Nigerian Peoples Party, with a base among the north-eastern Kanuris. The Peoples Redemption Party (PRP) was a rebirth of the defunct Aminu Kano's NEPU in Kano and Kaduna.

The Nigeria Advance Party (NAP), headed by respected lawyer Tunji Braithwaite, was newborn in every way and lost in every way. It was moribund at birth and bereft of hope in a field replete with tested and experienced hands. Awo playfully taunted the relatively younger Braithwaite that he was prepared to take a bet with Braithwaite that NAP would not win a single seat. Awo could have won the bet easily, as NAP lost in virtually every constituency in which it contested.

The Federal Electoral Commission (FEDECO) was put in place, and Michael Ani, a decent and thorough bureaucrat from Cross River State, was appointed chairman. He blew his whistle, and the game of politicking began. If the campaigns were vigorous and healthy, the aftermath of the voting was something else entirely. Obasanjo had warned, rather ominously and indiscreetly, 'The best man may not necessarily win the race.' To win under the 'geographical spread' arrangements, a presidential candidate must win by attaining a third of the votes in 'at least two-thirds of all the states'. As it was, there were nineteen states, and Shagari of the NPN was declared to have won twelve states and a sizeable chunk of votes in the thirteenth state, Kano, which was won by the PRP. The political dilemma arose from a legal twist: whether twelve and two-thirds or thirteen would be the more approximate number that would constitute two-thirds of nineteen. Awo challenged the outcome in court.

By a whimsical twist of fate, the erudite and transparently honest Darnley Alexander, who had been recruited into the services of the Western Region when Awolowo was premier, had risen to the position of the Chief Justice of the Federation. He was a West Indian. His allegiance to Awo must have brought about a nagging suspicion that he would swing the matter in Awo's favour. He was therefore deliberately eased out before the case reached the Appeals Court.

Judgment was pronounced by the newly appointed Chief Justice, the scholarly and bold Fatai Williams. He upheld clever Akinjide's submission that twelve and two-thirds should pass as two-thirds of nineteen, whereas, in the real essence of approximation, thirteen should have been more acceptable. Fatai Williams gave his judgment on the proviso that this mathematical adjudication should not in future be a legal reference point. That proviso, in itself, was not only a legal precedent but also a judicial faux pas. It is my considered view as a Nation that judgments should not shy away from the inevitable spotlight of reference or the unavoidable scrutiny of history.

Obasanjo took his initial bow riding tall in the saddle into the Abeokuta sunset in his triumphant entry. He became the first military ruler in black Africa to voluntarily relinquish power, having orchestrated and seen, to a logical and legal conclusion, all the due processes of an election. His jubilant and appreciative Egba kinsmen were thrilled by the magnanimity of the Alake of Abeokuta, who conferred on him the title of the Jagunmolu (the victorious one) of Egba land.

CHAPTER FIVE

SHEHU SHAGARI AND THE SECOND REPUBLIC: CIVILIAN RULE— OCTOBER 1979–DECEMBER 1983

Having been declared the winner, Shehu Shagari was of course sworn in by Justice Fatai Williams as the new president of my Second Republic. Shagari had been instrumental in confirming Fatai Williams's appointment as the Chief Justice of the Federation. He ushered in a new regime that brought a huge sigh of relief and introduced a new era that signified the possible termination of military interference in my governance.

However, the regime of Shagari was a rehash of the First Republic under Tafawa Balewa. This regrettable replication was on a scale that could only lead me back again to the waiting hands of rapacious men in uniform who were itching once more to have a piece of action in governance. The regime witnessed the perpetration of corruption and mismanagement at an unparalleled level. After the shamelessly rigged elections, it was to be expected that there would be but little to distinguish the political class from the civilian–military occupants who ensured the victory of Shagari and the NPN. It became obvious towards the end that the Shagari government was bent on turning me into a feudalized one-party state, without consideration for the sensibilities and inclinations of the other various groups I comprised.

Even though towards the end of 1983 I had begun to see military intrusion into government as an aberration, the voice of Sani Abacha was like a soothing balm for my anxious frame of mind and a lullaby in my ears at the turn of the New Year four years after the profligate rule of Shagari. If a dream in my sleep told me that Shagari's government was being sacked, I dearly wanted the sleep to continue. But it was indeed a reality. I woke up to the realization of the fact of Shagari's ouster. At least that was exactly how I felt at the time, because a well planned and brilliantly executed coup had taken place, almost bloodlessly. Only the gentleman soldier, Bako, detailed to arrest Shagari, was killed by Shagari's overzealous aide-de-camp. Nobody shed any tears when my Second Republic was sacked. In fact, there was widespread jubilation among my populace. The coup, which took place on New Year's Eve, December 31, 1983, was greeted with the convivial felicitations of 'Happy New Year and Happy New Government!' by church-goers and New Year Eve revellers alike.

The picture before the departure of Shagari was gloomy. There was a general malaise of indiscipline, nepotism, and maladministration. Also, there were burdensome foreign and domestic debts. Import bills were not paid. Letters of credit were not honoured overseas. The treasury was depleted, and the election into the second term had been won by a landslide. Barefaced manipulation of figures had been the order of the day. Umaru Dikko seized control of proceedings from the FEDECO Control Center, which was generally known to be out of bounds to all but FEDECO officials. He dared anyone to challenge his satanic computations that assigned comprehensive and unassailable victory to his NPN. The Minister of Information, Walter Ofanogoro, acting as the Lord and Master of all he presided over on Television, bullied into hapless submission, viewers who could not answer back. Ovie-Whiskey, FEDECO chairman, had doggedly and angrily denied accepting bribes. He declared point-blank that if he ever did set his eyes on a sum of 1 million naira (N1,000,000), he would faint.

Awolowo's observation that 'the ship of state was heading rudderless towards a rock' and the alarm he raised about the economy in shambles had been rebuffed by the repartee from Shagari that 'those who sowed the storm shall reap the whirlwind'. The storm became a hurricane in the feeble and shaky hands of Shagari and his advisers. Akinloye and Edozien had to travel to London to address a world press conference to facetiously refute Awo's allegations when they claimed that the economy was buoyant. Shagari and his government were blown away by the same whirlwind he had erroneously said Awo might reap. Awolowo was to eventually quit politics in disgust and frustration after the rigged elections of 1983. He warned ominously that the next generation of my citizens may never know the essence of true democracy.

When the great Zik, doyen of them all, cried foul on the outcome of the elections, the petulant Chuba Okadigbo dismissed his claims as 'the ranting of an ant'. The paradox was that the 'elephant' (Zik) had been derisively cut down to the size of an 'ant'. The mellowing ember in the aging Zik was ignited as he exploded in expletives and curses ending with the emphatic finality of 'Amen', 'Ase', 'Amin', and 'Isen' in all my ethnic languages he could muster.

CHAPTER SIX

MILITARY GOVERNMENTS: SECOND SET

BUHARI–IDIAGBON—
JANUARY 1984–AUGUST 1985

Welcome aboard my Ship of State with the helmsmasters, the much misunderstood and unfairly maligned regime of the 'terrible duo' of Buhari as Head of State and Idiagbon as the second in command and Chief of Staff. Desperate situations call for desperate measures, just as a painful malady might call for a painful therapy. They strove desperately to stuff discipline down my people's throats. Indiscipline had become endemic and, like cankerworms, had begun to eat deep into the fabric of all strata of society. Greed and the 'get-rich-quick' mania had turned some of my desperate citizens into drug peddlers. Corruption and general disorderliness were so pervasive that they constituted a brazen assault on the pillars on which a responsible society rests.

The new military regime acknowledged these facts and more. They were painfully aware that governors had used the so-called security votes to swell the coffers of their different parties for the purpose of contesting the elections and bribing the electorate. This led to a spate of repressive measures. Tribunal courts were set up to probe and recommend appropriate punishments for the erring former governors, commissioners, ministers, and some parastatal directors and operatives. The 'smart' ones fled and sought refuge in far away London, Washington, and other Western cities. Draconian laws and decrees were promulgated to punish the offenders. It seemed that losers in the political class bore the brunt of the Tribunal judgments.

Either by inexplicable coincidence or strategic ploy, the trials began first from my southern sectors. My erstwhile dashing governors were led from detention to prison cells. The old and revered Adekunle Ajasin, the experienced and seasoned Bisi Onabanjo, the brilliant and erudite Bola Ige, the 'Cicero of Esa Oke', were all jailed and sent to various prisons along with some of their commissioners. They were all from the West and belonged to the UPN. Then the popular Jim Nwobodo and 'weeping governor' Mbakwe of the NPP from the East received long jail sentences. Melford Okilo and the former popular Governor of Central bank who later became the Governor of South-Eastern State, Clement Isong of the NPN, both got jailed.

The searchlight that was directed up north was dim, half-hearted, and selective. Abubakar Rimi of the NPP cursed all the way to prison, having been sentenced to many years there. The outspoken and fearless Barkin Zuwo of NPP was also jailed, even after he protested and alleged that his 'security' oppressors had declared much less than they found in his house out of the millions of naira hidden in beer cartons. He had protested and explained that all he did was to 'keep government money in Government House'. Was there any better place? I shuddered with wonder and amazement! They, along with Solomon Lar and Aper Aku, were all members of the NPP and were sent to prison.

Discrimination and tokenism were displayed in the sentences meted out to Nadama, Anwal, and Adamu Atta. They were all northern government leaders of the NPN. Death took its toll on some of the arrested and detained political players during the regime of Shagari. Adelakun, the rascally 'Eru O bodo' from the UPN in the West, would die in jail. Barkin Zuwo, later christened 'banking' Zuwo for 'safely' 'keeping government money in Government House'; Ambrose Alli, from the Mid-West; and Bisi Onabanjo never fully recovered from illnesses worsened by their incarceration. They each died soon after. So did Aper Aku of the NPP. Indeed, a few days after the Buhari–Idiagbon regime came on board, a manhunt of political actors of the Second Republic was embarked upon, most probably on the regime's instruction. Awolowo's residence was invaded and placed under constant surveillance for spurious and tenuous reasons of 'state security'. His passport was seized, as were the passports of the venerable Ooni of Ife, Oba Sijuade, and the highly respected Emir of Kano, because of a reported visit to Israel.

Wary and alert British security agents scuttled a puerile and desperate attempt to abduct Umaru Dikko from London and repatriate him. He was to have been air freighted—in a crate—on a Lagos-bound cargo plane from Stanstead Airport. Some ministers were jailed. Two journalists, Tunde Thompson and Nduka Irabor, were imprisoned for an offence allegedly committed under the spurious and retroactively enforced Decree Number 4 (DN4). This was a sad reflection of the ominous threat at the inception of the regime that 'Freedom of the Press would be tampered with'. The well-intentioned War Against Indiscipline (WAI) programme was introduced. It was meant to instil discipline and promote a culture of orderliness and a decent moral code of conduct for all.

Retroactively enacted laws were employed to snuff out the lives of three cocaine pushers to serve as a warning and deterrent to would-be offenders. The culprits were Owoh, Bernard Ogedegbe, and Ojulope. There was an all-pervasive air of fear and trepidation, which made the social critic and Nobel Laureate Wole Soyinka say that the operators of the system had committed murder and that he could not see any sense in talking to deaf people. This was because Buhari and Idiagbon seemed to have become so impervious to criticisms and were adamantly incorrigible and spiteful of reasoned advice. The lives of the trio were wasted in the manner in which people were made to quote Wole Soyinka, who had declared in a moment of despair and exasperation that his was 'a wasted generation'. The regime had unwittingly laid siege against some sacred aspects of the tenets of fundamental human rights.

To fortify and strengthen my currency, the regime decided to change the colours and denominations of the notes. All currency notes in circulation were recalled and exchanged for new ones within a particular time frame. But some persons, favoured by people in the corridors of power, were allegedly able to smuggle in 53 bulging suitcases stuffed with old naira notes. This atrocious act was carried out despite the stiff resistance of an eagle-eyed Customs officer, who was almost predictably given a punitive 'transfer to Siberia' (a distant and remote area) for his affront. This was in addition to the officer's uncompromising stand, which was seen to be embarrassing to some people in authority. Idiagbon had promulgated a law to the effect that under-age children should not perform that year's Hajj in order to conserve the much-needed foreign exchange. When Idiagbon broke his own law and allowed his own under-age son to go on the pilgrimage, the idea was very insulting to the law-abiding citizens.

Buhari and Idiagbon meant well. They endeavored to enforce discipline. They preached public probity and accountability. They gave priority to cleanliness and strove to keep cities, towns, and villages clean by declaring the last Saturday of every month the Environmental Sanitation Day between 7 am and 10 am. On such Saturdays, everybody was supposed to stay within the environs of his home, sweeping, cleaning gutters, and cutting grass. This was a ritual observed diligently and compulsorily by all my citizens. They were, willy-nilly, restricted to the periphery of their houses, at the risk of being apprehended by the ubiquitous WAI Enforcement Brigade. The latter often dealt instant justice by way of fines or corporal punishment or by forcing culprits to do manual labour. Some were subjected to gruesome physical drills, including frog jumps and long periods of squatting in uncomfortable or contorted positions.

Buhari and Idiagbon dearly wanted to establish a government of law and order. They wanted a well-ordered society that would respect the rule of law regardless of status or class. Offences like 'bunkering', which is illegal oil-lifting; 'arrangee', which is foreign exchange manipulation in the black market; and cocaine and other drug pushing spelled disaster and public opprobrium for all apprehended culprits. Buhari–Idiagbon performed well, albeit behind a façade of doggedness and misapplied fixity of purpose. They wore, as it were, dour and unsmiling masks for 20 boring but harrowing months. They liked to call their regime an extension of Murtala–Obasanjo's regime. But the latter wore human faces and not dour masks; they blended condescension with attachment, diagnosis with therapeutic palliatives, and authority with humanism.

IBRAHIM BABANGIDA (MILITARY GOVERNMENT)— AUGUST 1985–AUGUST 1993

As a Nation, I breed fun-loving and adoring citizens, who would feel harassed by, and disdainful of, the scowling, cowering, and sullen looks permanently etched on the faces of Buhari and Idiagbon. My relieved citizenry heaved yet another sigh of relief when first Dogonyaro and then, inevitably, Abacha—in 'that familiar languid voice'—droned out the now-familiar announcement, 'Fellow Nigerians...' They rolled out the tanks to usher Ibrahim Babangida onto the stage with his gap-toothed smile and easy manners. He dangled the carrot and kept the stick slyly aloft or behind his back. He was greeted first with resignation and a feeling of déjà vu. As Babangida raised the carrot, he also wielded the stick by abrogating the notorious DN4 (Decree Number 4), jocularly pronouncing 'DN4' as if it were a chemical compound. He repealed the draconian laws. He also threw the jails and detention centers open to release jailed politicians and the suspects detained by the Nigerian Security Organization (NSO).

He made Rafindadi look like the Gestapo butcher as head of the notorious NSO. He was a taciturn career diplomat who was adept in the sleek espionage and security intelligence works and tactics. He eventually became the boss of that elite group of the national security network until he was appointed Ambassador to Germany (Bonn). Pleading collective responsibility, Rafindadi was literally thrown into the same dungeon from which his victims of various nationalities had earlier been liberated.

If ever there was a determined and deliberate populist, I have unwittingly played host to one in the sly, scheming, and calculating Babangida. He made it appear that he would carry everybody along in his decision-making processes. It became apparent that he built all his political edifices from the roof towards the foundation. It was like proving a geometric theorem from QED backwards. He knew what he wanted and where he was going, but he would start by making believe that grassroots views were sine qua non in importance, by first portraying a semblance of involving all of my citizenry in his decision-making process. He became the protagonist of national debates—a process in which topical issues that called for consensus and monumental decisions were thrown open for debates in order to sample various shades of opinions. Babangida's regime signified the beginning of political gimmickry, sophistry, and gerrymandering.

Proposed entry into the Organization of the Islamic Conference (OIC) became an open debate. Even though I was an acknowledged and avowed secular state, I had already attained an Observer Status, and my membership became perennially shrouded in mystery. This situation was made possible because of the powerful influential members of the Supreme Council for Islamic Affairs among my citizens.

The International Monetary Fund (IMF) reached for my economic jugular vein by imposing unacceptable 'conditionalties' before it would grant me access to more loans. Similar stringent conditions were imposed on the rescheduling of the repayment terms of my previous indebtedness. Plenty of energy was dissipated on debating the issue by courtesy of Babangida. My economy dangled ominously between the Scylla of crass devaluation of my currency and the Charybdis of the removal of subsidy from the sales of my petroleum products. It was a classic 'Catch 22' situation: Babangida knew I could not win; hence, he left the ball squarely in the court of my citizenry. He calculated that IMF would absolve him from the blame of inertia. He would be blamed, he thought, for neither inertia nor for not trying enough.

Bisi Onabanjo, the past master in satirical journalism, nicknamed Babangida 'Maradona', in his must-read weekly *Tribune* column. The cognomen stuck like glue to Babangida because it was so eerily apt. The Argentinean footballer, Diego Maradona, veteran of three World Cup finals, was a master dribbler who could easily maneuver his way out of tricky tackles and situations and cleverly score goals. He had scored one such goal with his hand instead of his leg or head against England before. He swore thereafter that the 'hand of God scored the goal'. Several times, throughout his eight-year rule, Babangida was to swear in the name of Allah that he would carry out an obligation or fulfill a pledge, only to ultimately renege.

He placed a ban and impulsively lifted the ban on politicians whom he categorized into 'old-breed and new-breed'. This turned out to be a grievous error, putting a spanner in the works of an ingeniously contrived scheme. This 'political engineering' of new-breed politicians would lead to a new breed of leaders, imbued with patriotism. They were like toddlers trying to walk, falling down and getting up without undue interference from the old-breed politicians. The older politicians were steeped in greed and corruption and always on an ego trip of the cult of personality. The old breed came back to destabilize and disorientate the new breed who, as should be expected, were ill-equipped and inexperienced. It became clear that the new breed politicians were not comparable with the old breed, who were more experienced and had stronger financial muscles. The new-breed politicians were never given the chance to put their acts together. The old breed heeded the frivolous and nebulous call of Babangida and swooped in on the innocuous 'new breed', exploiting their naïvety and dearth of initiatives.

First, Babangida established the Cookey Political Bureau to determine which system of government to adopt. Memoranda were called for, and as usual the idea was openly debated. Then the bureau laboriously collated various shades of opinions in an attempt to evolve a viable system of government. Babangida bared his fangs by withdrawing the dangling carrots and wielding aloft his big stick again when the *Newswatch Magazine* jumped the gun, pre-empting government by publishing the bureau's report, which had not been discussed and ratified by the FSMC (Federal Supreme Military Council). He proscribed the magazine for its temerity.

Then he allowed the formation of political parties. It looked as if he was going to allow 'a thousand flowers to bloom'. Many parties were formed, and there was a flurry of party registrations. He tinkered and experimented with this idea, and then threw it out the window. So he ruled me as a nation by whims and caprices. By so doing, he toyed with my political destiny. Babangida stunned political scientists and students of government by embarking on the unprecedented. He fashioned out two political parties, positioning them 'a little bit to the right and a little bit to the left'. There would be no 'founders' but 'joiners' of these two new parties.

The cerebral professor Omo Omoruyi was appointed the head of Babangida's Research Laboratory, which was called 'The Centre for Democratic Studies'. I was effectively turned as a nation into one vast political laboratory for unusual experiments, all in the name of the 'continuous learning process', which was the brainchild manipulation of the all-knowing Babangida. The manifestos of the two parties, introduced as the Social Democratic Party (SDP) and the National

Republican Convention (NRC), were written by the Centre. Having given them names, the two parties had their symbols designed for them. The colours of their flags were also chosen for them. SDP was given the horse symbol and green flag. NRC got the eagle symbol and white flag.

Secretariat buildings were erected for each party as administrative head-quarters, and government heavily funded both parties. They became, for all practical purposes, glorified government parastatals, which had to dance to the tune of the 'payer' of the 'piper', because he who pays the piper dictates the tunes. What a budding dictator!! What gave Babangida the notion that he could so denigrate my people's thinking faculties and pour scorn on their rights to free association? Did he think that they were bereft of initiatives and inept in the art of fashioning the rules and regulations under which they would operate? Babangida manipulated the string that made the two parties dangle and dance like the two legs of a puppet on a string.

Whether by accident or by design, Babangida placed thirteen 'egg-heads' (banned politicians) in the same detention camp at Epe for contravening the ban slammed on them. The outcome of the aggregation of the political sagacity of Jakande; the socialist inclination of Balarebe Musa; the recent invaluable sen-atorial experience of Saraki as leader of the Senate; the crafty and nihilistic scheming of 'Ogbuagu' Nzeribe; the rabble-rousing craftiness of the street-wise Ibadan strong man, Adedibu; the authoritative influence of the wealthy and am-bitious Shehu Yar'Adua; the calculating brilliance of Rimi; and the scheming and cultivated mind of Bola Ige could only result into an expected enforced 'session of patriots' at a retreat.

Any of these political heavyweights could easily become the president under normal circumstances. They promptly put their heads together in what looked like a round-table conference, brainstorming over the causes and cure of the political malady afflicting me as a Nation. By herding them together in that solitary environment, Babangida was unwittingly midwifing a new party ema-nating from determined, like minds.

Babangida thereafter released the banned politicians. He lifted the ban placed on them regarding participating in politics. By so doing, he virtually un-leashed them and their pent up political savvy on a waiting and stunned popu-lace. Classified as old-breed politicians, they were able to fraternize and come to a common vision for my political future from the place of their incarceration. It was soon discovered that every one of them declared for the Social Democratic Party (SDP). But that was after Babangida had allowed people to form political parties of various shades and leanings. Babangida later annulled the parties and the elections on a whim in a moment of sheer frenzy.

For eight years Babangida bestrode my landscape like a Colossus on feet of clay. He knew my citizenry and me inside out and could read us like the back of his hand. He seemed to have derived a sadistic pleasure in running rings around the politicians by banning, unbanning, and re-banning them at will in a manner that defied all reason until they were physically and fiscally broken. Many in the political class simply wilted and gave up in the politics of exhaustion. In fact, he even got to know how much everyone in the political class was worth and promptly placed price tags on each of them—not for sale, but for purchase. He created more states and multiplied the local government areas in his grandiose plan to bring government nearer the so-called 'grass roots'. He became adept at playing one group against the other and causing internal dissension within established groups.

The Nigerian Labour Congress (NLC) was rendered docile, tame, and compromising. The influential and highly regarded Nigerian Bar Association (NBA) was disunited when they most needed cohesion. The meddling hand of attorney general Clement Akpamgbo showed in the tendentious decrees that thwarted all genuine efforts to attain true democracy. The attorney general masterminded the disorder attendant to the Port Harcourt NBA conference and divided the close-knit association of 'learned friends'. The out-going president of the NBA, Priscilla Kuye, who was rough-handled and nearly assassinated, alleged that Babangida financed and gave tacit support to the imbroglio. Babangida and his minions had wanted the presidency of the NBA to change hands to the Kaduna-based Dalhatu. FGN-labeled cars ferried the lawyer conferees into Port Harcourt. The government paid their subscriptions and hotel bills to enhance their voting qualifications. They were therefore literally sponsored to do their master's bidding and unseat Kuye.

The National Association of Nigerian Students (NANS) was listened to when it barked, but was threatened, browbeaten, and finally ignored when it wanted to bite. Harassed vice-chancellors were virtually forced to close the universities hastily for fear of being held responsible for the inability and lack of foresight to quell or forestall looming riots or protests. Students were constantly rusticated, and universities closed down to such an extent that semesters were disorganized and sessional examinations lapsed into carryovers.

Academic Staff Union of Universities (ASUU) eventually boxed itself out of the tight corner into which Babangida seemed to have lured it. Babangida had to contend with the Bayero University lecturer Attahiru Jega when he emerged as the ASUU president. Under his positive and active leadership, ASUU took on the Babangida administration in a confrontation that was acclaimed as the longest in my university education history. ASUU confronted Babangida with a list of demands that were unassailably genuine in content and patriotic in all ramifications. These demands included

(a) Upliftment and betterment of education and research
(b) Renovation or rehabilitation of structures and edifices
(c) Improvement of library and laboratory facilities, not only for then, but for all time

Babangida tried to use brilliant Professor Nwabueze, Federal Minister of Education, as a foil to thwart the noble and laudable intentions of the Academic Staff Union of Universities. But both Babangida and Nwabueze reckoned without the crusading zeal of Attahiru Jega and his associates. For five months, Jega led the ASUU on a strike that was hampered by bureaucracy and legal intimidation. Government dished out a number of confusing decrees and illegal directives. The authorities entered into an agreement with the ASUU and then willfully reneged on it on a whim. The government tried without success to play the university teachers against the university administration cadre. But at the end of the day, the lecturers had their way. The strike outlived Babangida's regime, leaving the succeeding administration to recognize the striker's determined struggle.

The Nigerian Medical Association (NMA) flexed its muscles in sympathy with the ASUU and other crusaders against the intolerable administration. They had to calm down and resume work to lessen the suffering of their patients and the unhappy masses. Like a juggler, Babangida changed governors at will and reshuffled federal ministers with bewildering rapidity. He employed to the fullest his power to hire and fire. Out-going ministers, unaware that their services were being dispensed with, met their replacements at the latter's swearing-in ceremonies. The discarded ministers felt shocked, short-circuited, and short-changed.

Traditional rulers were cajoled, coaxed, and hoodwinked into dancing to Babangida's tune. He played to the gallery by distributing largesse and donations, spending government money as if it were from his private account and in his own dukedom. Grateful and indulgent governors gratuitously built presidential lodges in their state capitals in anticipation of a favored visit by the equivalent of a medieval 'Duke' visiting his fiefdom. These palatial presidential lodges were like those Middle Ages castles where the ancient kings were received and entertained with pomp and pageantry by their stooges and surrogates.

'Lagos Boy' Bode George, formerly of the Navy, made a life-size statue of Babangida, locating it at a conspicuous city square in Akure, capital of Ondo State, where George was governor. An embarrassed and flattered Babangida had to order his minions to reduce the statue to bust size. It was an unsolicited modesty, which the Akure people trivialized under other circumstances by reducing the bust to rubble at the first rumble of provocation that later led to a riot.

On a similar presidential visit to Ibadan, the Oyo State capital, the Military Governor, Adisa, appeared in heavily embroidered 'etu' (black woven) Yoruba attire. Adisa had ensured that his visiting potentate and benefactor Babangida would don similar dress by 'thoughtfully' having one made for him just for the occasion. Chameleonic soldiers suddenly turned from 'khaki' into 'agbada'. The regime brought new dimensions into governance and a new vocabulary evolved to perpetuate and institutionalize corruption. The word *settlement* took on a new meaning as a euphemism for gratuity and bribery. This system was freely used with careless abandon during the last days of Babangida's ill-fated Transition Programme. The 'Rent-a-Crowd Syndrome' became fashionable, and lorry loads of paid crowds demonstrated in support of government. Traditional rulers came in droves to implore Babangida to neither hand over nor go.

Better Life for Rural Women Programme

The National Commission for Women was established, ostensibly to institutionalize and legitimize the Better Life for Rural Women Programme (BLRWP). It was in fact the government's fulfillment of the global call following the Nairobi conference of 1985, which included the Declaration and forward-looking strategies, being a United Nations Programme for affirmative action on women issues. It was a well-conceived and well-intended programme, which Maryam, Babangida's wife, personalized. The programme was in furtherance of the perceived notion that women in the rural areas had been marginalized and neglected and that their lot needed to be bettered. Ibrahim Babangida, as president, encouraged Maryam in the pursuit of this exercise, to such an extent that fabulous sums of money went into its take-off exercise. She involved the governors' wives, both military and then-civilian, in galvanizing women in the rural areas to partake in this exercise, designed to improve their lot.

The Better Life Programme (BLP) actually made far-reaching contributions towards improving the lot of rural women, including the establishment of 10,000 cooperatives, about 2,000 cottage industries, 3,000 farms, 450 women's centers, and more than 200 health centers. Some people continue to doubt the veracity of these figures and dub them mere concoctions or self-glorification stunts and an image-boosting exercise of the regime's First Lady. It has also been said that the BLP was merely a forum for the display of power, influence, and prestige by pampered and privileged women. It was even being alleged that Maryam Babangida's style of running the programme was authoritarian and frankly militaristic as she issued orders which she expected to be obeyed without discussion, much less criticism.

The exercise reached a feverish pitch at which the self-declared opposition to IBB's government, the irrepressible Gani Fawehinmi, human rights activist and radical lawyer, challenged IBB in court, asking him to declare from which government vote the BLRWP was being funded. The action or inaction of the judiciary was predictably tame and half-hearted. The judiciary seemed to have behaved like a toothless bulldog that would not or could not even bark, much less bite.

The 'Maryam Babangida's Centre for Women Development' is a monumental edifice erected on the Better Life Street in Abuja to actualize this idea. There,

Maryam dominated the 'Hall of Fame for Nigerian Women' with 'his and her' larger-than-life framed pictures of herself and her potentate husband. The hall was also decorated with scores of trophies and awards which were stage-managed and given to her with fanfare to the applause of her sycophants and my unsuspecting populace. The awards, both local and international, included doctorate degrees from universities where, at the conferment, she would donate millions of naira to the fawning admiration of the scholarly tenants of the 'ivory' towers.

The wife of any popularly elected president in the American system of government, which I yearn to adopt, is referred to as 'First Lady'. Oblivious of the fact that her husband was catapulted into power backed by tanks and guns, Maryam wallowed in the exaggerated sobriquet of 'First Lady' with which the sarcastic Nigerian Press bathed her. It was soon to become 'feathering and tarring' like in the medieval days of countesses and miladies. In spite of heavy federal and state financial involvement and to the consternation of all, Maryam averred the obvious, by claiming that the Maryam Babangida Centre is a non-governmental organization (NGO), limited by guarantee and built by donation from public, private, and international agencies. This particular NGO was later to be handled by a Ministry of Women Affairs, newly created under the portfolio of a federal minister.

Maryam wielded so much power and influence that an office was created for her within the presidency. She demanded authority. She neither commanded nor earned it. She was always dressed up for every occasion with charming elegance and radiance. In doing so, not a few Islamic feathers were ruffled when her clothing did not conform to the demand that she should not expose any part of her body except her face. She could not stand the brilliance of other women who would outshine her. Hence, she was to know that an established and experienced hand—like that of brilliant professor Bolanle Awe's calibre—could do without the National Women Commission, which she chaired and which Maryam wanted very much to dominate. Francesca Emanuel, the first female Permanent Secretary, showed her dignity and self-worth when she refused to kowtow to 'She-Who-Must-Be-Obeyed' (Mrs. Babangida) as she made it known that she would rather take orders from her minister boss than receive instructions from the President's wife.

The Commission was established in 1990. Maryam Babangida promptly saw it as an outfit created for her. She would therefore not brook the brilliance and influence of Bolanle Awe. The Commission under the leadership of Bolanle Awe tried to establish itself as an autonomous body with full competence in handling all issues appertaining to women. This laudable move and the knowledgeable role of its leader seemed outrageous to Maryam Babangida. The latter was said to have harassed and undermined the influence of Bolanle Awe to ensure that she did not deflect the spotlight from herself.

Elections under Babangida

My previous military rulers had, at inception, taken the titles 'Head of State' and 'Commander-in-Chief of the Armed Forces'. Somehow, Babangida intentionally and deliberately forced out Domkat Bali by demoting him from the prestigious position of the Chairman of the Joint Chiefs of Staff to that of the less-significant Minister of Internal Affairs. He was excluded from the elite Armed Forces Ruling Council (AFRC). The amiable Army general from Langtang understandably resigned. The gentleman–soldier later jogged people's memories to the fact that Babangida had studiously taken the unprecedented title of President because he had higher ambitions than being a mere Head of State.

It became apparent that he was taking his cue from such other African sit-tight rulers as Abdel Nasser of Egypt, Ghadaffi of Libya, Mobutu Sese Seko of Zaire, Eyadema of Togo, and Mengitsu of Ethiopia. The unfolding drama confirmed Bali's view. Not only did Babangida want to rule, but he also desperately wanted to reign supreme. It was his desire to be in office for as long if not longer than the aforementioned military presidents. Rather vaingloriously, he had wanted to surpass Gowon's record 9 years in office.

Babangida's Transition to Democracy and Civil Rule programme was a classic example of squandermania and a projected exercise in futility. Gani Fawehinmi, ever alert and always showing the way, was the first to raise the alarm that Babangida, known as IBB, was 'transiting' to nowhere. As mentioned earlier, IBB had meticulously planned and mapped out his strategy. He knew exactly what he wanted, and he knew exactly where he was going. He held all the aces close to his chest. His cards were loaded and stacked against my unwary citizenry and me. He ditched the fine and principled gentleman naval officer Ukiwe because the latter would not read the lines assigned to his role as the Chief of Staff and the number two man in the unfolding melodrama.

A pliable and willing Augustus Aikhomu achieved this megaphone billing when he took over from Ukiwe, who had walked off the stage with his head held high and unbowed. The ovation will forever echo in the ears of Ukiwe. Aikhomu chose to become a pitiable mouthpiece, and as vice president had the unenviable assignment of issuing contradictory bulletins at hastily convened press conferences. Ukiwe had disowned any knowledge of my 'Observer' status at the OIC, even at his vantage position, and had flayed the recurring persecution of Christians in certain parts of my Northern Region. Ukiwe maintained that mine was a secular state and that in the protocol list and pecking order, 'No 2 was No 2, no two ways'. He stood his ground when Abacha out-maneuvered him on the queue and breached protocol on their way from Lagos to the Abuja parade grounds on Independence Day. So, Ukiwe had to go. Babangida tersely and curtly informed him on the telephone.

However, Babangida saw Ukiwe's departure as a little diversion and continued pursuing his inexorable course. He started from the grassroots by adopting the 'Zero Party' option propounded earlier by deep thinkers like Victor Oloyede Awosika, who had highlighted the divisive, progress-retarding, and corruptive influence of political parties. The chairman and councilors were chosen on their own steam, without any party bases. The Constituent Assembly met and adopted the Presidential system of government. Thirteen parties were formed, named, adequately funded, and mobilized with manifestoes. Symbols were assigned to the new parties. Beautiful buildings were designed and erected for the two parties in each local government area. Thereafter, the 'Zero Party' councils were dissolved, and civil-servant sole administrators were selected to run the councils. Another viable and evidently successful option was thrown out of the window without qualms.

The National Electoral Commission (NEC) was put in place. Professor Eme Awa, an experienced and knowledgeable professor of political science, was named as the chairman. In that capacity, he successfully organized the first series of local government elections. He repeated a similar feat at the subsequent Constituent Assembly elections. But when he handed over to the police some senior NEC officials who had inflated contracts and embezzled money, he incurred the displeasure of jittery people in authority. To call a dog a bad name so as to hang it, Awa was unceremoniously discarded for being an uncooperative doctrinaire idealist. Awa was to later say, 'If I had to open my mouth, Nigeria will burn' when he was asked about his reaction to his dismissal. He knew better than to start stirring the hornets' nest in a military regime that had scanty regard for finesse, elegance, and human life. He reluctantly let the cat out of the bag when he later averred that he was being influenced from the highest quarters to ensure that some serving governorship candidates were declared as winners. He knew that there would be no end to such instructions and shenanigans.

Humphrey Nwosu was Awa's former student. He was appointed to head the NEC. Nwosu was a very theatrical person who was given to grandiloquent and flamboyant expressions. He coined words to upbraid people who might be planning to rig the elections, saying, onomatopoetically for emphasis: 'No wuruwuru, no magomago', which literally means 'There should be no fictitious manipulations and no dubious under-the-table pranks'. He habitually delivered his lines dressed in designer wear and speaking in his deep booming voice. In the first series of elections, the open ballot system was adopted. Voters lined up behind the pictures of candidates of their choice.

One after the other and with the laudable efforts of Humphrey Nwosu, Babangida ostensibly recorded success after success in the stated agenda of the Transition to Democracy. However, he held the hidden agenda ace card, which he was going to play, close to his chest. Party congresses were held to elect party executives. Elections were successfully held into the 589 local councils. Party secretariats were built for each of the two parties in every local government headquarters. Much bigger party headquarters were then erected for each of the two parties at the state capitals and Abuja. Gubernatorial elections were successfully held to select governors. Elections were also held for state Houses of Assembly members. Then it was the turn of the National Assembly, which again was very well conducted.

All hell broke loose when the time came for the primaries to select the presidential candidates of each of the two parties. Presidential aspirants from both parties sought to meet the guidelines and conditions stipulated by NEC. Not only that, SDP and NRC requested each aspirant to pay huge sums of money as nomination fees. The subsequent electioneering campaigns were noisy and costly. In the SDP, there were Shehu Yar'Adua, Olu Falae, Lateef Jakande, Olusola Saraki, Arthur Nzeribe, Dele Cole, Biyi Durojaiye, and Lai Balogun among others. In the NRC, the more prominent contestants were Umaru Shinkafi, Adamu Ciroma, and Bamanga Tukur, although there were others. Presidential aspirants criss-crossed my political terrain and reached every nook and cranny with their campaign manifestos, slogans, and materials. There was a war of pictures and posters waged on the walls and billboards in all cities, towns, and villages. There was a blitzkrieg of advertisements in the electronic and print media.

States were grouped into zones, and the appointed days for the primaries were staggered to take place in the various zones at different times. This inevitably led to confusion, and as the primaries gathered momentum, the events careered into bandwagon proportions. The unfolding results reflected either states of origin or ethnic considerations in the support patterns for the candidates. The corrupting influence of money was very much in evidence, as voters seemed to have lined up behind the highest bidders' photographs. Electoral officers joined in the exercise as they manipulated votes to favour their candidates. The front-runners were seen as moneybags who would do anything and spend any amount of money to hijack and rig the elections. Yar'Adua, Falae, and Nzeribe held sway in the SDP with Yar'Adua as the front-runner, numerically.

Shinkafi, Tukur, and Chiroma were neck and neck as in a horse race in the NRC, with Shinkafi leading by a nose. When the aspirants began complaining loudly, they all played into Babangida's waiting hands. He promptly blew the whistle to stop the charade. Amidst claims and counter-claims, accusations and counter-accusations, the primaries were called off. Apparently, Babangida saw it coming. Each of the major contestants felt that he had the ear and goodwill of the President. Smart guy, that IBB! The botched primaries became the harbinger of the derailment of the Transition to Democracy programme. Babangida could always argue that his administration was invited to cancel the primaries by some of the presidential aspirants.

Ostensibly, he stuck to his guns and swore 'Insha Allah' that the military would not stay a day longer than necessary. He declared that the intention was to leave an enduring legacy of Democracy. Consequently, Babangida dissolved the Federal cabinet. He later handpicked and installed a transitional council under Ernest Shonekan, former chairman of United African Company of Nigeria (UACN). The Armed Forces Ruling Council (AFRC) was dissolved and succeeded by the Nigerian Defense and Security Council (NDSC) as the highest political arm of government.

Before this, it was unimaginable that such dissolution could be that easy. Babangida did it without batting an eyelid. He then declared a new date for the presidential elections. He executed these seemingly difficult arrangements with the ease of a past master in chicanery or a confidence trickster. Ernest Shonekan headed the 29-member cabinet Transitional Council that was put in place to ensure a smooth transition. IBB vowed that the council was on the threshold of alleviating the economic difficulties of my populace. Once again, Babangida ordered NEC to go back to the drawing board and come out with a viable and acceptable system that would ensure and guarantee meaningful and successful primaries.

After intensive deliberations, Nwosu's NEC zeroed in on Option A4. The system required that all aspirants from each party must make themselves available for consideration at the grassroots level of their local government areas. Successful aspirants from both parties at that local government level would then move on to compete with other aspirants at the state level. The winners at the state level would then proceed to the national conventions of the two parties. It was from this apex level that the victorious candidates would be declared as the flag-bearers to run for the presidency of my Third Republic. Perhaps not suspecting that they were playing on political quicksand, the NEC's Option A4 signaled the beginning of a stampede. Aspirants struggled to obtain the nomination forms. At the end of the day, the NRC had 110 and the SDP had 138 candidates vying for nomination as the presidential flag bearers. The race for the presidency along the various social strata was devoid of the usual malpractises or the nefarious activities of mischief-makers and moneybags.

It was remarkable that the Nigerian Guild of Editors met and appealed to media proprietors to *not* accept any advertisements capable of disrupting the transitional timetable. Everyone was eager to ensure or even hasten the uninterrupted departure arrangements of the military. It was in response to the Yoruba proverb that it is incumbent on the populace to plead with the villainous evildoer in their midst to effect the betterment of his society.

The only exception was the Association for Better Nigeria (ABN), which had mounted a blitz of campaigns for the extension of the military rule. The association was to claim later under the formidable Arthur Nzeribe that it had 25 million members whose signatures had been assiduously gathered. Nzeribe would amply demonstrate, as he was wont to do, that he was unsurpassable when it came to flaunting the strong points of views and courses he espoused. He was therefore one of the chief proponents and campaigners of the ABN.

Babangida described and decried the cynics of the military's intention to go on August 27, 1993, as 'blackmailers and fraudsters'. Aikhomu denied that the administration was behind the orchestration of campaigns to sit tight. But there were signs all over the place that there was tacit tolerance and acquiescence from high places. Huge billboards bearing IBB's picture in conspicuous places at Abuja proclaimed his virtues. Members of the ABN had a field day promoting, unmolested and unchallenged, the unspoken but manifestly evident desire of IBB to hang on to power.

The national conventions of the two parties took place at separate venues. At Port Hacourt, Bashir Tofa emerged as the candidate of NRC virtually by acclamation. But the SDP convention at Jos could not produce a clear winner at the first ballot. However, at the second ballot, M. K. O. Abiola, a billionaire business mogul, newspaper baron, and philanthropist extraordinaire, emerged as the SDP candidate. Tofa chose Sylvester Ugoh as his running mate, and M. K. O. Abiola chose Baba Gana Kingibe as his own running mate.

It is pertinent at this stage to analyze the chemistry between each of the candidates and his running mate. Tofa was a Muslim, born of Kanuri parents from the North-East but domiciled in Kano, where he was a successful businessman with powerful political and religious connections. He had once advocated that the military should rule till the year 2000, which was then some seven years ahead. His running mate was Sylvester Ugoh, a Christian from Imo State and a university lecturer who had once been the governor of the defunct Biafra Central bank. He was also a Federal Minister in the Second Republic. The 62-year-old Igbo man was 16 years older than Tofa, who was 46. Age and experience were expected to have a sobering effect on the ticket. Kusamotu, from Oshun State and with a doctorate in law, was elected as the new chairman of the NRC. He was a Muslim and a Yoruba man. The conservative NRC was determined to tread the well-worn path of ethnic and religious consideration to ensure victory at the polls.

Abiola was a Yoruba Muslim from Abeokuta in Ogun State. He was the vice president of the Supreme Council for Islamic Affairs in Nigeria and was one of the richest men in Africa. He was very powerfully connected locally and internationally. His philanthropism was legendary. His close friendship with Babangida was well known to everyone. His running mate was Baba Gana Kingibe, a Muslim Kanuri man from Borno State. He was an ambassador and former radio broadcaster with an engaging smile, a deep baritone voice, a cherubic face, and an infinite capacity to accommodate friends and foes alike. He was essentially a diplomat, having had a stint at the Ministry of External Affairs. He was the former chairman of the SDP. He gave Abiola a good run for his money during the race for nomination. Anenih, a Christian from Edo State and a retired police commissioner, was elected as chairman of the SDP.

It was seen that the bold and unusual Muslim–Muslim ticket was a rarity and a radical departure from the accepted and expected arrangement on a Muslim–Christian ticket. The SDP ticket was rare in its adoption and was also devoid of accustomed sentiments in its interpretation. When it won, it was hailed as revolutionary. In fact, any combination would have sufficed, so long as the intention was to get rid of the military regime.

I recall now with a feeling of bitterness that NEC released the Decree 13 on April 26, 1993, requiring the two presidential candidates to apply for security clearance before contesting the general elections slated for June 12, 1993. My suspicion grew stronger when, even at that advanced stage, the NEC declared itself capable of disqualifying any candidate whenever fresh facts emerged to make such disqualification necessary. Subsequent events were to justify my forebodings as the two parties took to the hustings with gusto and alacrity.

In the history of all the electioneering campaigns that ushered in my previous Republics, never had such spectacular display of fervent political activities and colourful show of blistering attacks and counter-attacks been witnessed. The candidates and their running mates criss-crossed my political terrain and carried their campaigns to every local government area across the land. Radio and television jingles ruled the airwaves. It got to a stage that even babies could hum the refrains of the party's songs because of their being repetitively played on radio and television. The NRC lustily sang

> Tofa is the answer, Tofa
> Tofa oh! Tofa
> Tofa oh oh oh Tofa, NRC go win O Tofa
> Patapata (completely) you go win O Tofa.

The battle song from SDP was

> On the march again,
> M. K. O.
> Is our man O!

And the battle cry was 'SDP PROGRESS!'

Abiola was virtually and literally living and operating in and out from his Aircraft for the duration of the campaigns. At a stage, some faceless opponents who were displeased and disturbed at the prospect of his looming victory were reported to have vandalized the plane at Kano Airport. He travelled with all the fanfare that could only be associated with a blue chip billionaire executive, with all his aides and the ubiquitous party stalwarts. At times, his running mate was also in his entourage. Tofa chose to travel mostly and modestly by road. He traversed the length and breadth of all the constituencies, in an attempt to bring himself near the grassroots. It is of historical significance to say that all these happened in an atmosphere devoid of thuggery and hooliganism, which had been the bane of such exercises in the past. People earnestly yearned for change.

Suddenly, strange things began to happen on the way to the June 12 elections. But I refused to be provoked. I would wish to go the extra mile to ensure that the aberrant Military Administration would be shown the way out. My greatest weapon was a ballot dropped in a box, 'Secret or Open' or 'Open Secret'. My articulate forte could be found in editorial columns of newspaper that unendingly preached the sermon of free speech and Fundamental human rights. Spanners were deliberately thrown into my wheel of progress and my path to the promised land of Democracy was strewn with thorns and brambles, betraying anti-democratic intentions.

New laws kept rolling out from the legal department of the administration. Some of these laws clearly showed the unmistakable attempt to hamper my smooth transition to civil rule. The Petroleum Secretary made some inflammatory policy pronouncements on the volatile issue of the prices of petroleum products. The government quickly doused the explosive situation a few days before the presidential elections. A massive protest planned by the NLC was averted. The protest would have scuttled the Transition Programme. This invidious pronouncement was reminiscent and similar in its probable repercussions with the one made in 1981, to the effect that 'the small size and populations of the oil producing people of Nigeria can never be a threat to the stability and corporate existence of Nigeria as a nation'. I got to know better and also got wiser to the explosive situation as my history unfolded.

Telltale acts and signs of oddity and insincerity began to rear their ugly heads. Babangida was not planning any farewell visits to the states. NEC busied itself with laying rules to the neglect of election logistics. The feverish recruitment and training exercises that usually preceded such elections were not seen to be done. NEC did not deem it fit and proper to conduct the mandatory exercise of the review of voters' registration to guarantee successful polling. The ever-watchful and effervescent Gani Fawehinmi characteristically cried out a few days before election day that there were no polling booths!!

The niggling ABN (Association for Better Nigeria)—banned and declared as an illegal entity in a Lagos High Court—moved up North and openly campaigned and organized placard-carrying rallies for the perpetuation of Babangida's military regime. This was in disregard and contempt for the Lagos High Court order. While ABN paraded unmolested its nuisance value, pro-democracy activists whose utterances and activities put the government into discomfiture were harassed and hounded by the state security operatives. The initiatives for the rule of law through litigation and demonstrations by the human rights activists were only matched by the consistency with which court orders were flouted or totally ignored. The press, too, was not spared. Journalists continually played the hide and seek game with the security agents.

The stage was thus set for the farcical moonlight court decision of Justice Bassey Ikpeme on June 10, 1993. An order was issued restraining the NEC from conducting the scheduled elections. Ikpeme stated that she believed the NEC should investigate allegations of corruption in politics, as mentioned by the ABN in their quest for an injunction restraining the NEC from conducting the June 12, 1993 elections. On June 11, 1993, less than 24 hours before the elections, Nwosu announced that the elections would go on. This announcement was made regardless of the badly timed and misleading court order. The court order would seem to have negated, as pointed out by Nwosu, the relevant section of Presidential Election Decree 13 of 1993, which states that 'no interim or interlocutory order of ruling, judgment or tribunal before or after the commencement of the decree in respect of any intra-party dispute or any matter before it shall affect the date or time of holding that specific election or the performance of the electoral commission (NEC) or any of its functions or any guidelines issued in pursuance of the election'.

It is on record that Augustus Aikomu, the vice president, had previously asserted, in consonance with the relevant part of the constitution, that no court could negate that particular decree concerning the elections. Confusion became worse as orders were countermanding orders. Let me quickly recall that a Lagos High Court had declared the ABN an illegal entity that lacked the *locus standi* to get a court injunction. In a similar vein, the Abuja Appellate High Court Judge Saleh ignored the ouster clauses in the decree that precluded the courts from entertaining any election complaints against the NEC. That was within the ambit of the election tribunals set up for the purpose.

Nature itself smiled on me and on my 'D-day' elections of June 12, 1993: My people's yearnings and aspirations were met when they went to the polls as scheduled. Nwosu had earlier defused tension by announcing on radio and television that the elections would go on. If he had not done that, there would have been confusion and doubt. The rains of June gave way to brilliant sunshine all over the land. If it had rained, most people would have stayed indoors, because there were no sheltered voters' booths under which voters could have performed their civic duty. The electoral officers, the agents of the two parties, the security agents, and both local and international observers would have been hindered by inclement weather from performing their monitoring functions. Even the heavens proclaimed the glory of June 12, regardless of the hidden agenda, which would have otherwise blossomed and flourished under rains and chaos.

Option A4 was a runaway success. The system was simple and straightforward. It was introduced to checkmate the rigging and other malpractises of the past. There were at most 500 voters at every polling centre. Accreditation procedures to identify eligible voters were conducted. Voters filed out in a single line towards a table containing a solitary ballot box. There, in the presence of NEC officials, party agents, security operatives, and local and international observers, voters put their thumb impressions on the voters cards and dropped the cards into the ballot box. At the end of the exercise, the NEC officials, in the presence of everybody, separated the thumbed 'horse' cards from the thumbed 'eagle' cards and counted each group, loud and clear, in the hearing of all.

It should be emphasized that the introduction of an election-monitoring group was a major innovation. Three thousand observers were involved in the exercise all over my territory. About 140 of them were foreign monitors from the United Kingdom, the United States of America, Denmark, France, Canada, China, Belgium, Italy, Jamaica, and Ethiopia. Results were announced on the spot and authenticated by the party agents and NEC officials. Every local government area had a collation centre from which results were conveyed to the state headquarters for further collation. The collated results from the states were prepared and put together for onward transmission to Abuja. There, at the Federal capital, the results were scrutinized and vetted, again, by the national executive of the NEC. This also was in the presence of foreign observers and local party agents.

The power to pronounce and announce the results was vested in the Electoral Commission. That was what was being done on June 14, when results of the elections from 14 states were announced and publicly displayed on a gigantic notice board in front of the NEC headquarters at Abuja. There at the Federal capital, the results were scrutinized and vetted by the national executive of the NEC. The results were in favor of the SDP. Results from almost all the states and the federal territory Abuja had been received. But curiously, the announcement was delayed. Because of the ease of collation, all results had been known unofficially except for that of Taraba State that had not yet arrived. Abiola had polled about 8.4 million votes, and Tofa recorded about 5.9 million votes (58.5% to 41.5%). Anxiety was at fever pitch among the electorate.

The NRC, clinging to the last straw, called for the cancellation of the polls, hanging the call on allegations of electoral irregularities. Whereas the Federal Government claimed that the suspension of the poll results was a judicial blind alley, politicians who knew the government beneath surface level thought it was an executive conspiracy. A new twist was brought in when the exercise was described as inconclusive, not only because of the tardiness of the Taraba State results but also because of the judicial conspiracy hatched in Abuja. Such a cancellation would of course be subjected to all sorts of interpretations.

'A catalogue of events that unfolded between June and August 1993 was like a river, the course of which is full of twists and turns. Nobody can stop it. No army, no force, can stop it from reaching its destination in the fullness of time'. On June 22, the Chief Judge of Abuja, Saleh, voided the presidential election results. According to him, a court order prohibiting the elections had been breached. I watched helplessly as Nwosu was gagged and browbeaten into silence and submission. I was also amazed as the NDCO purportedly 'met' to annul the 'transition decrees' that conferred wide powers of conducting the elections on NEC. The boat that had been conveying my people on a transitional joyride to Democracy floundered helplessly for about two weeks. To the consternation of all, it finally capsized. The international community felt bewildered and scandalized, having just witnessed the freest, fairest, and most peaceful election in my 33-year history.

On June 26, 1993, Babangida announced the annulment to save the judiciary from being ridiculed nationally and internationally. Protests and riots erupted in Lagos, Oyo, Ogun, Kwara, Ondo, Anambra, and Delta States. The Nigerian Labour Congress and the Campaign for Democracy led human rights activists who embarked on a series of 'sit-in' strikes which virtually paralyzed the commercial and business nerve centers in many cities and state capitals. Admitting his inability to guarantee law and order in Lagos, Governor Otedola yielded tamely to Defense Secretary Abacha, who unleashed armed guards on unarmed protesters, passers-by, and bystanders. One hundred sixty-five lives were lost in the process.

On July 18, a new NEC, headed by Okon Uya, another professor, was constituted, after Nwosu was sacked for electoral misconduct. When the press howled their disapproval in unison, Babangida's government promulgated the Anti-press Decree 35 of 1993, which prepared the way for the draconian treatment of journalists and the eventual proscription and sealing of media offices. Then, on July 18, Abimbola Davis dropped his clanger and spilled the beans on the ABN. In a hastily convened press conference before his hurried exit from Lagos Airport, he implicated Nzeribe and later, by extension, Akpamgbo, the Attorney General, who it was claimed was behind the judgments handed out by both Ikpeme and Saleh.

The plot was thickening. The noose was dangling dangerously close to Babangida as he allowed himself to be cajoled and entreated to hold on to the reins of power in a clandestine and stage-managed fashion. He attempted coercion and blackmail when he issued an ultimatum to the two parties to choose between having a fresh presidential election to be conducted on July 31 and risking the formation of an Interim National Government. This would mean that all the elected officeholders in the three tiers of government would be sacked. The two parties met and held a dialogue with the new NEC and signed the document with which they capitulated, opting for an Interim National Government (ING). The powerful voices behind this uncalled-for arrangement were those of Anenih, Yar'Adua, Obasanjo, and Kusamatu—and, of course, Babangida. A hard-won victory was sacrificed on the altar of conspiracy and meaningless compromise.

A Lagos high court, citing lack of jurisdiction, threw out a suit filed by Abiola to contest the annulment. Thereafter, and by proclaiming characteristically with a proverb that 'a bird does not tell another bird a stone is coming before taking flight', M. K. O. Abiola departed for London and the USA. He stayed abroad for more than 50 days telling the world the truth about the events in his homeland that sent him fleeing. It later became common knowledge that if he had waited behind, he would likely have been assassinated. His trip and his discussions riveted universal attention on me.

Conversely, people later frowned at the idea of Abiola's overseas trip. They felt that he was not worth dying for if he could not come home to wrest his mandate from the aberrant military junta. They alleged that he fled while his roof was on fire. Did Abiola 'turn tail' as did Ojukwu, in search of peace in the last days of the civil war? Was this a case of the good general who knows when best to retreat? Did he fight and run away in order to stay alive to fight another day? Time would soon tell in the unfolding saga of Nation building.

Abiola had made a series of political miscalculations immediately after winning the nomination of his party to run for president. He should have tried to entrench his interests in the internal political machinery of the SDP by injecting his own men into crucial party positions. Such a team would have established his firm foothold within the party in such a way that his men would ensure a definite pursuit of his mandate after the unpopular annulment. Instead, his journey to the presidency, strewn with thorns, led inexorably to looming tragedy of initial victory, annulment, his seeming desertion concerning his overseas trip, and on to the manipulative and skilful hands of the military cabal. Indeed, it was alleged that it was the cool and calculating Abacha who advised Abiola to travel abroad. The same Abacha and other vested interests were to promote the idea of the non-revalidation of Abiola's election.

The horrific killing of Kudirat, Abiola's wife, while he was in detention (on June 4, 1996) and the deliberate crippling of his businesses were part of the sacrifices Abiola made before he paid the supreme price with his own life. It has also been postulated by some of my great social commentators that when one examines the circumstances and considers the timing of the deaths of Abacha and Abiola, one is inclined to conclude that some highly placed people with vested interests simply saw both men as a problem and decided to get rid of them. People were known to have jubilated over the death of Abacha, but they agonized over the death of Abiola in a frenzied and mournful reaction that almost brought me to my knees. Memories of Abiola's death linger. Up to the very last days in office of Obasanjo's regime (1999–2007), calls were made to have Abiola recognized as the true hero of Democracy and to acknowledge the watershed status of the aborted election of June 12, 1993.

Uche Chukwumerije, Secretary for Information in the ING swung into action, trying to 'get the wind off Abiola's sail'. Chukwumerije resorted to giving alarming and false information. He alerted my entire populace that Abiola had gone to recruit an invasion army 'to attack his fatherland'. He alleged specifically that Lagos, Kaduna, and Enugu were being targeted to be bombed. He recreated the mass movement tragedy at the dawn of Biafra. If it was a mass movement in 1967, it was a stampede in August 1993. The two events were encouraged by the same alarmist in the bourgeois person of Chukwumerije, in the garb of a comrade, ever clad in what looks to be a Chinese workers' tunic.

However, Babangida made a self-serving decision on August 17, 1993 when he added new terminology by injecting a military marching order into my political vocabulary: He offered to 'step aside' as his own 'personal sacrifice' to end the political stalemate. He failed to get the support of his service chiefs. Not all the National Assembly members agreed with him. Some of the members had been allegedly 'settled'. Others were still tugging suicidally at the bait. Those who agreed kept trying to persuade him to continue in office. Babangida resigned from office in the midst of the simmering controversy. He relinquished the reins of power to a 32-member Interim National Government led by the hand-picked Ernest Shonekan and the cabinet that was forced into his hands. Babangida inelegantly 'left a knife stuck deep in the throat' of the ill-fated new administration.

Almost eight years later to the day—and N40 billion literally down the drain in a wasteful exercise in futility—Babangida fled. He was chased by the universal baying of the local and international news hounds at his heels to the safety of his hilltop mansion at Minna. But there could be no hiding place for the 'gold fish' dictator in my aquarium. In my political annals, Babangida's regime, particularly in its twilight, was an unmitigated disaster. The man was always probing into what was open in order to discover what was evident. He bewitched the citizenry with his gap-toothed, winsome smile and 'hail-fellow-well-met' ways, making believers of most of them. He continually disguised his autocratic disposition. He disarmed everyone with his personal charm only to deceive with his selfish ambition. The proliferation of decrees gave me a judiciary without jurisdiction. The decrees gave me a National Assembly that could not make laws because prohibitive 'no-go' areas hindered it. The docile and tame National Assembly was severely limited to debating Tourism, Archives, and other basically 'safe' subjects of little or no political import.

Babangida fought pro-democracy groups to a standstill and incarcerated the activists while promoting illegal organizations like the ABN to subvert all government plans towards democratization. It was as if he played the Maradona until the very end. He out-dribbled himself, whistle in mouth and acting the referee at the same time. He changed the rules in mid-play by picking up the ball from his own net after his opponent had scored a goal, which he had ruled off-side. At the end of the elongated first half of this macabre 'soccer' game, it would seem that Babangida had changed the location of the goal posts and changed the linesmen. He finally substituted for his own position a handpicked referee, Shonekan, whom he superimposed on the scandalized and weary spectators and players. He stuffed the mouths of the press with the dirty rags of DN35 and DN43, when he had released their gag of DN4 (Decree number 34) eight years earlier. Indeed, it was notable that these decrees (DN4, DN34, and DN35) were pronounced and dreaded like some tart chemical mixture.

It was happy riddance to an evil genius of a dictator. Babangida himself referred to the 'evil genius' tag when he admitted in *The Tell Magazine* a few years after his exit that he had gratuitously alleged that people had maligned him by seeing him as an 'evil genius' to whom could be ascribed the source of all evil and disingenuous machinations. It might also be that people saw him as the personification of all the woes and maladies that afflicted my political and economic growth throughout his long reign.

'THIS THING CALLED ING'

As a result of the monumental crisis that followed the annulled June 12, 1993 presidential elections, an Interim National Government (ING) was considered the best option and the only way out of the debacle. However, before settling for an interim government, several options had been weighed. Quite uncharacteristically of Babangida, in considering those options, my people were not carried along. It became clear that only a few people close to the corridors of power opted for the ING arrangements. At that stage of affairs, Babangida had boxed himself into a tight corner. He embarked on a desperate search for an escape route. He was virtually on his own because his military constituency had abandoned him. Even though the ING contrivance was distasteful to my people, they accepted it because they definitely wanted Babangida out of the place by all means, foul or fair, elegantly or disgracefully.

The reason for the call for interim government is not hard to find: Babangida had announced the annulment of the elections. No democrat in the true sense of the word would endorse ING. An interim government can be categorized as an aberration, as is a military government. Both systems were imposed on my innocent people who had no say in the matter. Interim or provisional government is usually a child of circumstance and is definitely not the choice of the people but that of only a select few. It is usually the product of decreed contrivance, when a nation is in distress. Hence, in such a situation, an imposed contraption like the ING was supposedly meant to steer the ship of state away from the rocks and divert it to the haven of a government of the people, by the people, and for the people, which is the anchor and safe harbour that democracy provides.

It is my fervent hope and prayer that historians and chroniclers will be lenient and kind in their assessments of the character and achievements of Ernest Shonekan. Fate thrust into his hands the short tenure of my governance. He attained the pinnacle of his illustrious career in the private sector and had made his mark as the chairman of the huge United African Company of Nigeria (UACN). In that capacity, his eagerly awaited views and comments on annual budgets, year in year out, were always predictable. Such views were invariably patronizing and (understandably) biased in favour of the succeeding governments in power.

He had a penchant for massaging the ego of the budget writers of other governments and unwittingly instilling a false and misplaced feeling of confidence in the masses. Shonekan always described such budgets either as 'a budget of redemption' and as 'calculated to usher in an era of economic progress and industrialization' or as a 'revolutionary budget'. This was because, when Shonekan spoke, it was with the voice and authority of the inveterate technocrat, the consummate bureaucrat, and the beneficiary of the colonialist commercial structure, made to measure for even the average initiate and devotee of such a system. Indeed, it was like his second coming: He had already experienced commercial power. Fate took over and catapulted him to the apogee of political power.

Having relinquished the pinnacle of power in the UACN, the time was auspicious for him to slide with a calculated degree of opportunism into the highest seat of power, which was left empty by the intransigence of Babangida. His march in the corridors of power began with the confusion and uncertainty that characterised the aftermath of the botched primaries involving 23 presidential aspirants in both parties. Accusations of rigging and big money changing hands between aspirants and voters rent the air, paving the way for Babangida to promote his ambition and prolong his reign.

Babangida was virtually invited to declare the cancellation of the primaries by defeated and 'unfairly treated' candidates. They felt done in, dispossessed, and inexplicably thrashed by the 'money bags'. For example, Jakande felt so humiliated by Shehu Yar'Adua in his Lagos constituency that he childishly challenged the latter to take a walk with him down a Lagos street in a popularity contest. Yar'Adua promptly advised LKJ to first challenge Sarumi—his (Yar'Adua's) Lagos surrogate, who had masterminded Jakande's defeat. Falae also felt the same way when Ibadan 'Strongman' Adedibu paved the way for Yar'Adua to win the Oyo State primaries. Nzeribe cried foul as Yar'Adua outsmarted him in some parts of the East, while Yar'Adua could not explain his loss to Falae in some parts of the North, particularly Kaduna. Falae's campaign manager had to flee from Kaduna to Abuja to escape the wrath of the defeated candidate's supporters.

As mentioned earlier, Babangida was boxed into a tight corner. He could run but he could not hide. His much-trumpeted programme of transition was in shambles and disarray as billions of naira had gone into its execution. But because power is a corrupting influence to the ambitious, Babangida became obsessed with the notion of perpetuating himself in power. He found a willing but unwitting tool in Shonekan, a gentleman and an incorruptible technocrat whom Babangida wanted to manipulate.

EARNEST SHONEKAN—JANUARY 1993 AND AUGUST 17 1993–NOVEMBER 1993

Although Shonekan reigned, it was Babangida who ruled, as his hands were still firmly on the reins of government. This was the setting in January 1993 when Shonekan was sworn in as chairman of the 27-member Traditional Council (TC). This turned out to be an amorphous body of strange and disparate bedfellows anointed by Babangida as a balm to soothe frayed and jagged nerves in both military and political circles. This group felt concerned over the postponement—from January 2 to August 27, 1993—of the ending date of Babangida's military government. Once again, Babangida had installed a puppet apparatus whose strings and remote controls he could routinely manipulate from Aso Rock.

Ordinarily, it did not seem that this should be a daunting undertaking for a man of immense and enabling background like Shonekan. Indeed, it turned out to be a correct observation in spite of the brilliant array of superstar technocrats that were on his team. They simply failed to click. This might be attributable to the personality of Babangida that loomed large, menacing, and intrusive in the background. Even though Shonekan was expected to bring into play his UACN experience in handling the 1993 budget as the head of government, the economic problems further worsened. This was in spite of his projected restoration of streamlining expenditure with realistic income profile and ensuring that the budget would again become an effective instrument of control.

In only six months, Shonekan's government had overspent the entire year's budget by more than N27 billion against an anticipated yearly deficit of N28.6 billion. There was no redemption and no economic progress. There was nothing revolutionary or innovative about his efforts. It was the virtuoso performance of a lover of the status quo who would rather not risk rocking the boat or ruffling a few military feathers. The situation was compounded by the recalcitrance of some of the secretaries in Shonekan's cabinet who were neither ready to listen to him nor take instructions from him. They would rather go over his head to report directly to Babangida. Some of them in fact felt bigger than Shonekan and saw the UACN captain of commerce as an upstart who was catapulted into an unsolicited position of preeminence. They thought Shonekan was perching uncomfortably on an unfamiliar terrain. A secretary like Chukwumerije (Information) made Shonekan realize that to all intents and purposes, Babangida, the President and Commander in Chief, was the one who called the shots.

Shonekan's other assignment was a monumental and enormous one. It was a fresh assignment that came about as a result of the annulment of the June 12 presidential elections. Babangida had wanted him to conduct another presidential election and leave the seat of power to a democratically elected civilian administration. It should be presumed that everyone knew that this was a charade, masking the ambition of Babangida to perpetuate himself in power. Most of all, Shonekan, who was a member of the NDSC, the highest ruling body, should have known better and could therefore not be exonerated from the events leading to the presidential election and its subsequent annulment.

If he was merely a head of government, a strange interplay of events combined to propel him up the ladder as the Head of State and Commander in Chief of the armed forces. In the face of mounting pressure, both domestic and international—and in spite of his last-ditch determined effort to cajole, coerce, and 'settle' the politicians regarding the recognition of the June 12 presidential election debacle—Babangida opted to 'step aside' from the highest seat of government as 'his own personal contribution' and perhaps sacrifice to the will of the people. Thus, Shonekan was installed as Head of the Interim National Government (ING).

Nobel Laureate Wole Soyinka dug out his poetic license and poesy to refer to the new government contraption as 'This Thing Called ING'. The same contrivance was described by Shonekan himself as 'the child of circumstances'. He admitted that the system was born out of the imperative to move me forward once more as a Nation 'united and indivisible'. As if he knew that he was toying with a ticking time bomb, he apologetically and philosophically averred that he was not in government 'to spoil anybody's joy', stating that 'it is God that has put me there'. He seemed to play the role of a 'kill joy' who desperately sought to be absolved from any blame. It was as if M. K. O. Abiola's joy, and the joy of more than 14 million voters, had not been 'killed' enough!

Credibility and acceptability were the twin problems that stared Shonekan in the face and dogged him throughout his 82 days in office. Being himself an Egba man like Abiola, pressure was put on him, even from his own Egba kinsmen, to resign and return the situation to the electoral verdict of June 12. He sought recognition and acceptability everywhere. As he courted the Sultan and Emirs of the core North so did he woo the unwilling and unimpressed people of the South, particularly, the South-West. He did not like that idea and retaliated by stopping the flow of money to states opposing him while pumping money to the friendly states of the North and parts of the East. He cajoled and courted Ondo State by confirming its rightful place as an oil-producing state and enabling it enjoy the 'derivative state' status which would earn Ondo State much-needed oil revenue allocation.

Although Babangida had gone to the smug comfort of his Minna castle, Shonekan kept in regular touch with him for support, advice, and solace. He operated from Akinola Aguda House at Abuja because the side-stepping erstwhile occupant of Aso Rock, Babangida, had probably departed with the keys when retreating to his Minna fortress. A week after he was able to get the key to a wing of Aso Rock and move in, Justice Dolapo Akinsanya, a fearless and erudite female judge of tremendous courage, delivered a landmark judgment that literally unseated 'this thing called ING'. Dolapo Akinsanya was the daughter of a similarly courageous and brilliant professor–father, Onabamiro (who conducted a research that discovered the steroid called onabamiroid).

Simply put, Dolapo Akinsanya ruled, in the best tradition of her calling, that 'you cannot place something on nothing'. Since Decree 61 brought in a transitional government had been abrogated and the master schemer's (Babangida's) ship of state had keeled over and been demobilised, the basis for Shonekan's 'ING' was no more. 'Let justice be done, even though the heavens fall'. With these words my illustrious and erudite ''Daniela' entered eminently into the judicial annals. She rattled it out, in bold Latin—*'fiat justice ruat colum'*. That was the premise on which she based her landmark judgment. Her remarkable understanding of legal semantics was matched by her in-depth interpretation of the law. It was said that 'She had ridden the proverbial ass on all fours, to its inexorable destination, where justice reigns supreme'.

It boggled the mind to watch helplessly as Shonekan—a lawyer and erstwhile boardroom super star—could not seem to know what was coming. I shudder to think that M. K. O. Abiola was not able to 'seize the hour' then. He could have grabbed the seat that was his by election but that was now declared vacant in an interregnum that brought Abacha steaming in to force Shonekan into submission. This was only after Shonekan had ignored Judge Akinsanya's ruling and after Shonekan had addressed a joint session of the National Assembly to the effect that 'this thing called 'ING'' was legal and had come to stay. A few days later, he repeated the same legal blasphemy at the judges' conference in Port Harcourt.

Shonekan showed his gratitude in many ways after Abacha, the 'most senior military officer' in his cabinet—as required by the offensive Decree 13—'bloodlessly' ousted him. His new role was more or less propagandist and apologist. It stemmed from his show of gratitude for the new regime retroactively 'annulling', by decree, the court ruling of Dolapo Akinsanya that judged the ING as illegal; thus the new order assured Shonekan a place in the 'revered pantheon' of former heads of state.

Some may describe Shonekan's new role as patriotic, but I view it seriously as the gratuitous role of an errand boy at the court of his tormentors and oppressors. A quiet, decent, and honest man, Shonekan tamely left office. It was said that the pennant on his car outside the Aso Rock Presidential villa was being removed even as he was being ousted inside Aso Rock. He did not go into oblivion, as some people would do. Imbued with a deep sense of patriotism and forthrightness, he extended his services to the Abacha government, who needed his support and name as bargaining chips in the conference rooms of the financial centers of the West—the World bank and the International Monetary Fund.

LAMENTATIONS AND FOREBODINGS: BEFORE AND DURING ABACHA'S REGIME

Quite apart from being a very wealthy man, M. K. O. Abiola was a very intelligent and resourceful personality. He was well known for his use of proverbs, allegories, anecdotes, instantaneous repartee, and deeply philosophical pronouncements. He could deploy any of these to achieve maximum effect, defuse tension, and assuage ruffled egos. Indeed, many times, in consonance with diplomatic parlance and usage, he had been known to 'say a nasty thing in a pleasant way'—that is, to be a smiling diplomat in his discourses. I must resort to borrowing from his wide repertoire of anecdotes and allegories to explain why my narration suddenly stopped at the sight and approach of the rampaging goons and nihilistic brutality of Abacha's security apparatus and personnel. Here are some of the utterances and pithy stories that are relevant to my being cautious:

1. A wealthy and popular man decided to go for a swim near his town. He undressed and waded into the deep end of the river and began to swim. While swimming, a raving lunatic passing by, saw and picked up the wealthy man's dress and ran away. On noticing this, the wealthy man rather decided on the side of decency, decorum, and dignity, not to give chase in his naked condition.

Or else, any beholder of such an unimaginable spectacle would be bewildered and might conclude that the wealthy man's insanity is fresher and more intense than that of the fleeing mad man.

2.   A knock-kneed damsel was asked why she was carrying her load at such an awkward angle on her head. She quickly pointed out that the reason was not hard to seek. Pointing downwards she said that this could be easily traced from the shape of her legs. Briefly stated, her bodily frame rested on a foundation that was wobbly and knock-kneed.

3.   A bold man who wanted to stop the noisy train from passing by the side of his cottage once stood in the way of the on-coming train and got crushed.

4.   Any one who dares to ride on the back of a tiger runs the imminent risk of ending up in the belly of the rampaging carnivore.

5.   A word is therefore enough for the wise. Quite unlike the wealthy swimmer, the knock-kneed woman, the man who dared an oncoming train and was crushed, and the one who chose to ride on the tiger's back, I would rather not count forwards and backwards, for certainty and in his pugnacious presence, the number of toes on the legs of a man with nine toes.

6.   Surely, decapitation is not the panacea for a worrisome headache, just as you would not want to cut off your nose in order to spite your face.

I would rather not narrate the events after the exit of affordable and innocuous Shonekan. I would rather, like the old, wise solider, fight and run away so that I could live to fight another day, because it is a wise and tactful general who knows when best to retreat. I do not want to self-combust and deny generations yet unborn the opportunity of knowing what went on in this momentous period of my history. I do not want to cut off my nose merely because I resent my face. I want to be alive to resume my narration of events as I see them. I want to tell the story of the kingmaker who became the king. I will talk about a grander deception; about the clone of the past master himself; about the renegade progressives and taciturn conservatives in government. I will not hold back my views on selected and elected constituent assembly members who laboured for one whole year only to have their work reviewed, re-engineered, and tampered with by a subsequent committee.

I will tell it all regarding the flight of NADECO members into exile: their escapades, performances, and pronouncements abroad. I will muse on the guile of the vanquished who later became the tormentors and villains, and I will extol the virtues of the victor who became the vanquished and the unwitting victim of his scheming captors. I will throw the searchlight on the perceived enemies and stumbling blocks who became prisoners through trumped-up coup charges. I will analyze the 'brief' stay which was planned to elongate into five years or into perpetuity; or transition at the presidential elections aborted by death, the ultimate terminator.

I will also talk about the TV melodrama and pantomime of alleged coup-plotters who were cajoled to confess their complicity on their way to the gallows. The giant carrot of remission and reprieve was dangled in their faces from the left hand of their executioner, who also wielded a menacingly raised cudgel aloft in his right hand. The cudgel was to batter them into the oblivion of long stretches in jail or the death penalty. Of course, they looked at the carrot and took the bait—hook, line, and sinker.

I will spill the beans on the terror unleashed on the Ogoni people, culminating in the supreme price paid by thirteen Ogoni activists. I will dwell on the international repercussions of the trial and execution of Ken Saro-Wiwa and the other eight Ogoni leaders. I will reminisce on my experience as a pariah nation, treated like a leper in the comity of nations. Will it be a dirge, a lament, or an exhortation? Time will surely tell. I will continue my narration presently. As M. K. O. himself would put it, 'If one prepares for insanity for 20 years, how much time is left to demonstrate the mad traits?'

CHAPTER SEVEN

MILITARY GOVERNMENT

ABACHA—NOVEMBER 1993–JULY 1998

Abacha seized power on November 17, 1993. He led a group of top army officers to demand the resignation of Ernest Shonekan, Head of the Interim
National Government (ING). The ING was the hastily contrived administrative
system which was put in place on August 17, 1993 by the 'stepping-aside' military president General Babangida. The ING itself, as earlier stated, was a disingenuous contraption contrived by Babangida ostensibly to complete his transition programme and conduct another presidential poll following the annulment
of the June 12, 1993, presidential elections. Ironically, pundits and political analysts alike had happily described the 1993 elections as the freest and fairest
ever in my history as a Nation.

My citizenry had become used to the automatic post-coup speeches of Abacha. The one he made on November 17, 1993, was the fourth of a similar genre.
I recall firstly that he announced the overthrow of the Second Republic, headed
by Shagari, and the takeover by Buhari in December 1993. Secondly, he had announced the toppling of the Buhari regime and Babangida's arrival on the seat
of power on August 28, 1985. Thirdly, he took to the airwaves again on April 22,
1990, to announce the termination of Orkar's frivolous and deviant coup.

Telltale signs of his veiled, lengthy takeover came in his maiden announcement. He promised a constitutional conference 'with full constituent powers'.
How soon this would be achieved was neither stated nor implied. At about the

same time, his second-in-command, Diya, glibly announced at the air officers' mess in Lagos that Abacha's new administration would be 'brief'. My doubts about Abacha's intentions and sincerity were ably articulated by Gani Fawehinmi's famous twenty questions concerning Abacha's credibility. Abacha became virtually the almighty power over an unwieldy government. The regime was outstanding in the way it sought the integration of all existing powers, influence, and authority under the 'supreme' Abacha.

The Constitution Decree number 107 of 1993 scrapped all the existing democratic structure left over from Babangida's transition programme. It placed the legislature and executive powers of governance in Abacha's hands. He was to share power equally with the Provisional Ruling Council (PRC) over which he would be the chairman. But since Abacha had the power to appoint members of the council and to dissolve it, to call meetings, and to act with the council's power when it was not in session, he was literally placed above the council. That is the stuff dictators are made of.

Abacha duly started manipulating the proposed conference by establishing the Constitutional Conference Electoral Committee, headed by Bernard Mbah. He also went ahead later to nominate a third of the membership of the conference. He meddled with the conference by funding a select group via slush funds channelled through the business committee. They frowned at the departure date of January 1, 1996, as proposed by Shehu Yar'Adua. They adopted the teleguided departure date of October 1, 1998. The conference was virtually beaten into a political tool for Abacha's future ambition. The stage was set for the clandestine ouster of Yar'Adua.

That was the known danger signal—a ruler who was bent on using guile to entrench himself on the seat of power. Hence, the June 12 agitators were convinced that Abacha built up this façade to buy time. They saw it as a ploy to teleguide the conference to their own political disadvantage. They therefore decided to boycott the new political programme. They also decided to vehemently oppose the Abacha regime through disruptive activities and well-organized civil disobedience measures. This led to the formation of the National Democratic Coalition (NADECO) on May 15, 1994. NADECO demanded the following:

1. Exit of the military within two weeks.
2. Revalidation of the June 12 poll outcome.
3. Swearing in of its winner, Abiola, who would immediately summon a sovereign national conference to debate the basis for my unity as a Nation.

NADECO and its supporters swung into action along with the labour unions, students and the human rights and democracy groups. The trade unions were quickly suppressed and gobbled up. The PENGASSAN as well as the Nigerian Labour Congress had their national executives dissolved. Sole administrators were appointed by government to take charge of the unions. Abiola declared himself president at Epetedo in Lagos and went underground. He resurfaced 12 days later on June 23, only to be arrested and later placed 'on trial' for treasonable felony.

After inaugurating the conference on June 27, 1994, Abacha pledged in a speech to be committed to ensuring a speedy and unimpeded transition to a civil democratic rule in which he and his colleagues would not be participants. He said it was neither in his regime's interest nor in that of the citizenry's for him to perpetuate himself in power. The pledge was not worth the piece of paper on which it was read. Abacha became committed to the exact opposite direction of his pledge made before the Assembly. He dissolved the existing two political parties. All processions, political meetings and associations of all types and in any part of my vast terrain were banned. All consultative committees, by whatever name called, were proscribed. These draconian steps were the very antithesis of Democracy.

Perhaps when Abacha referred to laying a very solid foundation for democracy, he must have had 'kleptocracy' in mind. He did everything within his powers to stand democracy on its head. He was enmeshed and neck-deep in massive corruption and looting of the treasury. All revenues led to his pocket and took flight with his henchmen and family members, into foreign banks. At the last count and estimates, he had siphoned abroad about $3 billion.

My suspicion of his self-succession motive, inherent in the implementation of the transition programme, was soon reinforced by the emergence of pressure groups, hired or sponsored by the regime. They started to clamour and canvass for Abacha to succeed himself as a civilian president under the auspices of the transition programme. Some of the pro-Abacha groups were supposedly made up of youths led by the calculating opportunist Kanu, who led the government-sponsored million-man march on Abuja. They also included traditional rulers, government contractors, sycophantic civil servants who wore Abacha badges, and some spineless politicians.

Even the five political parties were not left behind. They also joined the bandwagon by adopting Abacha as their consensus candidate for the projected August 1 presidential elections. The inimitable, extraordinary wordsmith Bola Ige had dubbed the political parties 'the five fingers on the same leprous hand'. Bluntly stated, the parties were like the leftover stumps of their previous whole hands, now stunted and emaciated. It would have been an almost farcical and tragic transition had fate not intervened mysteriously at the nick of time.

Abacha declared behind his fear-inspiring dark goggles that his regime would be firm, humane, and decisive. He drove fear into his critics as he threatened to deal decisively with anyone who doubted that pronouncement and attempted to test the regime's will and resolve. Thereafter, M. K. O. Abiola was detained. Shehu Musa Yar'Adua was arrested and detained, and he met his death, under macabre circumstances, in prison. Bola Ige was incarcerated and he smuggled a guiding piece of advice surreptitiously to Abiola, asking him to refuse to take any injection from anyone in order to avert the calamity that befell Yar'Adua. Unlikely and unbelievable phantom coup stories woven around top military officers like Abacha's second-in-command Diya, and Adisa, Fadile, and Akinyemi, earned them jail sentences.

It looked as if Obasanjo could not believe his ears and eyes as he heard and saw his accusers and witnesses against him at the seemingly spurious and fictitious coup trial. Only international pleas and the Pope's intervention saved Obasanjo from the gallows. Several journalists, including Chris Anyawu, were arrested, tried and imprisoned. Killer-squads trailed and assassinated the likes of Alfred Rewane, Kudirat Abiola, and Sulilat Adedeji. They trailed and wounded Alex Ibru, who was a member of Abacha's cabinet and owner of *The Guardian* newspaper.

Journalists became targets of nocturnal killers and assassins' bullets and were candidates for interrogation in various detention centers and police cells. Newspaper houses were shut down and sealed off. Wives and children were arrested and detained in place of fleeing husbands and fathers. The menacing and intimidating security apparatus put in place by Abacha spread fear and horror all around. Mysterious killings soon started occurring. Bombs surreptitiously planted in various cities exploded at intervals. Military officers who sounded like democrats were either summarily retired or implicated—or sent to jail. Anyone who looked or sounded like a potential voice of reason or a credible alternative was either detained or hounded into exile. These included Wole Soyinka, Anthony Enahoro, Colonel Sambo Dasuki, Dan Suleiman, and Bola Tinubu.

I was like a dying nation when Abacha presided over me. My fortunes dwindled as investors fled. The real sector became the operating theatre for crooks and speculators. My public facilities collapsed. An aggrieved international community, spearheaded by the ambassadors from the United States and Canada, spoke up in support of the fundamental human rights of my people. When Abacha responded by turning my foreign affairs establishment into a forum for shouting and abuse, and the Minister, Tom Ikimi, obliged by entertaining the international community with his 'area boy' (street-wise rascals) type of diplomacy, the world turned its back on Abacha and me, as a hapless Nation.

I was suspended from the Commonwealth, and my foreign affairs minister was hounded out of international conferences in both Scotland and New Zealand and even more so after the despicable politically motivated hanging of Ken Saro-Wiwa in Port Harcourt. I was denied the hosting rights of the 1995 Junior World Cup Championships. I was compelled to withdraw from the twenty-fifth edition of the Africa Cup of Nations, which took place in South Africa. I virtually became an island unto myself—isolated, ignored, unwanted, and despised. The era constituted what could rightly be regarded as my lowest foreign policy moments.

These were dangerous and unhappy days for me as a Nation. I experienced the nadir of misfortune and misadventure in the hands of a rabid dictator. I was treated like a pariah in the comity of nations. My public officials were banned from the major capitals of the world. Abacha's regime was one long stretch of misrule and disaster. Just when most critics were convinced that it was merely a matter of time before his agenda was actualized, this ambition somersaulted into an anticlimax as the news of Abacha's sudden death came like a thunderbolt from the blue on June 8, 1998. This brought to an end a regime that had been one long, dark night of bad dreams and horrific nightmares.

ABDULSALAMI ABUBAKAR: MILITARY GOVERNMENT—JUNE 1998-MAY 1999

The immortal William Shakespeare proclaimed his universal axiom in 'Twelfth Night' when he averred that 'Some men are born great, some achieve greatness, and some have greatness thrust upon them'. My own Abubakar achieved greatness in his own right. He rose to the rank of general in the army. He definitely had greatness thrust upon him when his peers in the corridors of power chose him to succeed Abacha, who had died under mysterious and scandalous circumstances.

Abubakar's ascension to the pinnacle of power as Head of State was providential. Abacha had embarked on moves to assume the post of the civilian president by handing over the office to himself on October 1, 1998. Abubakar was the Chief of Defense Staff in Abacha's regime. He was well known for his military professionalism. His friends and colleagues described him as an unassuming gentleman. They saw him as an officer who just wanted to perform his job well and according to brief. He was imbued with a fatherly demeanour and the strictness of a headmaster. He was also reputed to be a very patient individual. To his credit, he aptly demonstrated these attributes in concrete terms when, true to his word, he handed over power to his successor. He returned me as a Nation to much-needed Democracy. Expectedly, he took some bold and internationally applauded steps on assuming office as the Head of State:

1. He appealed to the international community for their co-operation and understanding. He reasoned that as a Nation, I deserved a fair hearing and constructive engagement and not isolation. He asserted my importance as a 'member of the international system through the framework of the United Nations, which is a veritable instrument of international cooperation'.

2. He appealed to all my citizens who fled into exile to return and join hands with fellow compatriots in the task of Nation-building. It would be recalled that some of my eminent citizens like Anthony Enahoro, Wole Soyinka, Bola Tinubu, and Nosa Igiebor created a 'NADECO' route through which they eluded the thugs and killers that the notorious and tyrannical Abacha's regime loosed on dissidents and critics.

3. The Press were unmuzzled. Journalists heaved a sigh of relief. They were able to resume, unfettered, their roles of news gathering, news dissemination, commentating, and critiques. Indeed, many of them were even released from prison.

Then Abubakar embarked on the delicate process of negotiation for the release from prison of Abiola, who was the universally acclaimed winner of the June 1993 elections, which had been inexplicably annulled by Babangida. Abiola had been languishing in jail since 1993 to gratify the wicked political ambition of Abacha. If the intention to negotiate the release of Abiola was conceptually laudable and magnanimous at the initial stage, it became increasingly clear that it was manifestly reluctant and half-hearted in execution. The plan did not come to fruition as Abiola met his untimely and mysterious death in July 1998 in prison, barely a month after Abacha's death and Abubakar's assumption of office. What was my conclusion? What gave me the impression that Abiola's death was viewed as good riddance to an irritant? Was he a cog in the wheel of progress, or a sacrificial lamb, deliberately slaughtered on the altar of an internationally promoted appeasement? These questions still beg for answers.

It looked as if the idea was to cajole and persuade Abiola to renounce his claim to the popularly won victory at the June 1993 polls. It was presumed that if he opted out, there would be a new and clean slate. To surrender his much-acclaimed victory would have been offensive and disappointing to his millions of supporters. They would have viewed him as a timid renegade and a manipulable turncoat. They would have reckoned that he was neither worth fighting for nor, even worse still, dying for.

I began to have fears of international conspiracy when, one after the other, the movers and shakers of the world and British Commonwealth along with the powerful and intimidating US power-broking apparatus and officials came pouring into Abuja. They all came with the same fervent resolve and avowed intent to persuade Abiola to relinquish his claim to the 1993 victory in order to establish a new beginning. Emeka Anyaoku was the first to come. His concern and intentions were understandable and patriotic. He was my own citizen who was then the internationally recognized Secretary-General of the Commonwealth.

The next to come was the newly appointed and immensely popular United Nations Secretary-General, Kofi Annan. The alarm button was triggered when the former American ambassador Thomas Pickering followed the two highly respected Africans. Susan Rice, who was the US undersecretary of State for African Affairs, also came. Some of these international visitors, particularly the

Americans, came with the same fervent resolve to request that Abiola renounce his victory. The Americans went a big step further, even as guests, to offer tea from their own double-layer flask to their 'host' and beleaguered prisoner. No sooner did Abiola partake of this proffered 'chalice' tea and the visitors depart than he began to convulse. He died thereafter.

Al Mustapha, the notorious henchman of Abacha, graphically and analytically highlighted the striking similarity of the throes of death suffered by both Abacha and Abiola. This arose during his testimony before the Oputa Panel on Peace and Reconciliation. He said that Abacha, like Abiola before him, had similarly convulsed and stiffened to death, after eating proffered apples from the hand of an expatriate prostitute. Mustapha should know. He was the notorious and dreaded top Abacha security officer who hastened to the venue to ascertain the death and observe the cause of Abacha's death.

I hasten to point out that all my government guest houses, whether at the Federal or State levels, are equipped with a full complement of furniture and with cooking and serving utensils. Furthermore, it is without doubt that the service personnel for such high-profile, august visitors and very important prisoners would be at the beck and call of government. The question of the guests 'serving' the host should not arise under normal circumstances; more so when the guests are not medical personnel. I therefore awaited the outcome of the Oputa Panel and the inevitable searchlight of research and history to either vindicate my postulation or expose more of the regime's dastardly acts. Meanwhile, I still consider the whole episode and the circumstances surrounding the mysterious death of Abiola as a stain on the otherwise white robe of Abubakar's regime.

Even then, Abubakar did not fail me as a Nation by any stretch of the imagination. He promised to complete the transition programme within 10 months and leave. He obliged. He proscribed the ill-contrived political parties, sarcastically dubbed 'the five leprous fingers', set up under the remote control of Abacha for his self-succession plan. Abubakar promptly dismissed the governors and legislators elected under the auspices of the parties. He embarked on a new transition programme on a new and clean slate. He rekindled in my people the dying embers of confidence in the military typified during the regimes of Babangida and Abacha. At the end of the promised 10 months, he did not 'step aside' as had been glibly and facetiously announced and enacted by Babangida. He was actually seen to have 'stepped out' by demonstrably handing over to a democratically elected President and Head of State.

It was not all rosy and smooth sailing in the regime of Abubakar. The economy was punctured resulting in blighting inflation. The value of the naira fell as the US dollar rose from N84 during the Abacha regime to N99.50k under Abubakar. The Foreign Reserve drastically fell. In retrospect and in extenuation, all these might be attributable to the prevailing oil glut in the world market. Inevitably, it was to be assumed that these factors caused prices to crash and Organization of Petroleum Exporting Countries (OPEC) to cut production quotas across the board. If Abubakar had an excuse and a justification for the fall in the Foreign Exchange Reserve, he had absolutely no justification in logic or reasoning for the continuous doling out of $1 million on daily basis for the peacekeeping activities of the Economic Community of West Africa Monitoring Group (ECOMOG) in Sierra Leone. This was an ill-timed arrangement, because my workers at home were hungry and therefore angry and on strike.

Abubakar did well by initiating steps to recover the loot stashed away by Abacha's family members, his Security Chief, and some of his Federal Ministers, like Ani and Dalhatu. Abubakar impounded exotic cars imported by Abacha that were meant as gifts for compliant and compromising traditional Chiefs. I am yet to know, however, what became of the recovered monies and the stolen cars. It is equally puzzling to ascertain what measure of punishment was meted out to the officials allegedly in possession of such monies. Suffice it to say, for ease of reference, that Abubakar, like Babangida, refused to appear before the Oputa Panel on Peace and Reconciliation. For good measure, Babangida pressed his rights and claim of refusal all the way to the Court of Law. Hence these questions also are still begging for answers.

The minimum wage issue also probably took some sheen off Abubakar's transition success story. Without thorough research and adequate consultation, he went ahead and announced a new N5200 minimum wage for my workers. After a lot of hue and cry from the paying authorities, particularly at the state level, he brought the minimum wage down to N3000. Even at that rate, some states still demurred, as they felt unable to pay. This unsettled issue was bequeathed to Olusegun Obasanjo, who became Abubakar's successor.

Quite apart from the successful implementation of the aforestated urgent and important aspects of the Transition Programme, it is worthy of note that Abubakar recorded some other concrete achievements. The Junior World Cup Fiesta, dubbed 'Nigeria '99', was successfully hosted between April 3 and April 24, 1999. The various elections to usher in Democracy were successful. The National Assembly complex and houses to accommodate the legislators were duly completed. My citizens therefore rose to hail and acknowledge Abubakar's achievements when he gallantly and successfully relinquished power to his successor, Olusegun Obasanjo, on May 29, 1999.

I am thoroughly satisfied with Abubakar for conducting the shortest transition programme in my evolving political history. It would, however, appear that history also has a double-edged place for him. His courageous and honourable step of voluntarily relinquishing power has earned him a golden space in my annals as only the second military dictator—after Obasanjo—to do so.

Conversely, history will wonder why Abubakar depleted my Foreign Reserve during his brief tenure. He also seemed to have turned a deaf ear to the will of the people until Abiola died under suspicious circumstances in prison. It looked like a grand international conspiracy to allow Abiola's body and blood to be used as fertilizer to make Democracy flourish. Moreover, Abubakar should have reconciled my fractured society rather than pass along the problems to his popularly elected civilian successor, Olusegun Obasanjo.

CHAPTER EIGHT

OLUSEGUN OBASANJO: SECOND COMING (IN CIVILIAN GOVERNMENT) —MAY 1999–MAY 2007

It always boggles my mind when I consider the circumstantial and providential emergence of Olusegun Obasanjo on the military and civilian stages of my evolving historical drama. He has always shown up in the nick of time and at those points in my history when 'the hour found the man'. He arrived opportunely at the war front to apply the 'coup de grace' that ended the civil war. He fit into the big boots of Murtala as assassination created a yawning gap in leadership. He was the general in charge of 'traffic signals' at the junction of change from a military government to a civilian one. He ultimately became the first head of a democratically elected civilian government to hand over to another similarly elected head of civilian government.

Obasanjo made a dramatic appearance at the war front when he assumed leadership of the crack troops of the Third Marine Commando. The previous commander from whom he took over was the swashbuckling war hero, Benjamin Adekunle. By Obasanjo's own account, he made himself more approachable to his troops. He removed a horrendous warning, which had threatened death to any uninvited intruder to Adekunle's 'situation report' office. He arrived at the scene and immediately began reorganizing and restrategizing in such a way that the Biafran troops were soon encircled and in disarray. Hence, the war was brought to an end, when Obasanjo mounted a cleverly contrived all-out attack, which turned out to be the coup de grace for the Biafran forces.

Some critics opined that he came at the critical junction of the war, when Benjy Adekunle was already on the glorious last lap. I share this view, because Obasanjo was essentially a child of fate and luck. Events continually played into his hands as he meandered his way from his conquest on the battlefield to Dodan Barracks as Head of State. Then he was thrown into prison as a perceived accomplice in a seemingly fictitious coup. Finally, he found his way back again into the highest seat of power at Aso Rock Villa as Head of State in his 'second coming'.

While Ojukwu was departing from the airstrip at Uli-Ihiala in search of peace at the haven of Yamusukoro in Ivory Coast, Obasanjo was honourably and deservedly recalled to Lagos. His mission was to obtain from the hands of Justice Mbanefo and Ojukwu's second in command—Phillip Effiong—the instruments signaling the end of the war. This landmark ceremony was conducted on the lawns of Dodan Barracks. Significantly, that was the military headquarters and the seat of Gowon's government. This milestone ritual turned out to be a watershed in the chronicle of events pertaining to the Civil War of 1967 to 1970, but it took place neither at the war front nor in any foreign territory. It took place in what used to be my Federal Capital territory, as both of my warring 'body parts' used to acknowledge it.

Once again, Obasanjo had to shake himself loose from initial doubt and misapprehension when fate compelled him to boldly stand in the gap after Dimka's bullets terminated the short but glorious and eventful reign of Murtala Mohammed on February 13, 1976. He assumed leadership when the mantle of power fell on him by the unanimous acclamation of his comrades in the military hierarchy. With characteristic gusto and panache, he embarked on the implementation of the programmes that Murtala Mohammed had mapped out with him.

Obasanjo had the foresight and sagacity to appoint lower-ranked Shehu Musa Yar'Adua as his Second in Command and went on to fortify the latter's position with accelerated promotion. He made all the right moves and capped them all by following through with Murtala's plan to return me as a Nation into the hands of a civilian ruler. He prepared the ground for conducting elections and handing over to a democratically elected government headed by Shehu

Shagari. In doing so, Obasanjo made history by becoming the first among a chain of military heads of state in Africa to cede power voluntarily to a civilian government.

Obasanjo's decision to relinquish power to a civilian regime was widely applauded. But many people, particularly among my vocal human rights activists, did not trust Obasanjo because military forces had cracked down on dissenters during his time in power. The ill-considered attack on the 'Ali-must-go' protesting students and the wanton destruction of the family home of musician Fela Anikulapo-Kuti immediately come to mind. My Yoruba people became almost implacable in their anger and suspicion that Obasanjo himself, being a Yoruba man, had allowed and might have surreptitiously worked with the Federal Electoral Commission (FEDECO) to rule in favour of Shehu Shagari of the National Party of Nigeria (NPN) when the 1979 presidential elections became mired in controversy.

The subsequent court ruling had to resort to mathematical acrobatics and stand the idea of approximation on its head to determine the more acceptably nearest figure to two-thirds of 19 states: $12^2/_3$ or 13 states? It should be recalled that Obasanjo had ominously warned that the best man might not necessarily win the race, whereas I have always opined that only the best is good enough for me. Incidentally, this was an election in which some of my most experienced hands—like Azikiwe, Awolowo and Aminu Kano—had participated as contestants. I still hold tenaciously to that criterion. The Yorubas believed that Obasanjo had assisted Shagari, a northern-based Hausa/Fulani, in defeating their man, Awolowo, in that particular election.

Obasanjo retired from the military following the unique and universally acclaimed 1979 hand-over of power to a democratically elected government. He began to run a chicken farm at Ota in his home State of Ogun. From October 1979 until his imprisonment by Abacha, he successfully cultivated the image of an international statesman with a social conscience. He expressed his abhorrence of corruption and cared deeply about my internal cohesion. He was a stickler for democracy and the rule of law, both within me as a Nation and for peace around the world. He combined this venture with a variety of international projects with the United Nations and other groups. Having handed over power voluntarily, he became a social critic and a moral voice in Africa, where many sit-tight military rulers held sway in their various territories.

He was a founder member of the Eminent Persons' Group, which preached and supervised good governance. He thus strengthened his relationships with other international institutions and leaders, such as the World bank, presidents, and prime ministers. The former United States' President Mr. Jimmy Carter had become good friends with Obasanjo when he was in power. These activities and powerful influential contacts considerably enhanced his international profile that, at one stage, he was considered for the prestigious office of the United Nations Secretary-General.

My civilian government under Shagari was overthrown in 1983 and was replaced by a succession of military governments, variously headed by Buhari–Idiagbon, Babangida, Abacha, and Abdulsalami Abubakar. All through those years of military rule, Obasanjo combined the work on his chicken farm with his international engagements and made occasional forays into local matters by offering comments and advice. He was an ardent critic of the military regimes of that era. He was known, for example, to have commented that Babangida's Structural Adjustment Programme (SAP) 'lacked human face'. He berated Shehu Musa Yar'Adua's adventure into civilian politics by asking if the latter had left anything behind which he was planning to retrieve from Dodan Barracks, the seat of government. Yar'Adua had contested for the presidential nomination, which elicited the wisecrack from Obasanjo.

On June 12, 1993, I witnessed the freest, fairest, and most peaceful Presidential elections that ushered in a new civilian government after 10 years. Watched, supervised, and monitored by local and international observers, the election was keenly contested between Moshood Abiola of the Social Democratic Party and Bashir Tofa of the National Republican Convention. The winner was Abiola, a billionaire businessman and philanthropist. Babangida annulled Abiola's much-celebrated victory, and the uproarious hue and cry that greeted the annulment ultimately led to Babangida's 'stepping aside'.

Babangida thus created a hiatus in the form of the whimsical and tendentious Interim National Government (ING) he set up. A thinly veiled line of succession was clandestinely inserted into the operative terms of the ING. It was to the effect that the most senior secretary in the cabinet would assume leadership in the event of replacing the head. This gratuitous contraption was quickly hijacked by the scheming Abacha, who was the most senior secretary. He wasted no time in toppling the ING headed by the civilian Shonekan, who had been personally and unilaterally handpicked by Babangida.

Obasanjo became a vocal critic of Abacha's government. In a bid to entrench himself firmly on the throne and in my peoples' psyche, Abacha embarked on a reign of terror. He hoodwinked the five political parties and got himself adopted as the sole presidential candidate in a projected presidential poll. He incarcerated Shehu Musa Yar'Adua. He hunted down and arrested Moshood Abiola. His thugs and goons went on rampages in which assassination became their stock in trade. Kudirat Abiola was assassinated. Suliat Adedeji was murdered. Alex Ibru was maimed and left for dead, but he lived to tell the story. Alfred Rewane was brutally assassinated at his home in Ikeja. Shehu Yar'Adua died in prison. Abacha was accused of judicial murder when Ken Saro-Wiwa and his fellow Ogoni agitators were hanged. Abiola was to die in prison after Abacha's own death. The voices of dissent were seriously muffled, and known human rights activists were hounded into exile. NADECO became a thorn in the flesh of Abacha's government, and bombs were intermittently exploded in city centers to drive fear into the people's minds.

It was in this atmosphere of fear and official molestations that Obasanjo was picked up from his Ota farm on seemingly spurious, trumped-up charges pertaining to a phantom coup. A pitiable Obasanjo looked, in turn, morose, taciturn, bemused, flabbergasted, and astonished as he faced his accusers inside the court. In hindsight, it looked as if Obasanjo tried to portray the victim, an innocent man who was being persecuted by the goons and knaves whom the Abacha regime had assembled to incriminate him and his second in command, Shehu Musa Yar'Adua.

In fact, pundits and analysts opined that it could be easily deduced from the testimonies of the coup plotters that they might indeed have approached Obasanjo and sought his understanding and probable support as their godfather. In spite of this seemingly covert agenda and in view of the prevailing atmosphere of doom and despondency, I shared the willingness of my sympathetic citizenry and gave the 'cornered and fallen' Obasanjo the benefit of the doubt. I had a presumption of his innocence and strongly condemned Abacha's plot to silence his own critics. However, Obasanjo was adjudged to have plotted a coup against Abacha and was consequently imprisoned.

Obasanjo's prison experience must have been spiritually edifying. It was alleged that he constantly read the Holy Bible and participated in prison church services. His wife, Stella, paid him regular visits while he was in prison. As fate would have it, it has been alleged that a highly placed civil servant, who would later become a close political associate of his in future, lent a hand by secretly smuggling an air-conditioner into his stuffy and oppressively hot Maiduguri prison cell.

Obasanjo was released from prison after Abacha's death in June 1998, thanks to the benevolence of Abdulsalami Abubakar, who succeeded Abacha. Abubakar promptly announced plans to hand over power to a civilian government in May 1999. Obasanjo initially greeted the suggestion that he should contest the presidential election with a rhetorical 'How many presidents do you want to make of me?' This alluded to the fact that he had already been a president from February 1976 to October 1979. He therefore demurred, but he later changed his mind by deciding to run as the candidate of the military-backed People's Democratic Party. The latter fact was attributable to the financial muscle and persuasive power of those people involved with the recent military government. They had literally put pressure on Obasanjo to decide to run. It was alleged that a substantial sum of money was placed in the Party's war chest to prosecute the presidential election battle on behalf of Obasanjo.

During the campaigns that led to Obasanjo's victory and ascendance to power in his second coming, he cast himself in the mould of a candidate capable of providing a bridge between military and civilian rule. But many people were wary of electing someone with such close ties with the military. My Yoruba people were still agonizing over the treatment meted out to Abiola. They looked forward to a new leader whom they thought might be able to protect their interests. They still remembered the seeming disdain and disrespect which Obasanjo exhibited towards Awolowo in his lifetime. They could still recollect the ease and contempt with which Abacha was able to depose and humiliate Sultan Dasuki from his imperial throne at Sokoto and hound him into exile. This latter fact made my Hausa–Fulani people wary and suspicious of anyone, however remotely connected with the military.

Moreover, in supporting Obasanjo for the presidency, it would appear that Babangida 'robbed Peter to pay Paul'. The presidential diadem that he snatched from Abiola's head, he helped to place on Obasanjo's. It was like making a penance or restitution to placate Abiola's disgruntled supporters. It was also seen as one of those deft moves by Babangida to massage the ruffled egos of the military establishment by enthroning someone whom they thought might be able to protect military interests. It was probably thought that Obasanjo would be able to provide leeway for them concerning any unseemly or untoward situations when the civilian government takes over. However, Obasanjo's military backers would seem to have foisted on my citizenry a capricious bat with a civilian head and military wings and legs folded in mid-flight.

Nevertheless, in the ensuing presidential elections, Obasanjo, as candidate of the Peoples' Democratic Party (PDP), defeated Olu Falae, who ran on the combined ticket of the All Peoples Party and the Alliance for Democracy, AD/APP. The people had goodwill toward Obasanjo when he was elected in 1999, and the euphoria that greeted the civilian government of Obasanjo was understandable. It was the euphoria of my people, who had groaned for 15 years under the most brutal dictatorships in my history. I was teetering on the brink of another civil war. The citizenry was eager to embrace democracy again, even if it meant entrusting the leadership to the hands of a retired general. Sadly, it was not long before that euphoria would turn, first into pessimism and then into disappointment, particularly from the second term. Then a reservoir of goodwill would have been wasted.

Thus, Obasanjo's 'odyssey' in the realms of power could be summed up in two phrases: 'From prison to power' and 'From prison to Aso Rock'. At his swearing-in ceremony, Obasanjo gave indications of what he would like to achieve and how he would set out to achieve them. He had declared, as a note of warning, that it would no longer be business as usual. He had also forewarned that he would step on some toes in the pursuit of his set objectives. He declared that he was determined to stamp out corruption and move the domestic economy rapidly towards economic recovery and growth. He appeared ready to take on the array of vested interests, the political jobbers, and careerists—the self-serving opportunists who were opposed to the reform measures, which could threaten their own perceived financial interests.

At the inception of Obasanjo's administration as a civilian Head of State, the picture was not so rosy. He was elected when I was a country in economical and political tatters. The military governments had militarized the polity and enthroned civic cynicism. The morale of my citizenry was at its lowest ebb. There was total decay of infrastructures. Public utilities that should bring comfort and conveniences were malfunctioning. There was an attitude of malaise. The institution of public pensions collapsed; huge arrears of payments accrued, bringing untold miseries to the homes of pensioners and retirees. State enterprises were inefficiently handled and suffered from neglect at the hands of inept people who were not seriously committed. Inflation took a strong upward flight. High unemployment led to general dissatisfaction, and it was a recipe for lawlessness, chaos, and an atmosphere in which the devil's workshop found use in idle hands. Of course, the situation would lead to general insecurity of lives and properties.

Obasanjo's administration embarked on certain fundamental changes otherwise tagged *reforms*. These were mainly in the socio-economic and political spheres. It became the case of a chronic ailment that required drastic therapy or even surgery to restore the patient to good health. Concomitantly, it is only an efficient surgeon who is well placed to handle a perfect surgery. One high-profiled appointment after the other, Obasanjo was able to place round pegs in round holes. He achieved this through a combination of diligent search and indisputable luck. He was able to employ the qualified and experienced hands to man the various programmes of reform.

His Secretary to the Federal Government, Ekaette, had built up a solid experience in civil service matters, as he cut his teeth in Gowon's administration and had subsequent postings at the upper echelons of the Federal Civil Service. Obasanjo appointed Ngozi Okonjo-Iweala as the Minister of Finance. She had worked with the World Bank and had experience in handling International Monetary Fund-related matters. In this capacity, the financial orthodoxy which she relentlessly pursued was part of the World Bank's financial agenda and strategy for poor countries. She drastically reduced my debt burden. She was an astute bargainer and negotiator. She brought sanity and order to budgetary planning and dispensation. She carried out measures that facilitated and enabled the Central Bank in active collaboration with the new Governor to shore up my Foreign Reserves. She also traced and reclaimed money stolen and stacked away in foreign banks by Abacha and his cronies.

Obasanjo's appointment of El-Rufai as the Minister of the Federal Capital Territory turned out to be a revelation. The new minister initiated moves that brought sanity and discipline to the original master plan for progress and development in Abuja. Commentators and critics alike, regardless of whether they adore or demonize him, all agree that El-Rufai ushered in an era characterized by high-tempo activism and revolutionary zeal in salvaging and transforming the capital city.

El-Rufai set out with a single-minded and tenacious determination to restore its abused and violated master plan and reclaim its integrity and authenticity. He succeeded in cleaning up the city. The conceptualized landscape was redeemed. The green areas were restored. The markets and shopping malls were reshaped. Intra-city roads were enlarged and repaired beyond any body's wildest imagination. He got rid of the ugly, grotesque, and illegal structures, the unsightly shanties, and the growing slums and ghettoes. He instituted a modern mass-transit system, which resulted in the expulsion of Okada (commercial motorcycle) riders from the city along with the attendant nuisance value and danger.

However, it is to be expected that El-Rufai in carrying out these tremendous assignments would tread on many toes. Also inevitably, there would be many pitfalls, land mines, and temptations along the path he found himself almost compulsively treading. The audacity in the extraordinary and revolutionary decisions he made while in office was alarming. I would have thought that he should prepare for retaliatory measures in any eventuality. Houses of the 'high and mighty', like those of Ahmadu Ali, even when he was the ruling Peoples' Democratic Party's chairman, and Emwerem, former Senate president, were demolished for contravening certain relevant regulations.

At the end of it all, when the new regime set in, there were inevitably obvious attempts to demystify and deconstruct his sterling qualities as the saviour of the Abuja master plan. His integrity was assailed because of the way and manner in which he allocated plots of land to himself and to certain individuals who were either very highly placed or closely related to him by blood. These accusations were examples of favouritism and nepotism. People began to lament the reign of impunity and illegality that characterized the twilight of Obasanjo's regime, and El-Rufai became the butt of ribald jokes and scurrilous attacks.

Obasanjo appointed Dora Akunyili as the Director-General of the National Agency for Food and Drug Administration and Control (NAFDAC). Seldom had any individual achieved so much success in an area so wantonly destructive of human lives. The accolades, citations, and encomiums she garnered in appreciation of her services in combating the dangers and importers of fake and expired drugs spoke volumes about her and, arguably, about Obasanjo, who appointed her. He also made a very good choice in appointing Bello as head of the National Drug Law Enforcement Agency (NDLEA) to curb the nefarious drug-related activity.

Chukuma Soludo's name is not only euphemistically synonymous with 'solution' but really with all that is excellent in my newfangled banking system. As the new Governor of the Central Bank, he drew up the outline for the banking deregulation in such a way that the stakes became higher. More viable mergers were formed to sanitize and strengthen the system. Before Soludo's consolidation of the banking system from 2005 to 2008, none of my 89 local banks were as large as the fourth-largest bank in South Africa. However, in the near future, my banks would be constantly rated among the biggest in the world. But for the consolidation exercises, my banking system would not have withstood the subsequent otherwise-catastrophic shocks that were globally imminent. Other shocks to my system were the collapse of the global oil market and the collapse of the domestic stock market. It is to Soludo's eternal credit that none of my 25 consolidated banks would collapse.

My foreign reserve rose from a meager $5 billion in 1999 to more than $45 billion in 2007 and had almost hit the $60 billion mark in 2008 before the crunching universal financial meltdown. The rise in the foreign reserve earlier was owed to the well-monitored strategy evolved by Soludo. His appointment became another feather in Obasanjo's cap, and a pointer to his proclivity for searching out the best people to appropiately handle certain intricate situations.

The debt cancellation of $18 billion by the external creditors of the Paris Club was, on paper, a great feat recorded by Obasanjo's regime. It remains arguably the greatest achievement of his presidency. It was hoped that the tremendous benefits of the cancellation would include the provision of other resources that could be invested in the other sectors of my economy. However, some of my discerning economic analysts debunked the ovation and euphoria that greeted the cancellation. They insisted that it was a known fact that $12.9 billion was already paid all at once, though some people argued that it was paid by instalments to the creditors before the much-vaunted foreign debt cancellation could be achieved.

Most of these debts were accrued in the 1970s and 1980s. For instance, it was during Obasanjo's first outing as a military Head of State that I was persuaded to obtain the first jumbo foreign loan on the specious ground that I was 'under borrowed'. This led me into a debilitating peonage that worsened the challenge of poverty and underdevelopment. They had remained largely unpaid and unamortized for a quarter of a century when the military ruled me as a nation. The capital and the accruing interest continued to be compounded until I arrived at a huge debt of over $30 billion. It emerged that some of the debts had been corruptly entered into by not being tied to specific projects. It has also been alleged that some of the monies did not leave the metropolitan countries and their banking institutions because of collusion between lenders and borrowers.

The rationale behind the idea of using foreign reserves to pay creditors who did not need the money remains faulty and questionable. The argument arose that payment of such a vast amount in one payment to the richest nations in the world belied the claim of debt reduction or part cancellation claimed by the creditor countries. The promise then was that, when I became free of this debt hangover, the money being used for debt servicing would then become available for infrastructural rehabilitation and development. Subsequent developments, however, showed that after the payment of the debt, the promised infrastructure money had not materialized. The origin of the debts was questionable. In a similar vein, beneficiaries of the accrued commission remain only a conjecture.

This leads me to the tragic notion of the surrender of my sovereignty and my enforced servitude to the imperialists' International Monetary Fund (IMF) and both the Paris and London clubs. Obasanjo's regime became subservient to the dictates of these bodies and the powers behind them. Substantial amounts of hard currency was needed to continue to service these debts. It was in these circumstances that Obasanjo embarked upon a series of damage-control measures. He used his considerable contacts and influence with foreign leaders and heads of international institutions coupled with his hectic and peripatetic travelling all over the world and the support of his economic team. There had been the erratic escalation of petrol, diesel, and kerosene prices and the devaluation of my drowning naira. Some of the other ripple effects of this tragic surrender were unemployment, lawlessness, insecurity, hunger, corruption, fuel palaver, and the seemingly intractable Niger Delta problem.

Combatting and reducing the level of corruption to the barest minimum within my polity was paramount in the mind of Obasanjo. Corruption was prevalent even in high places within my public and private sectors. The deplorable get-rich-quick mania became the bane of society. My citizens' efforts to hold their own in serious international business ventures were often treated with suspicion and downright contempt. '419', which was a euphemism for Advance Fee Fraud, became the stock in trade of cheats and swindlers who obtained money under false pretences for services not rendered and goods not supplied.

This evil reputation was endemic locally, and it globally preceded my citizens to major banking and commercial capitals. My name attained notoriety when it appeared high on the list of the most corrupt nations on earth. Money laundering became rampant as an easy way of transferring stolen or ill-gotten monies into the accommodating vaults of foreign banks. At times, such monies were brought back onto my shores via the back door of importation of various luxury items and goods. Obasanjo, with characteristic aplomb, set up the Economic and Financial Crimes Commission (EFCC) and gave it constitutional teeth and muscle to probe, expose, arrest, and prosecute the perpetrators of financial crimes. He chose Nuhu Ribadu, a lawyer by discipline and a professional police officer, to head the EFCC. In no time, Ribadu established the Commission as the financial and economic crime fighter and consummate investigator with a penchant for painstakingly pursuing a criminal matter to its logical conclusion of arrest and prosecution. He did become a thorn in the sides of such criminals.

However, it soon became clear that the awesome efficiency of the Commission could become a potent weapon of harassment and manipulation in the hands of an unscrupulous president enforcing his views and suppressing outspoken opponents of his regime. The effectiveness of Nuhu Ribadu was highlighted by the hue and cry that greeted his seemingly innocuous posting back to school at the Institute of Politics and Strategic Studies at Kuru in Jos. Some people felt it was punitive to either clip his wings or hamper his rising profile, as he was later to be demoted in rank. Indeed, he was later dismissed and the ripple effects of his dismissal became acrimonious on all sides.

Obasanjo retired all the military officers who had ever served in public offices as governors and administrators. He took such a measure to ensure discipline in the barracks. Otherwise, there would have been little or no discipline in the barracks, because some had become so rich as to be virtually uncontrollable. The Service Chiefs were appointed anew and ambassadorial appointments were made in such a way as to reflect my federal character. Justice was ensured and corruption highlighted for elimination in the Police when a huge sum of money in billions of naira was found in the various bank accounts of Tafa Balogun, an indicted Inspector General of Police. It was hoped that his ordeal would serve as a lesson and deterrence for members of my Police establishment, generally acknowledged to be corrupt.

Pursuing his mapped-out reform measures, Obasanjo created the Bureau for the Privatization of Public Enterprises. This removed inefficiency and bottleneck bureaucracy to achieve greater performance and growth. Efforts were made to encourage the participation of the private sector in rehabilitating decaying infrastructures and refurbishing malfunctioning utilities. He undertook certain measures for the liberalization of key sectors of my economy. Attempts were made to restructure the Public Service for more efficiency. The reviews of budgetary and taxation laws were carried out in order to entrench fiscal discipline in public budgeting and expenditure. Various measures were also embarked upon to reduce or alleviate poverty through the intensification of job and wealth creation.

To his great credit, Obasanjo tremendously improved the area of modern telecommunications services. It was not long after the frivolous and insulting assertion by one of my former federal ministers to the effect that the possession or use of the 'box telephone was not meant for the poor'. He had claimed that they could ill afford the exorbitant cost of acquiring a telephone. Those were the days when it usually cost a fortune to acquire a box telephone. Service was erratic and the heavy bills came in with annoying regularity. A telephone box could serve a whole household or a whole office establishment or even a whole neighbourhood. The innumerable and ubiquitous telephone posts linked by roughly intertwining and dirty telephone lines were present in every city and several selected towns.

Obasanjo's administration introduced and popularized the portable GSM cell phones. I soon outstripped South Africa in terms of 'teledensity' (or the number of hand-set units used by my citizens), in spite of my obtaining the technology much later than that country did. There are (at the time of this writing) more than 70 million units in the hands of my citizens. The effects of this modern telephone system can hardly be overemphasized. It enhances and accelerates business transactions. It has shrunken distances and minimized wasted time and rendered many delays in the postal system a moot point. It has brought much closer relationships within families, in business and social circles, and within communities at large.

In his first term in office, Obasanjo, in fact, somewhat successfully tackled the structural problems in the domestic economy. He attained a measure of stability in the macro-economy. He also reduced the level of Federal fiscal deficits through the stringent Demand Management Strategy. The entire income strategy was based on reformed measures aimed at diversifying the production base of the economy, restoring the balance of payment equilibrium, reducing public expenditures, and liberalizing the domestic economy. These reform measures based on reform management did not seem to work well as envisaged under Obasanjo. Stability in the macro-economy had been achieved at a great social cost, leaving the poor worse off than ever before.

Some major landmark achievements were recorded in Obasanjo's first administration. There was restoration of confidence among my citizenry in their government's policies, programmes, and activities. There was restoration of confidence within the comity of nations in my commitment to good governance and sound economic programmes. There was greater understanding and stability within the polity. There were signs that accelerated political and socio-economic development might take place, given the enabling environment made available and encouraged by Obasanjo's administration. All these seemingly laudable efforts turned out to be the proverbial lull that gathers ominously before the storm.

I consider Obasanjo's second term in office to be an anticlimax. The outspoken human rights advocate and crusader, Gani Fawehinmi, assessed Obasanjo's administration as a tragedy and a national burden. Gradually, he began to show his true colours. He seemed, with the benefit of hindsight, to know exactly what he wanted, his private ambitions, and how he planned to achieve them. His Peoples Democratic Party (PDP) had seemingly swept the polls in a landslide victory in 2003. My entire terrain became virtually one big constituency in the party's pocket. With the singular exception of Lagos under the bold and determined leadership of Bola Tinubu for the Alliance for Democracy (AD), the entire South Western zone fell into the hands of Obasanjo's PDP. This must have been due to a combination of alleged massive rigging, Obasanjo's clever sweet-talking, and the understanding reached between 'Afenifere' elders and the unwary governors whom Obasanjo had outfoxed.

The entire South/South zone was swept by PDP. Similarly, the whole of the South-Eastern states fell into PDP's hands with the single exception of Anambra State, which was originally declared won by PDP until the courts much later wrenched the victory from PDP in a long and persistent legal tangle before handing it to All Progressives Grand Alliance (APGA). The Northern zones struggled to retain just five states in the hands of ANPP, leaving the remaining states in the hands of the PDP.

Such overwhelming control of a preponderant number of states by Obasanjo's PDP seemed to engender a feeling of smug confidence. While some aspects of the reform agenda were in progress, abysmal failure in other areas became increasingly obvious. Power generation and distribution became an intractable problem that defied solution and gulped huge sums of money. In 1999, Obasanjo's government promised to turn things around within 6 months of being in power. It was projected that power generation would improve from 3,500 megawatts to 10,000 megawatts by 2007. Yet eight years later—after billions of naira had been expended on efforts to improve this vital sector of my economy and the welfare of my citizenry—there were no tangible results. Electricity in all my cities, towns, and villages was spasmodic and sometimes not even functional for weeks in some areas. Power generation at its best still fluctuated between 3,500 and 4,000 megawatts. Changing the name of the corporation from National Electric Power Authority to Power Holding Corporation of Nigeria was cosmetic and had not brought the much-needed changes in power generation and distribution capacities.

Towards the end of Obasanjo's administration, certain major roads were either still in total disrepair or completely broken down and impassable. It became very disheartening that such a road as the Benin/Lagos Road—which is a very important and strategic highway—had degenerated into a veritable death trap and robbers' operational route. Unwary travelers were daily delayed in seemingly inevitable traffic jams. The petrol supply situation had not fared any better than when Obasanjo took over. Supply was often erratic and ever costlier, and the commonplace queues were off and on again at fuel stations.

Strange things began to surface in the second term of Obasanjo's administration. They all concerned my political existence and the essence of my constitution. I watched how Obasanjo chose to operate in his second term in office: like an uncontrollable person who had tasted real power for the first time. It was more and more apparent that he had appropriated *for himself* more power than my constitution permitted him. Obasanjo's predilection for power aggrandizement became more worrisome when viewed against the essential kernel of my constitution and the rule of law, which he had sworn to obey.

For example, my constitution does not give him powers to amend laws from the National Assembly before giving his assent to them. Yet he often got into hot water with the Federal lawmakers for doing just that. It was nowhere stated in my constitution that the president has power to seize or withhold Federal allocation to any state for any reason whatsoever; yet Obasanjo adamantly withheld the N14 billion allocated to the Lagos State government, flagrantly disobeying even court order in the process. He had claimed that the governor of Lagos, Tinubu, had unilaterally created new local government areas in Lagos State. He had thus held the entire people of the state to ransom in an attempt to vent his spleen on niggling Tinubu.

Obasanjo took certain measures that were responsible for dismantling my federalism and enthroning unitary government in its place. This directly contradicted the true Federalism that had been painstakingly envisaged and fashioned by my founding fathers. It was sad to see the frightened, threatened, traumatized, and frequently deposed senate presidents and state governors who fell out of favour with the president as they were subjected to the humiliations of 'kangaroo' impeachments. They were virtually reduced to yes-men and errand boys.

Certain acts of Obasanjo's elicited a lot of criticism and seemed to have introduced ethics and morality on issues and events. As a sitting president, he launched a presidential library fund-raising ceremony in his Abeokuta hometown. During that ceremony, about N6 billion was raised either in outright payments or in pledges. I considered it morally questionable for him to have launched a fund-raising exercise while still in office. American presidents embark on such projects after the expiration of their terms in office. However, since one good turn may deserve another in return, it was to be expected that people who donated hundreds of millions of naira might sooner or later need one form of favour or the other from the obliged president. Consequently, donors tried to outpace one another during the fund-raising ceremony. This apprehension became manifest in stark reality when, later, both Dangote and Otedola, wealthy entrepreneurs who donated N2.1 billion and N2 billion, respectively, were mentioned as being favourably considered in the proposed sales of the oil refineries at Kaduna and Port Harcourt. Happily, common sense prevailed, and the proposed sales were aborted.

There was also the question of the census figures—mostly in my southern cities and towns—that not only defied demographic trends but also turned statistical logic on its head. I also considered it ludicrous and reprehensible that a sitting Head of State should take a bank loan to initiate the giant corporation known as Transcorp, which bought up a sizeable chunk of my public companies. These companies had gone under the hammer of the Bureau of Public Enterprises (BPE), which was originated by the Obasanjo's Administration.

In the twilight of his administration, the question of his probable successor as president at the end of his second term in office became paramount. The search for his successor was initially discussed, but without saying so, Obasanjo privately nursed his own ambition of attempting a third term in office. Cognisant of the fact that the idea could only be achieved through a formal constitutional amendment, Obasanjo got the pliant National Assembly to lumber the issue of tenure elongation with other topical and germane matters. Such matters included the creation of more states in specific zones and the highly contentious issue of a new revenue allocation formula. Regardless of the relative importance of the other genuine items to be ratified in the constitution, the amendment bill was roundly defeated. It was a case of throwing out the baby with the bath water. Obasanjo reckoned that he could hoodwink the National Assembly members with the aid of subterfuge and gerrymandering by retaining the 'baby' in the dirty and murky bath waters, already polluted with the hidden agenda of tenure elongation.

A new character trait manifested itself in Obasanjo after the happy demise of his ill-conceived third-term agenda. The constitution amendment which Obasanjo conceptualized and which he remotely manipulated through his backers in the National Assembly was a disguised attempt at tenure elongation. It was dealt a crippling blow on the floor of the Senate. The new character trait pervaded his second term in office. Having tacitly admitted the futility of his third-term agenda, he continually made pronouncements to the effect that he would ensure that his successor should not be a criminally liable person. His successor should be someone he could rely upon to continue his reform programmes, particularly his anti-corruption crusade. This wasteful and bitter quest for a third term resulted in the parting of ways with former allies. Even the anti-corruption campaign, which could have been the hallmark of his achievements, became mired in his politics of cronyism and vendetta. His international profile instantly nosedived. My men of goodwill took relevant steps to frustrate the ill-considered project.

The longer Obasanjo stayed in power, the more he was inclined to amass power rather than strengthen the pillars that would sustain democracy. Most of his failures can be traced to this reality. He made enemies of political opponents instead of building bridges and embracing compromises. This was neither weakness nor inanity. This was adroitness and superior diplomatic administration.

Rather than focus on my myriads of economic problems, he embarked on the time-wasting exercise of leveraging power. It became starkly apparent that he had failed to sufficiently shed his military toga and embrace the ethos of democracy in a civilian setting. Suffice it to say that my people seem to have expected rather too much from Obasanjo in terms of 'democratic dividends'. The expectation that Obasanjo could do more was rather misguided. My citizenry were of the view that democracy should instantly unlock the barn of national prosperity and have the goods tumbling down in torrents.

He had glibly declared that the April 2007 polls were going to be a 'do or die' affair, which was a clear indication that he was not willing to leave.

Incidentally, it would appear that he had personally and unilaterally determined who the 'criminals' were as well as who his successor should be. That came up at a time when the relationship between Obasanjo and Vice President Abubakar Atiku had floundered and suffered a severe setback because Atiku had tactfully and almost covertly championed the anti-elongation movement.

The unfortunate break in the relationship between my two topmost office holders brought me a lot of embarrassment and bellyaching. Mud-slinging and name-calling became the order of the day. Accusations and counter-accusations and references to the use to which the Petroleum Development Technology Fund (PDTF) had been put led to calls for the resignation of the Vice President, who had joined another political party, the Action Congress (AC). The party duly convened and nominated Atiku as its presidential candidate.

On many occasions, various issues which were fall-outs of the quarrel were before the courts for adjudication. The Vice President won such issues as whether or not he could continue to operate as a Vice President. He also won the verdict that the post of the Vice President was not vacant. Questions were raised whether Atiku could retain his entitlements in terms of security, his accommodation, and the continued enjoyment of the use of designated official areas, aircraft, and vehicles—Atiku won on all counts. Common sense, however, dictated that he should not force the issue on any relief granted him by the courts.

The battle line was definitively drawn when the Peoples' Democratic Party held its convention to nominate its presidential candidate for the 2007 presidential elections. Certain questions were raised which begged for explanations that I thought would be offered at the convention. There were the zoning issue and the contradictory claims made by the South/South and South/East zones. My Northern states saw zonal rotation of the presidency as between the North and the South. They recalled that there was an earlier tacit understanding that after Obasanjo, a Southerner from the South West, the presidency should revert to the North. To make a confusing situation worse, Obasanjo's personality and official clout seemed to have dominated the convention's deliberations.

This was the setting when an array of high-profile contestants for nomination as the PDP presidential candidate suddenly began to stop showing interest in the exercise. Governors Peter Odili of Rivers State, Donald Duke of Cross

River State, Victor Attah of Akwa Ibom State, and other candidates from the North, began, one after the other, to withdraw their names from the presidential race. Some were dissuaded; others were harassed and had the dreaded EFCC breathing down their necks. Then, Obasanjo showed his deft political hand by displaying his 'joker'—throwing his prodigious weight behind the candidature of Yar'Adua. It had become apparent that all the other contestants shied away from contesting by withdrawing in favour of Yar'Adua because of this development. He thereafter became the PDP candidate for the 2007 presidential election. As if that were not enough, Goodluck Jonathan, the rookie Governor of Bayelsa State—who had been sworn in as governor in place of impeached and disgraced Alamasiegha—was drafted as Yar'Adua's running mate. This of course was at the instance of the all-powerful Obasanjo.

Towards the end of the convention, the icing was liberally spread on Obasanjo's cake when he was elevated through very adroit manipulation to the status of Chairman of PDP's Board of Trustees. The implications of this appointment, as spelled out in the party's constitution, immediately became obvious. This would definitely turn him to the Alpha and Omega of the party. Even at retirement, he would keep calling the shots from his Ota farm or so he thought. Instead, he found out that he could not wield the influence of a party leader. Political analysts predicted rightly or wrongly at the time that Obasanjo would pull the strings from Ota and the puppets in Aso Rock Villa would dance.

By the terms of the party's constitution, only retired Heads of State are eligible for election to this powerful controlling organ of the party. I began to wonder when it became the sole responsibility and constitutional right of the president to appropriate the rights of my people to elect their choice as president in 2007.

It is incumbent on me at this stage to reflect the views and comments of my citizenry on this topical issue. They were to make a total break in changing from the military to military or military to civilian government. They wanted to embrace the change from civilian to civilian government for the first time in 28 years. I shared the views of those opposed to zoning the presidency to any geopolitical area. They argued that such an exercise would cheapen the presidency. They also pointed out that if too much emphasis were placed on rotational presidency, or the 'power shift' formula, there might be a danger of fielding candidates who neither had the prerequisites nor the talent for the job. I aver with paternal concern and a foreboding that such a backsliding scenario in this age of digital high technology would lead inexorably to putting one step forward and fifty steps back.

Some of my citizens opined that, at this early stage of my nascent democracy, no attempt should be made to trivialize the office of the president, which is the apex of power; that it is imperative for every potential candidate to possess adequate and impeccable presidential endowments and be popularly elected based on an unblemished track record. Placing their best foot forward, my people must always insist on the very best and brightest among the topmost contenders, regardless of whether or not a particular candidate comes from the east, north, west, or south. For this arrangement to be operable, individuals, groups, or institutions must be willing to sacrifice their interests for my general good as a Nation. If Bill Clinton, of the obscure southern state of Arkansas in the United States of America, could become president, I am patiently looking forward to the day when the best person who is eminently qualified, with sound credentials and general acceptability, would be elected as my president. Considerations of zonal affiliation, ethnic extraction, or powerful connections should not be the determinants of suitability for the office of president.

Some of the utterances and dispositions of Obasanjo on various issues and events—particularly during his second term—seemed to have cheapened the exalted office of the president. Finesse and diplomatic niceties were thrown overboard and substituted with crudity, peevishness, vengefulness, vindictiveness, and the arrogation to himself all-knowing divine powers. He dismissed the Christian Association of Nigeria's (CAN) criticism of him by saying to them, 'CAN, my foot!' He made impunity, arrogance, and lawlessness appear as demonstrations of statesmanship.

He advised anyone who did not like him to get a large copy of his photograph, hang it on a wall, and vent anger on it by pelting it with stones. This was an archetypal study in sadism, hypocrisy, contradiction, self-delusion, and narcissism. He loved to be appreciated and admired; yet he pretended to abhor sycophancy. As a president, he was authoritarian and flaunted the fact that the buck stopped at his table. In fact, he once brazenly and famously warned his advisers that as president he was not bound by, or compelled to heed, their advice.

There are certain facts that are better left unspoken and understood rather than being voiced only to be subjected to all sorts of interpretations.

Some people are of the view that the real clash that led to the abrupt parting of ways between him and Dr. Ngozi Okonjo-Iweala, his brilliant and popular Minister of Finance, was the tussle over who should take the credit for the successful negotiations that led to debt relief. Even though Obasanjo was the power behind her, everybody knew about the clout and connections of Ngozi Okonjo-Iweala. Her vast experience and brilliant high-profile exposure in the corridors and forums of the world financial centers made her stand out as a high achiever of international repute.

It would also seem as the record shows that Obasanjo revelled in the politics of divide-and-rule. He was invariably behind most political turmoils in the National Assembly and in the People's Democratic Party, which witnessed the reigns of a succession of chairmen from Solomon Lar to Gemade, Audu Ogbeh, and then to Ahmadu Ali. He successfully sweet-talked and hoodwinked the South-Western Zone's Alliance for Democracy (AD) governors, who literally went to sleep during the 2003 elections as their states fell into the hands of PDP. He paid an official visit to Anambra State, where his foreboding translated into reality. Indeed, a few weeks later, Peter Obi, the APGA party governor, was impeached in a clandestine exercise conducted at dawn by the Speaker of the Anambra State House of Assembly. All the impeachment exercises hatched and carried out in Plateau, Oyo, Ekiti, and Bayelsa states had the imprint of Obasanjo's background influence and acquiescence. Governors like Fayose of Ekiti State and Adedoja of Oyo State, House of Representatives Speaker Na'aba, and the Senate President, Okadigbo, had to bow out because Obasanjo's hands either gently rocked or violently shook the cradle all the way from the Aso Rock Villa.

Obasanjo issued instructions that the May 2007 Federal Allocations should not be shared so he could prevent the out-going governors from stealing from such allocations. But in actual fact, he himself engaged in a frenzy of last minute awarding of contracts. A few days before the end of his administration, the Federal Executive Council, under the commanding hands of Obasanjo, literally pushed out contract approvals worth N585 billion, much to the consternation of my citizenry. The hasty sales of government shares and interest in various business entities raised a furor, not only locally among my peoples but also amongst economic watchers worldwide. More worrisome was the fact that some of these seemingly unusual transactions ignored the essence of due process. The Bureau of Public Enterprises (BPE), which is set up by law to privatize public enterprises, was not appropriately positioned to carry out these transactions through competitive open bidding in my overall national interest.

What bothered me was that most of the areas covered by these frenzied sales and contracts included energy, housing, roads, water supply, and others. These were key economic sectors and sub-sectors that had hitherto remained neglected. They were fraught with all sorts of problems before 1999, when Obasanjo assumed office. When I consider the near-paralysis of the infrastructure which called for urgent government attention in 1999, I find it inexplicable why the execution of such projects that could help to remedy the deplorable conditions of my people had to be delayed until the tail end of his regime.

Obasanjo's administration was neither able to implement any turn-around maintenance of my four refineries nor was it able to build any new ones in the eight years of its tenure. The fact that governance is a continuum is enough justification that the succeeding government should have been allowed to re-energize the proposed execution of projects that would add value to the lives of my citizens. The hasty sales of these items generated suspicion. This became more so, coming only a few weeks before the administration's exit.

It was also manifestly clear that not only were the assets grossly undervalued but also that all the stakeholders—employees, creditors, and minority shareholders—were not duly consulted before the transactions were consummated. Some of the beneficiaries of the sales were well-known cronies and acolytes of Obasanjo who, in a different milieu, contributed substantially to his library project. The Port Harcourt Refinery was proposed to be sold to Blue Star Oil for a sum of $561 million. The company was a subsidiary of Dangote Group of Companies, an organization owned by one of the biggest financiers of the ruling People's Democratic Party. The chairman of Zenon Oil, Femi Otedola—who also tried to become another beneficiary of these sales—was also a financier of the ruling PDP. Fortunately for me, as a Nation, these deals were aborted.

Other sales were either proposed or considered. The Onigbolo Cement Company was sold to the Dangote Group for about $1.8 billion. The National Arts Theatre nearly went under the hammer, but the uproar made the auctioneers

settle for an arrangement whereby private companies would operate the theatre at the cost of N35.8 billion. The International Trade Fair Complex was to be
sold to Aulic Nigeria Limited for N40 billion. The Tafawa Balewa Square was to
be sold to a business group called BHS International for N9.5 billion.

Another company heavily invested in by government—Ayip-Eku Oil Palm
Investment—was to be sold to Wingsong M-House Palm Oil Investment Limited
for N527 million. The sale of the Kaduna Refinery could not go through as it was
still being contested between some local companies and Chinese National Petroleum which had bid less at $105 million. The Ajaokuta Steel Company Limited
was sold to Global Steel Holdings Ltd. under circumstances that made people
think that some vested interests close to the seat of power may have influenced
the sale. The Egbin Power Plant was to be sold to Korea Power Corporation at
$280 million.

It was revealed that a few days before the curtain fell on his regime,
Obasanjo granted myriads of lucrative mining leases and exploration licenses to
international and local firms made up of individuals and entities with powerful
ties within the PDP. The relevant Deregulation Law was hurriedly passed to accommodate the new Solid Mining Regulations. It was later explained that the
Deregulation Law was an attempt to attract much-needed private investment to
develop the so-called neglected sector. As rightly pointed out by the chairman of
the House of Representatives' Committee on Budget, Farouk Lawan, these
transactions were mischievous and in bad faith. He went on to further opine
that such major decisions should be left for the in-coming administration, so
that due process should be embarked upon and carried out in the overall interest of my citizenry. However, it was really gratifying and instructive to note that
some foreign investors and multinationals demurred and refrained from the
scramble for contracts and oil block deals. This was an indirect indictment on
the system employed in the deals.

Obasanjo's 'swan song' which left everyone puzzled, alarmed, and angry
was his bestowal of last minute 'parting gifts' of N75 per liter fuel hike, up from
N65. The hike in the price of petrol was the sixth in his eight years in office. He
also left an increase from 5% to 10% in the Value Added Tax (VAT) on all goods
and services. The price for kerosene went up from N50 to N60 per liter. All this
made my people wonder whether there was a sadistic and insensitive trait in

Obasanjo, as it was obvious that people were suffering, and it seemed he could not care less. Could it also be likened to the ploy of the departing nonnative oppressor who defecated on the chair before leaving the seat of government in order to make it repugnant for his indigenous successor to occupy?

There is no gainsaying the fact that Obasanjo carved a niche for himself, and for me, in the field of international politics. He had, indeed, repositioned me as a Nation into a place of honour and respectability within the global arena. Before his subsequent re-emergence as a civilian Head of State in 1999, I was a pariah nation, shunned by many members of the International Community. My rediscovered national grandeur was again largely attributable to the astute diplomacy of the Obasanjo administration. I often wondered why he could not deploy similar astuteness in his local administration at home. However, on assumption of office, he fashioned a 'Road Map' highlighting his administration's goals, which he diligently set out to pursue. They included my integration as a Nation into the international community; conflict resolution, especially on the African Continent; and the resuscitation of my economy through economic diplomacy.

Great success was achieved in dealing with these issues. On my reintegration process, my acceptance by the comity of Nations was seen in many ways. His appreciative counterparts from other countries reciprocated Obasanjo's visits made to several countries across the continent. Social and economic ties were forged with countries that once loathed me. This wholesome re-entry process was underlined by my speedy readmission into the Commonwealth within the first month of Obasanjo's government after a four-year suspension. I was immediately elected into the 8-member Commonwealth Heads of Government Meeting (CHOGM) committee in 2003. This act alone signified my full acceptance and the recognition of my importance by the world at large.

My incredibly rising profile as a powerful African State was indicative of my new status. I was consulted and involved once more in initiatives and issues that concerned and affected Africa and elsewhere in the quest for peace in places that were hitherto involved in crisis. Obasanjo's administration was constantly involved in mediatory efforts in enthroning peace, in such trouble spots as Sierra Leone, Guinea Bissau, Guinea (Conakry), Ethiopia/Eritrea, Democratic Republic of the Congo, Burundi, Western Sahara, Sao Tome and Principe, and Liberia. Essentially, it amounted to universal kudos to his administration's adroit diplomacy, which brought to an end the 15-year-old Liberian internal crisis and the devastating internecine war in Sierra Leone.

It became quite clear that Obasanjo's policy of conflict prevention, resolution, and management was borne of the imperatives of peace and security. These were necessary for sustainable democracy, my internal economic development, and the West African sub-region. His performance in this aspect justified the African adage that says, 'You should help put out the fire in your neighbour's backyard so that it will not spread to your own'. As a result of these successes, my leadership role and contribution to the maintenance of international peace and security was widely acknowledged.

Another outstanding performance of Obasanjo's administration in the area of sub-regional cooperation and integration was the successful inauguration of the Gulf of Guinea Commission (GGC) in Libreville, Gabon, in November 1999. The GGC is made up of the following countries: Gabon, Sao Tome and Principe, Congo Republic, Democratic Republic of the Congo, Angola, and Nigeria. Its principal objectives included the strengthening of economic and political cooperation within subregional organizations like the Economic Community of West African States (ECOWAS) and Economic and Monetary Community of Central Africa (CEMAC).

The Obasanjo administration's foreign policy objective—to make me a safe haven for foreign investors, particularly in those sectors that have suffered neglect under military rule—was a partially successful ploy. To promote greater inflow of direct foreign investment, the administration embarked on a policy of resuscitating bilateral joint commissions with countries that have been identified as exporters of capital. Some beneficial agreements, particularly the Investment Promotion and Protection Agreement (IPPA), were signed.

One of the silent but enduring achievements of Obasanjo's diplomacy was the increasing level of international development assistance that continued to come my way. At one time, I was seen as the least-favoured African country for the Official Development Assistance (ODA) grants or international aid. But where I had once been seen as profligate and wasteful, Obasanjo's administration laundered my notorious and wayward image. Foreign investors began to compete with one another to come and take advantage of my large market, friendly population, and efficient but inexpensive labour. It is quite unfortunate but also quite understandable that the activities of the militant groups in the Niger–Delta area would drive away some fearful foreign investors. The volume of my debt reprieve—by the cancellation of 60% of the original sum—was owing to the indefatigable and unrelenting shuttle diplomacy practised by Obasanjo and his intrepid team of finance experts, led by Ngozi Okonjo-Iweala. The debt cancellation was made possible through the persistent and astute negotiation with the Paris Club of Creditors, despite my controversial status as an oil-rich Nation.

At the end, and with the benefit of hindsight, Obasanjo's overall record was dismal. There was a noticeable period of rancour and division among the political elites. This was because of his divisive tactics, including sadistic revenge against his foes. He made some daredevil Machiavellian moves in the pursuit of his objectives. Infrastructures had declined woefully. The social sector, including education and health care, was rich in promise and planning at the beginning but ultimately tapered off in poor execution and abysmal failure. The lingering Association of Senior Staff of Universities (ASSU) strike was ignored, and Healthcare Delivery did not meet the standard the protagonists and planners envisaged. Cost of living soared with a concomitant drop in the standard of living.

My economy under Obasanjo reflected good intentions but yielded poor results. It was disheartening to watch the downward slide in the standard of living and to watch myself, as a middle-income country, recede into a low-income one. Half of my citizenry were categorized as living below the poverty line. Unemployment defied all solutions, such as the launching of such projects as NEEDS, NEPAD, and Africa Peer Review Mechanism. Projects such as privatization and deregulation failed to make the desired difference. To rank the regime of maximum dictator Abacha as better and as more acceptable than that of Obasanjo would be inadequate. Infrastructural decay and poor maintenance culture were the major causes or excuses for failures and reverses suffered either in business or social functions. Good roads were lacking and were poorly maintained where available. Electricity was minimally generated and erratically distributed. One could go on and on detailing the catalogue of woes that brought misery to my citizenry in the twilight of Obasanjo's tenure.

He had planned to add another feather to his cap by becoming the first civilian President to hand over to another civilian President in my political history.

The fact remains that Obasanjo's administration was civilian in name and content but was more military in practise and outlook. He demonstrated scanty regard and contempt for due process and the rule of law. He flouted the rulings of the apex court several times. The predilection for military usages was underlined by Ahmadu Ali, a retired military colonel and chairman of the ruling PDP, who glibly declared that 'garrison politics' was the order by which my people were being governed. He said this particularly regarding the political turmoil that festered unrestrained in Ibadan with the active connivance of the strong man of Ibadan politics, Lamidi Adedibu, whom Ahmadu Ali labelled as 'Garrison Commander'.

Obasanjo claimed that he never schemed for a constitutional amendment to facilitate the elongation of his tenure. This was contrary to generally known views on the matter. His body language and his 'loud and audible' silence on the matter, in spite of allegations and insinuations, spoke volumes. He revealed a 'trademark' of his leadership style by saying God would have granted him a third term if he had prayed for it, because He grants him any favour he asks of Him. This was vintage Obasanjo, who acted as if he were the divinely appointed Messiah. He had a penchant for insulting people, some of whom insulted him right back. He even employed in his administration some who exhibited crass insolence against those who disagreed with their boss.

2007 ELECTIONS
AND ELECTION CONTROVERSIES

Even before my Independence, elections that took place always generated a lot of controversy. The quest for political supremacy, the inordinate ambition for the acquisition of wealth and the appendages of power, and the tool for corrupt self-enrichment have always been the lure that attracted some into politics. The recurring by-product of such tendencies was always controversy after controversy. To be in power is to be in charge of government treasury and party purse strings. Such wealth that properly belongs to the people would then be used to illegitimately enrich party faithfuls—investors in elections, like 'godfathers', friends, clients, proxies, and allies. The introduction of the use of election-rigging, lawlessness, bribery, fraud, debauchery, and a culture of deception resulted in the evolution of a political culture of powerful politicians who constantly corrupted the system. Corruption literally became the trademark of the political class.

Some of these elections in the past featured several malpractises and blatant acts of rigging and thuggery. From the campaign trains and hustings to the ballot boxes, it was always time for thuggery, violence, and other maleficent practises. Voting cards were stolen and stuffed into ballot boxes to swell the number of votes. Result sheets were either manipulated or ignored, and fictitious results were announced to the consternation of fellow contestants. This reached its most horrendous proportions in my old Western Region in the 1960s. There was once a time when a politician would wake up in the morning to find an incriminating corpse deposited in his yard. The only imaginable option left for such a politician—as an alternative to being charged with murder and possibly being executed—would be to switch his political party allegiance without further persuasion. It was the worst and most indecorous form of arm-twisting tactic. It was the height of crude and insidious blackmail.

Voters were more or less browbeaten by overzealous party officials in certain parts of my federation as they were being observed, monitored, and guided when casting their votes. The 'observing' official would sit on a raised platform and monitor the direction in which the prospective voters moved. If one were found moving in the direction in which the opposition's ballot box was situated, an explanation would be demanded. Oppressive and severe punitive measures could be meted out to the 'erring' voter.

Election rigging and manipulation attained horrific proportions after I became Independent in the 1960s. Ballot boxes were stuffed with prestamped ballot papers. There were weird and obscene stories about women who appeared pregnant on their way into the polling booths having padded their tummies with ballot papers. They would then re-emerge with their 'babies' (voters cards) already safely delivered!! In my old Western Region, the leadership of the ruling Nigerian National Democratic Party (NNDP) made voting almost irrelevant as the bribed, coaxed, or cajoled electoral officials often declared rival politicians as having accepted defeat voluntarily by withdrawing from the contest.

The culture of 'awarding' votes and seats to competing political parties became a disturbing pattern of malpractise in 1983 when the ruling party, the National

Party of Nigeria (NPN), imposed its candidates on constituencies where the party's support base suggested otherwise. It was a rude shock when, 20 years later in 2003, international observers who wrote honest reports about the shameful practises witnessed the same rigging exercise. They reported on how recorded votes far out-numbered the names on the registered voters' lists. They also reported how the police customarily became accomplices in the rigging exercise. At that time, Obasanjo dubbed the international observers and monitors as 'detractors' who did not wish me well as a nation. Rigging reached such dimensions that my citizenry and I, and in fact the various international monitoring groups, have come to expect it as sadly unavoidable in any election.

The consequences and aftermath of blatant rigging of elections have always been grave. The notoriously violent protests that greeted the badly rigged elections in my defunct Western Region in the mid-1960s paved the way for the debut of military intervention in my political history. It is equally undeniable that these protests and upheavals resulted in full-scale civil war from 1967 to 1970. It is painful and regrettable that politicians seemed to have learned nothing from the incessant and persistent uproar that always greeted these nefarious activities characterized by violence, bitterness, and acrimonious controversies. Indeed, it would appear that some political jobbers stand to gain from the negative forces unleashed following every rigged election.

These dangerous and unacceptable electoral malpractises reared their ugly heads again in the 2007 elections. It turned out to be like a macabre dance in the theatre of the absurd. It was characterized by brigandage, massive electoral fraud, and deliberate result falsification. I was saddened and alarmed at the seemingly hopeless and helpless straits in which the overwhelming majority of my people found themselves. I watched and listened as my citizenry agonized and lamented over the scale and magnitude of fraud and chicanery that dominated during and immediately after the polls. It had been long feared that the 2007 elections were doomed to failure. Successful elections are not measured in terms of the results or the figures returned, but they are assessed and gauged through the processes from which the results are revealed. With this deduction at the back of their minds, my electorate, along with the army of international observers, went away with the conviction that we had just witnessed the worst election ever held in my political history.

The sheer brazenness and bravado which characterized the 2003 elections paled into insignificance in comparison with the blatant daylight robbery that was manifest in the 2007 elections. It turned out to be a no-holds-barred contest with Atiku, the Vice President who had emerged as the AC candidate—in spite of the interminable court actions to deter him. Atiku himself also saw it as a show of strength between him and his boss.

It is difficult to downplay the unfortunate utterance of Obasanjo to the effect that the election was to be a 'do-or-die' affair for his party. It was calamitous and out of character for him, as Head of State, to threaten categorically and publicly that anyone who rose in protest would curse the day he was born. By some of his outbursts, he laid claims on 'the prerogative of violence', and machete wielders freely roamed the streets in some cities like Ibadan. As he made these spurious pronouncements, his praise singers, dyed-in-the-wool supporters, and cohort of groveling sycophants and thugs egged him on. In Ondo State, he openly threatened to unleash the fangs of EFCC on Segun Mimiko 'Iroko' for having soiled his ministerial seat and for having the temerity to challenge the incumbent governor, Segun Agagu. He maliciously alleged that Mimiko must have been a domestic victim of his step-mother's malignant curse.

Under no condition could one absolve the chairman of the Independent National Electoral Commission (INEC), Maurice Iwu, from the confusion and imbroglio that characterized the travesty of an election that took place in April 2007. The election was conceived with ulterior motives. It was born into a predesigned shape and outlook. Compromised and teleguided electoral officials were the midwives. It was supervised and defensively watched over by the police, soldiers, and party thugs. The harassed, and the hapless electorate attended upon it. Sadly, too, the scandalized local and international observers and monitoring groups witnessed it. The independence of INEC was very seriously in doubt, and serious questions and court challenges surrounded Obasanjo's administration's attempt to use INEC to disqualify several key opposition candidates, including Vice President Atiku.

It was an exercise in which Iwu would hardly be able to extricate himself from blame and the negative criticism or condemnation of history. He swore repeatedly and unabashedly on his honour that he would conduct free and fair elections even if it were to be the last thing he would do in this life. It did not therefore come as a surprise to anyone when Iwu glibly awarded himself pass marks, amid the hue and cry that greeted the woefully conducted and rigged elections. He initially introduced an electronic registration of voters against the fiercely debated directives of the National Assembly. It was supposed to be the biggest computerization exercise in Africa.

The project was very expensive in terms of the huge amount of money spent procuring the equipment. Time was not enough for a proper display of the voters' register, and as a result, prospective registered voters could neither raise claims nor objections. This ineptitude in handling the equipment and the resultant delay, led eventually to the abandonment of the electronic voting and the adoption of the outdated and notoriously manipulable manual system. This led inevitably to the repetition of the ugly practises of the past in which snatching of ballot boxes and multiple thumb-printing of ballot papers in private places became very rampant.

Even though the INEC authorities created the impression that they were ready for the elections, fears and doubts were expressed about the operational possibilities of the election timetable. It was claimed and even underlined by the Federal Minister of Justice and Attorney General, Bayo Ojo, that

- The large number of parties contesting the elections posed serious logistics problems for INEC.
- 100 million ballot papers would need to be printed and distributed within the short span of time left to conduct the elections.
- Provisions would have to be made for 50 Party Agents representing 50 parties across my vast territory.

This seemingly official revelation from no less a personality than the attorney general, heightened the electorate's suspicion enough to make them fret and worry. They wondered if this were not an indication of an orchestrated plot for 'tenure elongation'. The people saw such claims as a deliberate ploy to subvert the constitution and subject their wishes to the whims and caprices of a power cabal. They rightly concluded that the timetable was a loophole that could be exploited by the planners. They also felt that it should be revisited and redrawn.

Comic relief was introduced to the serious matter at hand. It was rumored that the PDP candidate, Umar Yar'Adua, died in faraway Germany, where he had gone to receive treatment for an ailment. This death hoax created the distinct possibility of a postponement of the elections on the strength of a clause in the Electoral Act, which empowers INEC to postpone an election indefinitely on the death of any of the candidates. Such a postponement would have left the way open for term elongation for Obasanjo. Possible tension was defused by the humorous tattle and clownish intervention of Obasanjo. It was dramatically confirmed that Yar'Adua was alive after all when Obasanjo placed an international phone call to him at a public gathering and asked rather facetiously, 'Umoru, are you dead? They say you are dead!'

I aver that the culprit of these malpractises was the PDP, simply because it was in power. With the benefit of a deep analysis of the outcome of the 2007 elections, I have adequate reasons to believe that it was a situation which, under the prevailing circumstances, any party in power could have exploited. It was evident that the constitution and the prevalent circumstances of my nascent democracy virtually empowered the ruling party to return itself to power. The indubitable bane and constriction on free and fair elections was the constitutional provision which empowered the president to choose both the chairman of INEC and appoint the INEC resident electoral commissioners. All these appointees should have the same qualifications as members of the House of Representatives. This clause clearly and literally translated to mean that such appointees should be card-carrying members of 'appropriate' political parties. We should also consider the fact that another party may be in power in future. In effect, PDP as the ruling party would select mostly its stalwarts for appointments to INEC. The constitution had unwittingly allowed the choice of partisan umpires who would surely help the party in which they are interested.

Eloquent and instructive appraisal of signs of the times can be deduced from the lopsided results of the April 2007 elections, which eventually took place on schedule. The Peoples' Democratic Party won not only the presidency with a clearly overwhelming and almost embarrassing majority in which it outstripped its nearest rival, ANPP, by scoring over 22,000,000 votes out of an estimated 30,000,000 votes. It also won 30 of the 36 gubernatorial elections. The All Nigeria People's Party (ANPP) won 3; the Democratic Peoples' Party (DPP) won 2;

and the Action Congress (AC) won 1. PDP also won an overwhelming majority in both the Senate and the House of Representatives. Of course, it was to be expected that the badly beaten and upended parties would protest. They made all the usual allegations of electoral malpractise including blatant rigging, ballot-box snatching, thuggery, thumb-printing of ballot papers in private places, confusing and contradictory announcements of results from collation centers and Abuja, and the use of security personnel to harass and bully the voters.

The harrowing specter of turning me into a one-party State stared me in the face. I shudder to think of myself in the unlikely and unseemly company of some 'banana' republics that had floundered on the unsteady and storm-tossed ship of the one-party system of administration. The negative connotations are distinctive. Voices of dissent would be muffled or completely ignored. It would constitute an outright negation of the principles of fundamental human rights. It would create and fertilize a breeding ground for dictators and autocrats. Collective decisions might lead to mass failure if, and, as it is often the case, when it is 'follow-the-leader' option.

It became incumbent on the aggrieved parties to legitimately pursue their claims at the tribunal set up to examine such cases. It was open to educated conjecture that such tribunals might repeat the feat once executed in Anambra State, where after a wait of three years, the court upheld the claim of Peter Obi of APGA and reinstated him as the duly elected governor in place of Ngige of PDP. It was hoped, and it was equally advisable, that INEC should always, in the spirit of fair play and propriety, make available to all petitioners without delay all documents and materials needed to support their petitions to the electoral tribunals. They should also publish the detailed account of all the votes cast at both the state and presidential elections. Hopefully, the tribunal officials would heed the advice of the Chief Justice and refrain from being bogged down by the twin evils of corruption and under-the-table machinations of unsavoury government influence peddlers.

CHAPTER NINE

MY VISION AND
THE WAY FORWARD: POLITICS

Several factors combine to make some people draw certain harrowing conclusions. Given the circumstances of my diverse and distinctive cultures, the future might be fraught with the gloomy circumstances which could be ascribed to 'a failed state'. These circumstances have brought forth the need to view with concern the centrifugal forces that have posed a threat to my corporate existence.

Succeeding generations of my political leaders have failed abysmally to manage or even address the differences existing within me. Multiplicity of languages has definitely constituted a roadblock to unity and cohesion. These differences portend the twin evils of frequent religious and communal upheaval fuelled by ignorance, ethnicism, and inept leadership lacking true national spirit. Also, a preponderance of my citizenry have been impoverished by the chronic and widespread cankerworm of corruption that has eaten deep into the fabric of society, particularly among the leaders. The United Nations Development Programme (UNDP) recently placed me on the lower rungs of the ladder of living-standard parameters. Indeed, a report jointly issued by *Foreign Policy* magazine and the Fund for Peace listed me as a mass of people broken up into fragile states and in ferment—and the eighteenth most unstable country in the world.

Without any shadow of doubt, I realize that it is true that I have serious challenges to my nationhood, but they are not insurmountable. All hope is not yet lost. I am determined to turn these differences into formidable strength and to allow true federalism to take root. True federalism will allow each federating unit to develop according to its culture and values. It is my considered view that my diversity as a nation should not make me force my heterogeneous constituents to live under a homogeneous arrangement. I want my institutions to be strengthened to become neutral to religion and ethnicity. I will strive to place more emphasis on the doctrine of equality before the law. Since there can be no peace without justice, all my laws as a nation should be firmly applied.

Economic roots of the problem will be tackled by creating an inclusive economy that provides jobs and opportunities for the unemployed and idle youths in the cities and particularly in the oil-producing areas. Militancy and vandalism there have become a ticking time bomb that may ignite into a conflagration of unmanageable proportions. I emphasize that when a state is unable to guarantee the security and welfare of its citizens, it is inviting failure—and I do not want to fail.

I prayerfully aver with all modesty and hope that my future as a Nation is destined to be much greater still. The circumstances of my birth through the midwifery of my pioneering founders, fearless journalists, and dedicated politicians have ensured sustainable growth and greatness. Weaned by the British Colonialists and then nurtured on a staple diet of parliamentary democracy, I have marched inexorably through mischances and perilous adventure towards the promise of greatness in size, power, wealth, and preeminence in African affairs in particular and in world politics at large.

STRENGTH IN UNITY

Ideally, the truism that is applicable in my situation is that the bunched brooms reflect greater strength than one or two sticks in isolation from the bunch. The bunched broom will sweep with greater efficacy. It will much more easily kill or swat irritating flies. This is why it is advisable that I should jealously guard my internal unity—my 'bunched broom'—which is my strength as a nation. I should take good care of the cow that provides the milk and the goose that lays the golden eggs. The towns and villages and the occupants whose land belches out crude oil should be the focus of my attention and developmental projects. I will guard against secession and ensure stability and security of lives and property.

I should create an enabling and secure environment for residents and workers in the oil-producing areas. I should urge the foreign oil companies to plough back their profits much more than before for the improvement and upliftment of the lives of the indigenes. Oil exploration activities have robbed many indigenes of their means of livelihood on land and sea. Often they have had to resort to brigandage, kidnappings, and oil-pipe vandalism in order to attract attention, seek revenge, or even just to make ends meet. Massive injection of employment opportunities will go a long way to bring stability and ensure an atmosphere conducive to harmonious existence within the oil-producing communities.

While the Niger–Delta conflict is intensely connected to the control of resources, there is need to understand these conflicts within the broad context of international political economy of oil. It has been said that the US has projected that the bulk of its energy requirements in the next 10 to 15 years will come from the Gulf of Guinea rather than from the Middle East. This has made the Gulf of Guinea a strategic defense interest of the US. With its presence already in Liberia, Mali, Senegal, Cote d'Ivore, Ghana, Sao Tome, and Principe as well as in the coastal creeks of the Niger–Delta (at the invitation of my government under Obasanjo), the trend is ominous and fraught with aggressive implications. I, along with the other countries in the region, should be wary of the visible presence of the forces of recolonization or imperialistic interference. It appears that the issue involved, rooted as it were on resource control, has become very attractive to competing interests.

The interest and rights of the people of the Niger–Delta area must be protected and respected. A resolution based on those rights must be found. I believe that neither political repression nor misguided acts of brigandage and kidnappings on the part of the militants in the area would solve the problem. My government should be committed to the sovereignty of the people and a just resolution of their fundamental human rights can achieve the resolution. As much as possible, my Federal Government should refrain from using the armed forces to repress the activities of the militants. It is always better to 'jaw-jaw' than to 'war-war'. As proverb-loving M. K. O. Abiola would say, 'The panacea for a nagging headache is not decapitation, and you do not cut off your nose to spite your face'. Finally—and most importantly—'One does not use fire to ferret out and kill the lice in one's hair'. The situation in the Niger–Delta area therefore calls for extra caution and deft handling lest there be a conflagration which might send ripples and conflicting signals round the world.

CENSUS

It is universally acknowledged that there is strength in numbers. I was barely over 30 million in population around the time of my Independence in 1960, and I am arguably about 140 million at the beginning of the twenty-first century. Therefore, in about 50 years, demographers have assured me, the way my population is growing, it may reach as high as 200 million before the end of the twenty-first century. I expect more thorough and efficient census authorities to give me more accurate and operable census figures. The attendant benefits and accruing advantages are distinctive and desirable. Budgetary planning will be facilitated. Siting and distribution of amenities will be carried out in a more judicious manner.

The explosive nature of determining the biggest religious group and the acrimonious and often acerbic debates about which is the biggest ethnic group will continue to be 'no-go' areas among participants at such fora on constitution drafting or protocol recognition. It is thought-provoking to realize, for instance, that my Igbo-speaking citizens constitute the second-largest ethnic group in almost all cities and towns all over my Republic. It is also well known that Igbo people are industrious and productive wherever they live. The same thing applies to the religious groups in terms of numbers. But the fact still remains that statistical data based on census figures will establish once and for all certain undeniable facts that had previously defied logical conclusions or solution.

CONSTITUTIONAL REVIEW

There is a need to take a much closer look at certain parts of my Constitution. The need for the commitment to Democracy to be sustained but supported as well is already staring me in the face. The problem of sustaining the democratic project in my governance ceases to be a straightforward task. This is so because my road map of Democracy has been a product of military governments. They have been responsible for convening Constitution Review Committees, convening Constituent Assemblies, promulgating Constitutions establishing Party Certifying Bodies, establishing Electoral Bodies, funding Parties, creating States and Local governments, and arranging their own withdrawals back into their barracks. The military had been responsible for overthrowing with impunity governments that had been established by their constitutions. It is imperative that the civilian dispensation should allow the citizens to rise to the challenge of playing watchdog over the democratic process by insisting that the political class should live up to its responsibility to the constitution and to the people.

The constitution has to be revisited with a view to ameliorating some given situations or expunging certain offensive clauses. The obnoxious 'immunity clause'—which has hitherto protected corrupt officials from prosecution and promoted corrupt practises in high places—must go. There should no longer be 'sacred cows'. Also, I need a more acceptable formula of revenue allocation. The 'state-of-derivation' clause should take into consideration the needs of my displaced and impoverished citizens, especially in the oil-producing areas. Similarly, the VAT (value-added tax) should be made to plough back to states of derivation, appreciably and proportionately, the cash derivables from various states. I would rather like the grass-roots people to be more intimately involved in their own governance at the local government level. The people should not be suffocated with too much interference and bogged down by unwarranted intervention from my Federal Government.

Democracy presupposes that all the attributes of that concept are available and evident. Some of these attributes are periodic free and fair elections, an independent judiciary, a robust and vibrant opposition, a responsible and independent legislature, a responsible and free press, freedom of association, and focused political parties with functional and operable internal democracy. These are the attributes of democracy that grease the machinery on which good government gracefully glides. Therefore, adequate steps should be taken to ensure the survival and blossoming growth of democracy in my governance from generation to generation.

One indispensable tool for a smooth-sailing government is the availability of a well-fashioned and viable national Constitution. There is no substitute for clearly defined constitutional guidelines for each tier of government and for each arm within each tier. While it can be said that my 1960 constitution, which was revised in 1963, gave a fairly good direction, it was convulsed and dumped as a result of the 30-month civil war, which ushered in a succession of military regimes. There was no legitimate constitution until 1979. Every constitution that I have had since 1979 was imposed or midwifed by inept drafting and operated by people who were ignorant of the built-in pitfalls, booby traps, and land mines.

My 1999 constitution fared no better. It belonged to the same pedestrian and directionless genre as its predecessors. It was accepted that the constitution was faulty. The method of its preparation was criticized. The search and preparation for a new constitution must originate from a people-oriented foundation in which the preamble will justifiably take off from the premise of 'We, *the people*'.

The task of giving me an acceptable new constitution must be embarked upon as soon as possible. Such a constitution should evolve from extensive debates by a cross-section of my distinctive political, social, and cultural groups. The ultimate goal is to rectify the defects of the present constitution and make all necessary amendments to ensure my status as a truly Federal Republic.

First and foremost, the Electoral Laws must be reviewed. All stake holders, leaders of thought, and people responsible for putting forward the projected constitution amendment should shun self-interest. They should fashion modalities for free and fair elections for which the people yearned over the years. All genuine democrats should join forces to ensure that a thorough overhaul of the electoral system becomes a major target of political reform. It would be foolhardy, slipshod, and negligent to run subsequent elections under the same unwholesome rules that heretofore guided my elections.

The reviewed Electoral Laws should create a conducive atmosphere for holding genuinely democratic elections. Such elections afford my citizens the opportunity to elect the candidates of their choice. The political system that often rewarded corrupt and abusive individuals with public office will be reviewed and reformed. This is meant to discourage politicians from viewing unlawful behaviour as a necessary component of electoral success. Such Electoral Law criminalizes the activities of some politicians who hire political thugs to intimidate opponents yet generally enjoy impunity.

The new constitution should be such that it takes into account my federal structure, the humanity of my people, and the social structure in which they operate. Many of Obasanjo's programmes which were introduced without adequate consultations met with public resentment and protests. Incessant increases in the prices of petroleum products and the overt and often covert interference with the rule of law and other activities—ordinarily scheduled under the authority of other branches of government—cannot be acceptable in a truly democratic setting. Social dialogue by way of consultations and respect for joint agreements should be a welcome departure from the eras in which government reneged on virtually all agreements. The spate of retrenchment exercises which brought untold misery and mass unemployment in the past must be halted. All efforts at job creation must be stepped up. All infrastructural facilities—such as electricity, water, road, and efficient Health service —must be made to function optimally.

Remarkably, despite the billions of naira spent on these public utilities, no appreciable impact has been made on the social and economic lives of the citizenry. The ineffectiveness of these facilities will continue to affect the competitiveness of the productive sectors of my economy. Factors that led to the closure of factories, retrenchment of workers, and the unbridled importation of goods—especially Chinese products—must be seriously looked into. The textile, paper, electrical, and electronics sectors, which are some of the areas negatively affected, should be bailed out and spared from extinction. Agriculture should receive greater attention to the extent that the 10% growth in agriculture projected by Obasanjo's administration should be realizable.

I also foresee a yearning to revert to the days of Parliamentary Democracy. This was also the vision and the proposal of the quintessential political thinker, sage, and activist leader of Pro-National Conference Organization (PRONACO), Tony Enahoro. I also dream of the clamour for zonal, not regional, assemblies complete with Premiers and Zonal Ministers or Commissioners. I have seen that creating multiple states from the same tribe of people does not make economic or political sense. For example, why should the Igbos—who speak the same language and belong to a contiguous geographical area with similar tendencies and culture and have a generally accepted ancestral lineage—be divided into five states? The same thing as the Igbos goes for the Yorubas. Practically speaking, these have largely become parasitic states with equal numbers of executive governors and bureaucracy. Indeed, they can be politically welded into one viable, formidable and autonomous Zone.

The various zones already existing in the North could be similarly considered. There is the consideration of linguistic affinity. There is also the possible recourse to geographical contiguity. Some of the various tribes and cultures include the Hausas, Fulanis, Tivs, and Nupes. The fusion of some of the various tribes and cultures will considerably reduce the number of the existing states. There is no doubt that the management of such a multiplicity of states would inevitably constitute a drain of budgetary and financial allocations.

I am suspicious of the never-ending agitation for new states. This speaks to the fact that succeeding governments have progressively abandoned the Federal system of government and have embraced a unitary or, as it happened, a dictatorial system. It is a fundamental principle of government that federating units in a federal system cannot be dictated to by the center. Creating more and more states would be so ineffective and fragmented that they could not constitute a balancing counterweight to the center. Therefore, a major issue I see in any constitutional review is the return to true Federalism.

Federalism does not allow the center to create or fund sub-units or local governments from the federating units. In effect, this would translate into the geo-political zones transforming into the building blocks of the federation with each of these zones having the right to create as many states and local governments as it desires. The long list of items in the Exclusive Legislative List should be drastically pruned to a dozen or so manageable and essential ones. Revenue allocation formulas should tilt deservedly towards derivation rather than controversial and unverifiable population, population density, equality of states, land mass, and terrain.

My people will campaign against the concentration of power in the hands of one individual as evidenced in the presidential system. Healthy rivalries will develop among the various zonal assemblies, and this can only bring out the best from them, as it did in the early years of my independence when there were only 4 regional Houses of Assembly. I envision a government in charge of administration and a vigorous and effective opposition. I shudder at the thought of purchasable minority pawns prone to succumbing to the 'settlement' syndrome emanating from 'Ghana-must-go bags' (carrier bags used for clandestine or hurried conveyance of money or goods) in order to toe the government line, however unpalatable.

I have a dream in which other like-minded African nations averse to military coups will refuse to recognize and accept into the African Union any members who are products of 'fait accompli' coups. I have come to the unshakeable conclusion that military involvement in governance is an aberration. With the benefit of hindsight, I will ensure by all reasonable means, that never again will I be ruled by military edicts, decrees, and fiats. It has been a humiliating and harrowing experience that should be prevented and discouraged in this new century and beyond.

PITFALLS OF PREVIOUS MILITARY REGIMES

Four critical pillars that my successive military governments had to contend with were the rule of law; basic freedom of expression and association; electoral legitimacy; and accountability. Under military rule, I ceased to be a law-based state as military rulers performed as if they were above the law. They proscribed political parties and dissolved elected assemblies at will. They showed no respect for basic freedoms, particularly freedom of the press. They were accountable only to themselves. These were the main manifestations of my military dictatorships which were essentially antithetical to democratic norms. In theory, the restoration of elected governments and legislatures in May 1999 marked the end of military arbitrariness and the beginning of a new phase of apprenticeship to the democratic system.

For the benefit and guidance of those who will amend or redraft my constitution, I will outline the pitfalls that bedeviled my governance in the inept and untutored hands of the military rulers. Their exploits, misdemeanors, and serial maladministrations were inimical and simply unacceptable in any day and age. It was almost like jungle law in which *might equals right*:

1. Even Gowon, a soldier and gentleman, had his limitations. His lackadaisical approach towards the negotiation that led to the Aburi Accord initially exposed his lack of preparedness and good advice. The end result was that he came to rely, almost to a state of docility, on civil servants who literally exploited this awareness to emerge as a cabal of 'super perm-secs'. Flush with petro-dollars following my civil war, Gowon's famous exclamation (which he has repeatedly denied ever making)—that 'money was not my (Nigeria's) problem but how to spend it'—is a celebrated self-indictment of his ability to manage wealth. He made the same mistake—proposing elongation of tenure—that was to bedevil most of my subsequent military rulers. He said that a previously set departure date of 1974 was no longer realistic.

2. Buhari–Idiagbon set out on a bright note, and they were both determined to perform well. But their dour, unsmiling countenances and rigid enforcement of military rule on my citizens turned theirs into a reign of terror. Arbitrariness and unorthodoxy became their forte in governance. Buhari threatened and jailed journalists. He invoked laws retroactively to punish drug traffickers and foreign exchange manipulators.

3. Babangida's Structural Adjustment Policy (SAP) elicited the description of its lack in human face from Obasanjo. It was hastily conceived, unrealistic, and irrelevant. It was meant to be a kind of magic elixir for my economy, but it led to some negative results, including a *brain drain*. The Gulf War financial windfall was always in contentious debate. 'Settlement'—as a euphemism for bribery and corruption—was turned into an art. My citizenry still feel scandalized and let down over the annulment of Abiola's victory at the June 12, 1993, presidential polls and with the murderous aftermath and horrendous events which erupted after the annulment.

4. Abacha was the exact personification of the aberrations and of all that is ignoble and antithetical in military governance. Amid a spate of assassinations, murders, and sporadic bombings in city centers, he crowned his inglorious reign with the judicially sanctioned murder of Ken Saro-Wiwa, who was hanged along with his Ogoni fellows. He used his military might and dictatorial powers to stash more than $3 billion from my treasury into the accommodating vaults of foreign banks.

5. Abubakar mismanaged my economy and nearly depleted my foreign reserve. His poorly researched minimum-wage scheme was a failure. Still, he earns my commendation and the grateful admiration of my citizenry for not planning to overstay his welcome. He handed over power to a democratically elected civilian president.

The legacy of the military, particularly from the regimes of Buhari, Babangida, Abacha, and Abdulsalaam, has been one of abysmal failure compounded by colossal waste of resources and misdirection of my floundering ship of state.

Obasanjo was not the best that a civilian government should be, though he was probably better than were the military intruders before him. He failed with power generation and distribution; he failed with roads; he failed with his third-term misadventure. His contracts on railways and power plants were badly handled. He openly aided and connived with the incorrigible intransigence and rascality of the so-called Ibadan 'strongman', Adedibu. Finally, he left the naira too expensive against a weak dollar, and interest rates soared at the banks.

ECONOMY

I envisage an economy that would witness a positive transformation if efficiently planned and prudently managed. My annual budget in the year 1966, when I obtained my Independence, was the paltry equivalent of N72 million (about thirty-six million pounds) in comparison with almost N4 trillion I had already budgeted and would be budgeting much more in the years to come. Planners of my economy should look beyond my current mono-economy to a more diversified one. They should plan to develop *all* segments of my economy, especially agriculture, which has incremental effects on all other sectors. For instance, my Northern Region was noted for its massive production of groundnut (peanuts). The West was also noted for the considerable quantity of cocoa it produced, while the East had enormous advantage in palm products.

That was when my economy was mostly agrarian, and it was booming. The foreign exchange earning was on the upbeat. That was when the majority of my population was proud to farm as a genuine means of livelihood. That was when 'black gold' had not yet been discovered in Oloibiri and in present-day Bayelsa State. Furthermore, the planners should ensure that the healthy race for capitalization by the banks, flagged on by the Central Bank, will shift on to a faster lane. This will increase the shareholders' funds of each of the various banks to more than N100 billion.

I was encouraged to project positively into the future of my economy by the forward-looking Charles Soludo, my cerebral and indefatigable Central Bank governor. In 2004, Goldman Sachs (the global investment company) predicted that if the right things were done, my economy might emerge among the largest economies by 2020. Soludo also espoused that dream. The passion with which he expounded on this theme at every given opportunity injected a soothing dose of optimism in me that I would soon become the financial hub of Africa. When I transform into the twelfth largest economy in the world by 2050—ahead of Korea, Italy, Canada and others—I foresee a rebranding of my image from that of a clay-footed giant. This might sound utopian and optimistic because current statistics show that my GDP was $183 billion around 2007 with per-capita income of $1,418.00—which was one of the world's lowest—but by the end of the 1980s, I had fallen from being a *middle* income country with a per-capita income of around $1,000.00 per year to one of the world's *poorest*, with a staggering estimated per-capita income of only $250.00. Realistic estimates say over 50 percent of my working-age population are jobless or under-employed. But I like my citizenry to see the projections, nonetheless, as a wake-up call based on actual performance in the recent past.

It is an undeniable fact that the dynamic of my economy was fundamentally altered, particularly towards the end of Obasanjo's first term in office. There is the obvious need to take the achievement to a sustainably higher level. The experiences of other emerging economies which have made similar transition reveal that one of the ingredients of their success was doing the right thing consistently over a period of time. I need to ensure the continuous enthronement of democracy. I need a government that is guided by due process and obeys the rule of law. Such a government must continuously deliver on fiscal prudence, wage ceaseless war on corruption, and be guided by social equity. It must also deliver a workable economy and ensure wealth creation and its equitable distribution, as opposed to the cake-sharing mentality that has been the bane of my society.

Essentially, I see into the future and watch as such established institutions as the judiciary and the legislature strive with convincing performances that can stand the test of time. This quest to take me to a greater height and turn me into the heartbeat of Africa will be driven by the patriotic zeal of my citizenry. It should also be borne out of the conviction that the vision can indeed serve as a catalyst to propel me and position me among the largest economies in the world in the course of the century.

I have the potential and the capacity in terms of human and material resources to aspire to the heights attained by the 'Asian Tiger' countries of

Singapore, Malaysia, and others. The inimitable Lee Kuan Yew of Singapore showed the way and the will when confronted with a similar situation of creating a financial center. He succinctly captured the onerous task in his seminal work, *From the Third World to the First World*. Today, Singapore is one of the leading financial centers of the world. It has consistently made the list of the top ten emerging economies in the last few years.

In the future, well-planned vision painstakingly implemented will stand me in good stead. If my economic planners and leaders of government can exhibit sharp focus of where they want to be—and if the citizenry share the vision of a modern competitive market economy—my economy will attain new heights. They can rally my people to share in the political and economic vision, working together assiduously to achieve the dream. Focus should be shifted to the need to wriggle out of the quagmire of an underdeveloped state.

Power, steel, and the downstream petroleum sectors must be freed from the suffocating hands of the state. Government holding on tenaciously to otherwise-profitable enterprises *which it cannot run efficiently* continues to constitute a bane to my economy. A transparent bidding process will release the multi-billion naira enterprises—like the Ajaokuta Steel Complex and the moribund refineries lacking in turn-around-maintenance culture—into more efficient private holdings. The refineries have become a conduit for corrupt officials to siphon public funds in the name of maintenance. It is a national shame that I, as a leading crude oil producer and exporter, am in fact *importing* 80% of my domestic requirements of refined petroleum products.

The handlers of my economy should employ such basic economic principles as fiscal prudence and monetary discipline to foster a stable macro-economic environment in the pursuit of growth. Newspaper analysts have therefore identified a number of benchmarks that would catapult me into a financial hub in the scheme of things in world economies. The prerequisites include rule of law; independent judiciary; stable and honest government that pursues sound economic management; big, strong banks that are able to compete globally and are ranked by reputable rating agencies; a pool of skilled and adaptable professionals; risk-based supervision by the regulatory body to minimize systemic failure; reliable infrastructure; socio-political stability; efficient legal framework involving quick dispensation of justice and existence of commercial courts; and a thriving stock exchange and liberalized markets.

The prevailing situation and what it portends for the future makes it even more necessary than at any other time for my citizenry to rise up and take charge of my destiny as a Nation designated by the Almighty God to be great. Indeed, I am at the threshold of an enduring transformation. Failure to grab the chance now will probably lead to eternal condemnation by generations yet unborn. Testimony to the fact that history now beckons me is evidenced by the recent studies and forecast by Goldman Sachs Economic Research, placing me, all things being equal, among the largest world economies in the near future.

Liquefied natural gas would have fully come on stream. Bitumen that literally oozes out at Loda in Ondo State will become a vast revenue-generating source. Moribund factories will be reactivated and will operate at optimum capacity. More factories mean more employment opportunities, greater production, and less expenditure on imports. Flight of hard currency will be discouraged when the petroleum refineries and the petro-chemical plants are put to optimal use and less emphasis is placed on the importation of petroleum products. The turn-around-maintenance of the refineries, which was painfully neglected during Obasanjo's administration, should be dutifully and promptly carried out as, when, and where it is scheduled. In fact, it is my earnest wish that more refineries be built. More petroleum engineers should be recruited and better equipped to handle and maintain the refineries. The banks should be enabled to operate in a way that lending and interest rates would both suit the banks and attract more customers. Interest on lending rates in particular should be brought down to single-digit percentage.

ANTI-CORRUPTION MEASURES

Corruption is endemic among the rank and file in both my public and private sectors. Corruption is like a cankerworm that has eaten deep into the fabric of my society. It must be addressed with great urgency to achieve the desired goal of laundering my corrupt image abroad and enthroning probity and accountability locally. Efforts should be made to empower the Economic and Financial Crime Commission (EFCC) to enable it to perform with greater efficiency and without fear or favour. However, certain sections of the EFCC Act in my constitution should be amended to decrease the power of the executive president on the commission. It is feared that the statutory powers vested in the commission might be exercised recklessly or capriciously and subjected to manipulation or politicization by an overbearing, vindictive, and excessively powerful president. Also, my police should be better remunerated in order to minimize their propensity for taking bribes.

CHAPTER TEN

SOME HUMAN RIGHTS
ACTIVISTS AND SOCIAL CRITICS

My history is grossly incomplete unless I mention the tremendous roles played by the human rights activists in this saga of nation building. I should also highlight the quest of this breed of crusaders who gave articulation and animation to the struggle for the ideals and goals of fundamental human rights. Encapsulated in these ideals are the rights to life, basic dignity of the human person, personal liberty, fair hearing, freedom of expression and especially of the press, peaceful assembly and association, freedom of movement, and freedom from discrimination. These men and women were prepared to make their voices heard and their grievances known at the slightest flicker of suspicion that any aspect of this sacrosanct United Nations Charter was going to be abused, violated, assailed, or trampled upon.

The military administrations in particular sent out ominous signals when they continually resorted to the use of edicts and decrees that abused and assailed the people's fundamental human rights. My yearning for democracy heard the voice emanating from the indomitable courage and spirited articulation of the pro-democracy groups and the human rights organizations. These activists stood up to combat the dehumanizing effects of the aberrant military abusers of these rights. They would go to any extent to ensure that these essential ingredients of democracy are enthroned and enshrined in my constitution.

The activities of human rights crusaders long predated my arrival at the United Nations as a free and independent Nation. This therefore underscores my status as a signatory to the Charter on Human Rights. During the pre-Independence era and the struggles and agitations that preceded it, those whose ideas differed from the tenets of democracy the colonial administrators practised 'at home' and which they were demonstrably imposing on my colonised people were described as 'Communists' and treated with harsh suspicion. It was the 'Cold War' era, and the sensitive colonial administrators and their pro-Western collaborators always imagined communists in every closet.

TUNJI OTEGBEYE AND OTHERS

Bearded and unorthodox activists capable of moulding the characters and views of my impressionable youths were often haunted, harassed, and even detained. Tunji Otegbeye, a bearded medical doctor, became well known for his activist inclinations and his persistent efforts and moves to recruit willing youths to further their education in the so-called 'Iron Curtain' (communist) countries. The universities and other higher institutions of learning were the haven of ideas and targets both for the activists' nets and for the centers that attracted security agents' suppressive actions. There were radical student union leaders like Dapo Falase, Osita Okeke, Yomi Ferreira, and Edward Kobani of the University College of Ibadan (UCI) in the early 1960s. Red-capped and bearded Segun Okeowo of the University of Lagos—who was much later succeeded by the other Segun, the dread-locked Segun Maiyegun—was at the forefront of students' unionism, activism, and radicalism in the 1970s and 1980s.

Dapo Falase led the UCI students in a spontaneous protest against the Anglo-Nigerian Defense Pact in 1961. The protesters' war song was 'No Pact! No Base!' In the ensuing melee, which took place at the National Assembly (then in Lagos), seven students were arrested and later arraigned before the courts. They were hurriedly tried at the court, rebuked for 'youthful exuberance', and discharged by the presiding judge. The same Falase also led the invading hordes of protesting students—who arrived from Ibadan in a fleet of buses and then marched to the same venue in Lagos—to make their feelings known about the brutal murder of the socialist Congolese Prime Minister, Patrice Lumumba, in 1962. Towards the tail end of his presidency of the Students' Union, Falase also led the successful agitation for the expulsion of the misguided American Youth

Corp member, Miguel Michelmore, who had indiscreetly and carelessly dropped a U.S.-bound postcard conveying scurrilous and sneering criticism of my peoples' ways of life.

Segun Okeowo led the 'Ali Must Go' demonstration of 1978. It was a tumultuous demonstration by the students against the excesses and arbitrariness of the military government of Obasanjo in the area of education. This was during the tenure of Ahmadu Ali as the Federal Commissioner for Education. Okeowo and Maiyegun were arrested much later and under different activist circumstances. They joined other well-known activists like Gani Fawehinmi, Femi Falana, Beko Ransome-Kuti, and Baba Omojola in Kuje prisons. Their imprisonment was a result of their involvement in the uprisings that followed the annulled presidential elections of 1993 in which M. K. O. Abiola was the popularly acclaimed winner.

Much earlier, Adaka Boro, Nottingham Dick, and Samuel Owonaru rebelliously declared the Niger Delta a Republic in a 12-day revolution during the Tafawa Balewa regime in the early 1960s. They were radical activists who cried havoc at the treatment being meted out to the people of the Niger–Delta area. Their lands and waters were being subjected to acquisition and environmental abuses by the exploration activities of the oil companies. This became the harbinger of worse and inhuman treatment meted out to the people of the land and creeks with the 'black gold'. Ken Saro-Wiwa and the 'Ogoni-Nine' were doomed to hang for daring to confront the Abacha regime over the same issues.

Briefly put, before the advent of the Campaign for Democracy (CD), some pro-democracy groups and human rights associations had started establishing their presence. In the ranks of pro-democracy groups were professionals, student bodies, and women's organizations. The Civil Liberties Organization (CLO) was very visible and active. Its main objective was to highlight and protest against the human rights abuses rampant in the Second Republic and the succeeding military regimes.

GANI FAWEHINMI

The stoicism and the ability to be resilient and unflagging in the face of re-pression and harassment, a characteristic of the human rights activists, became personified in that quintessential activist and rare gem of a lawyer, Gani Fawe-hinmi. In this age and generation, and in future generations, whenever the his-tory of law and the rule of law is written and discussed, a golden chapter will al-ways be reserved for the irrepressible Gani. Whenever and wherever reference is made to the crusade against bad governments and oppression of the masses in any form in my historical annals, the quintessence of the one-man crusade would always be Gani. He was the self-appointed defender of the oppressed and the defenseless. Both his inveterate foes and his adoring admirers conceded these accolades to him.

He had the most distinguished record regarding the number of successful litigations brought against governments in the history of my judiciary. In like manner, he was being haunted, harassed, physically assaulted, arrested, and de-tained with the same fervour with which he fought successive governments. He was constantly on the defensive, particularly against Babangida's government, of which Gani proclaimed himself as the self-appointed leading opponent. Gani was detained 24 times and was continually hounded by the security agents of successive governments. He was arrested and detained in 12 different prisons and 9 police cells in as many cities. He was charged in court 18 times for various political 'offences'. His international passport was seized and held in the cus-tody of security agents 21 times. He was prevented from traveling out of the country 15 times. But he always survived to celebrate the demise of these governments.

His long and tortuous journey in the interest of justice and the rule of law started many years earlier. He had offered free legal services to a lowly factory worker whose wife was seduced to commit adultery by a powerful and highly placed civil servant. The lady had been lured with the display of power and money for sex. The unyielding persistence with which Gani doggedly pursued the matter earned him harassment and detention by the powers of the day.

It was this same crusading zeal in search of justice that made Gani challenge the then-military government of Ibrahim Babangida in a protracted legal battle.

He was convinced that government agents were somehow involved in the events leading to the death of journalist Dele Giwa on October 19, 1986, at Ikeja, Lagos. A parcel bomb was delivered to his house and marked 'from the Presidency' by unknown persons and abruptly took the life from Dele Giwa. This painful episode drew ire and fire from Gani to such an extent that he seized any and all available opportunities to point an accusing finger at the people he suspected to be involved in the murder.

Gani was the scourge of irresponsible governments. He became a legend in his lifetime. He caused numerous suits to be instituted against the government as means of curtailing excesses and abuses. Whenever such suits were adjourned, jittery and flustered government legal draftsmen responded to their masters' orders in various tame and subdued ways. They would correct the illegal acts, amend the offending law, or legalize government's questionable actions. They did this by enacting the specific law and making it retroactive. It became apparent that whenever government's legal draftsmen were at work in their offices, they took into consideration what Gani's reaction or assessment of their efforts might be. Governments imagined Gani breathing down their necks when formulating policies and drafting new laws. They always anticipated his usually well considered views and fearless criticism. He was always one step ahead of these government legal draftsmen.

Some repressive and unpopular government measures that attracted Gani's scrutiny and outright condemnation included Maryam Babangida's Better Life Programme; illegal dissolution of boards, including the Provisional Ruling Council and its membership; inexplicably delayed Budgetary Allocations; judicial killings; suppression of press freedom; and the extraordinary imposition of the Interim National Government.

Remarkably, Gani, a believer in the principle of physical nonviolence, could be very violent and virulent in his utterances in the pursuit of his ideals of justice and the rule of law. He could head for the courts at the drop of a hat when these ideals were abused. Anarchy and resort to physical violence, even under grim provocations, were alien to his culture and modus operandi. He always used the law to fight institutionalized illegality. Ever irrepressible, he was always the first to start the ball rolling, literally rushing in where it seemed angels feared to tread. It would not matter whether he had been right, but the debate he provoked would always be sufficient to ensure that issues were examined from all possible angles.

Gani practised, wrote, and facilitated the practise of law. He exuded brilliance. He facilitated brilliance and encouraged the achievement of brilliance in many eloquent ways. First, he awarded scholarships every year to deserving or indigent students at the secondary and tertiary levels. Second, he was reputed to have one of the best-equipped and computerized law libraries in Africa. Thirdly and definitely most importantly, he was the author and publisher of the *Weekly Law Reports*, which have become a sine qua non possession for all practitioners at the bar, the bench, and the law schools. It is to his credit that he was able to start and sustain this academic research and other endeavours with the assistance of capable aides despite opposition, especially from official quarters.

Like the other activists, he always emerged victorious, to the admiration and adulation of his teeming fans and appreciative clients. For his nagging activism, a feeble and amateurish attempt was once made to set his printing press ablaze. On another occasion, one of his night guards was maimed during a dastardly raid on his chambers, when 'official' attackers sprayed the place with bullets.

On his release from one of his 24 detentions, Gani said, 'It was my fifteenth arrest and ninth incarceration under Babangida's regime.' Even though he was suffering from an ailment aggravated by detention in far-flung places like Gashua, Jos, Kuje, Ikoyi, and Alagbon, he was ever ready for all eventualities. He was known to have kept three bags packed with his needed tablets, toothbrush and paste, books, and some clothes in each of the bags. A packed bag was placed in his chambers, inside his car, and in his house on the ready for security men who might come at any time to whisk him away for questioning and into detention—or perhaps into prison yet again.

Gani was a persistent gadfly to the judiciary. He was a fly in the ointment of oppressive governments. His fans and admirers hailed him as the die-hard defender of the oppressed. The consequences of his activities were inevitable. Year after year, despite the intimidating credentials which he visibly paraded and which manifestly recommended him, the nominating and appointing board refused to make Gani a Senior Advocate of Nigeria (SAN). However, he was undaunted. Contemptuously and out of spite for the board, the students' union of

Obafemi Awolowo University at Ile-Ife awarded Gani the Senior Advocate of the Masses (SAM). There is a Yoruba saying: 'If a felon shuns shame and dishonour, at least members of his household should show a modicum of guilt or shame'. Hence, in the fullness of time, when it was apparent that it was long overdue, the conferring authorities had to accord him the silk of a Senior Advocate of Nigeria (SAN). For his outstanding achievements in the area of human rights, Gani was unanimously selected for the famous International Bruno Kriesky Award, which he traveled to Austria to receive at the World Conference on Human Rights. That was the icing on the cake and the ultimate crowning glory for his relentless crusade, which spanned more than four decades.

Gani was perhaps the most hated, feared, and haunted of all the governments' critics. He criticized their poor performance in the areas of governance, respect for human rights, and the arbitrary uses of decrees and edicts. He maintained, with unyielding tenacity, that Babangida's transition programme was farcical and that he was 'transiting to nowhere'. Gani would be vindicated by the generally unacceptable annulment of the June 12, 1993, presidential election, which was globally adjudged to be free and fair. For Gani's persistence, consistency, and tenacity, Babangida expressed his grudging respect for him. But Gani sharply retorted that he would not let such diversionary praises go to his head or deter him from continuing his inexorable course of advocacy for justice and the rule of law.

In a special and peculiar way, Gani was almost a loner when it came to staunch adherence to principles. Even though he was a populist by inclination, Gani was not a man to be intimidated for his advocacy of unpopular ideas. He kept doing what he felt to be best, arguing his position with his trademark vehemence, oblivious or unmindful of what critics had to say. One commendable thing about Gani was that he never took a position without explaining his rationale behind it. This fact was very well known both to his admirers and critics. It made him always to be more at home with the impressionable youths, who identified with his ways and utterances, rather than the chameleon-like adults who would bend or soft-pedal their views to accommodate or placate any government in power. He criticized some of his comrades-in-arms like Tai Solarin, who accepted the position of chairman of People's bank. He frowned that Beko Ransome-Kuti accepted the title of Head of the Board of Lagos University

Teaching Hospital, even as the then-chairman of Campaign for Democracy (CD). He disagreed with Olu Onagoruwa for becoming, despite his warning, the Attorney General and Justice Minister in Abacha's government.

Similarly, he was not always readily comfortable with some of the other radical lawyers, because he disagreed with their methods. He once fell out of favour with his learned friends in the Nigerian Bar Association. This earned him some ignominy as he was placed on the dis-honour roll. However, it is certain that Gani was acting purely on principle. He had taken on the defense of a client in seeming defiance of an existing ban on members of the Nigerian Bar Association in order to protest the high-handedness of the military regime. He had come to epitomize the best in public-spirited intervention in topical matters.

He kept the public constantly informed of the activities of their leaders and how to involve and engage them in the unending dialogue on Nation building. I aver with sanctimonious insistence that every country, particularly in the developing world, needs its own Gani. I had my own Gani, and the truth of this assertion can be verified in the several ground-breaking and landmark cases he won through the courts. The law had always been Gani's forte; it was the anchor that always provided a safe berth for him. Like Walpole in English history, 'The rule of law!' was always his war cry.

TAI SOLARIN

People often eulogize a dead hero with the epitaph, 'Gone, but not forgotten'. Such is the similitude of this epitaph to the life and teachings of the educationist and human rights activist, Tai Solarin. He was an unrepentant atheist, a down-to-earth humanist, and, the very personification of honesty, incorruptibility, simplicity, and decency. He would march in protest against all forms of injustice and institutionalized corruption. He literally marched in protest to his grave. The sage and visionary Awolowo said of him, 'If the yardstick for assessing the qualifiers for entry into Paradise were the qualities and character traits which Tai had in quantum and exhibited all his life, he would gain entry much more easily and earlier than some Bishops and Archbishops'.

Tai Solarin embarked on his illustrious teaching career under the principalship of S. O. Awokoya, another 'star' in the realm of education, at the Molusi

College in Ijebu-Igbo. Tai had just returned from England, brimming with ideas, and eager to instill his brand of education and ideas into the impressionable minds of the young generation of students, who virtually adored and worshipped him in spite of his seemingly way-out ideas, Bohemian dressing, and dogmatically atheistic utterances. The school's Board of Governors and the conservatively rigid parents of his pupils, who were uncompromising in their belief in the existence of God, could not tolerate his ways and his utterances. This led to a parting of ways between Tai and the establishment at Ijebu-Igbo, which disagreed with him.

Ijebu-Igbo's loss, however, became his native Ikenne's gain. At Ijebu-Igbo, Molusi College's door closed against Tai and his wife Sheila. However, the entrance into Ikenne exposed to them a vast expanse of land, full of prospects and opportunities. Tai and his wife Sheila lived like hermits and frontiersmen in a little hut on the land. They dreamed and turned their vision into a mission. They mapped out plans that they later translated into the Mayflower School in Ikenne. The educational impact the school would make could be best expressed by the calibre of students that have passed through its portals who have enriched the reservoir of quality human resources available to move me on as a nation.

As a social critic and activist, Tai Solarin was a thorn in the flesh of oppressors and human rights violators. He strove at every opportunity to inject his atheistic views and mores on issues and the society. He gave full literary flight to these issues of his in his weekly newspaper column 'Thinking With You' in the *Daily Times* and his 'must read' newspaper column 'Tai Solarin' in the *Sunday Tribune*. He quoted lavishly and copiously from such inveterate iconoclasts as H. G. Wells and Robert Ingersol to buttress and disseminate his personal views, which propelled him all his life. No piece can be meaningfully written on Tai Solarin without reference, no matter how brief, to his atheism. This fact could not be over-emphasised or ignored because he could mould the minds of his students and had a wide and knowledgeable readership of his column in the *Sunday Tribune*.

He considered that the body of a dead human being lying unattended to by the roadside should be treated with reverence and decency. Lagos City Council officials learned such lessons the hard way from Tai. He would neatly pack such a corpse into a makeshift coffin and deposit it on the grounds of the City Hall's compound. The putrid odour emanating from the decomposing body would send the appropriate sections scurrying to do Tai's silent bidding by immediately arranging to evacuate the corpse for burial.

He took certain actions that clearly delineated his views on the events and the persons involved. He complained bitterly about Gowon's lack of sensitivity when he, as Head of State, got married with much pomp and pageantry during the fiercest period of my civil war. This was at a time when my troops and rebel soldiers were dying at the war fronts, and kwashiorkor was killing hapless and orphaned children. Tai resigned his appointment as the Public Complaints Commissioner when he was arrested for not having his driving licence on him. By such an action, he demonstrated a unique example of resigning to acknowledge and accept responsibility or culpability. This noble step is still a rarity among my highly placed public officials, who would 'sit-tight' and cling desperately to office in spite of the dictates of decency and common sense.

He practically demonstrated the illogic and senselessness of declaring locally brewed gin (ogogoro) illegal. He argued that it was inconsistent to allow the brewing (tapping) of palm wine and yet ban locally brewed gin. He led the agitation to get it legalized and made its production not liable to punishment. He berated and decried the establishment of Unity Schools and the profligate proliferation of schools by the armed forces and the police. He saw this as an unwarranted and unjustifiable expenditure of public money. Solarin resigned his appointment as chairman of the People's bank when he discovered what he described as 'daylight robbery' being perpetrated by the board's management in collusion with some board members. He promptly apologized thereafter to his constituency—the people and his fellow activists—for being on that board.

He did not spare any erring or cheating public official. He was a warrior on the side of Justice and Democracy. It was remarkable that he never ran away into self-exile over any of his critical views as some other harassed government critics did. He never shied away from any major issues of the day. He always took a clear and unambiguous stand on any burning national issues. There was no topical national issue that was too big for his commentary. He never regretted any of his detentions, although he was detained several times for criticizing government policies. Such periods of detention always gave him the opportunity to judge things impartially and put them in their true perspective.

In his accustomed knickers and short-sleeved shirt, Tai marched in protest beside Wole Soyinka a few days before he succumbed to the asthma that had afflicted him all his adult life. Indeed, he died the way, and under the circumstances, he had always wanted: working, walking, and in fact, climbing. He was, at his own requested, hastily buried in his 'uniform'. His larger-than-life statue in his familiar work dress adorns the Yaba Bus Stop Square, Lagos, where he marched in several protests. It is in silent tribute to him that marches and protests now originate from that spot.

DELE AWOJOBI

Dele Awojobi was a social critic and a crusader for probity and accountability in governance. He had participated in these efforts long before they became pet phrases on the lips of my people and in the press. He was a brilliant mathematician and an affable orator and iconoclast. He was always clad in an immaculate suit complete with bow tie. He was admired and feared by his colleagues, adulated and hailed by adoring university students, and much loved and highly regarded by the teeming masses for his forthrightness and outspokenness on all topical issues of the day.

Awojobi was never a lawyer, but by avocation, he possessed the erudition of the 'learned friends' of the court, and he assiduously busied himself in research and litigation. Though he was a professor of mechanical engineering at the University of Lagos, he spent more time in the courts than most lawyers of his day. He instituted more than 10 suits against the Shagari administration and some Second Republic government functionaries without winning a single one of them, invariably for lack of locus standi. He was sneered at as a 'professional litigant' and was given to weeping when he lost case after case at the Federal High Court.

But through it all, his obsession for justice and fair play was apparent. Unfortunately, unlike lawyers who are trained in the art, he always got too emotionally involved and absorbed in his cases, which he opted to personally handle. The end result was always predictable, because he did not have the patience, quiet tenacity, and rational presentation style of a professional lawyer. By his serial litigations, his doggedness, his logic, his steadfastness, and his patriotism, Awojobi sought to expand the terrain of patriotism and the space for principles and fundamental human rights. He was badly missed by his admirers. He was considered as another unique soul allowed to be wasted in my land.

KEN SARO-WIWA AND MOSOP

The diminutive stature of Kenule 'Ken' Beeson Saro-Wiwa belied the phenomenal driving force that propelled him to strut and prance like an agile giant on the stage of human rights activism, environmental protection, and theatre arts production. As a writer, he was known for his novels *Soza Boy*, *Songs in a time of War*, *On a Darkling Plain*, *Prisoner of Jebs*, and *A Forest of Flowers*, among others. He was also well known as a playwright for his humorous TV presentations of the comical and witty series 'Basi and Company', for which he wrote about 60 scripts.

However, Ken Saro-Wiwa was best known for his civil rights activism and dogged fight for his fellow Ogonis, asserting their rights as a minority group and seeking redress for the many problems created by the exploratory activities of the oil companies operating within Ogoni land. Incessant oil spillages plus pollution from the heavy equipment and machineries of the oil explorers caused the devastation of fish-food and crop production. Oil companies explored and exploited without paying back, neither by providing nor improving scarce amenities. Ken therefore led the fight against ecological and environmental degradation as well as economic and political enslavement. He described the struggle as against 'foreign and domestic Colonialists', because he viewed my various governments as equally culpable of the same exploitation and neglect being carried out by the foreign oil companies.

Through the dramatic interplay of intellectualism and brilliant articulation of the collective ideas of the Ogonis, Saro-Wiwa internationalized the issue of the deprivation thrust on the Ogonis. He pricked the conscience of the world in various appearances at every available international forum, including the revered United Nations. It was to be expected that this activism, through its high profile organization, MOSOP (Movement for the Survival of the Ogoni People), would soon come into frequent and open confrontation with government. On his way to international stardom, backed by the fervent and loyal MOSOP, Saro-Wiwa garnered a variety of awards, including the 'Rights Livelihood Award', which is generally referred to as the Alternative Nobel Prize. He was also a winner of the 'Bruno Kriesky Award for Human Rights', The Hellene/Hammett Award given by Human Rights Watch, and the British Media Environmental Awareness Award.

Four of Saro-Wiwa's moderate colleagues in MOSOP were brutally murdered in terrible circumstances. They were labeled as 'vultures', a euphemism for saboteurs. As a result of these murders, the fury of the military security apparatus was unleashed on the Ogoni people in the name of investigations and peace-keeping. In the ensuing military confrontation and civil strife between the two factions of the warring MOSOP agitators, villages were torched. Scanty utilities were disrupted, and many lives were lost. Saro-Wiwa and a number of his more militant MOSOP members were apprehended and detained. A protracted murder trial conducted strangely by a military tribunal, culminated in the death sentence passed on eight members of the movement, including Ken Saro-Wiwa. International disapproval and condemnation, in addition to the 'loud' local murmurings that greeted the death sentence, raged on for weeks and fell on deaf ears.

The pervading atmosphere of gloom and terror cast on their trial before the tribunal pointed inexorably to the gallows for Saro-Wiwa and his colleagues. Gani Fawehinmi, the irrepressible human rights lawyer who represented them, complained bitterly about lack of access to his clients. He also questioned the rationale behind the overbearing and intrusive presence of soldiers sitting in on the discussions between lawyer and accused client. He protested that the same soldiers would eventually become prosecution witnesses. For his audacity in asking questions, Gani was roughed up, slapped, and manhandled. He was thereafter banned from coming to the Port Harcourt venue of the trials. He was 'repatriated' on the same plane that brought him from Lagos for describing the Tribunal as a 'kangaroo court'.

The Provisional Ruling Council (PRC) was hastily convened before the stipulated three months and before the submission of the Tribunal's proceedings. The reason for this indecent haste became obvious as the PRC quickly confirmed the death sentence. The gruesome execution by hanging took place on the same eve of the inaugural meeting of the Commonwealth Heads of States in Auckland, New Zealand. The execution was ill-considered and ill-timed and made then-British Prime Minister John Major describe it as 'judicial murder'. It attracted universal ire and condemnation from the international community, and it led to the summary and ignoble expulsion of Foreign Minister Tom Ikimi from the Conference. It was a most inglorious exit for an errant Foreign Minister who chose to fiddle in Auckland while his own roof was virtually on fire in Port Harcourt. Ikimi stormed out of the venue and Auckland, like a spoilt brat caught in the act.

The aftermath was predictable. Nelson Mandela was understandably irritated. My previous governments fought for Mandela's freedom from 27 years of imprisonment in apartheid South Africa. Indeed, I was regarded as being one of the five warring front-line states against the apartheid enclave. In the interest of justice and human dignity, Mandela spearheaded and gave more bite to the move by the aggrieved Commonwealth leaders to suspend Abacha's government from that august body. The Economic Union (EU) of European countries and the United States of America clamped limited sanctions on the government of Abacha. On my soil, the voice of dissent was muffled; the radical press and the unofficial opposition consisting of the pro-democracy activists could only bark and could not bite. I practically became a pariah state in the comity of nations.

BEKO RANSOME-KUTI

Beko Ransome-Kuti was a medical doctor by profession. He came from a vintage pedigree of nationalists and advocates of the tenets of democracy and human rights. Both his parents were in the forefront of education, nationalism, and constitution making. What Beko wrote, spoke, and agitated for in his human-rights-activist role, his globally acclaimed 'Afro-beat' musician brother, Fela, sang in satire and discussed in his 'yabis' (lampoon) sessions at his popular Afrika Shrine in Ikeja. Fela sang of the aspirations of the urban poor and gave articulation to their pent-up anger.

Beko was more busily involved in human rights affairs than he was in his medical practise. However, he fearlessly championed the welfare and rights of medical doctors with Ore Falomo under the umbrella of the Nigerian Medical Association (NMA) between 1976 and 1979. He possessed a nerve of steel under his deceptive, disarming, and cherubic choirboy looks. His cool and calm mien could only be ignored at the risk of inviting the pent-up fury of the Committee for the Defense of Human Rights (CDHR), which he and other human rights activists established. It was under his leadership that the Campaign for Democracy (CD) successfully coordinated civil action, staged as an aftermath of the annulled presidential elections of June 12, 1993.

In this particular demonstration, Beko exhibited fantastic organizational ability. He mobilized and galvanized the people into an unusual frenzy of civil disobedience and 'stay-at-home' compliance. During the time, economic and social activities were totally paralyzed. It was a resounding success, particularly in the South. Beko's successful action was reminiscent of Funmilayo Ransome-Kuti's (his mother's) crusade that drove Oba Ademola, the Alake of Egba, into exile in 1947. Similarly, the Beko-led civil disobedience contributed in no small measure to the 'step-aside' exit of Babangida.

Beko was an unrepentant and heady advocate of human rights and democracy. He was noted for his recalcitrance bordering on stubbornness in the face of daunting odds. He refused to be intimidated by security agents even though it was known that his health was worrisome at the time of his arrest. The paralytic bedlam that the civil disobedience, which was masterminded by the CD under Beko and unleashed on the business and social sectors of major cities brought out the worst from the politicians and the most gruesome murders from the military. The tamed, subdued, and thoroughly browbeaten civilian Governor Otedola of Lagos State unabashedly owned up on television to his inability to maintain law and order in the Lagos metropolis. Based on this admission, the Chief of Defense Staff, Abacha, unleashed the fury of the Lagos Brigade of Guards on the defenseless people of Lagos, mowing down 165 of them in cold blood in the process.

During Beko's tenure, the CD—the coalition of human rights bodies—became a household code word. The mere mention of it was enough to send chills down the spines of Babangida's security operatives. Even after his unconditional release from detention was made possible by Shonekan, Beko remained a tenacious thorn in the flesh of the ING as he remained committed to the crusade.

He opted for a sovereign national conference to redress the apparent imbalances in the federal structure and was in the struggle for a just and democratic structure in the society. It was in pursuit of such a cause that he forwarded (via fax) the self-prepared defense of Ralph Bello Fadile to the Commonwealth fact-finding group. Fadile was convicted during the coup trial. The spurious charge, which amounted to a travesty of due process of law, earned Bello Fadile 15 years in jail. Subsequent political developments led to his freedom, and he remained a prominent advocate of democracy until his death.

1 Gani Fawehinmi. He was a well-known lawyer and a foremost Human Rights activist. 'The rule of law' was his forte and battle cry. He was a thorn in the flesh of dictators and oppressors. He was a friend of the underprivileged and the downtrodden. He customarily fed and clothed the poor and beggars. He was arrested and detained several times. He was the publisher of the Weekly Law Review *which is sine qua non for both the Bench and the Bar and Law students. **2 Tai Solarin.** Educationist and Human Rights activist, social critic, newspaper columnist, and founder with his British-born wife, Sheila, of the prestigious Mayflower School. He was a stickler for propriety and well-ordered society which values human life.*

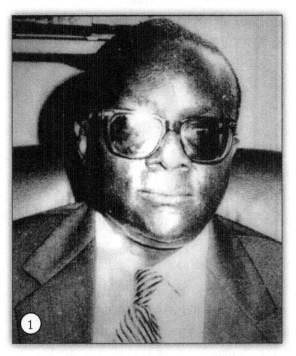

1 Beko Ransome-Kuti. *Chip off the old block from a family of Human Rights activists; agitator for propriety in governance. He was leader of Campaign for Democracy. What he agitated for in various marches his brother Fela Anikulapo-Kuti echoed in protest songs or during his 'yabis' in his African Shrine.* **2 Olise Agbakoba.** *Lawyer and iconic Human Rights activist; he was the first founding president of the Civil Liberties Organization. He deployed his vast knowledge of law against aberrant military governments and suffered all sorts of indignities and deprivations in the process.* **3 Femi Falana.** *Vibrant and outspoken lawyer, Human Rights activist, and President of Congress of Democratic Lawyers.* **4 Ayo Obe.** *President of Civil Liberties Organization. She lent a tough credibility as well as a feminine touch and charm to the activist's struggle against oppression and for fundamental Human Rights.*

FEMI FALANA

Femi Falana is a 'bird of the same feather' as the likes of Gani Fawehinmi and Beko Ransome-Kuti. The tough-talking and articulate lawyer—president of the National Association of Democratic Lawyers—is bold, erudite, and versed in the nuance of law, particularly as it affects human rights. He formed the third leg of the tripod on which my delicious human rights menu was being cooked. The Yorubas have a saying that 'A tripod on a furnace will never spill the boiling stew'. So it was with the formidable trio of Gani, Beko, and Femi, who were the first, second, and third legs of that solid tripod. They were usually marched together from police cells to prisons and detention centers. Falana was always persecuted and prosecuted for his persistent demand for the respect of human rights and the abrogation of unjustifiable laws.

Among several appearances in defense of the harassed and the oppressed, he successfully took up the case of *The News* magazine. In another instance, he won a landmark case brought by the *National Concord* editor, Nsikak Esien, against government closure of the newspaper's premises. During one of his arrests—following the struggle for the realization of the June 12 mandate—he expressed the hope that 'our political class will not betray our people this time around'. His hope was invariably misplaced. He was destined to be disappointed, because it appeared to him that the leaders of the winner's party blatantly sold their victory for a mess of pottage in the controversial Interim National Government contraption.

It was not by coincidence that some of them from the victorious Social Democratic Party (SDP) of M. K. O. Abiola were appointed as secretaries, either to assuage them or to keep their mouths shut. During his sojourn at Kuje prison—in the company of his usual co-travellers, Gani and Beko—Falana wrote to his wife and asserted, 'If they (Babangida's regime) decided to kill us, let them be prepared to be haunted by our ghosts. The struggle continues.' In a similar vein, when it was feared that the detained activists might be separated from one another away from Kuje prisons, Femi averred, 'Wherever we find ourselves, we shall remain as constant as the northern star. If they think they can cow us down with arrests and detention, they are deceiving themselves.' Such was the musing from the heart of a dedicated activist.

OLISA AGBAKOBA

Olisa Agbakoba is regarded generally as an icon in human rights activities. He was the founding president of the Civil Liberties Organization (CLO). He was instrumental in the struggle for democracy in my governance as a Nation. When the military had me in a stranglehold, Agbakoba stood out, deploying his knowledge of law in the fight against the arbitrariness of the military. In the process of the struggle, he paid dearly when he had to suffer indignities and deprivations. He was beaten up and incarcerated by the military junta for his role in the pro-democracy struggle. He was a prominent voice in the dark days of the military. He also led and took part in demonstrations and agitations for the military to return to the barracks.

There were other groups of activists that sprang up in the struggle for social justice and human rights. The names of their organizations, their characters, and their methods may differ, but they were all involved in the same clamour against hard-hearted governments bent on suppressing the voices of dissents and leaders of thought promoting the cause of fundamental human rights and social justice. These other groups included the Constitutional Rights Project (CRP) headed by Clement Nwankwo and the Universal Defenders of Democracy (UDD), founded and nurtured by the articulate Mike Ozekhome. The brilliant Ayo Obe led the CLO, bringing her charm and feminine touch to bear on the struggle. This feministic trend continues, with vibrant women like Okey Odumakin and Yemisi Ransome-Kuti meshing with their male counterparts and clearly demonstrating their civic competence and responsibility.

These groups exhibited unwavering faith in democracy and the rule of law. They pursued these twin tenets with immutable fixation, fighting their ways doggedly from the lower courts to the highest courts. Such was their determination in the interest of justice and democracy that neither temporary setbacks of justice delayed nor of justice denied deterred them. They became gadflies and menacing irritants which continually challenged the incessant constitutional aberrations of particularly the military governments. Several times, in defiance of the security harassments and the risks involved, they waged legal battles against bad legislations and ill-motivated decrees. They fought relentlessly against perceived military maladministration, executive irresponsibility, and arbitrary rules that run counter to democratic norms. Despite state harassments, intimidation, arrests, and detentions, the pro-democracy fighters remained unyielding. Their heads remained bloodied but unbowed, whatever the odds of pain, deprivation, or incarceration.

CHAPTER ELEVEN
APPRECIATION OF ACHIEVERS

As a Nation, I am blessed with an abundance of human resources. My exposure to education, particularly of the Western type, has broadened my outlook and increased the insatiable demand of my men and women to attain academic excellence and perfection in all areas of education and other academic endeavours. I appreciate excellence and bestow national merit awards to deserving individuals who excel in their various fields of academic or artistic endeavour—and particularly in the realms of science and the humanities. Alvan Ikoku, Obafemi Awolowo, Zik, Kashim Ibrahim, and 'The Teacher', Aminu Kano, were great pioneers and promoters of all that is best in education. I therefore indulge in some minor self-glorification by recounting the names and accomplishments of some of these men and women and bask in the sunshine of their achievements.

I am proud of the galaxy of stars in the legal profession. Since Sapara Williams blazed the trail as my first practicing lawyer ever, I have never had any regrets about my ability to produce enough lawyers not only to satisfy my demands but to extend their services to other African countries. By their sheer brilliance and erudition, some of my judges and lawyers can hold their own in name and reputation against or alongside their counterparts anywhere in the world. They display formidable skills and tremendous knowledge of the law, both when pronouncing landmark judgments or marshalling their arguments in support of their clients' claims. Some of them have long given meritorious service and achieved the highest honour in my legal profession: the Senior Advocate of Nigeria.

Take a bow, Teslim Elias, legal luminary and internationally acclaimed authority on Law and Jurisprudence. He bedazzled academia with his scholastic brilliance in many universities. He single-handedly set up and nurtured the Law Faculty in the University of Lagos, making it a nonpareil among the other universities even today. He initiated the idea of establishing the Nigeria Law School so that graduating lawyers may adapt their learning easily and practically to their local and indigenous environments. He rose from the position of the Minister of Justice and Attorney General to become the Chief Justice of the Federation. But Fate had played him a hard hand when he was summarily removed as the Chief Justice. Providence, the ultimate Judge and Arbiter, intervened and literally catapulted him to the exalted and sacrosanct Bench of the World Court in Vienna. He reached the apogee of excellence when he became the president of that august body. When Teslim Elias died, tributes from all over the world were showered on him in torrents from colleagues and staffers alike.

Rotimi Williams, legal icon and doyen of the legal profession of his era, earned his appellation 'Timi the Law' by virtue of his gargantuan presence and his prodigious expertise in constitutional law and advocacy. His keen and alert mind, encased in his eminently identifiable presence, made him a personality that could not be ignored in his legal role. Lawyers with such attributes normally have an edge in court. He had a personality which oozed respectability and confidence out of every pore. He was one of those in the legal profession whose names invoked fear in opposing lawyers and litigants while his reputation sent jitters down their spines. The crowning beauty of his distinguished career was his erudite advocacy.

In the legal field, one must admire the knowledge and masterly grasp of the theory and practise of law as exhibited by Louis Mbanefo, the clear thinking and incorruptibility of impartial Sir Charles 'Daddy' Onyeama, the erudition and scholarly chutzpah of Olakunle Orojo, the thoroughness of Andrew Obaseki, the linguistic grace of the quick-witted and philosophical Chukwudifu Oputa—fondly known as 'Socrates'—and the impeccable Udo-Udoma, who presided over affairs during one of the series of several constitution-drafting conferences.

In the same arena of law, one should not fail to mention the fearless and mercurial legal pundit, Akinola Aguda. Imbued with penetrating brilliance and intellectual depth, Aguda paraded his skills, first in far-away Botswana where he was appointed the country's pioneer Chief Justice and then returning home to head the Institute of Advanced Legal Studies. Aguda operated from an unassailably intelligent plane and expressed his views with panache and rare candour. He crusaded for legal purity. He was a thorn in the flesh of sit-tight military politicians. He could not hide his disgust for lazy, corrupt, and inept judges.

The tenacious logic of Anthony Aniagolu was most refreshing in an era of judicial activism under the pontificating influence of Ayo Irikefe, who then presided at the legal apex as the Chief Justice. Effervescent and scholarly Justice Kayode Esho became well known and highly respected for his in-depth analysis of any knotty legal issue because he always reasoned from his often unassailable minority stance. He boldly pointed an accusing finger at some 'cash-and-carry judges' who took money to 'guide' the course of justice. Olu Ayoola was another brilliant mind who moved on to preside over Gambian benches as Chief Justice. Ajose Adeogun similarly performed with distinction as the Chief Justice of Zambia.

Blessed with a coterie of brilliant and renowned economists, it is baffling that I have not been able to wade out of my troubled financial waters and find my way out of the morass into which the untutored minds of men in khaki uniforms have driven me. I stagger and wobble unsteadily, like a drunken sailor adrift on a rudderless ship on a stormy sea full of reefs and rocks of awaiting disaster.

The foremost economist of his time was the hoary-headed Pius Okigbo. He rendered useful advice and supported sound theories, which bounced off the undiscerning minds and ears of political and military administrators. Ayo Ogunsheye gave invaluable advice and service as Economic Adviser to succeeding governments.

Samuel Aluko advised various Western Regional governments during the era of Awolowo. His distinctive voice was the arrowhead which lent sobriety and commonsense to the old Ondo State government, which then included the current Ekiti State. He became a lone voice crying in the wilderness of confusion and aberration of the successive military governments. He gave teeth and fury to the barking bulldog that Abacha released to fight the cankerworm of mal-practice in the banking sector, Foreign Exchange manipulation, and general maladministration. Olakanpo was a brilliant economist whose ideas became in-valuable during the regime of Gowon.

Ojetunji Aboyade threw his weight and support behind Gowon's rehabilita-tion and reconstruction efforts following my painful civil war. Aboyade's genial warmth lit up the corridors of the United Nations when he went to the annual General Assembly meetings in an advisory capacity to my Permanent Represen-tative at the United Nations. He gave strong support and advice through which the indefatigable Samuel Adebo built a firm reputation for me and for himself on a dais of international adulation. This contributed significantly to Adebo's appointment as the director of United Nations Training and Research (UNITAR) after his retirement as my Permanent Representative to the United Nations. Aboyade was popularly referred to as 'our teacher' by his adoring students and other economists, who held him in the highest esteem. He was a foremost econ-omist, and he founded the Post Graduate School of Economics.

Akin Mabogunje became known not only as an expert in urban development but also as an authority on rural development. Along with Aboyade, he pio-neered the rudiments of poverty eradication and promoted small and medium-sized enterprises. They jointly co-authored programmes which they delineated in their book, *Optimal Community Development*.

Economists in the civil service should be recognised for their efforts to tackle the economic problems engulfing succeeding governments. Allison Ayida, who was first a permanent secretary at the Federal Ministry of Economic Devel-opment before becoming the Head of Service, embarked on the recruitment of young and brilliant graduates in the early 1960s. He showed his forward-look-ing adroitness in harnessing the best hands for government. He brought in 'young Turks' like the brilliant Dunni Teriba, 'International Yinkus' Orimolade, and the spectacularly brilliant Olu Falae, who later became a Federal Permanent Secretary, Head of Service, and a presidential candidate, in that order. Ayida also recruited Lola Osunsade whose economic genius was later to earn him a consultant status at the World bank.

Phillip Asiodu was another eminent Economist in my Federal Civil Service. The importance attached to his advisory capacity in the government of Gowon, was underlined by the fact that a plane had to be sent back to Lagos to fetch him to a Conference venue abroad, to offer advice on a knotty Economic issue. He was one of the elite permanent secretaries referred to as 'super perm-secs'. He later became the President of the Nigerian Economics Society.

Special mention must be made of Claude Ake, a renowned academic and activist of repute. He fought relentlessly for the down-trodden. Through his Center for Advanced Social Sciences (CASS), he canvassed democratic norms, values, purpose and structure. He was a member of the United Nations Economic Social and Cultural Organization (ENESCO) and a member of the 9-member team of African Directors of the World bank. He authored many books, including *Social Sciences as Imperialism*.

The Nigerian Institute for Social and Economic Research (NISER) was an engine room for powering the social and economic vehicle on which my economy rode. Among the brains who manned this engine house as director generals were the brilliant and resourceful H. M. A. Onitiri and the immensely successful and eminent scholar Dotun Duro-Phillips. Keziah Awosika was a Senior Research Fellow at NISER. She was the first African woman to obtain the Doctorate of Philosophy in Monetary Economics from Oxford University.

In the field of medicine, I have bestowed to the world some medical geniuses who commanded universal attention when they expounded on their specialties. Adeoye Lambo was a household name in psychiatric medicine. As a psychiatrist of international repute, he rose to become the Director General of the (United Nations) World Health Organization (WHO). He displayed his unique and sound knowledge in the admixture of the traditional and the orthodox in his treatment of psychiatric patients.

Lambo introduced the Aro village concept to the world. Aro is a sleepy little village at the outskirts of his hometown, Abeokuta. That was where he founded the popular Aro Psychiatric Hospital. Within the circles of world psychiatry, Aro probably had more name recognition than Lagos, Ibadan, or even Abuja. Aro's place on the world map was entirely due to the innovative and pioneering efforts of Adeoye Lambo. It has been said that by founding this centre, he had turned necessity into invention.

Rabid psychiatric cases were being cured at the Aro Psychiatric Hospital. He actually demonstrated his expertise on television when he held the viewing audience spellbound as he literally 'broke' and 'tamed' a raving lunatic. The patient became very tame and docile at the pristine incantations that poured out of the mouth of Lambo. He also delved into the use of acupuncture, thereby combining the occidental with the oriental and the indigenous African practise to evolve the sublime in medical healing.

Oladipo Akinkugbe is a world-acclaimed authority on hypertension, cardiovascular diseases, and nephrology. His gentle disposition, reassuring bedside comportment, and soothing voice are part of his therapeutic efforts that endear him both to his reassured patients and to the adoring clinical students who accompany him on his ward rounds, imbibing from him the knowledge and practise of medicine. He has the rare honour, distinction, and privilege of being the Vice Chancellor of two different frontline universities at different times. He was the first principal and then foundation vice chancellor of the University of Ilorin before he became the vice chancellor of Ahmadu Bello University of Zaria. He was later appointed as the Pro-Chancellor of the University of Port Harcourt. Because of his vast and knowledgeable developmental contributions as a university administrator, he is always invited to offer his invaluable experience and services in matters concerning universities and the setup of the colleges of medicine. Indeed, he was the first chairman of Joint Admission and Matriculation Board (JAMB).

Professor Akinkugbe became a member of various international medical and scientific panels and delivered series of lectures and papers at various conferences and universities all over the world. His expertise and vast knowledge based on scientific and clinical research made him a much sought-after intellectual in many academic fora in Europe, Asia, America and Africa.

Jubril Aminu was a gold medalist in medicine as a medical student at the University College of Ibadan (UCI). After a stint as a university administrator, he was appointed as the secretary of the National Universities Commission. He later became the vice chancellor of the University of Maiduguri. As a tribute to his versatility and enlightened nature, he was appointed first as the Federal Minister of Education, then later as the Federal Minister of Petroleum and Natural Resources. He had a stint in diplomacy, when he was appointed as my ambassador to Washington. Finally, as if that were not enough, he delved into politics and was elected as a member of the House of Senate.

Kayode Osuntokun was a distinguished neurosurgeon and medical scholar par excellence. He achieved a series of 'firsts' as the first African to obtain a doctorate (DSc) in neurology from the University of London. He was the first black to win the Charles Drew Medical Prize and the first black examiner at the Royal College of Physicians in London. Osuntokun became a professor at the relatively tender age of 35. He was acclaimed in 1994 as one of the 10 best neurosurgeons in the world. This global recognition acknowledged him as a surgeon at the apogee of excellence. He was an outstanding medical scholar imbued with sheer and almost effortless brilliance. The foundation for this dazzling brilliance had been laid at Christ's School, Ado Ekiti, where he set an all-but-unbeatable record of 9 distinctions in 9 subjects at the (Cambridge) School Certificate Examinations in 1951. He made outstanding contributions in the general field of medicine and in neurology in particular. He put African neurology on the world map. He was an astute administrator as the Provost of the University College Hospital, Ibadan. International health organizations, especially the World Health Organization (WHO), held Osuntokun in high esteem. He served the world body for over 20 years.

Bello Osagie was an eminent and professionally well connected gynecologist. He is long remembered for the fact that he was best known for delivering almost all the babies born at the State House since the era of Gowon. Vincent Aimaku was another reputable gynecologist, and he rose to become the first vice chancellor of Ekpoma University. Olikoye Ransome-Kuti was the protagonist and nurturer of the Primary Health Care Service. He became Federal Minster of Health.

Olugbenga Fadayomi possesses a very lucid medical mind and has run some of the best private medical diagnostic centers in Africa. He is a cardiologist of international acclaim. His clientele includes the movers and shakers in government and industry. It became a curious fact that the entire neighbourhood of the vast Tafawa Balewa Square complex in Lagos where he operated his clinic was almost always thrown into a frenzy of security activities whenever any of his powerful patients came in for consultation, particularly during the military regimes. It is proof positive of his competence and global acclaim that doctors from the popular Harley Street clinics in London, reputed for their professional competence, often refer Nigerian patients back to him for his expert attention.

Ashiru and Shobowale are the fantastic duo that embarked on, and actualized, some of the most successful test tube experiments in IVF (in-vitro fertilization) in Black Africa. Adeloye was a neurosurgeon of wide acclaim. Oluwasanmi became the first plastic surgeon in Nigeria.

Eneli, Kuku, and Obioha are three industrious medical geniuses who established a joint medical hospital in Ikeja. The Eko Hospital was named as an acronym of the first letters of their names. The hospital is so well organized and so efficiently run that it was recommended for use as a clinical education center for clinical students and housemanship from the university teaching hospitals. The Eko Hospital soon became the first publicly quoted of its type in the Capital Market.

In the mid-1980s, quite a good number of brilliant medical doctors migrated into the fabulously lucrative services of the Saudi Arabian kingdom medical institutions. The movement towards greener pastures by the medical 'flock' soon became a stampede, and my colleges of medicine were to suffer avoidable losses as a result of the ensuing 'brain drain'. Fortunately, this mass migration soon became a blessing in disguise through the resultant exposure of these professionals to the vastly superior and more sophisticated equipment available in Saudi Arabia. The migrating professionals simply acquitted and excelled themselves there. They attested to the fact that they could hold their heads high and rub shoulders with the best anywhere in the world in their chosen fields, especially when given the right equipment and environment. Indeed, some of them have moved on from there to take up positions of great eminence at the World Health Organization (WHO) in Geneva, Switzerland. The most outstanding example is Oluwole Akande, who was once the provost of the University College Hospital (UCH) in Ibadan.

The list of profound intellectual minds and scholarly administrators is endless. Kenneth Dike, a trail-blazer in his own right, became the first indigenous vice chancellor of the first and premier University College of Ibadan (UCI). He encouraged and instilled confidence into the senates of subsequent universities to put the mantle of academic leadership on more indigenous academics, both male and female. Dike was a historian of great depth and was adept at research education.

The prestigious list of university administrators and vice-chancellors includes the affable and knowledgeable Ajose; the world acclaimed psychiatrist Adeoye Lambo; the deep-thinking scientist Eni-Njokwu; Saburi Biobaku, who reigned as the vice chancellor of the University of Lagos with scholarly brilliance; the agricultural scientist Oluwasanmi, whose pioneering efforts saw the University of Ife, now Obafemi Awolowo University (OAU), through its teething stages. The others were the scholarly Oritsejelomi Thomas, the historian Tamuno, and arguably the most versatile of them all, Oladipo Akinkugbe, whose pioneering performance at Ilorin eminently recommended him to occupy the 'reserved' seat at the Ahmadu Bello University, which had hitherto been the exclusive preserve of foreign scholars and Northerners.

Professor Ade-Ajayi was so versed in African history that he made the teaching of the subject very attractive to myriads of adoring students. He had the neat and scholarly mind of an authority in his specialized field. The custodians of tradition in Yorubaland have been known to consult him in order to set the record straight on certain contentious traditional and historical issues. He rose to become the vice chancellor of the University of Lagos. Ishaya Audu was a professor of obstetrics and gynecology. He became the vice chancellor of the Ahmadu Bello University in Zaria. He later gave a good account of himself when he was appointed Minister of Foreign Affairs. Professor Wande Abimbola, a proficient Ifa (occult) exponent, was a vice chancellor and later a member of the House of Senate. Colleges of medicine have provosts at the apex of administration. Such positions have been graced in the past by the likes of the pioneering Elebute, the distinctive and erudite Oladejo Dosekun, and the world-acclaimed scholar Kayode Osuntokun.

I have had still other high achievers in their respective fields. The cultured and internationally acclaimed structural engineer, Professor Ife Oladapo, whose vast knowledge was tapped by construction firms for the delicate art of making foundation structures for bridges, also became the first vice-chancellor of the University of Ado Ekiti. The incisively brilliant geologist, Fred Adegoke, the legal luminary, Arthur Nwabueze, and the creative, artistic, and historically popular sculptor Ben Enwonwu, who sculpted the magnificent statue of Queen Elizabeth that sat majestically in front of the old National Assembly buildings in Lagos, were among my most brilliant minds.

Chike Obi was one of the foremost mathematicians of his time. He was born a genius and died a genius. His legacies in the world of mathematics are unforgettable. He was also involved in politics and had a stint as an elected member of both my Federal House of Representatives and the Eastern Regional House of Assembly. He lectured first at the University of Ibadan before attaining the post of an associate professor and full professor of mathematics at the University of Lagos in 1971. He was dean of the faculty of science in 1980 and became emeritus professor of the university in 1985. At one stage, his name became synonymous with brilliance in mathematics. Any schoolboy who showed brilliance in his mathematics studies promptly got nicknamed 'Chike Obi'.

Chike Obi was a Fellow of the Nigerian Academy of Science. He won the Ecklund Prize from the International Center for Theoretical Physics for original works in differential equations and for pioneering works in mathematics in Africa. During the twilight years of the last century, he astounded the world when, without the aid of a computer, he solved a 358-year-old puzzle: Fermat's Last Theorem, posed by the Frenchman Fermat. What made the achievement more outstanding was the fact that Obi's research was conducted at his Onitsha-based Nanna Institute of Scientific Studies. His celebrated work was published in many international journals.

The unsurpassed innovation of Phillip Emeagwali in the Internet world placed him on the pedestal of great inventors in the field of computer technology. He was the unsung icon and the undisputed father of massive parallel computing technology, which spawned supercomputers and the Internet phenomenon. He was a mathematician and scientist, also described as 'the father of the Internet'. The former American President Bill Clinton called him 'the Bill Gates of Africa' when he visited me in 1999. Emeagwali earned these accolades because he discovered a formula that enabled supercomputers, powered by 65,000 electronic brains called 'processors', to perform the world's fastest calculations. This formula inspired the reinvention of the supercomputer, which cost about $400 million apiece. Powered by 65,000 processors, these machines performed a billion calculations per second and were pivotal to the operation of the Internet.

Through research, he found a machine called the Connection Machine at a laboratory in Los Alamos. The machine had sat unused after scientists had given up trying to figure out how to make it simulate nuclear explosions. The machine was designed to run 65,536 interconnected microprocessors. Emeagwali set the parameters and ran a programme. The result was the correct computing of the amount of oil in a simulated reservoir. This fantastic machine turned out to be capable of performing 3.1 billion calculations per second.

The crux of this prodigious discovery was that Emeagwali had programmed each of the microprocessors to talk to each neighbouring microprocessor at the same time. This record-breaking experiment meant that there was now a practical and inexpensive way to use machines to speak to each other all over the world. Within a few years, the oil industry had seized upon this idea then called the Hyperball International Network. This virtually created a worldwide web of ultra-fast communication.

This discovery garnered Emeagwali about 30 awards within 15 to 20 years. The prestigious Gordon Bells prize, the 'Nobel Prize' of Supercomputing, was awarded to him in 1989. His fantastic invention helped pave the way for the Internet, and this generated headlines across the world. It made mathematicians rejoice and caused the whole of Africa in general—and me in particular—to beam with great pride. In 1998, he received the Distinguished Scientist Award from the World bank. I feel very proud that by his outstanding achievements, he was not only one of the greatest Africans who ever lived but also one of the greatest scientists of all time. He is in the distinguished company of the greatest scientific minds, like Isaac Newton and Archimedes.

I can also boast of some dazzlingly brilliant women—academicians and geniuses who have excelled in various fields. The strict mathematician Grace Alele-Williams was the first female vice chancellor of a University where she stood at the helm of affairs at the University of Benin for two four-year terms. There was the brilliant professor of law, Jadesola Akande, who became the vice chancellor of Lagos State University. Reading through Jadesola's *curriculum vitae* was like reading an engrossing paperback novel. Her learned contributions to the various international and local journals of law were a reflection of her neat and distinguished scholarly mind. She later became the president of the Association of African Women for Research and Development. She was an eminent member of the International Federation of Women Lawyers and of the International Law Society. She was an unrelenting women's rights crusader. She used various platforms and opportunities to advocate for an end to all forms of gender-based discrimination and violence. She continually strove to change the lot of the average African woman, starting with the girl child. She was appointed as the pro-chancellor of the Federal University of Technology in Akure.

Another woman of unique distinction is Adetoun Ogunsheye, the first female professor in my academic annals. She was for many years the chief librarian of the magnificent University of Ibadan Library. Francesca Yetunde Emanuel became the trailblazer for women's progress and development as she was appointed the first female Administrative Officer in 1959. She later became the first Federal Permanent Secretary in 1975. She became the first female Federal Permanent Secretary in 1975. She brings flair, integrity, and a solid work ethic to her job. Parenthetically, she is also an acclaimed singer. Bolanle Awe was an erudite, refreshingly brilliant, and well-versed professor of history. She also distinguished herself at the Institute of African Studies, where she left her mark indelibly as an authority and reference point on the course of African history then, now, and in the future. Abimbola Odugbesan became the first female rector of the Yaba College of Technology. She owned an impressive array of academic and professional laurels as a master city planner.

Dr. Hajia Ladi Kwali, the gifted pottery artist of Kwali and Suleja, was honoured with a well-deserved doctoral degree from Ahmadu Bello University. She thereafter reached the acme of her distinguished and creative career when she was honoured with my National Merit Award. Because she was not literate, her dexterity in pottery-making and the general artistic development of her natural talents was not polluted by the caprices of modernity and schooling. She made high-quality pots, delicately beautiful earthenware containers, and other pottery creations of various shapes and descriptions. Her works and creations were smuggled at giveaway prices to Europe and America where they attracted fabulous prices. Some of her works still adorn the Suleja Pottery Center, some State Houses, the National Museum, and the Institute of African Studies. Her works have been an eloquent testimony to the painstaking self-development of raw and natural talents.

CHAPTER TWELVE

AUTHORS AND LITERARY GIANTS

I see myself as a Nation blessed with an array of literary giants, prolific writers, and highly imaginative authors. One of my favorites, D. O. Fagunwa, had a fertile brain that created spell-binding yarns about the *Ogboju Ode ninu Igbo Irunmale*, which Wole Soyinka (whose literary efforts will be discussed later—see Chapter Thirteen) translated literally as Forest of a Thousand Demons. It is also remarkable that Wale Ogunyemi produced the stage adaptation of Fagunwa's *Oke Langbodo*. His 1949 *Igbo Olodumare* (Forest of God) was a masterpiece in which Fagunwa's imagination soared and created some awesome images in folklore. Though his works were written in the Yoruba language, Fagunwa was a master in the art of cliff-hanging narration and an authority on Yoruba cultural folklore and tradition. He authored many books, all of which turned out to be masterpieces. In his writings, he usually conjured picturesque cultural settings and backgrounds. He displayed masterful use of proverbs and pithy sayings. He also employed rich and flowery expressions and imageries in coining memorable names and nicknames.

Some of his highly imaginative and meaningful appellations included the following:

- *Kako, oni kumo ekun* (Kako, the one with the tiger's cudgel)
- *Alagbede Orun* (hell's blacksmith)
- *Ajantala* (alias for a fabulous wrestler)
- *Ojola Ibinu* (the irritable python)

- *A ta koro wo'nu ado* (the blithesome one that romps into the small gourd)

These images and mythical characters brilliantly created by Fagunwa were beautifully sketched and captioned in Fagunwa's books. For example, the harrowing sketch of Ojola Ibinu, the irritable python, has a head with the contorted and hideous face of a human being popping out on top of the spirally coiling body and tail of a long python. This fearsome image could only be the brainchild of a literary genius.

I am a Nation blessed with literary icons like Chinua Achebe, who sat daintily on the highest pedestal in the gathering of my literary giants. I have become a nation that revels in the successes and remarkable achievements of my eminent citizens. Achebe was an internationally acknowledged writer and novelist whose works achieved universal acclaim and wide readership in about sixty languages. President Jimmy Carter of the United States of America once pointed out that his reading of Chinua Achebe's *Things Fall Apart* afforded him a much deeper perspective of the African cultural setting. Achebe's writings reflect culture, dwell on the morés of society, and emphasize the bond that holds them all together. Achebe's redoubtable corpus was his smooth-flowing prose.

Achebe was best known as an eagle—an eagle that perched atop the Iroko of Africa's literary forest. His books stand out as referential materials on African literature. Though he was essentially a writer and a teacher, Achebe's greatest legacy to African literature is the founding and editing of Heinemann's African writer series. This became the launching pad from which budding African writers could take off on their flights of fancy and carry their creative imagination to other parts of the world. Through this medium, he offered an outlet to such talents as Flora Nwakpa, Chinweizu, Chidi, and the late soldier–poet, Maman Vatsa.

Achebe founded the Association of Nigerian Authors (ANA) in 1980. The association forms an umbrella for young authors, affording them the opportunity that enables their literary acumen to blossom and flourish. It is the literary works from such authors that explore my literary horizon to the fullest. Annual prizes were instituted to realize these objectives. Beneficiaries of such awards include Osofisan, Bode Sowande, Zulu Sofola, and the late Ken Saro-Wiwa.

Achebe exhibited a high-voltage talent in the exploration of his themes and in the conceptualization of his plots, which were always excellent. There is a sort of literary continuum in his books, as one theme leads to another. His stories are gripping, suspenseful, and punctuated with irony and captivating cultural and political anecdotes. His three early works, *Things Fall Apart, No Longer at Ease*, and *The Man of the People*, present the picture of pre-Colonial and post-Colonial African society in an exciting style that is vintage Achebe.

It is clear that all the ideas embedded in *Things Fall Apart*—the major and minor characters and the scenes and plots—were all fiction. Yet it is no longer disputable that the book, in its entirety, has come to represent the story of the African people: African peoples came across their white counterparts in the form of a marriage of cultures. As a result of this, one culture tried to subsume the other. This situation led to the death of the people's hero, Okonkwo. With his death, a yawning gap was created in his native Umuofia, a local place that in many ways represents the totality of the black race.

Achebe received my National Merit Award in 1981. *Things Fall Apart* not only showed the way but challenged the many misconceptions and misrepresentations of Africa by the Europeans. The book also inspired other African writers to see their own history as authentic and worthy of being documented for posterity. The book attained a pinnacle of excellence that incontrovertibly ranks it among the foremost African literary books of all time.

Gabriel Okara is an award-winning poet and a profound thinker. As one of the patriarchs of my indigenous literature, his deep land-marking contributions made him worthy of the accolades and honour bestowed on him in the *Encyclopedia Britannica*. He was listed as the first significant English language Black African poet to write in a modern style. He became my first writer to publish in and join the editorial staff of the influential journal *Black Orpheus*. His writing was further described as a link between colonial poetry and the rigorous modernist writing that manifested itself around the time of my independence in 1960. Okara's short story, 'The Iconoclast', won him his first prize in 1954. His poem, 'The Call of the River Nun', won him yet another prize towards the end of the 1960s. The poetry collection, 'The Fisherman's Innovation', won him the Commonwealth Prize in 1978 and established him as a distinctive voice.

Okara's remarkable novel, *The Voice*, was published in 1964. The novel attempted to directly convey and translate his thoughts and stories from his mother tongue into English. He believed that language was a vehicle of thought

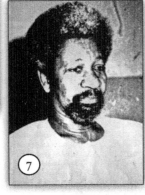
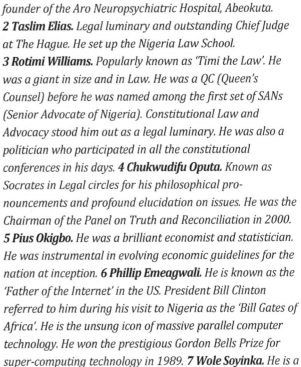

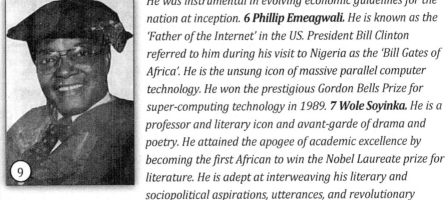

1 Adeoye Lambo. *Internationally acclaimed psychiatrist and founder of the Aro Neuropsychiatric Hospital, Abeokuta.*
2 Taslim Elias. *Legal luminary and outstanding Chief Judge at The Hague. He set up the Nigeria Law School.*
3 Rotimi Williams. *Popularly known as 'Timi the Law'. He was a giant in size and in Law. He was a QC (Queen's Counsel) before he was named among the first set of SANs (Senior Advocate of Nigeria). Constitutional Law and Advocacy stood him out as a legal luminary. He was also a politician who participated in all the constitutional conferences in his days.* **4 Chukwudifu Oputa.** *Known as Socrates in Legal circles for his philosophical pro-nouncements and profound elucidation on issues. He was the Chairman of the Panel on Truth and Reconciliation in 2000.*
5 Pius Okigbo. *He was a brilliant economist and statistician. He was instrumental in evolving economic guidelines for the nation at inception.* **6 Phillip Emeagwali.** *He is known as the 'Father of the Internet' in the US. President Bill Clinton referred to him during his visit to Nigeria as the 'Bill Gates of Africa'. He is the unsung icon of massive parallel computer technology. He won the prestigious Gordon Bells Prize for super-computing technology in 1989.* **7 Wole Soyinka.** *He is a professor and literary icon and avant-garde of drama and poetry. He attained the apogee of academic excellence by becoming the first African to win the Nobel Laureate prize for literature. He is adept at interweaving his literary and sociopolitical aspirations, utterances, and revolutionary commitments.* **8 Oladipo Akinkugbe.** *Professor and Internationally acclaimed academician and authority on hypertension and cardiovascular diseases. He has the unique distinction and honour of being Vice Chancellor of two different Universities, the University of Ilorin and Ahmadu Bello University. He is an experienced University Administrator and was the first chairman of JAMB.* **9 Kayode Osuntokun.** *He was a distinguished neurosurgeon. An outstanding academician who was the first black to win the Charles Drew medical prize. He became a professor at the age of 35. He was also acclaimed to be one of the best 10 neurosurgeons in the world.*
10 Kenneth Dike. *The first and indigenous Vice Chancellor of the premier university, the University of Ibadan, where he had also been the Principal when it was then the University College of Ibadan. He is a trail blazer for subsequent string of Nigerian dons that became University Vice Chancellors.* **11 Chike Obi.** *He was a professor and the first indigenous mathematician of vast international acclaim and a Fellow of the Nigerian Academy of Science. He won the Ecklund prize from the International Center for Theoretical Physics for his work on differential equation.*

1 HMA Onitiri. *He was the Director- General of the Nigeria Institute of Social and Economic Research, which was the engine room of the Nigeria Planning Commission.* **2 Grace Alele-Williams.** *Strict administrator and professor of mathematics, she became the first female Vice Chancellor of a university in Nigeria when she served two 4-year terms in the University of Benin.* **3 Jadesola Akande.** *She was a professor and the first female Vice Chancellor of Lagos State University. She was also the President of Association of Women in Research and Development.* **4 Ngozi Okonjo-Iweala.** *She rose to the exulted position of World Bank Managing Director. She was also Federal Minister of Finance and briefly of External Affairs, 2003-2006.*
5 Keziah Awosika. *The first African woman to obtain a Doctorate of Philosophy in Banking and Money from Oxford University in 1973. She was a Senior Research Officer at the Nigerian Institute of Social and Economic Research. She is also a Director at the Nigerian Women Law and Development Center.* **6 Liadi Kwali.** *The gifted pottery genius of Kwali and Suleja. She made with sheer dexterity high quality pots and beautiful earthenwares. She was honoured with a doctoral degree at the Ahmadu Bello University, Zaria.*

and culture. He saw his use of language as one of the important tools to retain my peoples' culture, despite the intimidating ubiquity of Western civilization. Cultural preservation is made possible by language. He saw my languages going into extinction as a result of the wholesale adoption of the English language as my *lingua franca*.

Cyprian Ekwensi's writing career began with his first published work *When Love Whispers*, which explained the episodic nature of his subsequent novels. The graphic details of his settings might have projected his works to the league of realism. In his exploration of the appeal of city life and the treatment of ordinary folks, which he sometimes drew from the rural settings, his works attained the level of great significance. He had a down-to-earth way of writing about the natural behaviour of people from my various tribes. In his widely read novel *Jagua Nana*, Ekwensi explored the life of a middle-aged prostitute, Jagua Nana, and compared the old, traditional life and its modern urban equivalent. It is the reflection of a movement amidst the corrupt and pleasure-seeking life of the city and the pastoral rural life.

He continued with this preoccupation in some of his other novels. These included *Burning Grass, People of the City, Locotown, Beautiful Feathers, Restless City and Christmas Gold, Survive the Peace,* and *Jagua Nana's Daughter*. In recognition of his writings, he received the Dag Hammarskjöld International Peace Prize for literary merit. The icing on his cake of literary achievements was a lifetime award given to him by the Nigerian Academy of Letters (NAL).

Amos Tutuola's *The Palm-Wine Drinkard* broke new ground in combining folklore with imaginative narration. London-based Ben Okri won the prestigious British Booker Prize for *The Famished Road* in 1991.

The emergence of Grace Itayemi with her *Nigerian Folklore Stories* in the 1950s underlined the well known literary fervour and skill of my female authors, which blossomed and flourished with comparative elegance and fluency as did their male counterparts' styles. The contributions of women like Florence Nwakpa, Mabel Segun, Zulu Sofola, Buchi Emecheta, Helen Ovbiagele, Catherine Acholonu, and others were noticeable ones. However, women's impact on the scene seemed to suffer a setback. Critiques opined that at one point, they seemed to be more preoccupied with topical feminist concerns, which impeded their literary acceptability. For instance, it was erroneously thought that a situation in which female intelligentsia and academicians devoted much of their attention to gender issues would numb and stultify their interests and creativity in other areas. Happily, it became increasingly apparent that the end would justify the means. Their noble goal was to gain political leverage and ascendance in order to ensure that doors would be open to allow women take their proper places in the scheme of things. This made the brilliant and enterprising Dora Chizea suppose that a woman should be one of the vice presidents in my Fourth Republic.

In an effort to enhance the possibility of attaining loftier heights, an association of female writers known as Women Writers in Nigeria was created. It was formed to create literary awareness among them and to provide common ground for the actualization of literary dreams among prospective female writers. The association was also planned to provide a forum for the polishing of literary skills and ideas among prospective female writers. It planned to publish a biannual journal of women's writings and critique female literary writing and women-related literary works. Its future is still very rosy, and I look forward to the day when my female writers take their proper places in my literary scene. Happily, I now have a generation of new writers and artists who are attracting international rave reviews. These include Chimamanda Adichie and Helen Oyeyemi among others.

CHAPTER THIRTEEN

CULTURE: DRAMA AND MUSIC

Many notable actors and actresses have contributed their share to drama-
tizing and portraying my culture on stage and in some theatres and halls
across my territory. The ancestors and progenitors of various clans and communities were animated in stories told under the moonlight. These stories were
adapted into plays and dramatized by gifted and versatile actors and actresses.
Hubert Ogunde was the undisputed father of theatre artists and the doyen of
stage and drama. He was the first person to put together a drama troupe, which
travelled far and wide, showcasing the richness of my culture in operatic dramas.

Ogunde in his dramas mirrored the society of his time. He reflected the beauty,
grace, elegance, and diversity of songs, dances, attire, and values of that era. He
used the stage on several occasions to comment on current affairs, to articulate
the views and criticisms of the common man, to offer advice, and to comment on
the morals and mores of society, particularly those of his Yoruba tribe. Ogunde
created an operatic satire on the bullets that mowed down the Enugu coal miners, who met their untimely deaths in the hands of the colonialist agents in
1949. This was during the time the mine workers were on strike for better pay
and better working conditions. Ogunde put on stage an operatic drama which
sermonized that 'Bread is better than bullets'.

He bemoaned the internal wranglings which rocked the unity of the Yorubas when the excesses perpetrated during 'operation weti e' (riots and arson)
of the middle 1960s led to the declaration of a state of emergency in the defunct
Western Region. He promptly went on stage with a message urging the Yorubas

to 'put on their thinking caps' (*Yoruba ronu*). To drive his message home, he composed and recorded a song of the same title, which he rendered in his rich and distinctive baritone. The lyrics of the song were offensive and irksome to the fidgety and oversensitive powers of the day; the sale of the record was banned. Playing the record on the State Radio was definitely out of the question. The pain of censorship and bans became gain for Ogunde as the record became so popular and sought-after that they were sold heavily from hidden shelves.

Ogunde graduated from stage to cinema screens. His works and productions packed the cinema houses in many towns and cities. It was remarkable that in an attempt to keep his team of talented stage and film actresses intact, he married some of them. He made both the actors and actresses happy, well exposed and well remunerated. He kept the troupe together, particularly the actresses, for about four decades. Like vintage wine, the troupe got even better with age and experience. They enjoyed greater adulation and admiration from their teeming and adoring fans. Ogunde endeavoured with enduring success to portray my culture on stage, in costumes, in the invocation of my ancestral spirits, in the use of pithy sayings and adages, and in glamourizing my heroes of yesteryears.

Both Ogunmola and Duro Ladipo learned and perfected their stagecraft under the tutelage of the incomparable Ogunde. It is noteworthy that Duro Ladipo's scintillating presentation of 'Oba Ko So' re-enacted with chilling similitude the circumstances that led to the death of the legendary Alaafin. This particular stage and screen presentation attracted rave reviews locally and internationally. As a creative theatre practitioner, Duro wrote and staged more than 30 plays, which had the potency of recreating and celebrating black African culture and awareness.

Other actors and actresses were to follow on stage, in cinema, and on television. The versatile cultural icon, Segun Olusola, created the 'Village Headmaster' television series. The series brought joy, laughter, and eager viewing into many homes on the National Television Network. The cast included fabulous actors like the punctilious headmasters Ted Mukoro and Femi Robinson; teachers 'Jegede' Shoyode and 'Oghene'; the discerning and fatherly 'Oba Fagade'—Dejumo Lewis; the mercurial and quarrelsome 'Chief Eleyimi' Funso Adeolu; and Wole Amele, the argumentative and irascible 'Mr. Know-all' counsellor, Balogun—the last two actually became Obas in real life in their respective towns later in their lives.

Some other 'Village Headmaster' stars included the tattling gossip 'Amebo' Ibidun Allison; the stern matronly seamstress' Aunty Clara, Elsie Olusola of fragrant memory; the palace messenger and jester, shaven-headed 'Gorimapa'; the rascally and smart-talking 'Lakunle' Lai Ashadele, (who showed immense aptitude for drama and honed his art from his Ibadan Grammar School days); Justus Esiri, who continues to ply his genial and expressive role as a Nollywood star; Joe Layode; the store keepers and exponents of pidgin English 'Bassey' Jab Adu and Ekaete; and grim faced Igbo pidgin English speaker, 'Okoro', Jimi Johnson. Most remarkably, the drama series depicted the customary setting of a typical but imaginary village where people of various ethnic backgrounds relate and cohabit. The fictional activities of some of the villagers featuring the headmaster and his wife, the Oba, local Chiefs, local councilors, and the village dispenser were highlighted.

Many soap opera actors and actresses have been seen to strut across television screens in serialized dramas like 'Mirror in the Sun', 'Checkmate', 'Supple Blues', The Third Eye', 'Ripples', 'Behind the Clouds', 'Cock Crow at Dawn', 'Fortunes', and the popular and hilarious 'New Masquerades'. The latter play brought together a collection of actors and actresses whose accents and intonations reflected the accents and mannerisms of various ethnic groups different from theirs. The play also exemplified the day-to-day use of 'malapropisms'—when the English language is juxtaposed with the local dialects to evolve a ludicrous and very funny misuse of words. The most notable exponent of this is Chika Okpala, popularly known as 'Zebrudiah' alias 4.30.

The brain behind these productions must be recognized. Bayo Oduneye came into prominence during FESTAC and later became the director of the National Troupe. In this capacity, he produced several stage plays and led the National Troupe to perform and to display my culture in faraway lands. Also, Ola Balogun wrote and directed many stage and screenplays, and he won some awards and citations at international film festivals. Ola Rotimi is another ace at play writing and directing. Rasheed Gbadamosi, an economist, industrialist, and versatile and accomplished personality, is also a playwright. Lola Fani-Kayode and Zulu Sofola were successful stage directors and playwrights. Lola became a talk show host on television during which she exuded dignified simplicity in her impeccable taste.

The beauty of my cultural background and the impact which it has brought to bear on the local and international scenes cannot be adequately discussed if I do not make an eminent mention of one of the greatest literary icons of our time. After all, a popular adage says, 'The big masquerade reserves his turn to dance till the very end of the show to bring the curtains down'. He is the effervescent and prolific literary giant and Nobel Laureate, Wole Soyinka. He bestowed to posterity such memorable and hilarious plays as 'Kongi's Harvest', 'The Road', 'Death and the King's Horseman', and 'Brother Jero' among others. Soyinka's forte is both drama and poetry. He is a multi-faceted genius—a writer, a poet, a dramatist, and a humanist. 'Our own WS' (wasn't William Shakespeare also 'WS'?) was celebrated here within my territory and highly honoured and recognized for his literary works on the international plane. Indeed, he held international press conferences from his Abeokuta homestead. His path to the pinnacle of intellectualism and international acclaim was rough.

An *enfant terrible* of sorts as a youth, he had the temerity to hold up the Ibadan Radio Broadcasting Station to draw attention to or arrest the drift towards the abyss into which the Western Region was being shoved. He was said to have produced his own prerecorded cassette, revolver in hand, not only to prevent a recorded broadcast by Premier S. L. Akintola to the beleaguered people of the Western Region but also to halt and negate the announcement of the alleged winner of the massively rigged election which bestowed victory to S. L. Akintola's National Democratic Party. Soyinka's penchant for bravado was evident when he joined the Victor Banjo-led 'Third Force' during my civil war. This resulted in his subsequent arrest and extended incarceration by Gowon's government. He wrote his memorable book, *The Man Died*, during his confinement. It was a reproachful dialectic on contemporary events.

During his short sojourn as a student in the University College of Ibadan (UCI), as it was then known, he founded the Pirates Confraternity. Of course, he could not have known at the time that he was unwittingly creating a heinous monster that was to bedevil and blight my universities in later years. His Confraternity splintered and mushroomed into notorious secret cults, which have now become the bane of these universities. The original club 'WS' founded was viewed at inception as a brotherhood of happy-go-lucky and fun-loving revelers. They dressed like sea pirates, answered to the popular names of legendary pirates, and revelled late into the night. There was nothing cultish or diabolical about them at that time. Soyinka explained that 'it was not [his] intention to breed this generation of decadent and over-pampered brats.'

As Africa's first Nobel Laureate for Literature, literary icon, and avant-garde dramatist and poet, Soyinka always interwove his literary and socio-political aspirations and endeavours. His works were vehicles for his genius and his revolutionary commitments. He wrote as a visionary, using his dreams about the future to expose the present with clarity and veracity. He used the English language with unique sublimity, charging his words with high voltage in a way that classified him as a true genius. His choice of words emanated from a very fertile, subtle, and refined mind. It is said that Wole Soyinka's greatest works will be read and studied by scholars and students alike just as long as works like *Hamlet* and *Oedipus Rex* are read.

On his 50th birthday, Soyinka blasted members of his generation—his critics, friends, colleagues, and admirers alike—with a scathing indictment of what he called a *wasted generation*. A decade later, amidst the uncertainties and brouhaha resulting in the spurious and universally decried annulment of Abiola's election as president, he had another unusual 'present' for those who gathered for the celebration of his 60th birthday. He avowed that he could not find the least cause to celebrate anything, least of all a birthday, because of his disenchantment with the state of affairs of his beloved fatherland. He lamented my situation as a Nation by saying that 'for most of the 35 years of our post-colonial existence, a noxious cloud has hung between the Nation and the sun; this miasma wears the military features of General Abacha and an incorrigible cabal of predators; therefore marking this 60th birthday would be celebrating a birthday that represents years of frustration and waste.' Having gone through a widely judged and universally acclaimed 'free and fair' election that was annulled by the military government, Soyinka waxed poetic in an elegiac outpouring:

> The scattered chutes regroup, release their toxin and blight the tentative shoots of social landscape…

'Kongi', as Wole Soyinka is fondly called by his admirers, dug deep into his repertoire and coined such unforgettable phrases as 'The man died', 'Justice is the first condition of humanity', and 'Agents of a depressing eclipse of our culture'. All his utterances and pronouncements were geared towards excoriating or eliminating military dictatorships. Such was his impatience with and aversion for the military's ineptitude that he resignedly described Babangida's government as 'deaf and dumb'. He made his utterances in distinctly measured phonetic fashion, and the words tumbled out in his deep and clear diction.

On another occasion, an elated Babangida's government bestowed on him the award of Commander of the Federal Republic (CFR). The particularly worrisome and disconcerting event, the magnitude of which Soyinka called 'Vatsa's murder', led him to smash the award to smithereens in anger at the height of the military misrule. The French government honoured him with the highest award given to any foreigner: Commander in the Legion d'Honneur. The German government gave him the Order of Merit of the German Republic. Soyinka was among those responsible for stampeding Babangida off his imperial pedestal. He had fallen out with Babangida's government in disgust over the execution of soldier–poet Vatsa, who was said to have been involved in Orka's frivolous attempted coup that threatened to oust the government of Babangida.

Soyinka unleashed venomous arrows of caustic words on the annulment of Abiola's election by saying it was 'an elongation of IBB's farce in a diabolical soap opera'. His passport was impounded on several occasions. It got to a frenetic stage at one point when he had to raise an alarm that plans to eliminate him were at an advanced stage when a suspicious aircraft hovered menacingly over his homestead at the outskirts of Abeokuta.

He transferred his venom to Abacha, who clandestinely took over from the innocuous Shonekan. The latter had been planted in government when Babangida 'stepped aside' and made his hurried exit into the safety of his Minna castle. He described Abacha as a 'latter-day despot' and fled into exile on a motorcycle via what became known as the 'NADECO route', when he sniffed a Gestapo-like attempt by the Abacha goons to kill him. He became more dangerous to Abacha's government living in exile than he could ever have been at home.

The beauty and cadence of Soyinka's English language, both written and expressed, constituted an aspect of his works that does not cease to elicit comments. Once it is understood that 'only the deep can speak to the deep', then that aspect of his works explains itself. It is only the discerning mind or one that stands ready to learn that can understand the nuances and peculiarly spawned figures of speech in some of his literary works. It should be added that most serious students like to 'drink deep from the deep'. Just as English writers occasionally injected foreign phrases or words into their writings to achieve required depth and stylish effect, so also did Soyinka achieve the height of language for himself by reaching into the depths of the Yoruba language to convey the exact meaning and inference of a given situation. He would then deftly translate such inferences into English.

Kongi decided to *pitan fun* (delve into history for him) his fellow Egba kinsman, M. K. O. Abiola, who had approached him with a request to lessen or stop his severe criticism of Obasanjo—this cessation would aid Obasanjo's bid to become Secretary-General of the United Nations. Soyinka, however, meant that he would reveal to Abiola the genesis of WS's caustic criticism, which would make Abiola's request boomerang. Another reason for this was that Obasanjo had berated and decried the presidential ambition of Abiola by saying that Abiola was not the 'Messiah Nigeria wanted'.

Soyinka also concluded that Abacha suffered from 'second fiddle syndrome' after silently operating in the background of Babangida's regime. This attitude of quietly awaiting his turn and then grabbing it with calculated alacrity when it finally arrived made Soyinka satirize with poetic license, in both Yoruba language and pidgin English, '*Nwon a gan pa* (they will swagger, strut, and pose) and marvel at their newly acquired power by saying, '*Na me be this*' (can this be happening to me?).

MOVIE-MAKING INDUSTRY
Nollywood and Other Movie-Making Enterprises

The United States of America has Hollywood, the kingpin of the world movie industry. India subsequently created *Bollywood*, and it has been acknowledged as the world's second largest home of film producers and movie makers.

Here, I have evolved my very own version: *Nollywood*. I predict that, given the necessary support, my Nollywood will take the world by storm as the authentic voice and mirror of the black race. My movie industry has taken such phenomenal strides that producers and filmmakers churn out hundreds of movies and home videos annually. It has also been estimated that around 54 titles are created every month. The introduction of Nollywood films in the twilight of the twentieth century and the dawn of the twenty-first century would seem to have affirmed the cinema-going culture of my people. Gone are the days when people flocked into cinema theaters to watch Hollywood westerns and the ubiquitous but popular Indian films (Bollywood).

When Hollywood held sway globally, particularly during my colonial era, film producers here were nonexistent or were too amateurish. That was the era of films like 'African Queen', 'Tarzan', and 'King Solomon's Mines'. These films were gratuitously foisted on my film-goers, and even though these were made from the books of the same titles, the films were stereotypical and horrid. When my earliest film producers ventured out on their own, they were slowed down by some major factors. They dealt with subjects such as colonialism and other African issues. The films were mostly elitist in presentation and viewership. The masses were in the main excluded because of the prevailing circumstances of poor production values and lack of social awareness. Because the films were shot at prohibitive costs and the sophistication which 35 mm demanded, the film makers had to raise funds from patronizing and condescending international agencies and reluctant and unwilling governments. Nollywood's answer was to start releasing directly to video.

The question remained: How can a country establish a film culture when it excludes the very people for whom the films are made? It was neither reasonable nor advisable to continue shooting on 35-mm film in an environment where cinemas were being variously converted to churches, warehouses, restaurants, and stores—or being simply allowed to waste away in disuse and abandonment. Major popular cinema houses like Casino, Rialto, Rex, and Penn in Lagos and Odeon and Scala in Ibadan no longer held any fascination or attraction for viewers. These and other issues were to be addressed by the emergence of Nollywood.

The Nollywood phenomenon was made possible by two main ingredients: the entrepreneurship of my Igbo citizens and the reign of digital technology. In the late 1980s and early 1990s, Lagos and some other major West African cities witnessed the growing epidemic of crime and insecurity. People avoided going to the movie theaters, as they were reluctant to be out in the streets after dark.

Videos for home viewing, imported from the West and India, were only mildly popular. Nollywood was born and made quite a big difference. It created a whole new exemplar against which emergent African films would be measured. It addressed issues that found relevance in people's reality. It created an avenue for the projection of the people's cultures and mores. It identified with their trials and ordeals. It destroyed the miasmic fantasy and the stereotype created by Tarzan, in particular, that my ancient cultures belonged to a race of apes and savages.

The opportunity therefore arose for these entrepreneurs to fill the void with their own products. The trailblazer was the release of 'Living in Bondage', in 1992. The movie was a tale of the occult, and it turned out to be an instant and huge-selling success. This was a clarion call for up-and-coming producers to jump on the bandwagon. They currently produce at a rate of about 2,000 movies a year. It is an astounding fact that these movie entrepreneurs have what it takes to salvage any situation and make it entertaining with their creativity and ingenuity.

Nollywood films and home videos have gone into cities, towns, and villages not only within my territorial spread but also across similar settings in English-speaking Africa. Though made on the cheap, Nollywood films and home videos have become huge hits with stories, themes, scenarios, and faces familiar and akin to other African settings. My Nollywood movie-making has attained a frenetic pace with low-budget movies, which are typically filmed in a short time with just one digital camera. However, the movie makers and producers themselves admitted that by the leverage of years of experience and a fledgling relationship with technical partners in the United States, they have been able to provide first-class video experiences that were unparalleled in Africa.

Nollywood stories are not essentially different from those found in Hollywood movies. However, it would seem that Nollywood movies—and in particular traditional Yoruba and Igbo movies—have African-specific themes with what I think of as too much emphasis on spectacles like ritual killings, witchcraft, and elaborate voodoo settings. The worrisome prevalence of witchcraft and violence may encourage the worst example of stereotypes about Africans. Many foreign and local critics have criticized Nollywood for its banal plots, poor dialogue, and awful sound systems with often loud and disturbing background music and poor production values.

These movies flood the markets and are sold for as cheap as N350 (just over $2) per videocassette. Such movies are shown to the public for a few naira in restaurants, video centers, and private homes. This industry has created many employment opportunities for the young ones. An average movie will sell up to 50,000 cassettes, and popular blockbusters have been known to sell well over 250,000. The growing popularity of the movies, formerly dismissed as exploitation by intellectuals, has changed the traditional perception of acting and perceptions about actors.

The first Nollywood movies were made on shoestring budgets of about $15,000. Yet in just under 20 years, my movie industry has grown spectacularly from very modest and humble beginnings into a huge $450 million industry employing thousands of people in the various activities of movie making. Bulky and rather clumsy video cameras gave way to the digital innovations, which are also now being replaced by handy and portable high-definition (HD) cameras. The producers and movie makers have moved to a superior level, using computer-based systems in editing, music, and post-production work.

It has been said that my Nollywood films are so popular and so widely accepted in many English-speaking African countries that they have won many awards at film festivals. It is also a well known fact that not only do Nollywood actors and actresses gain instant recognition both locally and in distant lands, but also people in some African countries have begun emulating the Nollywood actors' speech and fashions. This is reminiscent of the bygone days of Hollywood westerns and the influence the American slang of the cowboys had on my young people of those days, specifically in the way they dressed and spoke. It was even reported that when one of my visiting Heads of State walked into a foreign gathering in another African country, he was hailed as 'Igwe!'. This was comically reminiscent of the reception accorded an Igbo Eze, as depicted in many Nollywood movies.

I was amused to learn that some actors of Yoruba extraction were contemplating creating their own 'Yoruwood' version of the industry. This was likely in answer to the preponderance of my Igbo actors plying their trade in Nollywood. There is no doubt that fantastic stories and themes characterize

D. O. Fagunwa. *He was a prolific and highly imaginative author of spell-binding Yoruba folklore.*

*The sketch of '**Ojola Ibinu**' (the Irritable Python), which is one of the products of Fagunwa's inimitable genius.*

Chinua Achebe. *He has been described as an Eagle that perches atop the giant Iroko tree of the African literary forest. He has bestowed to posterity the imperishable* Things Fall Apart, *which has been translated into over sixty languages.*

Cyprian Ekwensi. *In his writing, Cyprian Ekwensi explored the appeal of city life and the treatment of ordinary folks. He had a down-to-earth way of writing about the natural behaviour of people from the various Nigerian tribes. His popular* Jagua Nana *has been widely read.*

the presentations of both styles. Most if not all of the Nollywood movies are in spoken English language, whereas the Yoruba movies are in Yoruba language with English subtitles, reminiscent of the older but popular Indian movies. Happily, both versions have reached an accommodation in the crossover appearances and performances of some of the actors and actresses who are either bilingual in both Yoruba and Igbo or whose popularity and track records fit the demands of the plots and the roles.

It is necessary at this stage to highlight certain critical tendencies which may militate against the popularity and international acceptance of the products of my film industry. The emphasis on voodoo, witchcraft, and excessive facial and body makeup and painting may have the effect of stereotypes. These may provoke or promote a *déjà vu* feeling of watching a familiar and boring series of scenes. Repetitive and excessive use of incantations, panegyrics, and pithy sayings, particularly in Yoruba films, may confuse or even bore the audience.

It is becoming increasingly apparent that the once-lucrative industry is gradually receding towards a comatose state. Some notable factors are responsible for the seeming lull. Apart from the uncoordinated number of newly released movies, the storylines are monotonous. Furthermore, the productions lack technical depth and the characters and principal actors are overly recycled. In spite of the frequency and sheer number of movies being churned out, the themes were so similar as to be predictable and boring. If the producers were not dealing with love stories and sizzling romance with the same set of characters, they were dealing with themes celebrating rituals, voodoo, covens, pastors, imams, and visits to shrines.

Some notable male actors who have appeared in several 'blockbuster' Nollywood and Yoruba movies and home videos are Pete Edochie, Olu Jacobs, Richard Mofe Damijo (RMD), Zack Orji, Jide Kosoko, Olumide Bakare, Laz Ekwueme, Justus Esiri, Enebeli Elebuwa, Segun Arinze, Funso Adeolu, Sunday Omobolanle (Pappy Luwe), Desmond Elliot, Yinka Quadri, Hanks Anuku, Kola Oyewo, Nobert Young, Lere Paimo, Chidi Mokeme, Emeka Ike, Jim Iyke, Kelvin Ikeduba, Mike Ezuruonye, Femi Branch, Taiwo Al-Hassan, Adebayo Salami ('Oga' Bello), Odunade Adekola, Bolaji Amusan, and the popular and inimitable duo of 'pocket giants', Osita Ihime and Chinedu Ikedieze, also known as Aki and Pawpaw.

Some notable Directors, Producers and others who combine directing, producing and at times acting include Zeb Ejiro, Tarilla Thompson, Fred Amata, Teco Benson, Tchidi Chikere, Muka-Ray and Lasun Eyiwunmi, Lancelot Odua-Imasuen, Mac Collins Chidebe, Funso Adeolu, Fidelis Duker, Tunde Kelani, Ifeanyi Ikpoenyi, Dele Odule, Tade Ogidan, Afam Okereke, Saheed Balogun, Sunday Nnajuide, Antar Laniyan,

Some of the very popular actresses are Patience Ozokwor, Joke Silva, Bukky Ajayi, Rita Edochie, Ngozi Egwuonwu, Liz Benson, Bukky Wright, Fausat Balogun, Dupe Jaiyesimi, Kate Henshaw-Nuttal, Omotola Jalade-Ekeinde, Stella Damasus-Aboderin, Stephanne Okereke, Genevieve Nnaji, Gloria Anozie-Young, Laide Bakare, Thelma Okodua, Ronke Ojo, Binta Ayo-Mogaji, Omoni Oboli, Chioma Chukwuka, Ini Edo, Mercy Johnson, Mercy Aigbe, Liz Dasilva, Empress Njamah, Monalisa Chinda, Oge Okoye, Fathia Balogun, Shade Kassim (Lepa Shandy), Funmi Holda, Idowu Philips, Moji Olaiya, Lizzy Anjorin, Iyabo Ojo, Rita Dominic, Ope Aiyeola, Benita Nzeribe, Tonto Dike, Toyin Aimakhu, and Sola Kosoko.

Emem Isong, Ronke Akindele, Uche Jombo, Fathia Balogun, Bukky Wright, Ego Boyo, Omoni Oboli and Stephanne Okereke, are some of the versatile actresses who also double as playwrights and producers.

Nollywood: The Way Forward

It is my fervent hope and expectation that Nollywood would attract wider international viewership and worldwide attention. It is only a matter of time before my fledgling movie industry attains such tremendous impact as to be able to flex its competitive muscles in the world of show business and cinematography. Interplay of a variety of factors will be at work to enhance production, encourage and expose budding talents, and promote interest in viewership and patronage.

The distinctive aspects of my culture are waiting to be tapped and scripted into stage dramas and screenplays. My folklore and traditional themes are inexhaustible sources of themes for wholesome stage and screen performances. Modern cinematography equipment is now available to facilitate quick and efficient production of movies. Many tertiary institutions offer courses in theatre arts. This of course would swell the rank of actors and actresses who would enliven Nollywood and raise standards immeasurably in terms of production values and acting. My film stars will be primed to garner many prizes and nominations, locally and internationally, for acting and producing prestigious film awards.

If my various governments were to support the film industry and its positive impact on my socioeconomic development, it would be well worth it. There should be effective legislation to protect the property rights of creative artists with an anti-piracy campaign. In view of the global popularity now attained, it is imperative for the film practitioners to maintain their steady rise to higher and higher levels of quality production. Some of the major developments in the industry include a certain level of professionalism and guidelines for the establishment of a film village and a National Film Development Fund.

MUSIC (MY REMINISCENCES)

Music is the melodious expression of the distinctive aspects of my culture. Music forms the background of my cultural activities. It is like the cry of a baby at birth—it signifies life and vivacity, bringing joy, smiles, and a sense of expectation to the new mother who was groaning in excruciating labour pains only a few moments earlier. Music is used to praise Almighty God. It is also used to invoke the favor of the gods and to similarly appease their ire. Music is used on special occasions. During the inter-tribal wars in the past, it was used to give inspiration as the men went off to the war fronts. It was also used to extol the battlefield prowess and celebrate the triumphant return of victorious warriors. My people bemoaned their losses in somber and mournful music. They bewailed their losses and poured out their lamentations in dirges at funerals. My music is also the expression of joy, particularly when it is meant for dancing and entertainment. It is a pleasurable vehicle for the effusive conveyance of satire, comments, and greetings.

The famous musicologist Sammy Akpabot opined in his submission to the FESTAC Colloquium that the sound of music in my culture can demonstrate a commonality of purpose and usage among peoples of my various tribes. In his research, he found that four drums are used for the Ofala Festival of the Obi of Onitsha; that the Yorubas used four drums for the worship of Obatala;

that four-gourd rattles are used by Hausa women in harems to serenade their husbands; and that four horns are used by the Ibibios to form an Uta. When the Emir of Katsina is being turbaned, the tambari drum is struck twelve times to inform the people.

The same large drums are called ugbaji in Ondo, and they are used on important occasions in practically all the palaces across the land—Benin, Oyo, and Tiv, to mention a few. The *gbugburuke* drums are used in Ondo to announce the death of the Oba, an Ewarefa (one of the six high chiefs), or any of the high-rank chiefs. When these drums are rolled out, it is believed that hearing the drumbeats would spell certain death for a living Oba or Ewarefa. The high chiefs and Obas were known to have taken certain precautionary or remedial measures to avert looming calamity. They would either stuff cotton wool into their ears or retire into the innermost recesses of their abodes so that the ominous sound would not filter into their ears. They would, in fact, hurriedly make their exits out of town, just to avoid the doleful death knell being sounded from the drums.

Drums are very relevant and significant to my cultural expression, from community to community, all over the land. The changing sounds of drums in my musical culture dictate the pace and rhythm relevant to the events being celebrated. The sounds go through slow, somber, prayerful, or mournful adagio to a rising crescendo and ultimately to the loud, fast-paced and energetic tempo of zestful jubilation. The sizes of the drums vary. They are made from the trunks of woods made hollow through delicate chiseling. One or both ends are covered with dried hides made taut by pegs and ropes to attain various pitches. The Yorubas call some drums covered at both ends *bata*. They also use the 'talking drum' with which they express words and render songs.

Drums are beaten either with specially carved and curved drum sticks or with dried and flattened rawhides. At times, drums are beaten with bare hands. The Yorubas in the former Western Region and parts of Kwara and Kogi States commonly use the talking drums. They are also used by peoples around the old kingdom of Benin and among various tribes and communities in the old Eastern Region. Just as it sounds, talking drums were used to convey messages and announcements. This has been used perennially as jingles to identify radio stations as in the popular 'this is the Nigerian Broadcasting Service' of the early 1950s and 1960s. Such drumbeats also announce the continuity services of various radio networks.

The big *iya ilu* (lead drum) dictates the rhythm and tempo to the rest of the band. It introduces the next tune, lyrics, and pace for the drummers and singers. It also dictates the tempo and movements to the dancers. In some places, the drummers are accompanied by the *sekere* maracas. Sekeres are made out of big gourds encased in tasseled cowry beads. When rolled, shaken, or beaten by dexterous players in accompaniment to songs, the beaded gourds give good rhythmic sounds, which motivate and spur the dancers to fiercer gyrations. The supremely skilled sekere player, in moments of sheer ecstasy, would occasionally toss up the sekere only to attain perfect synchrony and demonstrate acrobatic agility as he catches the gourd that rattles with cowry-beaded tassles. The display of this acrobatic performance is very entertaining.

In some parts of my old Eastern Region, drums are made either from hollowed woods or from big gourds or solid clay pots with openings covered with taut rawhides. When beaten, the drums resonate deep and melodious sounds. The larger the gourds or hollowed woods, the deeper the sounds. Some drumming contraptions that look like xylophones are also made from neatly arranged flat woods, joined together by string cords and beaten with sticks by ambidexterous players. This type of drumming was being used as a 'talking' device or a medium for conveying or relaying messages from village to village.

In my Northern Region drums are very widely used. The drums are different shapes from the ones in the West. The northern drums are roundish and bigger. Long horns and trumpets are the major musical instruments, particularly at big occasions like turbanning or any event that is graced by the presence of an Emir or the Sultan. It is always entertaining to watch the trumpeters perform, their cheeks swollen and faces distorted as they blow the trumpets. The cheeks swell like full-grown apples, reminding any knowing on-looker of the trademark of the famous Afro-American jazz trumpeter, Dizzy Gillespie, when he blew his trumpet.

The Yorubas call trumpets *kakaki*. In Yorubaland, when the Obas emerge from their royal palaces in their royal splendour, they are usually greeted and hailed by the trumpeters and drummers. Carved and trumpeting horns are used in chanting the Obas' praises and inspiring them by their appellations. Similar

1 Hubert Ogunde. He was the doyen of stage drama in Nigeria. Ogunde was the first person to put together a drama troupe which travelled far and wide to showcase, in operatic dramas, the richness of Nigerian culture. *2 Segun Olusola.* Ambassador Segun Olusola became the first TV producer in Africa. He created the hilariously successful soap opera 'Village Headmaster'. He is also a great exponent of Nigerian culture.

practices are enacted and displayed when the Emirs come out with their heavy turbans and in their flowing gowns. Such horns are also widely used by the Igbo flutists and horn blowers to announce the presence or sing the praises of traditional rulers or eminent personalities.

The practitioners of various professions are usually enabled by performance-enhancing songs to rise to higher levels in whatever they are doing. The oarsmen performing during cultural displays in a Regatta, rhythmically paddle their canoes and sway to heartily rendered songs; the labourers cutting grass, the brick-layers arranging blocks or bricks on walls of houses being newly erected, and farm-hands making mounds and ridges burst into hilarious and invigorating songs as they wield their tools. The yam and millet pounders evolve a rhythmic sound of their own with pestles and mortars; the lumberjacks sing cheerfully as they saw the big tree trunks bringing joy, zest, and enthusiasm into their tasks. The storyteller under the big tree and the starry moonlit night sky laces his yarns with songs that tickle and keep the listeners agog with the expectation of happy endings. Such songs are full of refrains and sing-along choruses.

Songs enrich my culture. Songs enhance traditional rites during naming ceremonies. Songs and choruses accompany the new bride at a wedding ceremony, as she moves into the home of the bridegroom. She is similarly received by a waiting troupe of singers at the bridegroom's home. Libations are poured to begin a festival, or at the beginning of a house-warming ceremony. These rituals were usually carried out with evocative songs, beseeching the spirits of the ancestors to preside over affairs. The introduction of Christianity has come to underline the significance of songs as the vehicle conveying our praises, pleas and requests to the throne of the Almighty God. My first National Anthem at my independence began with the line 'Nigeria we hail thee' before the more inspirational and clarion-calling 'Arise O Compatriots' took to the air waves, followed by the verbally rendered reassuring National Pledge: 'I pledge to Nigeria my Country'. Every festival affords an occasion for the outpouring of joy and conviviality by way of songs and dancing.

'Were' and 'Waka' brands of music are rooted in the Islamic culture. 'Apala' and 'Sakara' were then the indigenous airs. Harouna Ishola was arguably the greatest exponent of *apala* music. That brand of music also comes from the 'Doje' and 'Molo' instruments in the North. The amusing aspect of the apala music is the culture of praise singing in which the virtues, prowess, antics, and heroics of the Obas, Obis, Emirs, Nzes, and prominent people in the gathering are extolled and lauded to the skies in songs. In such songs, prayerful incantations are chanted. Repetitive mention of their names, appellations, and aliases are brought in for emphasis and in refrains.

Juju, Were, Apala, and Sakara were very much in vogue at about the same time. Other brands of music that made their short-lived appearances were Konga, Kokoma, Agidigbo, Mambo, and Apola. One after the other, they bowed out of the musical scene, yielding ground to new fads. Konga was the one that seems to have permanently left the most emulated dance form and song. The song goes thus:

Adebisi Konga,
Ko Ko Konga
Ko Ko Ko Konga.
Onibata Konga,
Ko Ko Konga.

The interesting thing about this song-and-dance tune is the fact that the graceful wiggling movement still forms the basis of all the modern-day dancing. The dancer places both hands akimbo on the hips, sways this way and that with the hips, and at the same time looks left and right as rhythmically dictated by the pace and sound of the accompanying drums.

Juju and the new craze, 'highlife', became the contemporary music and form of dancing in those halcyon days of my newly won independence. Azikiwe, my Governor General at that time, was so thrilled by the performance of I. K. Dairo, the inimitable accordionist and ace juju exponent, that he recommended the maestro for an M. B. E. award in the Queen's New Year's Honours List for 1963. Victor Olaiya, trumpeter, vocalist, and foremost highlife music exponent of that era, brought a new dimension to that brand of music. He captured the prevalent mood and activities before and during the first federal elections, which preceded Independence in his highlife music when he sang

> December 12, 1959,
> Federal Election day in Nigeria,
> Happy to sing about the election,
> When we all learn to say,
> 'Baakodaya'.

The Action Group (AG) party had boycotted the elections in certain parts of my Northern Region. However, both the electioneering campaigns and the actual elections went on in other parts according to schedule. The outcome was predictable. It led to a massive victory for the Northern Peoples' Congress (NPC), particularly in the North. In the ensuing announcement of the election results on radio, high figures were reported, mostly for the NPC, far fewer numbers for other parties, and nil votes—in Hausa language, 'Baakodaya'—for Action Group. The repetitive and continuously derisive nil returns of votes reported for AG left the word indelibly in the minds of listeners and found its place in history and in the peoples' vernacular when Victor Olaiya used it as a refrain in his memorable song. He carried the highlife musical culture beyond my shores and was awarded an honorary doctoral degree in music from the Republic of Czechoslovakia.

Musicians traditionally played 'jam sessions' at popular nightclubs and performed at beer parlours. Musicians were then more preoccupied with entertaining club crawlers, wayside party makers, and occasional ballroom dancers and giving them the opportunity to listen and dance to new styles of music. Nightclub performances were given free of charge. Token gate fees were charged at the 'Sunday Jump' or 'Tea Time' dance sessions at the famous Ambassador Hotel located in Yaba, Lagos. That was where the grandfather of highlife music and the doyen of the music of that era, Bobby Benson, presided and performed. Billy Friday was another popular performer and entertainer at the same venue. Similarly, E. C. Arinze and later Victor Uwaifor entertained with highlife music at the popular Kakadu nightclub in Yaba. 'Tea Time' dances were held at the Paradise Club, Oke Bola in Ibadan where Eddy Okonta held sway and at the Central Hotel, Ekotedo, where Roy Chicago entertained similar crowds of revelers and guests.

Nightclub performances by the popular bands and orchestras of the day were mostly held in places like Lagos, Ibadan, Enugu, Jos, Calabar, Port Harcourt, Kano, Benin, and Onitsha. The artists played pure, original, creative, and unique Nigerian music. This later became adulterated, albeit modernized with Western instruments, which gave it jazzy flavour. The horns, trombone, electric guitar, and guitar-bog were the new instruments introduced to make highlife music more melodious. These along with tap dancing were the innovations which Bobby Benson used to take highlife music to a new jazzy level. He brought all these new instruments into play in his rendition of the classic song 'Taxi Driver':

Sisi Siju,
You no dey shame,
Plenty money dey for me hand.
If you marry taxi driver,
I don't care,
If you marry Lorry Driver,
I don't care.

He later built the popular Caban Bamboo Night Club as his operational base on Ikorodu Express Road in Lagos. The exponents of highlife with their distinctive styles included Victor Olaiya, who sang such songs as 'Iye Jemila' and 'Omo Pupa'. Eddy Okonta popularized the dance step called 'bosue' with his 'Oriwo o' and 'Sisi Bisi'. Roy Chicago held his audience spellbound with scintillating rhythms in 'Aisan Aba' and 'Yoyo Gbe'. 'Cardinal' Rex Lawson crooned to them across the land with his own uniquely melodious brand of highlife music. He came into the limelight with his unforgettable 'Ibinabo'. People were enraptured by his voice as he entertained audiences with his serenading voice and danceable music. His new records came out in rapid succession and were all instant party hits and chart busters, played regularly on most radio stations. Rex Lawson's music had a distinctive quality of its own that made him sound like a cross between Ghana's Black Beats, E. T. Mensah, the Star Gazers. and the Ramblers Band of those days.

Some other great musicians then were Chris Ajilo, King Kennytone, 'Baby face' Paul Isemade, Zeal Onyia, the ace trumpeter of 'Vic Yemokumo' fame, and Bala Milla, who zestfully blew his trumpet in the North into his ripe old age. Victor Uwaifo blew his trumpet and strummed his guitar in 'Guitar Boy', 'Mammy Water', and the ever-popular 'Joromi', which became his musical signature. Uwaifo was always dapper and immaculate in his performance outfits. He was dexterous and adept with his guitars, which were many shapes and colours. He popularized the highlife dance step called 'panlogo'.

Osita Osadebey had little education but an abundance of musical talent. He started with rudimentary instruments and graduated into the musical superstar that he became. He was in the limelight of highlife music for almost sixty years. His musical style still lingers on. He had a folksy way of singing. Though he did not sing in English language in the practical sense of it, he did make his music speak the language of the people. Everybody yearned for his music because they understood it. He perfected the use of the various instruments that dominated the music at various stages—his Master's voice, turntable, piano, and even modern computerized sounds.

Adeolu Akinsanya sang his satirical limerick in 'acada' in which he highlighted the attributes and characteristics of the new breed of educated and glamorous Lagos girls. Oliver de Coque and Etim Nyang Ete were great exponents of highlife. The music-loving Oba Adeyemi, the Alaafin of Oyo, once crowned Oliver de Coque as the King of Highlife. Bright Chimeze was the highlife 'Zigima' master whose stagecraft, showmanship, and performances were agile, dexterous, and electrifying. His highlife dance form and choreography made him the audiences' delight.

Musical entertainer Godwin Omabuwa sang the calypso as if he hailed from the West Indies. He performed to the delight of fans and patrons of the Gondola and Maharani Nightclubs. The former was located at Yaba and the latter on Martins Street, Lagos. Bongos Ikwue's music was soothing and with his mellifluous voice, he rendered and recorded many 'hits' in the 1970s and 1980s. Keyboardists and crooners like Jimmy Solanke, Tunji Oyelana, and 'Yom Yem' Yemi Ogunsanya always gave good performances at luncheons and in-house parties where they dished out 'oldies–but-goodies'.

Juju music stars illuminate my musical firmament with a glow that is very original and rousing. Juju music itself evolved from Yoruba folklore. Early in the twentieth century, Lagos was the place where local peoples encountered freed slaves from the 'New World'. Together they created a recreational music that came to be known as Palm Wine Music in an atmosphere of drinking and merrymaking. Guitars, banjos, and hand drums were played to the accompaniment of lilting tropical songs. The old juju maestros and exponents were Tunde King, who was the first to call his music *juju*. The others were Irewolede Denge, Theophilus Iwalokun, Ojoge Daniel, Ayinde Bakare, Julius Araba (of 'easy-motion-kelele' fame), and Tunde Nightingale of the high-pitched voice. These past masters established the core repertoire that would shape the fast evolving juju music.

The deep voice of Agun of 'Why Worry' orchestra was a pleasurable throwback to another era of homegrown Ondo juju music that acquired widespread acclaim and prominence. The late octogenarian Fatai Rolling Dollar continued to play juju music with special emphasis on ballads. He seemed to have cast a look back at the performances of his compeers of bygone years and drawn a comparison between those past masters and the contemporary crop of juju artists who are the raves of the moment. His verdict was as humorous as it was biased. He made a record in which he sang 'Nwon kere si number wa', which literally translated means 'They are inferior to our own billing'. The old man sounded convincing but seemed oblivious of the facts of the past and the present: Back then, there was only inferior equipment. Now, the superior gadgets enhance and ensure greater and more efficient performances and better recordings and recording facilities.

Modern acoustics-enhancing electronic equipment has elevated juju music to new heights. Performers and dancers have enhanced their entertainments with the type of music which encourages delightful viewing. The fantastic duo of the vintage and evergreen 'King' Sunny Ade, popularly called KSA, and Ebenezer Obey ruled the roost until the twilight of the twentieth century. The artistic performances of both Obey and KSA were gripping and engaging to their listening audiences and fans. The seeming competition between them fuelled the evolution of the juju sound to include drums, trap drums, guitar synthesizers, and even more percussion instruments. Obey later ventured into the hallowed areas of Christian evangelism, singing gospel music, and preaching. KSA still marches on, waxing stronger and turning out records and CDs and best-selling video performances. For the past three decades, KSA has been thrilling audiences and listeners with dynamic live performances, creative videos, and innovative recordings.

These two juju musical maestros are both adept with their guitars, and they can always be identified by their uniquely distinctive styles and voices. Obey's type of juju and dance form was called 'Miliki System' and that of Sunny Ade was called 'Synchro System'. Both became melodious and vibrant refrains in their juju musical compositions and performances. It is remarkable that Obey shunned praise-singing in his newfound love of evangelism when one considers that this type of song earned him millions of naira. It also won for him many famous friends and the admiration and ecstatic gratitude of towns, groups, and revelers about whom he sang in his recordings. In one such song, he made praise-singing references to the culture and people of Egba, Ibadan, Ijesha, and Ondo. Now, he says, all praises belong to God.

There were also other juju stars. Dele Abiodun's answer to the 'Synchro System' of Sunny Ade was his 'Adawa Super'. The beats and dancing steps are similar and the musical arrangements attract responding fervour from the dancing audience. But Sunny Ade remains the king in his beautiful musical compositions, his dexterous handling of the guitar, his fantastic footwork, and gyrating body movements.

Some of the great juju players that made the entertainment arena bubble with hilarious performances included Prince Adekunle; Orlando Owoh, who possessed a deep and serenading voice; Sina Peters, who was called the 'musical rave' of his era and creator of the 'Afro juju beat'; Dele Taiwo, who made hay

Pete Edochie

Fred Amata

Olu Jacobs

Richard Mofe Damijo

Jide Kosoko

Tchidi Chikere

Odua Imasuen

Hanks Anuku

Joke Silva

Patience Ozokwor

Ngozi Egwuonwu

Genevieve Nnaji

Fathia Balogun

Stephanne Okereke

Laide Bakare

Bukky Ajayi

Omoni Oboli

Emem Isong

Kate Henshaw-Nuttall

with a punchy keyboard-rich sound that he called 'funky juju'; Olu Fajemirokun, who adopted the phrase 'E get cover' in his songs and performances; and Segun Adewale and Y. K. Ajao. The newest sensation, however, is the wheelchair-bound Aiyefele, who had been involved in a debilitating motor accident. The sound and rhythm of his songs are unique. He sings thought-provoking ditties and twines new songs around old tunes to revive sweet memories. Guitarists and drummers who provide vibrant rhythm and danceable beats supply very engaging background music.

Comfort Omoge was a very popular and special bandleader. She was special in the sense that she was a woman in music, a field essentially dominated by men at that time, as it is even now. Her specialty was the 'Woro' music played with juju flair. She sang in her beautiful Ikale intonation, a derivative of the Yoruba language. A queen in her own right by marriage, Omoge combined beauty with grace, elegance, and poise. She was always regally attired in hand-woven native dress. She radiated charm and royal grace when singing and dancing.

Dan Maraya Jos, also known as Adamu Wayya Mohammed, is a very popular Hausa musician. An indigenous musician, he is a rare breed—a one-man band. He twangs the local guitar contraption called 'kuntigi' to which he sings and dances. His famous and much sought-after musical renditions offered in his mellifluous voice are a rare combination of his own poetic compositions and the deft use of his peculiar kuntigi.

Through the use of the tiny harp-like stringed instrument, Dan Maraya catapulted himself to popular national demand and international recognition. He became a leading light in Hausa traditional music and an untainted icon of Hausa folklore. Dan Maraya uses his music as a weapon to capture and decry the root causes of societal problems. These include drug addiction, divorce, drunkenness, corruption, and lasciviousness. He admonishes the culprits and proffered solutions to these issues in his songs. Some of his songs are about such varied topical issues as my population census, various elections, the activities of MAMSER and WAI (programmes embarked upon by some military regimes to instill discipline and maintain order), Operation Feed the Nation, currency exchange, and FESTAC.

Dan Maraya virtually turned himself into a self-appointed disseminator of government policies. His songs assist in enlightening the citizens about the vital issues of the day. He is like a journalist who takes one on an excursion through his writings. He conveys his messages with the melodious twang of his kuntigi, using his unique brand of music to prickle the minds of his listeners. They enjoy the sedative tinge in his songs that at the same time indulge in critical self-examination. At his citation during the conferment of a doctoral degree on him at the University of Jos, he was referred to variously as the 'Nigerian Nightingale', an African Mozart, a drummer, a violinist, guitarist, composer, poet, philosopher, and ambassador. Indeed, he is all of these rolled into one.

Israel Njemanze's name conjures an admixture of sad and historical memories in people's minds. Some remember him for his melodious songs, which were a cross between highlife and calypso. But the older ones would recall his gruesome death in Lagos by murderers whose celebrated trials remain memorable in the annals of murder cases. If Njemanze's voice was melodious and well modulated, the voice of Joe Nez, who sang similar ditties, was deep and sonorous. They were two of a kind, who operated in different eras and in different octaves.

Ambrose Campbell, the London-based bandleader, lived in London for a long time. He formed an orchestra called 'West African Rhythm Brothers'. The orchestra was made up of his compatriots who were also based in London. Their regular venue of operation and performances was the 'Club Afrique'. The orchestra played a unique brand of music that was a cross between calypso, rhumba, cha-cha, juju, and highlife. They also sounded more sophisticated because they were in Britain, using the prevailing standard equipments that were not available in my territory at that time. Their long sojourn abroad made them sing the homesick and popular juju/highlife piece, 'Irin Ajo la wa' (We Are Travellers):

Irin Ajo la wa yi o (We are travellers on a trip)
Ori gbe wa de'le (May fate lead us home)
B'Olorun fe awa a de'le (God willing, we'd be home)

Their other widely popular song euphemistically gave them their name, 'Ero ya' (Passers by, stop by and watch our show).

The influence of the personality and music of Ambrose Campbell on the up-and-coming musicians of West African origin in general, and my indigenous Nigerian ones in particular, can hardly be over-estimated. Campbell's brand of music, characterized by beautiful rhythm and heavy percussion, was an instant hit with music lovers and at parties all over my major cities, particularly in the Yoruba-speaking areas. Campbell himself extolled the influence which the encouragement of people like Awolowo and Azikiwe had on his life and music, particularly during their frequent visits to London for the Constitutional Conferences. He capped this with the memorable visits and performance tours to various cities and towns within my territory towards the end of the 1950s. Notable musicians Bobby Benson, Fela Anikulapo-Kuti, Zeal Onyia, and Falana were known to have made guest appearances with Campbell's West African Rhythm Brothers when they were in London.

Towards the end of the 1960s, the musical pendulum swung from local and indigenous highlife to the imported Western-oriented pop music. It was the era of the Beatles, four incredibly successful and globally acclaimed musicians from Great Britain. It was not strange, therefore, that my impressionable youths and teenagers quickly caught the bug of 'Beatlemania'. They formed themselves into groups such as the Clusters, Soul Assembly, the Hykkers, and Johnny Haastrup's 'Monomono'. Geraldo Pino became very popular as a fabulous song-and-dance man. Some of these groups were located in the old Eastern Region, but most were in Lagos.

It was also the era of Chubby Checker during which my youngsters resorted to 'twisting the nights away' at parties, picnics, nightclubs, and organized musical shows and performances. The all-action 'Godfather of Soul', Afro-American James Brown, crowned this golden era with his unforgettable visit and tremendous performances at the Onikan Stadium, Lagos. His universally chorused 'I'm Black and Proud' hit song was energetically rendered. During that era, this particular song influenced the famous Civil Rights Movement in the United States of America. It was the era that witnessed the dropping of the 'Nigger toga' and the glorification of the American black cultural movement. James Brown gave marvelous displays during the performances of his hip-swinging and body-shaking dance called the 'boogaloo'. It was a visit that was unique and so successful that it soon became the reference point for future successful foreign artists' organized performances.

The stars began to emerge and flicker from the 1980s through the middle of 1990s. My musical culture took a dramatic turn when the then Nsukka undergraduate Kris Okotie erupted onto the musical scene with his 'I Need Someone'. This was followed by a series of solo acts. Okotie was to veer into full-time pastoring as he founded the 'Household of God' Church, where he preached to his adoring followers, holding them spell-bound with his fiery sermons usually delivered with grandiloquent expressions.

Sunny Okosuns began to sing the song of freedom in his crooning voice. It was the era of freedom fighters in the apartheid enclave of South Africa. His song 'Fire in Soweto' riveted the world's attention on the African freedom fighters and their plight and living conditions in the hellhole slums and settlements around Soweto. This was quickly followed by 'Papa's Land'. He was vociferous in the universal clamour for the release of Nelson Mandela, who was then moving towards the end of the third decade of his incarceration at the isolated Roben Island detention camp, established by the overlord champions of apartheid in South Africa. Then Okosuns turned his prodigious musical talents into the realms of gospel singing. He recorded many albums and won awards for his efforts.

Some musical stars of this era enriched my musical culture and heritage. These include Dizzy K. Falola; Stella Monye; Felix Laberty; Tony Okoroji; Jide Obi; Onyeka Onwenu, the 'elegant stallion', who sang 'One Love'; the 'lady of songs', Christy Essien-Ugbokw; the 'singing Regent', Bunmi Olajubu; the inseparable and identical twin Lijadu Sisters; Vera Morinoghe, who sermonized on my behalf in her sweet voice that 'Nigeria Go Survive'; and the enchanting Funmi Adams, who serenaded her adoring audiences with her emotional songs which she rendered, for good measure, in my three main languages.

The distinctly unique and incomparable Fela burst onto the scene as Fela Ransome-Kuti with his Koola Lobitos Band in the 1960s. He began to blaze the trail with the pulsating and acerbic lyrics of his Afro beat music. Even though he metamorphosed into Fela Anikulapo-Kuti by renouncing the foreign part—Ransome—of his double-barrelled family name and changing the name of his band from Koola Lobitos to Egypt '70 and then Egypt '80, his Afro beat rhythm remained essentially and unmistakably the same. Fela was a very peculiar person who liked to do things his own way. The meaning of his adopted name *Anikulapo* speaks for itself—'the one that carries deadly arrows in his sheath'. He was also referred to as 'Abami'—a 'freak of nature'—which he sometimes appeared to be in his weird ways. He was a non-conformist bohemian with the eccentric proclivity of a highly talented artiste.

Fela brazenly smoked marijuana, the dopey herb, which he habitually referred to by its Yoruba name of 'Igbo'. He always appeared clad only in skimpy attire or swim suit at home and ceremonially married 27 wives at once. He was the son of father who was a disciplinarian, an educationist, and an Anglican clergyman and a mother who was a tempestuous political activist. Operating as a high priest from his popular club Afrika Shrine, he became an iconoclast and an irreverent songster who berated the Pope, the Bishop, and the Imam in one of his songs. His musical compositions marked him essentially as an arranger, a polemic, and a satirist.

He was the voice of the underprivileged. He was nemesis to those who peddled injustice and exploitation. He was a fierce critic of the many aberrant military regimes. It has been said that Fela was a freakish genius with a mission. It would appear that his music always carried the message for the black man to learn how to discover himself and bear his cross. He inveighed against the notions and practises that had vitiated the efforts of the black man and prevented him from taking his destiny in his own hands. He was generous and hard-working, but he would not spoon-feed anybody, and neither would he tolerate laziness or dishonesty.

He reached the acme of his disdain for the military in his beautifully composed and brilliantly choreographed song/dance 'Zombie'. It was a very sarcastic description of the soldiers as strait-jacketed, unthinkingly regimented, and servile. For this, the 'unknown soldiers' descended in blind obedience to 'directives from above' with wild and uncontrollable fury on his family home, Kalakuta Republic, in the Ojuelegba area of Lagos. They burnt down the house and destroyed everything in sight, maiming and wounding the occupants, including Fela's aged mother. This atrocious invasion led to the death of his mother, Funmilayo Ransome-Kuti, the tempestuous 'lioness of Lisabi', as I earlier referred to her.

To reach a much wider audience, Fela embraced the use of pidgin English in conveying his messages. He did so either in songs or at his frequent 'Yabis' sessions at the Afrika Shrine. During such sessions at the shrine, he played to full houses of his numerous fans, churning out such pieces as 'Jeun Koku' (chop and quench), 'Open and Close', 'Overtake Don Overtake Overtake', 'Confusion Break

Bone', 'Clear Road for Jaga Jaga', 'Suffering and Smiling', 'Beast of No Nation', and 'Demoncrasy'. These songs discussed and often criticized contemporary events. Some of the words and usages mentioned in the songs are still in vogue and have again become relevant, current, and applicable in the unfolding series of contemporary events.

During his 'Yabis sessions', Fela would embark on the heinous task of excoriating and lampooning any targeted person however highly placed or any event however highly sponsored. He was even known to have berated and warned his activist younger brother, Beko, to be wary and mindful of his utterances about the maximum dictator, Abacha, at the height of his megalomania or else 'Abacha go bash am' (Abacha would bash him). Such sessions always afforded him the opportunity to voice his radical views on any topical issues.

At the frequent Saturday night gigs in the shrine, Fela always conjured and enacted a dramatic scene of occultism and ancestor worship. With the atmosphere fully charged, he would suddenly change the tempo of his music. Then, with curiosity mounting and smoke belching from the inner sanctum of the shrine, Fela would appear, flanked by two hefty men carrying calabashes. He would then perform the choreography of appeasement to his ancestors and gods, much to the admiration of his fans. He would dance and gyrate as if possessed. His lyrics would become esoteric and suggestively stimulating.

The international scene was beckoning, and the exciting news about his Afro beat musical releases and stupendous performances at his shrine preceded Fela. West Africa and various countries in Europe and America waited, agog with expectation, to watch him and listen to him. Consequently, he played to capacity audiences and packed music auditoriums in far-flung places. He rose into a musical class all by himself. Fela's music redefined Afro beat in contextual terms. His musical arrangements and repertoire included frenetic percussion, double-bass guitar, and rhythmic syncopation. All these combined to launch Fela into a unique national and international prominence.

On the personal level, Fela was a rebel who seemed to doubt the good intentions of everyone. His entire life was a history of continuous wrangling with all sorts of people and situations. It was a notorious fact that he was rigidly unforgiving. He had a running quarrel with M. K. O. Abiola to the bitter end. Obasanjo was not spared the fury of his antagonism after the demolition of Kalakuta Republic and the resultant death of his mother. The duo of Abiola and Obasanjo,

1 Bobby Benson. Doyen and father of highlife music in Nigeria. *2 Victor Olaiya.* Highlife maestro and vibrant trumpeter who rendered the historic 'December 12, 1959' highlife music, which highlighted the Federal Elections and ushered in Independence in 1960. *3 Victor Uwaifo.* He sang the unforgettable 'Joromi' and was the creator of the dance form called 'Panlogo'. A dexterous guitarist and an agile showman and dancer. *4 Fela Anikulapo-Kuti.* Musically talented and internationally acclaimed Afro-beat king. *5 Lagbaja.* Versatile, masked singer and entertainer. *6 Femi Kuti.* He is an Afro-beat musician in his father Fela's footsteps. He built and modernized the new African Shrine. *7 Ebenezer Obe.* Juju Music super star and the initiator of the 'Miliki system'. He veered into evangelism. *8 King Sunny Ade.* High-flying Juju music super star who started the 'Synchro' system. His stage and dance performances are fantastic. *9 Oliver de Coque.* The lively and amiable performer of high-life music was crowned 'The King of Highlife' by the Alaafin of Oyo.

1 Dan Maraya. A rare breed—a one-man band. His unique guitar is called 'Kuntigi'. He is an untainted icon of Hausa folklore. He uses his music to disseminate governmental campaigns against indiscipline and the abuse of drugs. 2 Sikiru Ayinde Barrister. He was the veteran exponent of 'Fuji Garbage' music.

both Egba kinsmen like Fela, were to have their names chorused repeatedly in the song he recorded and dubbed 'I.T.T.' (The abbreviation of the International Tele-Communications outfit was euphemistically referred to as 'International Thief Thief'.) They both performed regularly at the popular Jazz 38 Night Club on Awolowo Road, Ikoyi, until the untimely death of Fran.

He quarrelled frequently with his promoters and recording companies like Decca and EMI. On one occasion, Fela resorted to taking up residence inside the premises of the recording company in order to settle a score over his financial entitlements with the establishment. It was alleged that Fela and some members of his band constituted such a nuisance that they started cooking their meals and defecating in the premises. His demands were quickly attended to, and he was convinced to vacate the premises. Until he built his own house at Gbemisola Street in Ikeja, he and the landlords of the houses he rented were always at odds. In the final analysis, the police and the army were the objects of his deepest hatred. They were also the favourite themes of his bawdy and ribald jokes and his scathing and sarcastic songs.

Given that genius and talent as vast as Fela's can hardly be hidden or ignored, it is an accepted fact that he lived his life for all to see. Granted also that Fela's music had great rhythm and entertainment value, its lyrics could be lewd and immoral, and the dances and choreography could be indecorously suggestive and downright obscene. His lifestyle was socially unconventional. His unprecedented marriage to 27 wives on the same day and in the same ceremony was viewed with outrage and alarm even by his fans.

His defiant use of drugs like marijuana, his glamourization of sex, and his irreverent reference to highly placed religious leaders of similar callings to his late father's all portrayed him as an immoral and defiant deviant and nihilist. When death finally came, after his physiognomy was in rack and ruin, looking frail and fragile, no one was surprised when it was announced that he had succumbed to AIDS. His funeral was a celebration of his life. When he died in October 1998, he was universally mourned. He was buried with fanfare by myriads of his wailing fans that adored him when he lived. His fans still celebrate the anniversary of his death every October, in what they call a 'Fela-bration' of his life.

Music runs in Fela's family veins. The beautifully composed Egba national anthem was the work of Fela's grandfather. Femi and Seun, his two sons from two women, took after their father in looks and musical talents. Their forte was their consummate handling of the saxophone. Femi and Seun eventually blossomed into giving virtuoso stage performances which only clones of Fela could enact. Even though Femi humbly admitted that Fela's shoes were rather too big for him to step into, he paid his dues handsomely in various exquisite ways.

Fela acknowledged in his lifetime the arrival of Femi on the musical scene when the latter released his chart buster 'Wonder Wonder'. In this song, he vented his feelings of impatience on the seemingly intractable unity of Africa. He also trod the sacrilegious trail already blazed by Fela when he took a controversial swipe at Christians who await the second coming of Jesus Christ. He formed his own orchestra, 'The Positive Force', around himself and his sisters, Yeni and Sola. His sisters doubled as accomplished dancers and complementary background singers. Femi went a step further when he built his own version of the Afrika Shrine. It is a far cry from the ramshackle house and surroundings which characterized Fela's previous nightclub. It is well known that Femi did not indulge in the excesses which spelled the doom of his father. Indeed, he appeared on advertising billboards to draw attention to the dastardly effects of the dreaded AIDS.

Interestingly, Femi has assiduously worked his way into universal stardom. Events played superbly into his hands when he stood in successfully and admirably for Fela at a much-publicized performance in Los Angeles. Fela had been detained at home for a currency trafficking offence. Femi perfectly rendered Fela's favourite songs and performed as if Fela himself were onstage. Rave reviews and global acclaim of his performance made people wait with baited expectation for his own debut. He in fact arrived, having evolved his own distinctive style and developed his own vigorous dance steps. He won the coveted CORA award. He was also nominated for the distinguished Grammy award in New York.

Art Alade was a rare gem of an artiste as an accomplished jazz pianist, a consummate concert impresario, and humorous entertainer. It is gratifying that Art Alade would seem to have bequeathed his son Dare to my entertainment world. The latter repeatedly gave heart-warming performances to emerge as a promising singer, pianist, and entertainer at the 'Project Fame' competition on television. Tunde and Fran Kuboye were a fantastic couple, both of whom were jazz-playing musicians who complemented each other with ease and grace in the Extended Family Band. They both performed regularly at the popular Jazz 38 Nightclub until the untimely death of Fran. While Tunde twanged his guitar with an air of fulfillment, Fran, who was a niece of Fela's, crooned and serenaded in her deep guttural voice.

There is no gainsaying the fact that highlife and juju, predominantly popular then and now, will continue to be the basic types of music that propel my culture to higher international realms. Calypso and reggae have been imported from the Caribbean Islands. Artists like Majek Fashek used reggae to 'invoke the rains' in his beautifully rendered song; Ras Kimono used the new musical fad to ask 'Whats gwan' (what is going on?); the Mandators, dread-locked as were the earlier-mentioned two, were the adherents of *Ja* as Rastafarians. Mike Okri, Alex Zitto, and Daniel Wilson effectively combined calypso and reggae to evolve a brand of music that was danceable and unique. Some of the other artists in this mould were Evi Edna Ogholi, Isaac Black, and Rammy Anderson. All these singers and entertainers contributed in no small measure to my musical heritage and culture.

A gangling, precocious kid, muscular and dread-locked, emerged from the Ajegunle ghetto to glamourize his environment in reggae music. He extolled the 'jungle city' tutorials and experiences which make the ghetto kid rugged, durable, and smart in his 'E jo o in the ghetto'. His name is Daddy Shokky, and he is still recording with his deep and moving rich voice.

Lagbaja is a great musical sensation in every sense of the word. He is as 'nameless' as he is 'faceless'. He is nameless because the Yoruba meaning of his name is just 'Mr. So-and-so'. He is also faceless because he is perpetually masked and covers himself from head to toe like a masquerade. He wears colourful tight-fitting long-sleeved shirts at times under colourful capes attached to the mask. His brand of music is unique in sound, and his lyrics make him stand out as very creative, original, topical, and contemporary. Lagbaja successfully fuses a jazz sound and rhythm with indigenous Bata and talking drums to achieve the type of melody that is identifiable as him only. He is quite at home and skilful with the tenor saxophone. His popular recorded composition, which is a 'party buster', is titled 'Konko Bilo'. His choreographed performance and rendition of this song made the dance form extremely popular with the young and the old. Particular mention should be made of his duet partner, Ego. Imbued with a sweet voice, Ego adds glamour and scintillating performances to Lagbaja's choreography.

Fuji music is highlife, juju, and apala rolled into one. It therefore has the potential of being classified as original and creative music. 'Mr. Johnson', Adewale Ayuba, called it 'bonsue fuji' and danced to it the same way people used to dance to bonsue in a bygone era; Wasiu Ayinde 'Marshall's' own version was called 'talazo fuji'. These last two types of dances were very popular among the youths and in the university campuses. But the big names that make fuji music very popular and in demand at parties and other social functions were the veterans 'Fuji Garbage' Ayinde Barrister, Wasiu Alabi Pasuma, Ayinla Kollington, the inimitable 'Waka Queen' Salawu Abeni, and the boyish-looking Obesere.

Gospel music has become very popular. Its general acceptance and spiritual significance are manifested in the fact that the songs come in various languages and dialects. The ambiance and milieu of the rendition and performances of these songs are always similar. Choral groups and individual artists perform in churches and concert halls. Essentially, the themes are always the same: Basically, they are songs of thanksgiving and praise-worship to the Almighty God.

Some of the popular gospel artists are Panan Percy Paul, Dele Bamgboye, Heleta Felix, Sola Rotimi, Deniran, Ori Okoroh, Bola Are, and Tope Alabi. Choral groups include the Light Bearers, Karis Band, Glad Tidings, and the Good Women Choir. The Steve Rhodes Voices were a group of disciplined and well trained singers, conducted and guided by the impresario and conductor, Steve Rhodes. They rendered spiritually uplifting and melodious gospel songs at music halls and on television. Sunny Okosuns also demonstrated his versatility by singing some beautiful gospel songs which were easily danceable. He rearranged and brought more danceable flair to the music of well-known Christmas carols. Okposo is a great and impressive gospel singer with a very powerful and sonorous voice. He won nominations and awards at international level.

Open-air concerts and music jamborees have become the vogue since the 1980s. Public holidays marking such Christian and Muslim religious festivals as Easter, Christmas, Eid-el-fitir, Eid-el–kabir, and Eid-el-maloud are usually marked with these musical fiestas. The popular spots and designations featuring these events are Lekki Sun Splash, Badagry Beach, Root Rock Reggae Revue, Poatson Music Jamboree, Unity Concert, Pepsi Promo Concert, Golden Tones Concert, and Harp Concert.

The completion and opening of the prestigious MUSON Center (Musical Organization of Nigeria) has ushered in an era of musical renaissance in my exposure to the modern trappings of international cultural excellence. The MUSON Center has become the Mecca of concert-goers and patrons of arts and culture. It is a magnificent edifice of beautiful architecture and modern grandeur, comparable in concept and essence with any of its type anywhere in the world. It is appropriately designed to accommodate a variety of events and performances. The founding patrons under the cultured and capable leadership of the well-respected doyen of chartered accountants, Akintola Williams, had a vision and concept of incomparable magnificence for the place as it continued to grow and expand. Ayo Rosiji was also another founding member of the elite group, which gave great support to the noble cause that the center stands for.

The Performing Musician Association of Nigeria (PMAN) was the umbrella organization under which my enterprising and industrious artists and musicians converged to promote and protect their undertakings. At the initial stages the programmes and activities of the association were laudable and very ambitious in propagating and promoting their interests and agenda. They were meant to augur well for the future of music and musicians. Indeed, the PMAN's greatest achievement then was the inauguration of the Music Award Night, during which talents and great performances were displayed. Deserving artists and budding talents were recognized and rewarded. Such an exercise was meant to develop to the status of the prestigious Grammy Awards of the United States of America and the nascent Kora Awards of South Africa. It was in recognition of their importance and cultural relevance that the Babangida government handed out a generous donation to PMAN to build a befitting musical plaza in my new Federal capital in Abuja.

Laudable as the programmes of the association were, execution of such programmes was constantly impeded by a variety of seemingly intractable problems. Piracy remained the bane of their recording zeal and acumen. Profitability constantly eluded their efforts and genuine expectations. Songs and beautiful recordings made in authorized and professional studios found their way into the hands of miscreants and unscrupulous racketeering pirates. They would in turn carry out mass faked and unauthorized recordings. The end result attracted more sales and profits for underground marketers who undercut legitimate sellers, thereby leaving the genuine artists and producers short-changed and impoverished by these nefarious practises.

Leadership tussles within the hierarchy of the association made the confusion worse. Bitter acrimony was to usher in and usher out succeeding executive boards, leaving the work of combatting piracy through the proper government channels unattended to. Leadership of this august body changed hands from Tony Okoroji to Mustapha Amego and then to the delectable 'Lady of Songs', Christie Essien-Ugbokwe.

The activities of PMAN became more publicized when an acrimonious rift nearly tore it apart. The colourful and irrepressible Charles Oputa—'Charlie Boy'—was elected its president, and events took a new and dramatic turn. He attacked issues head-on and on two fronts. He criticized the activities of the outgoing executive under Okoroji by accusing it of financial malpractises. At the same time, he took the reins of administration with a strong hand, and in a whirlwind fashion he fought the pirates by taking the fight straight to their doorsteps. The struggle and intrigues to select a generally acceptable leadership seemed to go on interminably. Finally, the end of the road was reached with the election of the level-headed and experienced classical flutist, Tee Mac.

Some Traditional Rulers

I cherish the dignity and majesty personified in my traditional rulers. They were the *sine qua non* of grassroots administration and were the most effective and influential players in the Indirect Rule system during the colonial era. The traditional rulership institution has been instrumental in the modernization of the civil society and in applying soothing balm on the ravages and anxieties unleashed on my post-Colonial polity. My people from various tribes were ruled by traditional rulers. Some of these titles are Emir, Oba, Obi, Igwe, Eze, Olu, Shehu, Amanayanbo, Etsu Nupe, Obong, Gbong Gwon, Tor Tiv, and the uniquely paramount Sultan of Sokoto, who combines religious leadership with his traditional roles. These traditional rulers are generally ably supported and assisted by other chiefs bearing various traditional titles.

The Obas hold sway among the Yorubas and the Edos. They derive their kingship through ancestral lineage and inheritance. Selection rotates among ruling houses made up of members who are in some cases related to one another. After the due processes of selection, Obas are made to go through the rigors of initiation followed by elaborate enthronement or coronation ceremonies. Ibadan operates a distinctly peculiar system in which accession to the throne of the Olubadan is by seniority. This is why at times the Olubadans are very old at the time of their installations. It is like a game of 'Dancing Chairs', in which a departed Olubadan is substituted by the next and highest-ranking remaining chief. Thereafter, the other chiefs move a step higher on the seniority list and new chiefs are duly appointed.

The Oba is the most venerated person in the land. In the pantheon of Yoruba deities, he is second only to the Orisa. The Orisa in turn, is the equivalent of God's (Olodumare's) agent on earth. The Oba's authority is unquestionable, and this fact is implicit in his title as the 'Alaiye', the supreme owner of his immediate environment on earth. The Almighty God is known as 'Olorun Olodumare' who is the Supreme Owner of Heaven and Earth. The Oba is Orisa's god's second in command. The Oba's appellation is Kabiyesi (ka bi o o si), which means 'the one whose utterances and powers are neither challengeable nor questionable'. The Oba's decisions are respected, and there are some utterances that are taboo in reference to him. For instance, the Oba does not sleep—he merely relaxes. To sleep for him is to die, and you do not say the Oba dies—he only goes through the ceiling to join his ancestors. He does not behold a dead body. He is not sup-posed to be seen to be eating publicly. When he eats, he is actually supposed to be performing a ritual.

The traditional rulers respect all religions particularly in the South where Christians, Muslims, and animists freely worship God, as the Christians and Ani-mists call Him. The Muslims call Him Allah. The traditional rulers also accord re-spect to tradition and culture by accommodating their subjects' worship of other gods. Of particular note was the Osemawe of Ondo, Oba Festus Adesanoye. He was a practicing Christian who hardly ever missed the Holy Communion ser-vice on Sunday mornings. Revival services were regularly conducted at the cha-pel he built in his magnificent palace where his born-again wife, 'Olori' Anike, was always present. Oba Adesanoye attended the mosque when occasion war-ranted it, essentially out of respect for Islam and love for his subjects. He per-formed all the rituals, which the animists and tradition occasionally demanded of him, particularly during the Ogun festival.

Still in Ondo Town, the new Oba, Kiladejo, ascended the throne of his ances-tors by incorporating into the enthronement procedure the idea of receiving the prayers of Christian priests and Muslim Imams along the route leading to the various ritual sites before his installation. He also emerged from his hibernation quarters and made straight for the church, to attend a Thanksgiving service be-fore accepting the Staff of Office from the Governor of Ondo State. Indeed, he of-fered a gift of the Holy Bible to a sectional head of an ancient quarter in Ondo. This was in order to commemorate the reconciliation between the Osemawe of Ondo and the Oloja of Ifore, the latter being the head of the Ekiis, whose progen-itors were the aboriginal dwellers in the town. The significance of mutual re-spect and cordiality between the two was emphasized during the ceremonies and rites that led to the installation and the Oloja of Ifore's proclamation of Ose-mawe as the new Oba.

During the reign of the former Olubadan of Ibadan, Oba Michael Adeyemo, he held high laity offices in the Anglican Province and the Ibadan diocese. He was also highly respected by both his Muslim subjects and the animists. Eze Ibiam was a knight of the church and was one of the protagonists of Presbyteri-anism in my religious culture. The same thing applied to Muslim Obas like Oba Matanmi Ataoja of Osogbo, who was a practising Muslim who respected the views of Christians and performed his official ritual duties during the Osun Osogbo annual festival. The Oba of Benin, the Olu of Warri, and the Asagba of Asaba are typical examples of Christian Obas who did not turn their backs on other religions and always upheld the dictates of traditions, particularly relating to ancestors and established 'precedence'. This attitude to religion is common among all the traditional rulers in the South and some parts of the Middle Belt, where an unavoidable degree of religious tolerance is understandable.

The Emirs are strictly Muslims. But it is an acceptable fact that they have been known to exercise a reasonable degree of tolerance towards other religions while upholding by example and by precepts the tenets of Islam. The Sultan of Sokoto is unique in his own title and peculiar lineage. Heavily turbaned and imbued with the dignified aura of a spiritual ruler, the sultan combines his awesome powers of the caliphate with the revered headship of the Islamic religion. His word is final regarding the interpretations of the tenets of Islam. He attained his authority via his legendary ancestral lineage of Usman Dan Fodio. The sultan exudes authority and exemplifies the essence of Islam. His confirmation of the sighting of the moon signifies the beginning of Ramadan and the beginning of the fasting period, which is one of the five pillars of the Islamic Religion.

Traditional and Professional Titles

I am a Nation of people who adore titles. Some titles are inherited; some are competed for; some are bought outright. Some titles are earned by professional qualifications and others are conferred on merit. My people answer to titles like Prince, Otunba, Chief, Alhaji, Daud, Ogbuefi, Mazi, Mallam, and others in different tongues. They like to be known and acknowledged by their professional titles like Dr., Arch., Engnr., Barrister, Deacon, Rev'd., Sheik, and even by military rank: General, Commodore, or Captain. Some people are referred to by the nature of their professions. They therefore answer professionally to such callings as barber, tailor, mechanic, plumber, rewire, vulcanizer, carpenter, bricklayer, and other such descriptive names stemming from various professions.

Modes of Greetings and Salutations

Greetings and salutations vary from place to place. The Yorubas portray the culture of respect by using the plural forms of some words. For example, it should be 'You' (Iwo) for a peer or younger person. It is also 'You' (Eyin) for an elder person or for many people. While the male Yorubas prostrate or bow respectfully to their elders and people in authority, the females kneel down in greeting and a show of respect. Curtseying, particularly by the female Yorubas when they receive or give something to their elders, is an acknowledged sign of good up-bringing. People, specifically males from my Northern ethnic groups, crouch and bend low with raised clenched fists in salutation saying 'Ranki ya dede' to their elders and in obeisance to people in authority. They greet one another by saying 'Sannu', shaking hands once or twice, and touching their chests after each handshake.

The Muslims in the North and the West often exchange the religious salutation of 'As-Salamu Alaykum'. The Igbos are less formal but still very warm and expressive in their greetings. Their chiefs and elders give one another the back-hand handshake three times and cheerily end it with frontal handshakes, at times using fans or walking sticks. The Igbos greet each other saying 'Kedu' with a cheery handshake and touching their chests. This mode of salutation exudes warmth and respect.

CULTURAL CELEBRATIONS

Events and Significance of Prayers and Ritual Items

There are always many causes for celebration within my various ethnic groups. The birth of a new baby and the naming ceremony, house-warming, marriage, funeral rites, burials, and anniversaries are all events that are celebrated and remembered when the calendar turns. These events are often celebrated at lavish parties where one hears the sound of music and watches dancers at village squares, city halls, and private homes. However, lavishly equipped and decorated events centers have now sprung up in some major cities.

Kolanut is a very important item in my culture. It is a very meaningful gift item. When the slices are cast on the ground, diviners expertly interpret the meanings of the positions assumed by the cast kolanut slices. The thrown slices are used for the invocation of the gods and for their blessings, favour, and guidance. The kolanut is a food gift for the gods during prayers both at ceremonies and settlement of quarrels. Some tribes place equal value on the kolanut as on money, and as the saying goes, 'Money is kolanut, and kolanut is money'. Others animate the kolanut, giving it life and essence, by re-echoing Chinua Achebe in *Things Fall Apart*, saying, 'He who brings kolanut brings life'.

It could be very instructive to explain the significance and relevance of some of these food items as they impact my culture, particularly in the South. Events like naming ceremonies for infants, weddings, engagements, building a new house, freedom ceremonies for successful apprentices, and launching a new planting season call for the use of some items as token gifts in offerings to God or invoking the assistance and blessings of the ancestors. For example, the sweetening and chastening properties of salt make it a requisite item for prayers. The use of honey or sugar as sweeteners and the indestructibility of the sugarcane during a fire outbreak make both items useful for prayers at wedding ceremonies and house-warmings. Palm oil is used as a balm and an appeaser, just as water is reputed to 'have no enemies' as rendered in Fela Anikulapo's song 'Water No Get Enemy'. Hence the attributes of both oil and water are desirable in the lives of infants, the future of a bride, reconciliation between disputants, and a smooth ride for travellers. The pod of the alligator pepper contains plenty of seeds, and this has formed the basis for the prayers of a productive life for a new bride and a very productive and abundant harvesting season for farmers.

My cultural heritage is rich, colourful, and expressive in many ways. Various aspects of my culture are portrayed in rituals, events, dramas, songs, and dances. The Atilogu dancers speak for themselves when they take native choreography to new dimensions of agility and dexterity. The jangling tinsels around their wrists and ankles supplement the drums and songs their dances interpret. The Obitun dances with the aesthetic grace of a semi-divine nymph. She radiates the confident charm of a virgin beauty. The Obitun enriches the culture of the Ondos and the Owos. It was a kind of festival held for young girls for the purpose of introducing them to adulthood. It was a kind of initiation that incorporates the universal concepts of change and acceptance into the more active, responsible, and productive membership of the community to which the young girl belongs.

Apart from the sociocultural significance of the rites, the Obituns' artistic performances have become an art in which the dance troupe now functions as a medium of entertainment in schools, social functions, and cross-cultural festivals. The Obituns tie 'aso oke' (indigenous hand woven clothes) as their wrappers to cover their chests, leaving the neck, the shoulders, and arms bare. They are draped in ornamental beads and have their hair elegantly woven in neat corn-rows. Chalk powder and camwood lotion are used to smear their bodies. The climax of the dance is reached when the star dancers dance with two or three china plates intricately balanced on their heads and on their hands.

The Mbopo or Mbobi puberty rites of maidens among the Efik/Ibibio communities of my riverine areas of the East and the Mgbede rites amongst the Igbo are comparable in essence and ritual significance with the Obituns. The Bata drummers and dancers gyrate to melodious rhythms; the exponents are from Oyo, Ibadan, Ogbomosho, Oshogbo, and Ikirun.

Festivals

My cultural heritage is very rich and beautifully diversified. I have successfully resisted all attempts to be overwhelmed by the corrosive influence of modernity. Efforts have been made to ensure that originality is maintained and procedures and rituals remain undiluted. In the absence of documentary history up to a time, habits and systems evolved practically from oral history enacted and practised from generation to generation.

Such is the Durbar, the celebration of equestrian splendour in honour and remembrance of great people and events, used as an entertainment for visiting potentates or royalty. It is a major component of Hausa tradition of cultural display and a traditional evolution dating back to the earler part of the sixteenth century. It was a traditional military parade, showcasing the military might of the Emir of Kano, particularly during the Eid-el-Fitir celebrations. Significantly, the military parade of skilful horsemen was a pointer to the culture's resilience in the face of colonial onslaught as it stood the test of time. It is even being considered to showcase and elevate the Durbar festival to international status by enlisting it as a United Nations Economic, Scientific, and Cultural Organization (UNESCO) World Heritage Event.

The Durbar reached the climax of superb performance and demonstration of an aspect of my culture during FESTAC '77. Thousands of horsemen in colourful dresses exhibited picturesque, traditional, and skilful horsemanship. It was the parade of various emirates with the Emirs resplendent in their heavily embroidered robes and precisely arranged turbans. They rode under colourful and big umbrellas and were ushered in turns around the pavilion grounds. When the parade reached the front of the assemblage of dignitaries, which featured the venerable Sultan of Sokoto, everybody in the parade groups paid obeisance. Then the horsemen cantered away amidst hysterical yelling, ululations, and fierce drumbeats. This type of event is occasionally celebrated in some parts of the Northern Emirates.

The Regatta naturally belonged to a different milieu from the Durbar. It was also one of the fabulous events on display during FESTAC '77. If horsemen on horses on dry land celebrate the Durbar, the regatta comes alive with canoes and oarsmen on the water. Because of its cultural setting, this event is celebrated by my people who live in the riverine areas like Port Harcourt, Warri, Okitipupa, and Lagos. The regatta is the formation of a gaily bedecked and festooned armada of canoes, with oarsmen paddling rhythmically to the percussion of drumbeats and melodious singalong songs and choruses.

The Argungu Fishing Festival has become a very important annual festival in my cultural calendar. It started in August 1934, when the then-Sultan of Sokoto, Mallam Hassan Dan Mu'aza, made his first historic visit to Argungu. In appreciation of this visit, a grand fishing festival was organized. It has become a highly recognized international event held between February and March each year. The event attracts people from different nations in a spirit that transcends international barriers. It is a spectacular event in which about 3,000 fishermen participate in a fishing expedition.

The participants are equipped with only hand-nets that have hooks at both ends and a large round guard with a small opening at the top. Then they form a line about two kilometres long. The most thrilling moment of the show is when the signal is given for fishing to start. Then the fishermen would charge into the river to the loud blare of music, songs, and ululations.

Once the fishing is over, fishermen are ritually forbidden from fishing on the spot again until the next fishing festival. In essence, this is a ruse to enable more fish to grow in larger quantities and sizes and make ready for the following year's festival. Big catches are usually weighed in competition, and the lucky fishermen with the biggest catches are duly recognized and rewarded. People are also attracted to the festival because of its other cultural displays such as local boxing and wrestling, cultural dances, and local swimming competitions.

The New Yam Festival is a cultural event celebrated in every village and town all over the South, particularly where the staple food, yam tubers, are cultivated. In Akure, the New Yam Festival is celebrated as an annual ritual in the official residence of the High Chief Ojomu. In some places the yams are arranged in competitive displays, and the biggest ones are determined in competition. It is always an occasion for festivity and jubilation with drumming and dancing and feasting.

The New Yam Festival is a very important one in the cultural calendar of the Igbos. Whether at home in the villages or away in the cities and towns, the occasion is always marked with prayers, feasting, and merriment. The festival itself in Igbo cultural history is an annual celebration originated by my Nri people of the South East since the introduction of yam by Nri about 2,000 years ago. The celebration comes in two major parts, with the second and final ceremony usually taking place in the eighth month of the year. This may be the reason why some people refer to it as the 'Onwa Asato', meaning Eighth Month Festival. In Nri culture, when yams are cultivated, immediately after the first and second post-harmattan rains in January or February of each year, the farms are repeatedly weeded five times within five lunar months. During this time, the farm is expected to have produced new yams. This happens around July. The green leaves of the yam would have changed progressively from yellow to brown. They then mature, and the yams are ready to be harvested.

The first set of yams thus harvested could not go into the market or be consumed by the people unless 'purified' by the titled man called 'Ozo Nkpu', who is the designated purifier. He performs the purification and sanctification by carrying the new yam into the market. This official act would drive out old yams from the market in compliance with the people's custom.

The celebration of the New Yam Festival is held five native weeks after the 'Ozo Nkpu' has been selected. The yam is regarded and celebrated as the king of crops. It is eaten in various ways. It can be eaten when boiled, roasted, fried, or pounded. My Igbo people have set aside a day to celebrate the beginning of eating the new yam. The origin of this festival is traceable to the republican nature of the Igbos. The vitality of the convivial atmosphere is conducive for giving thanks to the Almighty God for bountiful harvest, for effecting reconciliation, and for settling quarrels.

The Ogun Festival is a big cultural annual event in most parts of the West. It is celebrated like a carnival in some places like Ondo, Ile Oluji, Akure, and Oyo-Ile. Ire, in particular, is where Ogun, the god of iron, is deified and worshipped. The drink of Ogun is palm wine. Under the influence of the intoxicating palm wine, its adherents cover themselves with knitted palm fronds and dance wildly as if possessed. The food of Ogun is dog meat. During the festival in Ondo in particular, it is happy riddance to stray dogs that cross the path of Ogun revelers. Such dogs are immediately decapitated, and they often end up in Ogun worshippers' pots of soup. It is that time of year when dog meat is a necessity for the devoted adherents of Ogun. But times are changing, and the Ondos have claimed that dog meat no longer holds any particular culinary pride of place or interest in their menu.

The name by which a dog is called in Ondo is 'Lokili'. Fiction has it that the name was coined when a serving colonial district officer (DO) had wanted to replace his dead Labrador dog allegedly bitten by a snake. The DO had asked his gardener to go into the market to buy a 'locally' bred dog—'lokili', as the gardener pronounced it, which could bark and chase away intruders. The gardener rushed to the marketplace and announced excitedly that the DO (Oyibo) wanted a 'lokili' dog that eats bread and barks. The name stuck. For a very long time the Ondos used to summon their dogs by calling out 'Lokili gba! gba!'—the dog that eats bread and barks.

The Igogo Festival at Owo is a cultural festival during which the virtue of womenfolk in community support and protection is celebrated. The festival was instituted in remembrance of one of the queens of an Olowo of Owo. She was supposed to be a goddess named Oronsen. The Olowo, who reigned more than 600 years ago, was called Rengenjen. Queen Oronsen had delineated the tráditions and rules of the Igogo Festival. Apart from the celebration, the festival also marks the start of the eating of the new yam at the Oba's palace.

The Igogo Festival is celebrated with regal fanfare and pageantry in Owo. This is a festival built around the Oba, Olowo of Owo, with himself prominently on parade as the cynosure of all spectators' eyes. The Olowo is usually dressed in his royal 'pakato' regalia, heavily beaded around the waist, wearing a white loincloth, and carrying an ornamental sword. His hair is plaited in neat rows like that of a woman. A special feather that gives him a distinctive look is stuck into the hair, distinguishing him from other chiefs who may also have their hair braided.

It is the only time all year when the Oba's head is uncovered, as it is never exposed except on that one day of the Igogo Festival. Men are not supposed to wear caps, and women, for the duration of the festival, are not to wear headgear. Besides these caveats, there should be no beating of leather drums or iron gongs, and the shooting of guns must also stop. Children participate in sheer jubilation by singing songs and beating sticks together, as drum-beating is forbidden. It is a day in which the Oba goes around the various designated quarters rendering prayers for peace and growth of the town and for fertility and good harvest. It is also supposed to be a binding time for all Owo sons and daughters at home and abroad, irrespective of their religious persuasions. It is a cultural celebration of the peoples' collective heritage. The festival usually attracts thousands of visitors and tourists, thereby giving the festival an aura of a carnival.

PLACES, PEOPLES, AND EVENTS

There are some facets of my features that speak volumes about me. They have continued to attract wholesome study by researchers and have become the object of curiosity to sightseers and fun seekers. Some are natural and others are manmade. The obelisk of Oranmiyan literally sprouts from the ground and looms like a giant ivory tower. The Yorubas believe that it was there at the beginning of time at the place of their cradle, Ile-Ife. The town is quaintly referred to as the 'source'.

There is the ancient footprint impression at Akoko Ikare around which a myth has been built. Chameleon-like, the footprint accommodates, measure for measure, all other footprint impressions except those belonging to witches. Hence, this permanent footprint is also seen as a witch hunter. The spa water at Ikogosi in Ekiti State has been turned into a holiday health resort. The cold and hot waters run side by side in an amazing manner. My people believe that the waters have healing powers because of their natural soothing effect on the body. Of course, the state government is exploiting the revenue-generating possibilities of the place to the fullest. As can be imagined, a holiday resort for health seekers has been set up there.

The fattening houses in Calabar turn out the aspiring bridal debutantes. Young unmarried ladies who are of the same age brackets are kept together in the same place and placed on a dietary regime to make them robust, vivacious, and curvaceous in the appropriate places that would make them attractive to menfolk. The young ladies celebrate the festival of their coming out as debutantes with dances in dresses that expose only their waists and necks.

In some parts of the North, young able-bodied suitors wield whips made from cowhide to whip each other silly in pairs while competing for a young lady's hand in marriage. The fights are often conducted at village squares under the watchful supervision of the umpires and family members of participants and interested spectators.

The placid Oguta Lake is the haven of tourists and sightseers who flock there for holidays. Decent hotel accommodations are provided, and the ambience of the entire resort provides delightful serenity. There are many game reserves and national parks where animals roam free in simulated natural habitats. The Yankari Game Reserve is the most popular. Others are the Borgu Game Reserve, Faro Game Reserve, Udu Niger National Park, Fazoro Game Reserve, Kainji Games Reserve, and Komoe National Park.

The sprawling Obudu Cattle Ranch, which is full of green pastures, is a home away from home. Even though the place is now fast metamorphosing into my tourism pinnacle as the Obudu Ranch Resort, it would be worthwhile to look at the historical significance of the old ranch. The name Obudu Ranch is a misnomer, stemming from the use the place was put to when it was first discovered. It was used as a cattle ranch because the flat top of the hill was free from tsetse flies. It is situated on a wide expanse of land, perched on top of the hills, and well over 1,500 meters above sea level.

The visitor journeys to the ranch on ascending roads which are not too steep. It is suffused with sharp upward corners, one of which is referred to as 'Devil's Elbow', which poses terrible danger to motorists. A notable side effect of the trip would be the gradual closing of eardrums.This is the type of experience one occasionally has in an aircraft cabin from the build-up of pressure and the increasingly rarified air. One literally walks through the air in Obudu as if it were a unique 'moon-walking' experience.

It is a place that could be described as having natural pristine beauty— rolling hills, ravines, and rainforest. It enjoys a temperate climate all year. It has a climate that ranges between 15° and 22° (centigrade) between November and January. Night temperatures, especially during the peak of the rainy season between June and August, often drop to 4° centigrade—refreshingly chilly. The periodic appearances of the crimson red moon on the horizon always conjure a spectacle of breath-taking allure. The days are peaceful and staid, just as the nights are calm, secure, and serene. Misty mornings soon yield to mild and bright afternoon sunshine. When the sun is at its beckoning brightest, the trees afford loving protection from its rays.

All forms of games to while away the time by tourists and sightseers are made available. These include chess, billiards, darts, Scrabble, draft, ludo, table tennis, and Monopoly. One of the great attractions of Obudu Ranch is its inclusion of a 9-hole golf course. There is a grotto which is a natural swimming pool and waterfall where fresh springwater continually gushes out. There are standard-size lawn tennis courts and many other sporting facilities. Perhaps I will emerge momentarily from history and mention the cable car facility that was recently installed at the ranch. It is reputed to be the longest of its type in the world.

All around the ranch are ravines which lead into canyons. In all these places are spa waters which are crystal clear and free of chemicals. The water tastes better than the chlorinated water drunk by residents in my other urban areas. There are parks for children to frolic and play. A gorilla camp has been created not far away so that the gorillas can be viewed in their natural habitat.

Nature displays its occasional quirks in the environs of the ranch on some extraordinary days when the sky is very clear. On such days, the rare sight of the sun and the moon at the same time and in different places on the firmament holds the viewer spellbound and eerily confused with sheer marvel. This is not like the usual partial or reluctant embrace of the two as it occurs in an eclipse. The sun and the moon together at the same time of the day stare down on earth in their heavenly splendour. There is no doubt that the Obudu cattle ranch is a tourist's haven and delight which has been made accessible by all sorts of communication facilities.

The special features of Plateau State, especially its hilly landscape, are of a breath-taking nature and are renowned worldwide. Apart from other notable sites in the state, one of the most prominent that attracts local and international attention is the serene Shere Hills. It derives its name from the traditional community of the Shere people. The name means 'home to rocks', as the indigenes call it. It is reputed to be quiet and unique in nature. It is a range of undulating hills and rock formations. The hills are reputed to stand tall amongst other hills that are found in the area with the highest point placed at 1,829 meters above sea level. The peak of the hills is reachable via a challenging meander that attracts both tourists and climbers. Though there are quite a number of rock formations that are scattered all over the area, two stand out. They are the Shere Peak and the Shere Magog.

The Shere Peak and Shere Magog have a special unique features. The formations at the top attract curiosity as they are so craftily arranged. Climbing the hills involves all types of odd contortions through narrow paths, bending and virtually crawling through cavelike shapes, and standing and stretching between the walls that separate the rocks. From the summit of the hill, climbers and hill walkers are assisted to descend to the base of the hill through the use of ropes that are tied to one of the rocks from the eastern side.

The popular Shere Hills Training School was opened in 1951 and is now known as the Mountain School of Citizenship and Leadership Training Center (Man O' War). It is located within the precincts of Shere Hills. The school is being used for the training of both military and police officers, who graduate from my Defense Academy and the Police Academy. It serves the same purpose for the National Youth Service Corps. About 7 million officers and youths had since received leadership training in Shere Hills.

Scattered over my geographical terrain, nature has generously endowed me with hidden treasures and places of relaxation and tourist delights. My diverse

cultural heritage and numerous museums are stacked with priceless and irre-
placeable artefacts that attract tourists and students of anthropology and sociol-
ogy from far and near. Apart from those places earlier mentioned are the Gurara
Falls, jutting out waters in rainbow colours, and Zuma Rocks in Suleja; the
Birikisu Sungbon Shrine (the legendary Queen of Sheba); Qua Falls and the Graf-
fon Snailery in Akwa Ibom State; the suspended lake at Ado Awaye in Oyo State;
my first-ever museum in Kaduna; Gbobaran Minaret in Katsina; Erin Jesha Waterfalls in Erin; the Slave Transit Hall in Badagry; Isaac Boro Park and Oloibiri
Oil Museum in Rivers State; Lake Tillar in Borno, Ogbunike Cave with the mar-
vellous sandstones, and Igbo Ukwu in Anambra State.

Ojude Oba Festival

The annual Ojude Oba festival is a unique and spectacular event where the
sons and daughters of Ijebuland pay homage to their monarch in a carnival-like
atmosphere. It is also known as Obanta Festival. It is a very important and festive occasion in the social and cultural calendar of the Ijebu people. The annual
celebration of Ojude Oba is a colourful ceremony which is usually celebrated
three days after the Muslim festival of Id-El-Kabir (Ileya). The festival affords an
opportunity for the people to turn out in their best to honour the Oba Awujale
according to various age groups. It portrays beautiful performances and radiant
display of cultural activities. The festival brings home all Ijebus who live and
work in cities and towns all over my territory.

The festival is a portrayal of the radiance of culture, full of elegance and fanfare. It is always a demonstration and expression of Ijebu nationalism and a celebration and acknowledgement of excellence, wealth, arts, and culture. It is
named after Obanta, the acknowledged founder and revered Oba of Ijebuland.
His cenotaph stands gracefully in a prominent city square at Ijebu Ode. Whether
home or abroad, the Ijebus always look forward to joining their kith and kin at
the lavish ceremony. The occasion, which dates back about 100 years and has
its origin in Islam, has grown so big in scope and dimension that it has cut
across all religious and political affiliations. The festival has now metamorphosed into a big carnival, which attracts not only the Ijebus but also visitors,
tourists, and people from all walks of life. It has virtually put Ijebu on the world
map. It has also been instrumental in forging a bond of unity among the Ijebus.

The festival is marked with 'woro' dance round the city and the eating of the popular Ijebu cuisine, 'ikokore'. The most colourful aspect of the festival is the age-group parade. Dressed in beautiful uniforms, the different groups accompanied by drummers move towards the Awujale's palace. In some cases some of the group leaders ride on horses to the parade grounds outside the palace. Though the festival has its origin in Islam, it emerged as a show of gratitude from the first set of converted Muslims who thought it fit to extend greetings and felicitations to the Oba to whom they pay homage and obeisance as they march or dance past him. This was also because the progressive Awujale at that time had given them a free hand to practise their new religion without hindrance. This liberal gesture was very significant, even in those days when African traditional religion was in vogue.

Olojo Festival

The Ooni of Ife epitomizes the cultural heritage of the Yorubas. By his appellation as the 'Arole Oduduwa', he is the acknowledged homegrown progeny of the Yoruba ancestral progenitor, Oduduwa. The other sons of Oduduwa became rulers over some of the other parts of their sire's domain. The Ooni therefore performs all those rituals that are sacrosanct to the throne of Oduduwa and for the spiritual upliftment of the Yoruba people. Hence, the Ooni celebrates the Olojo festival annually. He remains incommunicado for a few days before the festival begins, 'fasting and communing with the other 200 gods' as only he could.

The event takes place annually towards the end of October. It is, without doubt, the most important festival of the year, celebrated in honour of Ogun and Oranmiyan. Ogun is one of the deified personalities in Yoruba tradition. He is referred to as 'his majesty whose labyrinthine mansion (Onile Kangun Kangun Orun) is in heaven'. He was a hero during his lifetime. He was a fierce hunter who took extreme delight in warfare. He was also a cultural hero and the god of metals and was fond of wearing fiery dress soaked in blood.

History has it that Ogun had an affair with Ija, a woman of exceptional beauty and attractive physical attributes. The father of Ogun also had an affair with the same paragon of beauty, Ija. The father, Oduduwa, was fair skinned;

Ogun was ebony black. The resultant 'streaked' issue jointly procreated by father and son was Oranmiyan, born streaked down the middle, half black and half light complexioned. There is usually a dramatic representation of this 'freak of nature' during Olojo festival when every 'Emese' (the servants) of the Ooni paints his body half white (efun, made from a chalky liquid) and half red (osun, made from camwood).

Oranmiyan became the founder of the dynasties of Oyo and Benin. History has it that one of his misguided and misdirected wars ended in a bloody fiasco. In annoyance and great disappointment, he remorsefully drove his staff into the ground and left Ile-Ife forever. The ferocity and might with which he drove the staff into the ground was a testimony to his tremendous size and power. That staff was the legendary origin of the Opa Oranmiyan, the stone monolith situated on the old Ondo road at Ile-Ife.

The Olojo Festival is significant in many respects. It recalls the birth of Oranmiyan who, during the three days of the festival, worships and pays homage to Ogun, his father. The Olojo Festival recounts how Ogun abdicated the throne of Ife. He resettled at Okemogun, where he is still worshipped in the traditional way. The day on which the Ooni emerges from his pre-Festival hibernation is marked as a festive occasion. He wears the ageless 'are' beaded crown that was first worn by Oduduwa himself. Everybody then waits with excitement to glimpse the Ooni. This excitement was mixed with trepidation in the olden days. It has been said that the essence and personality of the Ooni, by virtue of his having to wear the Oduduwa's crown, would have transformed beyond the mortal realm in which he had normally been seen. Hence, the first uninitiated person who caught a glimpse of the 'reinvigorated' Ooni might die. The crown has longish white striped tinsel cascading down the Ooni's face and partially covering his visage. That is the only day of the year he wears that crown. The Ooni worships at the Ogun shrine at the Oke-mogun area of Ile-Ife. All his traditional chiefs, including the chief Priest of Ogun deity and traditional drummers, accompany him. This is the occasion during which the Ooni showers prayers and blessings on his subjects.

The day is marked with general merriment, feasting, and dancing. It is a day on which chieftaincy titles are conferred on deserving sons and daughters of the land who have contributed to the development and well-being of the society. In recent times the Ooni Sijuade has introduced greater grandeur and panache to the festival by awarding and conferring chieftaincy titles from 'The Source' on my worthy and deserving citizens from far and near, including Yorubas and non-Yorubas alike.

Osun Osogbo Festival

The Osun Osogbo festival is celebrated in Osogbo. It is a cultural event to honour the goddess of Osun at the grove by the bank of the Osun River. That was where one of the forefathers of Osogbo and the goddess reportedly had an encounter. It is generally agreed that in modern times, many cultural festivals have either lost steam or become extinct.

However, the Osun Osogbo remains a cultural heritage driven by an unwavering willingness of my sons and daughters in Osogbo to be faithful to a pact that dates back to 1370. The re-enaction of the pact of benevolent association with the River Osun deity between Osogbo ancestors and the Osun goddess who inhabited the grove is essentially the reason for the festival. The pact is said to have made Osogbo peaceful, progressive, and free from the ravages of war and pestilence. It has gained an international reputation as one of the truly rich cultural events in black Africa and even in the Diaspora that reaches across the seas to South America and the West Indies. A recreation of this cultural celebration was enacted in 1995 in Philadelphia with Oba Sijuade, Ooni of Ife as host.

Thousands of visitors annually converge on the junction city of Osogbo as suppliants to the river goddess of Osun. Some people come for the beneficial blessings and the fascination for ritual process. Others come as ministers and priests of the guardian goddess of the river. She is known and regarded as the goddess of fertility. Many more come to implore the goddess for wealth, children, happiness, bounteous harvest, and good health. It is generally believed by the ardent adherents that no one goes away empty-handed after paying obeisance to the deity. It is essentially a festival of love. It is an invocation of the primal forces of the ancestors of deeply religious adherents.

The festival usually kicks off a few days before with 'Iwopopo', the clearing of the main footpaths to the town. The Oba Ataoja of Osogbo leads his chiefs, members of the royal family, Iya Osun, the Aworo Osun, and other worshippers to the Gbaemu crossroads for prayers. The 'clearing' of the roads signifies that traditional security and spiritual cleansing have been put in place for the coming festival. This is followed three days later by the lighting of Osanyin's ancient lamp that will be kept burning until daybreak. The sixteen-eyed lamp (Olojumerindinlogun) is mounted on a piece of metal about 17 centimeters high. The elephant hunter Olutimehin allegedly seized it at the Osun.

On the morning of the festival, the traditional coterie of priests and priestesses meet at the Oba Ataoja's palace for a very important assignment. They go into consultative divination to determine by means of casting kolanuts which virgin damsel will be selected to carry the calabash. They will also use the same process to find out what the goddess wants as the contents of the calabash. The calabash itself is covered in the richest damask fabric with beautiful designs and patterns. The cascading fabric is made to partially veil the face of the maiden. She is chaperoned by the previous year's virgin and the newly selected Iya Osun.

The virgin 'arugba' first pays homage to the Oba Ataoja, who himself is an acolyte of Osun and who has kept his inheritance of the 'ojugbo' in his palace. Then the arugba (calabash carrier) and the priests and priestesses with the Oba Ataoja in tow lead the way to the Osun Grove, which is about a five-kilometre walk from the Oja Oba (the king's market). A crowd of supplicants, adherents, and tourists joins the procession to the Osun River. Everyone eagerly and gingerly follows the graceful footsteps of the virgin arugba. Once there, the contents of the calabash are cast into the river to be swallowed by the fish called 'IKO'.

The priests and priestesses offer prayers for the whole community for good harvest, successful trading, and fertility. During the long walk, it is taboo and generally portends ill-will for the damsel to trip and fall on her way to depositing the calabash on the lap of the goddess. Hundreds of people, including local and international visitors, gaily dressed in vivid colors that typify the picturesque and spectacular atmosphere of the festival then head back to the palace in a gay mood. It is usually a fascinating sight to behold as children, men, women, drummers, singers, and acrobats mingle with the faithful and tourists alike to partake in an orgy of festivities.

I must admit that the cultural history and significance of Osun Osogbo will not be fully told if I do not make a special mention of Susan Wenger and accord her a place of pride. She had settled in Osogbo for over five decades because of her 'love and adoration' for the goddess of Osun. Because of this, she became known as Adunni Olorisha. She brought traits of her culture and intellectualism to my setup in the early 1950s. She opted to be a full devotee of the Osun shrine. From that time forward, she played a prominent role in keeping the ancestral home of the shrine holy and sacred.

Without Adunni Olorisha's sense of commitment and painstaking efforts, little would have been available to ensure the enlistment of the grove as a UNESCO World Heritage Site by the that organization in 2005. This listing by the world body thus elevated the Osun Osogbo Festival to international prominence. The Osun devotees' tangible and intangible legacies and landmarks are found in the bizarre and grotesque carvings adorning the Osun grove and a flock of followers and devotees of Osun.

There is no doubt that the ambiance of the grove is one of the few places within my terrain that has retained its original vegetation. Adunni Olorisa became a special person in the scheme of events surrounding the worship of the goddess of Osun. She was known not only as an artist but also as a priestess of Osun. She designed and built a mausoleum for a celebrated theater practitioner which she calls the 'Oju ori oba koso, omo Ladipo'. The artwork on it symbolizes the ritual and emotional attachment of the god and goddess, Sango and Oya, respectively.

The Annual Festival of Azu-Ofala

My ancient City of Onitsha annually plays host to its sons and daughters and visitors from all over—both locally and internationally—to celebrate the Ofala Festival. The two-day event usually provides the participants, particularly the sons and daughters of Onitsha, the opportunity to revisit their roots in a bid to recapture those cherished elements of their rich cultural heritage. The essence of the festival, which is one of the most surviving traditional ceremonies of the Onitsha people and my Igbo race, is to mark the climax of the new yam festival, which is an occasion for family reunions and merrymaking.

Rich and spectacularly amazing cultural displays usually precede the main events at the Ime-Obi, as the Obi's palace is called. The glamour of the drumming, dancing, and singing that heralds the arrival of the various red-cap chiefs

'Indi-Ichie' to the palace grounds provides a splendid spectacle to behold and treasure. Eminent sons and daughters, including those visiting for the event, endeavour to remind celebrants how much they value the Ofala and the Igwe. The interior of the palace comes alive with an enchanting panorama of colour and motion. Gaily dressed individuals and groups begin to take their places in preparation for the commencement of the event. The event rolls on amidst a medley of drumming and musical performances from various cultural groups and entertainers.

Expectation of the arrival of the Obi rises to a feverish pitch as soon as the red-cap chiefs have taken their assigned exalted seats. The deafening staccato of gunshots and explosions from rockets and canons then announce the much-awaited appearance of the Obi. The grandeur of his sensational appearance on the scene is always in consonance with tradition. When the Igwe emerges from his inner chamber, it is a signal for him to be ushered to the palace arena by the chiefs. Then it is his turn to take the first dance round the arena to the great admiration of his people whom he had come to greet.

When the Obi starts to dance, he usually cuts a spectacular picture in his elaborate ceremonial regalia, which has its intrinsic designs complemented by royal beads, brass anklets, and a brass royal sword. His headgear is elaborately decorated with a profusion of bright feathers and many-faceted little mirrors. When the ceremony goes into the second day, the Obi and members of his cabinet of red-cap chiefs may not be as ceremoniously attired as on the first day.

The Obi, for instance, may be clad in simple white material, red neck beads, horsetail flywhisk, and his ceremonial bronze sword. The crown on his head is adorned with white feathers. The crown is fashioned to reflect his insignia, which has as its main features the dove representing his desire for peace and the rays representing the nine main clans of Onitsha Ebo Itenani that make up Onitsha Town.

As the Obi mixes with the people in order to greet them on the first day, he dances with majestic poise and sways with dignity and grace in tune with the rhythmic throbs of drums and other local instruments. The excited and mixed crowd of celebrants responds to the Igwe's gesture by calling out, 'Agbogidi! Agbogidi!' That is the royal appellation with which they enthusiastically hail him. The Obi then returns to his reception chamber in the palace after the chiefs would

1 The Olojo Festival of Ile Ife,
with the Ooni of Ife wearing
the once-a-year ageless beaded
crown inherited from Oduduwa.

*2 **The virgin Arugba** surrounded by*
devotees during the annual Osun Osogbo
*cultural festival. The virgin Arugba **is** the*
cynosure of all eyes as she carries the
ritually significant calabash during the
procession to Osun Grove.

3 Igue Festival. *A ceremony celebrated in Benin kingdom in an atmosphere of peace, accord and hospitality with the Oba as the object of praise, support and prayer for a peaceful reign.*

Susan Wenger/Aduni Olorisha. *An Austrian-born devotee of the goddess of Osun. She worked assiduously and successfully to get the Grove recognized as a UNESCO World Heritage Site.*

2 Azu-Ofala Festival. *The annual celebration of the Azu-Ofala Festival in the ancient city of Onitsha. The Obi of Onitsha is welcomed and hailed by his subjects, whom he also goes round to greet in his familiar regalia.*

have taken turns, one after the other, dancing and trying to outdo one another with adroit and intricate dance steps and graceful body and hands movements. The festival then ends with the speech of the Obi in which he takes stock of overall development in his domain during the year. He thereafter itemizes his plans, hopes, and aspirations for the years ahead.

The Traditional Igue Festival of Benin

This is a festival that is always elaborately celebrated in praise and support of the Oba by my people of the Benin kingdom. It involves certain ritual performances usually carried out in an era and atmosphere of peace and general accord. The origin of the festival dates back many centuries. It has over the years become a time to celebrate peace and love in Benin. Coming at the end of the year, the Igue festival usually provides my people in Benin the opportunity to reflect on the past year, effect necessary reconciliations, and look ahead to the coming year with hope for peace and progress. Apart from celebrating with the Oba in his palace, the people of Benin are enjoined to host their friends and sojourners within the community and in their respective homes.

The Regatta: The festival of aquatic splendour usually celebrated by people who live near water. It is the formation of gaily bedecked and festooned canoes and boats with people dancing and rowing rhythmically to drumbeats.

The period is generally one of peace in the kingdom. It is a time during which the people do not engage in war or any form of attrition. Story also has it that the British expedition of 1897, which led to the overthrow and exile of Oba Ovoranwem, succeeded primarily because the Oba was celebrating the Igue festival. That was at a time when, unfortunately, the Oba was not disposed to waging war or attending to extraneous matters of State.

Specially Designated Days for Local Cities and Towns

Cultural resurgence has manifested itself as a new fad among various communities and towns. Such activities reflect the richness and diversity of my culture. Hence, Abeokuta declares Lisabi Day in honor of the acknowledged founder of Egbaland. Ondo declares Ekimogun Day on the first Saturday of December each year. Akure has its Oyemekun Day; Ibadan celebrates Okebadan. Ikorodu celebrates the Ikorodu Oga Day in honor of their illustrious founder. On

The Argungu Fishing Festival is a festive but hilarious fishing extravaganza involving hundreds of participants. The biggest fish caught when weighed attracts prizes and praises for the winning fisherman.

such days the cultural format is the same everywhere. The general atmosphere is one of festivity, feasting, dancing, parades by age groups and clubs, cultural displays, and the acknowledgement of excellence through conferment of chieftaincy titles and awards on deserving sons and daughters of the particular community.

Masquerades

I do have masqueraders whose abodes are supposedly in the 'other world' but make appearances in far-flung places, tribes, clans, and within families. In Lagos, the Eyo is a symbol of ancestral dignity and the respectful remembrance and celebration of heroes of bygone era. Clad in white from head to toe and donning a flat-topped ten-gallon hat, the Eyo wields a long roundish pole, gently tapping the object of his adulation and uttering prayerful incantations in the process. Some prominent Eyo groups are the Bajulaiyes, the Kosokos, and the Oluwas. They are popularly referred to as the Adamu Orisa, Alagere, Oniko, Eyooba, and Ologede. Eyo has been adopted as the symbol of Lagos State. The larger-than-life imprint of an Eyo is etched on the Lagos House at Abuja.

The Igunnus are a different species of masquerade. They hail from and represent the ancestral families of the Tapas that have their roots in the Oshodi quarters of Lagos. The essential characteristics are their unusual heights and cylindrical shapes. They come out in celebration during festivals and anniversaries. They are also invited to appease an offended ancestral deity or in prayers and thanksgiving for perceived and received blessings.

The Geledes are a very interesting and amusing genre of masquerade. They stuff their buttocks with big round objects to add more curvy bulk to their body movements, which are even more evident when dancing. They are from the Badagry and Ado Odo areas of Lagos. They are also referred to as *Isangbetos*. The fleet-footed masquerade that runs as if it were airborne is the Ofe from whom the women flee into hiding. The Ageres are the stilt dancers who can dance with unusual mobility on carved and ornamented stilts and are capable of giving spectacular displays. The Agemos, also from Lagos State, assume various shapes and contortions from their mat coverings.

Throughout my southern parts, the masqueraders are generally regarded as persons from the other world. They are seen as the media through which the people communicate with their ancestors. The masquerades are supposed to represent incarnated ancestral spirits, visiting their descendants to entertain, give guidance, and exorcise evil spirits.

Some of my people in the South who believe in the culture of masquerades hold the view that the souls of the departed are in a state of permanent immortality. They believe that the process of dying is never complete as it is a continuous passage. I should add that some of the people are under the erroneous impression that this is one African cultural heritage of mine that dies hard. They believe that it has survived Western influences. It is my considered view that the exposure of my people to 'civilization' and 'enlightenment' and the advent of foreign religions—particularly Christianity and Islam, which frown at such beliefs and practises—will reduce such beliefs and practises to the banality of merely a fun-filled carnival.

However, this explains why the masquerade's peculiar 'other-worldliness' has made it imperative for them to have all parts of their human bodies covered either with palm fronds or sisal hemp. The hands, the legs, and the faces are covered with knitted materials to facilitate movement, breathing, and vision. Most of the masqueraders wear masks which can only belong to the other world and which give them weird appearances. They carry whips with which they flog targeted on-lookers. Carved heads of animals with distorted faces and bared teeth shaped into masks are worn by the masqueraders. When they talk, they disguise their voices gutturally as only they can—'being not of this world'.

At Arondizuogu, in my South East, an annual cultural festival called Ikeji is celebrated. During the festival, masqueraders of various forms and sizes entertain the people. Of particular interest is the Nwaburja, whose main interest differs from ordinarily entertaining or dancing for spectators. The masquerader trickishly sneaks out of the gathering and stealthily enters people's houses to 'steal' chicken, goats, foodstuffs, and other household items.

In Awka, the capital of Anambra State, week-long celebrations of masqueraders attract people from far and near. Apart from the heavily bedecked and gaily festooned masqueraders, others are made to look like various animals of larger-than-life sizes. Dancing, drumming, and general merriment are the order

__Annual Ogun Festival__ in Ondo. Ogun is the god of iron who is sacrificially fed on dog meat and celebrated with palm fronds and smearing of faces with all sorts of coloured powder.

of the week. The Mmanwu festival features an assemblage of over 2,500 masqueraders of various designs, shapes, and sizes from different communities in Anambra state. It is arguably the largest concentration of masquerades in any such festival in the entire world.

TRIBES, TRAITS, AND DRESS

My face is like a prismatic mirror, reflecting a variety of tribes and clans. You can look at me and see Waziri with the Kanuri facial marks or the neatly woven hair and the ringed nose of his wife, Fatimat. He can be a nomadic cattleman, a Koranic teacher, and a trader, a Christian, or (most often) a Muslim. Facial marks are the distinguishing brands on some of my Yoruba people, particularly the Ibadans, the Egbas, Oyos, Ogbomoshos, and the Ondos. The Itsekiris, the Ebiras, and the Yagbas have unique tribal marks on their faces. Some people in Benue and Sokoto states also have tribal marks. The facial marks on my Igbo people are always faint and not pronounced. The marks are usually made on the side of the head between the eyes and the ears.

Indeed, there was a time when a person's origin, background, and clan could be traceable from the tribal marks on his face. Apart from the various ethnic groups, families, clans, tribes, and societies have not only their faces marked but also decorated their bodies with tattoos to beautify and to distinguish one from the other. Abikus (the returnees) in some parts of Yorubaland had a single line etched across the nose to the cheek in the presumption that when the child (abiku) came back again as a newly born baby, the mark would expose and announce its re-entry into the world.

Some individuals even go a step further by inscribing their names or the tattoos of fish, herbs, or flowers on arms, stomach, legs, and buttocks. Marks also determined what position a person held in a family or a clan. Since tribal marks are no longer in vogue, young men whose faces are marked tend to hide the outstanding 'scars' with their beards. Women in similar situation resort to bleaching in the vain hope that the marks might be obliterated or thinned out. Bleaching can worsen their condition.

You can look at me and see different traits and telltale pointers to my origins. You could see Chukwuemeka Nwanze walking down the streets of Aba, where he could be dealing in stockfish or tending to customers at his second-hand clothing booth by the wayside. But essentially, my Aba people are very industrious and very enterprising. Aba itself is the acknowledged commercial nerve center of the East. You can visualize Morenike Osadiya working dexterously at her weaving loom in Iseyin. You readily apprehend that young Aminu Mohammed, cuddling his slate, is just emerging from his Koranic School at Kano. You can see the faces of the ubiquitous Almajiri youths who roam the streets at the behest of their Koranic teachers to beg in order to supplement their food allowances. Often times, unscrupulous politicians use them to cause riots and mayhem.

Hair weaving by all tribes owes its beginnings to the dexterous Yoruba and Kanuri women who fashioned the neat and stylish cornrows. Other people who will immediately catch the eye in villages and hamlets that abound all over my terrain are the palm wine tapper from Ila; the palm oil dealer from an Urhobo village and Okitipupa; the cattle rearers from Katsina and Jalingo; the tie-dyers of Oyo and Abeokuta; the itinerant '(Esusu) collector of Somolu' who walks on the side streets of Lagos to collect money from participating contributors; the Igbo auto parts dealers in almost all cities; the countless farmers, with their hoes on their shoulders; and hunters with guns across their shoulders.

Apparel and caps are some of the distinctive items that portray my people as Nigerians. These items are also indicative of what part of my territory is mirrored in me. The Igbos, the Ijaws, the Itsekiris, the Efiks, the Urhobos, and the people in the riverine areas at times tie wrappers round their waists. On top of the wrappers, the men often wear long sleeved shirts or round-neck singlets and put on felt hats or top hats. Some of the shirts are adorned with fanciful golden buttons or chains. In addition to their colourful wrappers, the women also wear blouses and dainty 'George' head ties. The Yorubas, the Guaris, the Ebiras, and the Ilorins wear agbadas made of hand-woven materials or cotton, damask, brocade, and ankara. Their caps are made of the same materials. The women use these materials for (Iro) wrappers, buba, and head ties.

The Hausa/Fulanis wear 'babariga' (big garment), either simply cut or heavily embroidered. They wear either plain caftans or the ones adorned with fringe embroideries. The cap, called 'tagia', forms part of their most celebrated attire. The design of the tagia is usually created with artistic flair. The turban is a mark of titular honor donned ceremonially by the deserving person who is supposed to have been 'turbanned'. The babarigas, caftans, tagias, and turbans are all commonly used throughout the North. Being mostly Muslims, the women wear simple cotton print dresses, which are supposed to cover most parts of the body and hair, except the face.

The Igbos, particularly the chiefs, are known for their red caps. Beautifully woven caps that look like knitted nightcaps are worn on top of fashionably de-signed colourful shirts. They wear agbadas and sokotos made of printed ankara or cotton materials. It must be emphasized, however, that after all is said and done, the conventional work-a-day suits, trousers, and shirts with ties—and lat-terly, 'french' or 'conductor' suits are the generally accepted and usual attire of my average worker. Basically, clothing was used as a clear delineation between a civilian politician in Agbada and a military ruler and personnel in their khaki uniforms.

The women have their own distinctive and characteristic way of dressing, deriving from ethnic or cultural background. The cotton fabrics and ankara or adire (tie dyed) materials are common and very popular all over. Embroidery, particularly on *bubus* for women, is in vogue. There is no denying the fact that my fashion-conscious females have successfully merged the foreign with the traditional to evolve styles that are distinctive, trendy, and aesthetic. They are also at home with foreign styles and fashions.

The evolution of the culture of *Aso Ebi* (social uniform attire) has achieved a phenomenal dimension that cuts across class and ethnic boundaries among my various peoples and cultures. It is quite different from the distinguishing as-pects of school uniforms and college blazers worn by students in the various schools and colleges. The Yorubas are inveterate proponents and consummate exponents of the *Aso Ebi* culture. The explicit meaning and connotation of *Aso Ebi* is 'family uniform'. It has its origin among the Yorubas when members of the same family, professional group, age group, and members of the same society and club would appear in the same attire on specific social events. These events include wedding ceremonies, house-warming ceremonies, and funeral ceremo-nies, particularly for departed older ones.

Such attire is made from various fabrics and textiles, ranging from ordinary materials like ankara and cotton to brocade, lace, satin, silk, and damask materials. Aso oke is the popular hand-woven material generally used by elite groups. It adds glamour and distinction to a woman's dress when used as head tie and loin wrappers. Men mostly use the heavily embroidered aso oke big 'agbadas' on very special occasions. They are often referred to as 'alari' for the red or purple colours, 'etu' for the black, and 'sanyan' for the beige or light brown colours. Aso ebi has also acquired a new designation as 'dress code', when those invited to particular types of events and celebrations such as weddings, festivals, and parades are specifically requested on the invitation to come dressed in specific colours for men's caps or women's dresses and head ties. The effect of such uniformity in dress at events is always picturesque and spectacular.

CHAPTER FOURTEEN
ARTS AND SCULPTURE

M y archives and museums contain the works of some of my great sculptors, artists, masons, potters, and artificers. My museums, where famous works of experts and past masters are preserved for posterity under the umbrella name of National Museum and Monuments Commission, are located in Lagos, Ile-Ife, Benin, Jos, Kano, Oron, and Esue. The war museum is located in Enugu. Ojukwu's bunker, built with great creative imagination during the Civil War, is preserved as a museum piece at Umuahia. Efforts are being made to retrieve my ancient and historical carvings which were surreptitiously carted away to decorate or equip the art galleries of faraway European countries. A typical example is the adopted logo of FESTAC '77, which is the carved head of an Ife prince and the very popular Benin Bronze.

The various museums are involved in many aspects of collecting, conserving, and preserving works of art which have been painstakingly researched and documented. These collected items are then exhibited to the people at formal exhibitions. This is how my people got to know about my Nok peoples' terra cotta culture, the art of which depicts the life, times, the kind of society, the culture, and even the religions of the people portrayed in the artifacts.

Some museums are famous for many art forms and historical works. While Esue Museum is noted for its famous stone sculptures, Jos and Kano are well known for the dexterous handling of pottery art and culture. The ancient Benin kingdom prides itself on its bronze, ivory, and stone works, while the 'source' city of Ife parades the Ife bronze and the gigantic monolithic totem pole traditionally known as 'Opa Oranmiyan'—the staff of the prince warrior, Oranmiyan.

The ancient town of Badagry contains various historical sites and items of monumental significance in my cultural evolution. The foundation of the first-ever story building within my territory was laid there by the British missionary Henry Townsend in 1842. It was completed by another missionary named Gollmer in 1845. The building still stands intact, attesting that durable materials were used in its construction. The building itself was home to a number of historical items. It was used as accommodation for the first teacher I ever had in the person of Mr. Claudius Philips who established the first primary school.

The building also contains my very first Bible. It was brought in by Townsend in 1842. The first Yoruba Bible, which Bishop Ajayi Crowther translated from Townsend's Bible, is also in the house. On the wall of the historical building, beside where the Bibles are placed, is a picture of Crowther and his great-grandson, Herbert Macaulay. The first safe where the missionaries kept their money in cowries, shillings, and pence is still there, intact and operable without oil or grease. It is over 150 years old. The first well, dug in 1842, is still situated within the premises. It is reputed to be fresh, tasteless, colourless, and drinkable. The Mobee Slaves Relics Museum houses pictures and relics of the dark ages of history and is also located in Badagry. The original irons used to chain the necks, legs, hands, and mouths of the slaves in the sixteenth century are still pitifully visible. There is also the big iron basin from which scores of slaves were made to lap water like dogs in groups at the same time.

Oron Museum has a rich historical collection of ikpu, and it is the oldest surviving work of its type in Africa. They are carved from hardwoods, which have stood the test of time and are not easily assailable by destructive termites. The Museum of Colonial History in Aba was built in 1905. The historical and well documented contents are mostly pictorial, depicting the precolonial images of the slave trade, missionary and colonial administration, and the important era of amalgamation.

Skilful and artistic Ben Enwonwu has done me proud by his great works, which always look so real and near perfect that one can visualize them in flesh and blood. His countless works of genius adorn several places within my culture and abroad. The Sango sculpture in front of the former National Electric Power

Renowned sculptor Ben Enwonwu standing in front of one of his works, "Anyawu", at the United Nations in New York City. His popular works include the famously sculpted statue of Queen Elizabeth, who sat for him in London, and also the "Risen Jesus", located at the University of Ibadan's Chapel of Resurrection.

Authority (NEPA) building on Marina Street, Lagos, depicts the god of thunder sculpted as muscular, magnificently proportioned, and oozing with thunderous energy, forever clasping an axe as if ready to strike in a flash. Enwonwu's artistic and expressive wall murals on the Nigeria Ports Authority (NPA) building adjacent to NEPA are a marvel to behold. Similarly, the bronze sculpture of the water goddess Yemoja dropping anchor stands as if the anchor were literally being dropped into the lagoon.

Queen Elizabeth II of Great Britain actually sat for Enwonwu in London. Today the gargantuan and majestic portrait sits protected in the strong room of the national museum. The statue looks so real that it seems to breathe and grow, sitting straight in regal carriage and with a majestic mien. When critics in Britain doubted the resemblance and critically ventured an opinion that he should have 'sculpted' the exact impression that he had 'penciled', Enwonwu waxed philosophical as he explained that he was 'not preoccupied with resemblance but engrossed with the burden of representation'. The works of Enwonwu as an artist and a sculptor always capture the being, essence, awareness, and other life forces only the interpretative genius of an artist can discern and describe. Hence, as she grows older, the Queen over the years has grown to look more

like the statue. The statue conjures exciting memories in those who saw the
Queen when she paid a visit to my territory in 1956. It seems therefore that Enwonwu conceptualized and projected Her Royal Majesty, Queen Elizabeth II,
into eternity and for all time.

The Chapel of Resurrection at the University of Ibadan is eternally graced
by Enwonwu's statute of the Risen Jesus. Both the great Zik and Kenneth Mella-
mby, founding Principal of the University College of Ibadan, sat for him. The
'Anyanwu' statute brilliantly sculptured by the master himself had focused and
riveted world attention on his work at the United Nations building in New York.
He was the winner of my 1980 National Merit Award for fine arts and culture.

Some of my other illustrious artists included the so-called 'Zaria rebels',
made up of a group of highly original art students of the late 1950s at the School
of Arts and Technology in Zaria, where they had rebelled against prescribed
norms and charted a style of their own, peculiar in its aesthetic principles, down
to earth and quaintly domesticated in content. The group included Demas
Nwoko, Uche Okeke, and Bruce Onabrokpeya. Uche Okeke became the leading
figure in the Uli movement, a style essentially derived from the Igbo wall painting technique. Bruce Onabrakpeya invented a print style that is remarkable and
brilliantly artistic. Demas Nwoko is famous for his works in terra cotta, theatre

*Twins Seven Seven (Taiwo Oyewale-
Oyelade) was a consummate artist: a
painter, musician, actor, dancer, and
writer. His works embraced the
cosmology and mythology
of the Yoruba culture.*

designs, and architecture. He also constructed the magnificent Cultural Centre Studios in Ibadan.

I am very proud of my naturally talented daughter, Hadjia Ladi Kwali, who was so dexterous in pottery that she became also the proud recipient of my National Merit Award. Twins Seven Seven was a fabulous and freakish prodigy from Oshogbo. He was versatile and creative in all realms of culture as an artist, drummer, musician, writer, and dramatist. Others were Yusuf Grillo, Okpu Eze, Ben Osawe, Kunle Fakeye, and Ben Edokpaiye.

Statues in Lagos

Statues of the great men and women who have left their footprints on the sands of time are notable, particularly in Lagos. First is the statue of the grand old man of journalism, politics, and nationalism, the redoubtable leader and protagonist of the struggle for my Independence, Herbert Macaulay. The statue with its twirling moustache looks unmistakably like him as he surveys Broad Street and the street named after him in Yaba. Obafemi Awolowo's statute flashing his famous 'V' sign and wearing his round-rimmed spectacles graces the roundabout at the Allen Avenue–Obafemi Awolowo Road in Ikeja.

1 The Three Greeters at the Ketu-Ojota end of the Ikorodu Express Road, seemingly welcoming new arrivals into Lagos.

2 The imposing and magnificent statue of Obafemi Awolowo flashing his famous victory sign; situated at the roundabout of Allen Avenue and Obafemi Awolowo Road in Ikeja.

The genial nature and 'city-gent' posture of the amiable philanthropist Mobolaji Bank Anthony is brilliantly portrayed in his statue, beautifying the front of one of his many worthy causes, the Ayinke House, named after his mother and donated by him as a gynecology unit in the General Hospital at Ikeja. The hospital has now been elevated to the status of a teaching hospital for the Lagos State University (LASU). He also donated a fully equipped wing to the Orthopedic Hospital at Igbobi. The statue of the famous 'Idumota Soldier' with his companion of the 'bald pate' was moved to the parade grounds at Tafawa Balewa Square. Its place in Idumota now accommodates the statue of the Eyo masquerade, which has also been adopted as a mascot and logo by Lagos State.

The statues of the Three Greeters at the Ketu–Ojota end of the Ikorodu Express Road leading out of Lagos is a study in the art of hospitality and welcoming gesture. This is made up of three Lagos 'white cap' chiefs sculpted in standing positions and mounted on a pedestal, stretching out their arms in a gesture of greeting, reception, and hospitality. Significantly, they seem to have their eyes trained on the road leading to Lagos for visitors arriving there for various reasons. It is as if they are emissaries from the palace of the Oba, bidding hearty welcome to every arriving visitor to Lagos.

CHAPTER FIFTEEN
RELIGION

My religions manifest themselves in distinctive modes and in various de-nominations. They are truly multi-dimensional. It is a phenomenon that cuts across my entire territory in one form or the other. There are more than 60,000 churches and mosques in the cities and towns, villages, and hamlets. My people worship the Supreme Being whom they call, variously, God, Allah, Ubangiji, Olodumare, Chineke, Osanobuwa, Oghene, Tamuno, Abasi, and several other names in other tongues and in every nook and cranny of my vast terrain. Day and night in all these diverse places, if one were near enough to the various sites, one could hear the voices and songs of worshippers in cathedrals, churches, and vast auditoriums; the chants and voices of prayers in the mosques; the high-pitched exhortation to prayers from amplifiers affixed to mosques' minarets; the hysterical shouts of 'Hallelujah!' and the cacophony of resonant utterances of prayers emanating from the huge gatherings in Pente-costal churches; and the muffled incantations of the animist priests and the jin-gling eerie sounds made by their adherents at the innumerable shrines and co-vens of the animists and cultists.

It is manifestly clear and significant that the two prominent imported ver-sions of religion—Christianity and Islam—preach peace and tolerance. There is no doubt that they share a commonality of awareness and acknowledgement of the existence of God, whom they refer to as God (Christianity) and Allah (Islam). Their doctrinal incompatibility and the differences in orientation, outlook, dress, concepts, and modes of worship have always seemed to be the causes of many misunderstandings, misconceptions, arguments, upheavals, and riots among adherents and practitioners. From the political point of view, these upheavals and riots constitute the niggling bane of my much-needed unity and cohesion as a nation.

Churches and mosques often become the targets of rioters at the slightest provocation. Ironically, the animists, who could visibly wield more malevolent occult powers and are more dangerously lethal, are the least belligerent. In practical forms, they could easily be fetishist and diabolical. They operate usually under the cover of darkness in covens and isolated shrines. They were the indigenous idolaters on whom the Colonialists and the Moors unleashed their proselytizing zeal when they arrived on my shores.

It is also a notorious, painful, and condemnable fact that some of the adherents of the two foremost religions run to the animists for succour and assistance under the cover of darkness at some remote shrines. Some pastors and alfas have been known to attempt to enhance their spiritual powers and crowd-luring ability by engaging the services of diviners, the use of herbs, and animist's incantations and concoctions. Some heed the diviner's instructions to deposit prescribed sacrifices in pots and calabashes at T-junctions or under designated trees in the forest. There was once a story in one of my widely circulated newspapers that a priest in a new generation church had to ritually bury a live animal inside the altar in his desperate and outrageous bid to attract more adherents and followers to his church.

CHRISTIANITY

The churches have become modernized and reshaped in doctrine, organization, and hierarchy. Sects are multiplying at a competitive rate. They emerge under various hierarchical orders. Essentially the greatest common denominator is Jesus Christ, to whom all adherents are beholden. He is celebrated and adored at Christmas in honour of His miraculous birth, which was a result of Divine incarnation. His death on the cross is mourned, lamented, and later celebrated along with His burial and victorious resurrection at Easter. He is also remembered with gratitude and thanksgiving at harvest festivals. Every devout Christian also awaits the Second Coming (Advent) of Jesus Christ.

The oldest Christian sects are the Roman Catholic, Anglican, Methodist, Baptist, Cherubim and Seraphim, African Church, Christ Apostolic Church, and the Aladuras. The newer and rapidly expanding Christian sects come under the umbrella of Pentecostal churches. They answer to such exotic sounding names as the Deeper Life Church, the Redeemed Christian Church of God, Latter Rain Assembly, the Redeemed Evangelical Mission, Mountain of Fire and Miracle Church, Winners Chapel, Christ Embassy, The Household of God, and many others.

The hierarchical order in the various Christian sects include the popes, prelates, cardinals, archbishops, bishops, general overseers, archdeacons, monsignors, canons, pastors, padres, reverends, and deacons. Some adherents affectionately refer to each other as 'brother' and 'sister'. Some leaders and general overseers wax paternal by fondly referring to members of their flock as their children. But it is equally reassuring that both leader and flock humbly acknowledge God as 'our' Father.

The Catholic church is well entrenched and enjoys a fervent and very large and faithful following all over my territory. The Catholic priesthood hierarchy has attained such impressive and commendable heights that I can boast of three indigenous cardinals. Dominic Ekandem was the first to be so appointed. It is also to its credit that at crucial points in the history of Catholicism, one and then two of the cardinals were in the College of Cardinals that sat to elect two successive new Popes. Indeed, to my great joy and utmost pride, one of them, Cardinal Arinze, was in great contention for the exalted post because of his seniority and his universally acknowledged effectiveness as a co-coordinator at the Vatican. Olubumi Okogie was the other high-profile and respected cardinal. His views and opinions on topical and contemporary matters, public and moral issues, religion, and societal mores were always eagerly sought and forthrightly given.

As applicable to Catholics worldwide, my Catholic Christians have stuck resolutely to Christian orthodoxy in theory and in practise. Those tenets and original beliefs are still paramount and given prominence in their mode of worship. Mary, the mother of Jesus Christ. is hailed and worshipped. Her statue adorns every Catholic church and compound. She is acknowledged in prayers and held in universal adulation. Those core issues, against which Martin Luther 'protested', are still religiously adhered to. The source language, Latin, is still in use during the celebration of High Mass. The Catholic Charismatic Renewal has sprung up within the Catholic Church. Members of this group are devout prayer warriors. They believe in the healing powers of prayer, and they are also involved in interceding between worshippers and the Almighty God.

To further the solemnity and sober piety as formerly practised in the orthodox churches' mode of worship, very little emphasis was given to drumming, dancing, and gospel music. It is arguable whether sticking to the rather rigid orthodoxy might have been responsible for the mass movement of the flock into the warm and boisterous practise prevalent in the newfangled Pentecostal churches. Through it all, the Roman Catholic church marches on, popular and respected within my territory as it is all over the world.

The history of the Anglican church in my territory is as old as the history of British colonial interest in my affairs from birth through infancy to independent manhood. The Church Missionary Society introduced to my people the Anglican Christian denomination, its doctrine, and its mode of worship. The British colonialists used the United African Company to foster trade and commerce. Similarly, they used the Church Missionary Society for evangelizing and education. The area of influence of the Anglican church used to be known as the Province of West Africa. The prelate, the Archbishop of Nigeria, now heads my Anglican community. While there were only four Bishops and only one Archbishop in the 1960s, there are now more than 100 dioceses with as many Bishops and a dozen Archbishops with the Prelate as head. The hierarchical order sees an Anglican priest climb the ladder from reverend to canon, archdeacon, bishop, and archbishop in the Anglican church in England. The same system still applies within my Anglican Church community.

Changes and differences in the doctrine and practise of Anglicanism inevitably crop up because of the divergence of culture, background, and traditions. The lackadaisical approach to such doctrinal issues as divorce, the consecration of women as bishops, and the methodology of worship that caused the split from Rome in the first instance in the sixteenth century is now threatening to cause a row between the Church of England and the Anglican community in Africa. On the surface, homosexuality is the bone of contention. A liberal Archbishop of Canterbury has seen nothing wrong in the idea of hobnobbing with a consecrated homosexual bishop in the United States of America. Homosexuality is alien and repulsive to African culture and the people's way of life. My people reject homosexual practise, which they regard as incompatible with the scriptures and alien to their culture. They are also not open to the ordination of women. The Anglican community, particularly in Africa, waited to see if the Prince of Wales (Charles, who was divorced from his wife, Princess Diana, before she tragically died) would have his marriage to another divorcee approved by the authorities.

The prelate of the Anglican Church of my Anglican community, Archbishop Akinola, was in the forefront of the opposition to a homosexual bishop. The threat of a split on this account is very real. The prelate seemed to enjoy the support of other African bishops. A boycott of the 2008 Lambeth Conference, which is a once-in-a-decade world Anglican Conference in England, was very much in contemplation. The Anglican Church referred to the 1998 Lambeth Conference decision as it applied to issues of homosexuality. It was then the conclusion that my people in the Anglican community cannot advocate the legitimizing or blessing of same-sex unions. They also refused to be involved in the ordination of those in same-gender unions. This might lead to a chain of unpalatable reactions that could spell doom and disintegration to Anglican Christendom.

Songs, drumming, dancing, and all the show of jubilation and felicitation that come under the umbrella of praise worship and thanksgiving are now very common practises in my Anglican churches. The same practise now also goes on in the old established churches like the Catholic, Methodist, Baptist, and the white garment churches. This is probably in answer to the deeply entrenched practise of the Pentecostal churches, where emphasis is on clapping, singing, dancing, and gospel songs. It is also probably a successful attempt to win back those who flocked into the Pentecostal churches, particularly the youth.

Pastor Oschoffa founded the Celestial Church of Christ. The sect is unique in the theory and practise of worship. The robes and garments are all white with blue motif to denote rank and order. Members of the sect worship barefooted and move about with their long and seamless 'sutana' robes. The more committed ones put on felt hats in the manner of the founder and leader Oschoffa. The aroma of burning incense and candle waft through every 'Cele' church and compound. Spiritually cleansed water is their forte; candles, palm fronds, eggs, and olive oil are the essential ingredients of their mode of worship and purification. They sing lustily and clap continually. Every once a while, an engrossed

worshipper falls into a convulsive trance and begins to speak in tongues, fore-
telling and forecasting about people and events.

The demise of pastor Oschoffa after a freak accident signaled the beginning
of an acrimonious and unbecoming struggle for leadership. At the end of the
struggle, Pastor Bada, the next in rank to Oschoffa and his confidant of many
years, won the mantle of leadership after a very sad, inglorious, and avoidable
court intervention. This later brought a measure of sanity into a worthwhile and
creditable system left behind by the leader and founder, 'Papa' Oschoffa, as his
adoring flock called him. When Bada died later, the struggle for leadership again
cropped up. There were claims and counter-claims and some breakaway threats
and attempts by those who claim to support a favourite leadership candidate
over the others. The mantle of leadership eventually fell on the much younger
shoulders of the son of the late Pastor 'Papa' Oschoffa. Ironically, the leadership
struggle raged on for some time between Pastor Oschoffa's two sons.

Kumuyi, the brilliant mathematician, warmly embraced and espoused
Christianity, preaching and rekindling the idea that unless one is 'born again'
and accepts Jesus Christ as one's Saviour as recommended by Jesus Christ to Ni-
codemus, one will not enter into the Kingdom of God. His adherents believe in
this concept (as all other practising Christians do), and they practise in every
material particular the tenets of his belief: preaching the gospel, sharing fellowship through Bible studies, and leading an austere life of utmost simplicity. They
are a marvelous crowd to behold as they troop out as worshipful adherents
from the bowels of their cavernous Deeper Life Church in Gbagada, Lagos. The
men and children wear very simple work-a-day dress without wristwatches or
rings. The women's dresses are simpler still and completely devoid of all adorn-
ments—necklaces, earrings, and makeup.

The greatest revelation of all is the Redeemed Christian Church of God as
pastored by the incomparable Enoch Adeboye. He has been adjudged by a popular American magazine as one of the 50 most influential persons in the world.
Like Kumuyi, Adeboye was a lecturer of mathematics at the University of Lagos
before he heard and heeded God's call to His service. The harvest of his efforts
could be seen along the Lagos–Shagamu Express Way, where he built the Holy
Ghost Camp of the Redeemed Christian Church of God. The original founder of
the RCCG was Akindayomi. It would appear that the type of the 'double portion'

of power passed on from Elijah to Elisha must have been passed on to Adeboye by Akindayomi when the latter was about to die. The 'double portion' seemed to have been wrapped around Adeboye. He thus became the general overseer of the popular sect, which is world-wide.

Pastor Adeboye acknowledged with his usual humility and often-expressed gratitude to God that RCCG has been responsible for about 3,500 parishes, 50 of which he personally nurtured within my territory and overseas. The assembly hall was so vast that it accommodated more than 200,000 people in its monthly night vigils. The 'Redeemed' Church, as it is affectionately called, has won converts from all religions. Members of other Christian sects flock by the thousands into the fold of the RCCG. Pastor Adeboye's sermons are always spiritually uplifting and instructive, spiced with many appropriate quotations from the Holy Bible. His intermittently rendered two-minute prayers fill the cavernous interior of the massive auditorium with palpable presence of the Holy Spirit. At the end of each monthly session, grateful and affected worshippers always give testimonies of answered prayers and fulfilled wishes.

Adherents attest to the revivalist atmosphere that envelopes and pervades the new Pentecostal churches, including that of the Evangelical Redeemed Christian Church of God (ERCCG). Adeboye, the general overseer of the sect, speaks with a deep, rich, and sonorous baritone voice, which always seems to flood the vast auditorium with an awesome tide of spiritual power. When he enters the vast auditorium on the monthly Holy Ghost night vigils, he always holds the congregation spiritually enraptured by intoning 'Let somebody shout alleluiah'. Then all respond by shouting accordingly with ecstatic delight. He preaches that the spiritual rivers of heaven are overflowing its banks with the awesomeness of the Almighty God. This has resultantly produced in the Church a sense of divine majesty, the power of which compels both Christians and non-Christians to stand in awe. To his adherents, Adeboye preaches that the awesome aura of God is no longer an expression but an experience.

The newfangled, praise-worshipping church of Chris Okotie is called the Household of God. Okotie literally transmogrified from a performing artiste into a modern-day pastor, bringing into the worship of God the glitter and the razzle-dazzle prevalent in the world of showbiz. For a church, Okotie converted and merged two sprawling warehouses in Oregun, Lagos. The colour motif of the entire compound was formerly white but was changed to lemon. All the walls of the huge interlaced buildings and the long stretches of the surrounding fence walls are painted in eye-catching white. The vast compound is usually decorated with starry twinkling bulbs and buntings at Christmastime, and this has established the reputation for attracting visitors and worshippers who flock into the compound every year to marvel at the fabulous decorations.

The interior decor of the church is exquisite. The floors are beautifully tiled. The air conditioners whir silently, giving the big hall a cool, relaxing ambiance. Scores of hanging fans neatly dot the ceilings. Okotie is so fluent and articulate that one often wonders if the less educated ones among his flock would be able to cope with his often bombastic choice of words and flowery expressions.

Okotie claims with fervour to have a dream like the legendary Martin Luther King. He dreams to rule me as a Nation. He dreams that someday, with the right leadership, I would have a true Federal Constitution devoid of flaws, where Federalism would be given a proper definition. He dreams of me as a Nation endowed with a new leadership, full of love, compassion, and empathy for the people. He looks forward to the day when youths would be given the opportunity to lead me as a Nation in order to establish an atmosphere of brotherhood, equality, faith, hope, and security. To this extent, he continues to nurse the ambition of one day becoming my president.

He dreams of me as a Nation in which tribalism and money politics are a thing of the past; as a Nation in which the people would vote for their leaders irrespective of their tribes, religion, or political antecedents. He also dreams of me as a Nation in which the youths and people of the Niger Delta (where he belongs) would be given their due in the scheme of things and be freed from the shackles of exploiters from outside and traitors from within. He sincerely craves to be involved in my affairs as a nation which he believes is crying for God and that there is scriptural evidence that God has a purpose for me as a Nation.

Tunde Joda founded the Christ Chapel and Bakare established the Latter Rain Assembly. Benson Idahosa, Oritsejafor, and Okonkwo have their own Christian adherents under the 'Worldwide' label. They are firebrand preachers who hold followers in their churches and viewers on television spellbound with their religious oratory and moving prayers.

Pastor Temitope Joshua is another prodigy. He is a spiritual healer who founded the Synagogue Church of All Nations at Ikotun-Egbe in the Lagos suburb. Cancer and AIDS patients whose ailments had defied all orthodox medicinal cures were alleged to have been miraculously cured by Pastor Joshua in his church. It is remarkable that news about the exceptional miracles performed at the synagogue and as seen by many on television continue to attract many people from far and near across the globe to witness the miracles or to be recipients and beneficiaries of the healing powers of Pastor Joshua. Visiting heads of state and world leaders and kings continue to perform the pilgrimage to Joshua's Synagogue.

Flocks of praise-singing and hand-clapping adherents patronize the Pentecostal churches. They are mostly young and devout religious sloganeers and banner-waving decent people who worship God with a singularity of purpose. They liberally sprinkle their talks and discussions with prayers and quotations from the Holy Book. They are mostly young and upwardly mobile people, and they range in ages between 18 and 40. Their practise of religion is devoid of the pretensions and conservative rigidity that have come to characterize the established sects like the Anglicans, the Catholics, the Baptists, the Methodists, and the older ones from whom these new sects attract worshippers at an increasing rate, particularly the younger ones.

It is notable that the older sects in a desperate attempt to regain adherents have now embraced drumming and dancing inside their churches and during services and thanksgiving sessions. These practises were in the past forbidden as anathema. It should be mentioned that Pastor Adeboye, the general overseer of the Redeemed Christian Church of God (RCCG), warned his other parish pastors not to lend their pulpits and stages to gospel artists who have not professed accepting Jesus as saviour and redeemer. But as earlier mentioned, the Roman Catholic Church has relaxed its mode of worship by minimizing the use of Latin. It has also accommodated drumming, singing, and dancing, which has become a habit born of practise, in order to lure back Catholics lost to the newer churches.

Theophilous Olabayo founded the popular Evangelical Church of Yahweh. He has been called the modern-day Nostradamus because of the uncanny accuracy with which he predicted events and occurrences as they would happen all over the world. He was known to have correctly predicted the collapse of communism as practised by the United Socialist Soviet Republic and its COMECON (Council for Mutual Economic Assistance) satellites; the literally earth-shattering earthquake disaster in California; the release of Nelson Mandela from about three decades of incarceration; and other major events. The accuracy of his predictions boggled the mind. He received his foreknowledge of things to come from Mount Taborah, where he retreated every year with his flock of devout adherents. Up there, he would fast and pray for many days for inspiration and extraordinary perception of future occurrences.

He made it a habit to emerge from this annual ascent and descent from Mount Taborah to make a series of forecasts and pronouncements which he would thereafter release in booklet form. But he was not 100% accurate—several times, he was known to have missed with his predictions. He had argued that some of the predicted adverse effects of catastrophic events had been averted through prayer and fasting. For example, he had erroneously predicted the victory of the elder George Bush over William Clinton in the US presidential elections, the victory of Neil Kinnock over John Major at the British Parliamentary elections, and the death of famous personalities who did not die but instead were alive long enough to be in a mood to threaten him with court action.

Some of the other sects include the Rimmer Chapel, Church of Liberty, Four Square Gospel, Church of Eckankar, Seventh Day Adventists, Olumba Olumba, the Redeemed Evangelical Mission, and Christ Embassy, which was founded and led Chris Oyakhilome. The Christ's Embassy is a fast-growing church, still expanding by leaps and bounds, particularly among younger people, largely owing to the charisma of the founder, Chris Oyakhilome, and his visibly demonstrated power of miracles and powerfully delivered sermons and incisive prayers at various convention centers and on television. Christ Embassy built a vast administrative headquarters and also constructed a massive and magnificent church, both at Oregun in Lagos. The Christ Living Spring Apostolic Ministry under the leadership of Wole Oladiyun also gained many followers in the Ojodu area of Lagos.

ISLAM

The practise of Islam is encapsulated in the famous Five Pillars of Islam. All my devout Islamic adherents answer the call to prayer five times a day facing the east towards Mecca as they pray. It is the wish of every Muslim who can afford it to perform the Holy Pilgrimage to Mecca. This practise among my Muslim adherents automatically earns a pilgrim the title 'Alhaji' or 'Alhajah'. Jumat services on Fridays are always followed by the practise of Zakkart in which wealthier Muslims distribute alms to less fortunate people, who are mainly beggars. It is also obligatory to tithe to the mosque. Fasting during Ramadan is a binding injunction and a solid pillar of Islam, and every true Muslim must undertake it during the prescribed period. It is also a very important code that Muslims must accord respect and honour to their parents and elderly people.

Schools for Koranic studies are found in some cities in the North and West and in Lagos. Children enter these schools young to imbibe the knowledge of Islam through Koranic studies and writing. They learn the Koran by heart and recitations of the Koran are often rendered in competitions at religious ceremonies. Deserving scholars earn various rewards, both in cash or other kinds.

There are different sects of Islam. The best-known and earliest ones are the Ansar-u-deen and the Nawair-u-deen. There are also the Ahmadiya and the Zumratul Islamiya. They are all believers and adherents of the Holy Prophet Mohammed, who derives his power and mysticism from the Almighty Allah, the Omnipotent, Omniscient, and Omnipresent.

However, of recent, the fundamentalist zeal of some of the adherents and practitioners of Islam has come into focus bristling with violence and passion. This can be traced to the all-consuming, all-pervading fire of zealotry that has burned its way from across the Sahara Desert and the Middle East, shaking governments and leaving terror and death in its wake against any Arab Potentates and governments who might be seen to have been adopting a compromising and lackadaisical attitude towards the practise of Islam.

Maitatsine followers are fanatics of this veneer and would not brook the presence or opposition from any other religion. They are implacable apostles of the Sharia Law. They believe in and acknowledge only governments that adopt the theocratic and sectarian system of governance and judicial dispensation.

1 National Mosque *at Abuja*   ①

2 National Ecumenical Complex *at Abuja*   ②

They unleashed a reign of terror that killed many in my northern cities like Maiduguri, Kaduna, Kafanchan, Katsina, and Bauchi. The Zango Kataf riots erupted into a raging inferno, destroying the properties of a whole community and setting Christian natives against Muslim settlers in a bloody orgy of maiming and destruction.

The whole of my eastern flank is occupied mostly by Christians with quite a few Animists and a negligible sprinkling of Muslims, quite apart from traders and settlers from the North. The North is predominantly Muslim, particularly in the Hausa/Fulani axis. It is also the seat of the revered Sultan of Sokoto, who is acknowledged as the spiritual head of the Muslims. The North also contains the second-largest religious group of Christians, particularly in the Middle Belt and in some cosmopolitan cities like Kaduna, Kafanchan, Gboko, and others. Here, Animists are few and far between and are found mostly among the illiterate not manifestly touched by either of the other two predominant religions.

The West and Lagos have the three religions well spread and identifiable within the various states. While Ondo and Ekiti states are preponderantly full of Christians, the Muslims and Animists share a lower percentage between the two of them. Oyo and Osun states are a veritable salad of the three religions. While Ibadan, Ikirun, and Shaki have more Muslims than Christians, Ogbomosho is the haven of the Baptists. The Seventh Day Adventists have established a strong foothold in Ile-Ife and Ilesha. However, there are also many Muslims in these areas. There are more Christian mission schools in the West and Lagos than in all the other parts combined. Osogbo is well known for its Animists who worship the goddesses Osun and Oya.

Lagos is a potpourri of all the religions and their various sects. There are churches and mosques in practically every neighborhood. It is remarkable for example that there are more than twenty churches located on Akowonjo Road (in the suburb of Lagos) alone. The degree of tolerance among the various religions is a shining example of the type of happy coexistence that should exist between the adherents of the religions. This position of interaction and unwritten but acknowledged compromise between Christians and Muslims has left Lagosians with little choice other than mutual accommodation and respect. Often, members of the same nuclear family fervently embrace either of the two very different religions. They also participate actively in the other ancestral Animist celebrations. In Lagos, this makes tolerance and the easy accommodation of religious leanings a very interesting and unavoidable exercise in intra-family relationships.

Islam as a religion is very popular within my boarders. The Sultan of Sokoto is at the apex of the Islamic hierarchy. The chief imams are Islamic scholars who are versed in the knowledge and interpretation of the Holy Koran and are steeped in the ennobling spiritual traditions of that religion. Every city or town has its Chief Imam. The *alfas* and *mullahs* are the heads of the community mosques. Just like the churches, once you have seen a mosque, you have seen them all. Where the cross is the symbol of the Christian religion, the crescent symbolizes the Islamic religion. Their minarets are constructed in the shape of domes. The arcs and pillars are essential features of a mosque, just as the towers, belfries, and arced multi-coloured stained-glass windows are characteristics of a church.

In their collective wisdom, the designers of the questionnaire that formed the basis of various census exercises have cleverly sidetracked any effort to determine, assert, or establish the numerical superiority of any religion. This is a source of great relief and satisfaction to me as a Nation. To assert the numerical superiority of one religion over the other is to court bitterness and rancour. There would be no end to the acrimony. Accusing fingers would be pointed at the perpetrators of what would be perceived as a calculated attempt to foist on the people an arrangement which can upset the applecart of 'religious spread', 'geographical spread', and 'federal character'. Should I let this monstrous sleeping dog lie? Am I not sweeping this issue under the carpet? Time will tell.

RELIGION AND FESTIVALS:
FUTURE INDICATIONS

It may sound altruistic, utopian, weird, downright naïve, and maybe simplistic, but as a Nation desirous of promoting harmonious co-existence between the various tribes, clans, and families within me, I have a dream of a rapprochement between the two main religions of Christianity and Islam. The two must evolve a system of accommodation and tolerance never known before in any part of the world. If their teachings center on love and tolerance, which they both claim is integral in their religious tenets, the resultant assertion of superiority in number will recede into the background. Peace will always prevail in an atmosphere of love and tolerance, devoid of rigid complex or maniac obsession.

The voodoo, fetishism, and mysticism exhibited and celebrated during some traditional festivals will continue to be watered down and trivialized. Hard-core traditionalists may be bent on retaining the status quo, but the inevitable metamorphosis from festival to carnival is already taking place. The gods like Ogun, Sango, Amadioha, and others are adored and worshipped in festivals. Their worshippers flock to the shrines in adoration and in great expectation of obtaining help and assistance. The masqueraders invoke the spirits of the ancestors, and ancestral worshippers are supposed to be their followers. The carnival atmosphere that pervades the air at such festivals is unmistakable. Such festivals as Osun Osogbo, Ogun festival in Ondo, the Ojude Oba festival in Ijebuode, the Igogo in Owo, the Okebadan festival in Ibadan, the Olojo in Ile-Ife, the traditional Igue Festival in Benin, and the festival of Azu-Ofala in Onitsha have become tourist attractions. The festivals draw crowds of fun-seekers and tourists from near and far in a carnival atmosphere of fun and merriment. Inevitably, the themes and reasons for the festivals will gradually recede into the background. The carnival atmosphere will become more pronounced. Emphasis will shift from the festival of worship and adoration of these gods to sheer merriment and gratification which pervade the atmosphere at carnivals.

It is instructive to note that, year in year out, more and more people, both local and international, attend the various festivals. The aura of carnival has become inevitable. Everyone comes with a singularity of purpose to have fun and a feel of the various 'shows'. The private sector, commerce, and industry, spearheaded by the advertising agencies, usually have a field day promoting the sales of various products. Quite significantly, my people are increasingly aware of the various efforts to recognize, harness, and celebrate what gives them fun and togetherness in a convivial carnival atmosphere.

The essence of the carnival atmosphere of the events is amply demonstrated by the presence of colourful and entertaining sideshows. Masqueraders go to the festivals to demonstrate the spirit of the ancestors and why it is necessary to accord them their proper places in the day-to-day scheme of things. Football competitions, raffles, and fashion shows are often packaged to accompany and spice up the carnival atmosphere of the festivals. The thin line between festival and carnival will soon vanish. Sooner rather than later, festivals will attain the status of all-comers carnivals.

CHAPTER SIXTEEN

EDUCATION AND THE
INSTITUTIONS OF LEARNING

At the last count, I could boast of about 100,000 schools and colleges at the primary, secondary, and tertiary levels. Through the assistance of the missionaries, the colonialists laid a solid educational foundation that has stood me in good stead over the years. The introduction of education seemed as if the missionaries switched on a light, its glowing rays piercing through the prevalent dreary darkness and scattering the forces of ignorance, backwardness, and gloom in favor of enlightenment. Education was the most effective weapon wielded by the colonialists. They bequeathed a legacy of basic and fundamental education which has blossomed profusely over the years in various aspects of my development.

Evangelization was one of the intentions of the colonialists. Expansion of their trading and commercial vista was their motivation. Education was the spotlight with which they found their way through the labyrinthine and often vexatious paths of deep-seated tradition, ignorance, complex taboos, and idolatry. The colonialists came, they saw, and they conquered. They used education as their greatest dragnet in a vast catchment area. Education conquers all. It most certainly took a lot of convincing and cajoling to educate and evangelize the people so that they could stop worshipping their idols and follow either the Christian master or imbibe the teachings of Islam.

Where there are no laws, there can be no sin. The opposite of order is disorder. The proper administration of a society is always based on set guidelines, regulations, and binding codes of conduct. It was not as if the colonialists came to meet an administrative vacuum. Indeed, it was a case of educating the 'natives' in the new system of administration and fine-tuning existing practises. In a similar vein, the language and practises of commerce must be taught. In fact, the ordinary system of 'Trade by Barter' required the ability and knowledge of negotiation, calculation, and the language of communication. It could thus be seen that education was a barrier-breaking tool in the hands of the colonialist nation builders.

The setting and the characteristic features of an average town or village could be easily conjured up and relived: the native authority building which the civil servants used as the secretariat; the church, the mission school, and the vicarage with its inevitable belfry from which chimed both the exhortation to worship on Sundays and the reminder to attend school punctually during the week. The post office was built not far away, and the 'CMS' bookshop was close by. These were the unforgettable vestiges of education in the early days, particularly south of the rivers Niger and Benue. For a picture of what occurred in the North, substitute the churches with mosques and the belfries with the minarets from which regular calls to prayer were made. The schools multiplied in number as education caught on. Side by side with the Christian mission schools of various sects and the Muslim schools were the local or native authority schools.

The renowned and highly rated educationist Afolabi Ojo expatiated expansively on missionary legacies, the vestiges of which still abound all over my cities, towns, and even villages. He claimed that 'to the casual observer, missionary legacies are exemplified by imposing physical structures within expansive and well laid out compounds. But to the enquiring mind, such legacies include both visible structures and the considerable invisible input towards the integral development of individuals and the society, materially and spiritually'.

The missionaries were God-inspired, and all their activities, including the founding of schools, were God-centered. They made the knowledge of God in various fields of learning the primary objective of their teaching. Another noteworthy aspect of the missionary legacy was their foresight concerning education as the arrowhead of total human development. They always took quick action to set up educational facilities in their areas of operation. Special provisions were made for the grooming of essential human resources that would assist in their educational programmes.

UNIVERSITY EDUCATION

The picture has changed dramatically and almost unmanageably. Statistical data and comparison of the pre-Independence budding infants with the post-Independence educational blossoms would suffice. The tertiary level of education will be considered first, in order to emphasize the extraordinary and gigantic leap education has taken. There existed only the University College of Ibadan (UCI) to award University College of London degrees before I attained Independence on October 1, 1960. Subsequently, UCI gained autonomous status in 1962 and became known as the University of Ibadan (UI).

I pride myself in the smug awareness that there are now about 100 universities and more are still under consideration for approval. It is said that this number nearly equals the total number of universities in all other West African countries combined. This number does not include colleges of education, polytechnics, and other specialized colleges in agriculture, meteorology, and various courses offered in other tertiary institutions.

It seems paradoxical that there should be far more university undergraduates than the number of students of polytechnics and colleges of education. This confounds the Ashby prescriptions and recommendations on the eve of my Independence. It was established that the key to national manpower development rested more on my broadening the base in technical middle education than in the unbridled expansion of my university system.

This unbridled expansion was questioned when, in his valedictory lecture at his retirement after almost 30 years of meritorious and record-breaking service as a lecturer–professor and university administrator, renowned Professor Oladipo Akinkugbe expatiated on the consequences of uncoordinated development of the tertiary process. He said it was grounded on enduring pitfalls in primary and secondary education. Then he opined with professorial finality that

1. There were too many conferences and seminars with volumes of reports written but little evidence of a coherent and internally consistent programme of implementation. The reports were infinitely long on planning but short on execution and monitoring.
2. The credo of free education at all levels has worn thin. It is imperative, if not downright compulsory, that education should be partly borne by the consumer by way of national cost-sharing, while at the same time, scholarships should be

made available to outstanding students at all levels of government, even if it involves refundable bursary awards.

3.   Parents should not by default consign the upbringing of their children or wards to house servants and nannies at home and teachers at school. All appropriate hands must be on deck to rear and guide them along the right lines.

The undergraduate and postgraduate population of these universities continued to grow by leaps and bounds. Most of the universities were either federally owned or state owned. However, the foundation laid for the establishment of privately owned universities began to yield enormous interest and success at the beginning of the 1990s. It appeared that ownership or proprietorship of a university became a status symbol and a parameter by which the importance and efficiency of a state government were adjudged.

Looking at the youths seeking education at the higher level, one may be tempted to conclude that I was in need of more universities. It was becoming increasingly clearer that the existing universities were inadequately funded. Basic infrastructures were lacking in some of them. Libraries were not well equipped. Research facilities were not conducive to encourage future university lecturers and administrators. It was proposed that instead of allowing more universities, we should equip and update the existing ones. If universities were properly funded and well administered, one university could conceivably accommodate two or three states at a time. I also observed with concern and alarm the proclivity of some prominent politicians for turning the establishment of universities into some kind of business enterprise or personal status symbol. It appeared that the motivation was not perhaps the genuine desire to educate the people but instead to profit from the fees charged.

Because of the vast numbers of applicants wishing to gain admission to these universities every year, and with many fewer places available within the faculties, the scramble for admission was streamlined and brought under the controlling body called the Joint Admission and Matriculation Board (JAMB). The name was later changed to Universities Matriculation Examination (UME). It was this board that conducted general examinations for all prospective undergraduates who indicated in prescribed application forms the universities of their choice in order of preference. With advice from the various universities' registrars, examination mark goals were set, and admission policies were geared towards standards of merit and based on first choice, catchment areas, availability of places in the various faculties, and other concessionary considerations.

The arts and humanities had pride of place over science and technology at the onset. As an emergent Independent Nation, I needed personnel of appreciably high standards to fill the administrative posts left vacant by the departing British administrators. They were also needed to satisfy the widening demands of an infant nation. Therefore, the universities had to create teachers not only for arts, education, law, government, and general administration, but also for science, even if it was at its very elementary and rudimentary stages.

It reached a stage when the teachers of the classics (the study of ancient history and languages) were a unique and highly respected faculty at the University of Ibadan. Then the classical discipline declined, having been driven into insignificance by the more meaningfully relevant departments such as language, where modern languages like French, German, and Spanish were taught. Happily, emphasis again shifted to the sciences with attendant wholesome relevance to agriculture, engineering, medicine, industry, and geology. These are vital and relevant areas and essential for my economy in terms of food production, development, construction, health, social amenities and services, and the exploration of my greatest source of income—crude oil and other mineral resources.

It is desirable to have a preponderance of science undergraduates and graduates. Universities offer the humanities with emphasis on education to train teachers, administration classes that will produce civil servants and businessmen, and an economics curriculum to train bankers, accountants, and economic planners, as well as law and arts-oriented vocations. The ratio of relevance and comparison between the sciences and arts and humanities still seems to tilt the balance in favour of arts and the humanities at around 60% to 40%.

It is certain that, given time and the new craving of my emerging generation of intrepid scientists for scientific knowledge, barriers will be broken down. My new vanguard of all-conquering and science-oriented entrepreneurs will lead me to join the big league of technologically advanced countries of the new millennium. It is now being appreciated that computer science and information technology, which are already in vogue, will greatly facilitate the gathering and storage of data to enhance studies and research in all spheres of education.

SECONDARY SCHOOLS

If there are about 100 universities offering a few thousand places for hundreds of thousands of Joint Admission and Matriculation Board's (JAMB) examination candidates, then the number of secondary schools can be reasonably reckoned to be about 60,000. The colonial administrators laid the foundations for the foremost and oldest secondary schools through the efforts of the zealous and selfless missionaries. The prestigious pioneering institutions of this system speak volumes in the meaningful and suggestive names they bear. Kings College was unmistakably named as a mark of honour to the English monarchy. It remains the only one so named and still based in the then-capital city of Lagos. A similar status could be accorded the CMS (Christian Missionary School) Grammar School in Lagos. The only significant difference being that CMS Grammar School was moved from Broad Street in Lagos to Bariga Street in mainland Lagos. It was the hallmark of the missionary secondary school educational foundation within my territory.

Girls' secondary schools that go under the umbrella name of Queens College were established in Lagos, Ede (later Ibadan), and Enugu (Elelenwa). The one in Kaduna later became known as Queen Amina College. Then the government colleges were established as satellites in the various provincial headquarters like Ibadan, Umuahia, Benin (Edo College), Enugu, Zaria, Keffi, and Bida. Competitions to gain admission to these popular government colleges are always very keen.

The missionaries entered the educational field with their usual dedication and meticulous zeal for planning. Inevitably, the seed of the Christian religion was painstakingly sown into young and impressionable minds. The missionaries cultivated both brain and character, and the effect was outstanding and noticeable in the days before schools were taken over by the government. These were the glorious days in which grammar schools were liberally established and funded by the Christian Missionary Society (CMS) in the South and parts of the North. While the name CMS Grammar School still applies to the Lagos branch, it is called Grammar School or Anglican Grammar School or College in other areas.

Apart from the Anglican missionaries, many other Christian sects participated in the educational field. The Christian sects that were mainly involved included the Anglican, Catholic, Methodist, and Baptist missions. The educational activities of these other sects led to the establishment of such secondary schools as Baptist Academy, Methodist Boys or Girls High School, Holy Child, Saint Gregory's, Saint Finbars', and Reagan Memorial Anglican Girls School and Girls Seminary, all in Lagos; Sudan Interior Mission; Saint John's College in Jos; Mary Immaculate Conception in Ado Ekiti; Christ the King's College in Onitsha; Saint Leos College in Abeokuta; Dennis Memorial Grammar School; Hope Waddel Institute and Mary Slessor College both in Calabar; Saint Josephs College in Ondo; Stella Maris in Abuja; Saint Faith; and Saint Anne's in Ibadan. Other secondary schools are named after established missionaries, sects, saints, or other notable missionaries who served meritoriously in many towns and villages.

If the Colonial administration-backed missionary secondary schools were Western in orientation and imbued with Christian ideals, the Muslim secondary schools were Islamic-based and Arabic in ideals. Since the insatiable thirst for education defies the coloration of the waters of religious sects, the two main religions soon learned to accommodate each other as they trooped to the fountains of knowledge. In their quests for knowledge, the interaction and crossover mentality between the Muslims and the Christians has been phenomenal. The two religions drink knowledge from the same watering hole. The language of science and technology defies the suffocating limitations of creed and ideology.

Unfortunately, all the rich legacies began to wane rather than wax. This was brought about by the gradual dampening of the missionary spirit, following the abrupt unilateral governmental takeover of schools from the voluntary agencies after the civil war. The erstwhile missionary agencies have been downplayed ever since. Despite the frequent hue and cry of my concerned citizens and the protests of many high-powered organizations like the Catholic Laity Council of Nigeria and the Catholic Bishops of Nigeria over the unjust and unfair action of government in hijacking the schools from their owners without compensation, the loud and persistent protests largely went unheeded. There is no doubt that the consequences have been damaging to my educational system as well as to my other educational institutions. Devoid of the moral and religious foundation on which the missionaries built the schools and trained the students, the acquisition of the schools wreaked incalculable damage to these institutions. They have become riddled with disorder of unimaginable proportion. Some of them have become the dens of cultists and the practise grounds for examination malpractises. There is no doubt that vigorous and effective participation of the private sector will be needed to help unburden the problem of management solely by government.

The Muslims started training their youths in the Koranic and Arabic schools. The way was then paved for the establishment of a number of secondary schools. The most outstanding ones are the Ahmadiya secondary schools, the Zumratul Islamiya secondary schools, and the Ansar-u-deen secondary schools. These are mostly located in Lagos and the old West and parts of the Middle Belt. Having secondary schools named after them has immortalized some of the great Muslim leaders. Typical examples are Dan Fodio and Abiola. One was the great founder of the Sokoto Caliphate and indisputably a pioneering front-liner of the Islam in the region. The other was a devout Muslim and high-ranking official of the Islamic movement—a philanthropist, who held the idea of education in very high esteem.

It is worthy of mention that Tai Solarin and his wife Sheila founded Mayflower School at Ikenne. On its own, Mayflower School became a model school founded on discipline and on the bedrock of self-help, self-development, science, and humanism. These were the ideals for which Tai Solarin lived and died and of which all 'ex-Mays', as they proudly call themselves, are flag bearers in the realm of nation building. The schools' student orientation was pragmatic and its leadership concept participatory and demanding. No boy or girl who passed through Tai's Mayflower would have cause to regret having it as an alma mater. They always pay glowing tribute to it with passion and nostalgia.

Similarly, Igbinedion single-handedly founded a model and modern comprehensive secondary school in his native Okada in Benin. It is a school that heralded the modernity and uniqueness of what the Igbinedion private university would look like. He set a very high standard and also personally subsidized fees by awarding scholarships. Much emphasis is placed on science, technology, culture, and a good atmosphere conducive to learning. Other private schools of high standard began springing up in the other states.

Communities and towns took their cue from the government and mission schools by building community grammar schools named after their environments, after some illustrious sons and daughters, heroes and heroines, or after memorable events and places. Barewa College in Zaria is the elitist educational beacon in the North, producing the best of the best to man public and private sectors. Others in this mould are St. John's Secondary School in Jos, government College Bida, and Keffi government college and the Defense Academy in Kaduna. The latter is the teaching ground for the officer corps of my elite military forces.

My federal government used the establishment of government colleges conceptually to foster unity and encourage not only co-education but also the breaking down of barriers between states and the eradication of inward-looking ethnicism. Hence, these unity schools are located in most states with some having one for boys and another for girls and in a few cases an additional one for co-education (for both boys and girls together). Entrance procedure to these secondary schools is very competitive, and the examinations are conducted under the auspices of the Federal Ministry of Education. At the last count, there were about 102 of these secondary schools. Plans to privatize the secondary schools somehow engaged the attention of education planners. Reasons for such plans range from emphasis on the qualitative education prevalent in the private secondary schools to involving parents in the financial aspects of running the schools. The disapproval and resentment that greeted this proposal made the proponents quickly apply the brakes.

The states soon joined in the same trend by establishing state or model secondary schools. Unfortunately, the unifying purpose of having children go to school in distant states outside their home states seems to have been defeated by the astronomical cost to convey such students by air or land to various far-flung destinations and the attendant risks involved.

A classic example of unbridled duplication or proliferation of secondary schools can be cited in the establishment of Command Secondary Schools for the various military branches—Army, Navy, and Air Force. In addition to these formations, some universities established international secondary schools as appendages to their campuses. These schools cater to the interest of the university teachers' children and those of the international community who like to patronize such schools because of their locations within the citadels of higher learning.

Private secondary schools are springing up in every major city, all in search of superior and better-supervised education. They come in all sorts of names, systems, and environments. They can be found mostly in major cities like Lagos, Ibadan, Abeokuta, Enugu, Onitsha, Benin, Offa, Ilorin, Ondo, Jos, Minna, Abuja, and Port Harcourt. The fees are exorbitant; concomitantly, standards are in most cases very high and impressive, and results are always very encouraging and attractive.

PRIMARY SCHOOL EDUCATION

The fundamental significance of primary schools as an essential ingredient of education can hardly be overemphasized. Indeed, in the olden days, the first two years that a pupil spent in school were in the so-called 'infant schools'. Nowadays, the two preceding years to the primary schools are spent in nursery schools, which are usually attached to the mushrooming private nursery/primary schools. The 6-3-3-4 system of education adopted in the 1980s envisaged that the pupil would spend 6 years in the primary school, 3 years in the junior high school, 3 years in the senior high school, and 4 years at the tertiary level. Before this system was adopted, however, the practise was to spend the first two years in the infant school learning the alphabets in the local language and how to read and write in the mother tongue. All these have now been sandwiched into six years during which a pupil undergoes all the basic introductions into reading and writing to calculate and develop aptitudes in objective studies.

Just as a primary school education is equal to the first tottering steps of a child towards greater and higher accomplishments, it is also the first and most meaningful blow against illiteracy and ignorance. This is why there are primary schools in every nook and cranny of my vast terrain. There are thousands of these primary schools, which are the veritable gateways to the wider vistas of knowledge and erudition that are available at the secondary and tertiary levels.

The defunct Western Region—under the distinguished leadership of Obafemi Awolowo and the erudite, brilliant, and forward-looking planning and advice of Adekunle Ajasin and S. O. Awokoya—was the pioneering protagonist of free and compulsory primary education. Lateef Jakande, the former 'action' governor of Lagos State, went a step further by eradicating the 'double shift' system (morning and evening schools) through construction of more school buildings. Even though the buildings were jeeringly described as poultry sheds, 'Jakande schools' showed subsequent governors the way.

Assured of greater financial support from successive military governments, the military governors erected ultra-modern structures to replace Jakande's 'poultry sheds'. Mudashiru Lawal, an Air Force officer, was the most successful among the military governors in building the new structures. In Lagos, neighborhood primary schools were created to feed neighborhood secondary schools. Understandably, all the other states tried to emulate Jakande's system, making schools available to all and within an easy distance for pupils.

All states and local governments place a great premium on primary education. Though the goal of meeting the universally acceptable level of literacy is yet to be attained, efforts are being made to make up for lost time by establishing adult education centers. Condensed programmes are offered for willing adults, who are urged to come forward to learn in arrears in order to broaden their outlook and promote better understanding of the current trends in their various vocations and professions.

EDUCATION: THE WAY FORWARD

The picture of my educational sector, even at the beginning of the twenty-first century,was rather pathetic. It is a shame and a source of genuine concern that some children are still studying under trees, in dilapidated structures, and on bare floor. I see this as a *dis*incentive to learning. It strips my citizenry and children of their dignity. Indeed, available statistics have indicated that the enrolment level of children in primary, secondary, and tertiary levels were 60%, 37%, and 3%, respectively. There should be mass determination to remedy this unseemly trend. According to my former Federal Minister of Education, Obiageli Ezekwesili, 'If a nation does not get the product of such inertia in the educational sector, it runs the imminent risk of breeding weapons of mass destruction'.

The foundation for the eradication of illiteracy and ignorance seemed to have been laid or so it was assumed by people in the sector. I thought that the hundreds of thousands of children who were in schools receiving education in the twilight of the twentieth century would all grow into literate adults in the nascent twenty-first century. This would have signaled the total eradication of illiteracy along the lines of my dreams as the century progresses. However, it is better late than never. The massive education drive that would produce thousands of schools and pupils from primary through tertiary levels would guarantee that illiteracy will soon be a thing of the past.

The modern 'high-tech' world of gadgets, educational aides, and information technology will go a long way to instill awareness and maintain and sustain steady progress in the acquisition of knowledge and expertise in all branches of education. I would like to resuscitate the study of history through out the various stages of education. Awareness and knowledge of the past, in terms of people and events, will beneficially and positively influence my people's thinking, actions, and planning now and in the future.

I foresee a major breakthrough in the field of research leading to the discovery of medicinal cures for ailments that continue to defy treatment. The interaction between modern medical research and trado-medical practitioners may be the key to those discoveries. As I earlier postulated, I still believe that efficacious medicinal herbs—leaves, buds, flowers, nuts, seeds, tree barks, and roots of trees—which abound in my forests may provide the solutions when subjected to microscopic and scientific analysis and experiments in the laboratories.

I am a stickler for education in all its ramifications. My vision is for qualitative rather than quantitative education. While my desire for massive education and eradication of illiteracy might have been satisfied by quantitative education, I want to ensure quality in education. The 6-3-3-4 concept was introduced as a response to the agitation for a more functional and qualitative education system. However, sadly, after about ten years of it, analysts came to the conclusion that the system, among other things, lacked consistency. A higher level of transformation was needed to achieve the desired standard of educational development. The perennial problems of lecturers' strikes, university closures, and cultism in the universities must be properly addressed and contained to minimize such incidents in future. Proliferation of universities may become counter-productive. This may cheapen the glory and splendour of education and accentuate falling standards. The employment market may become saturated if concomitant job creation and production sites are not set up. Too many hands gunning for very few available positions may lead to poorer pay. It is certain therefore that the answer lies with the improvement of the economy in order to create more employment opportunities.

CHAPTER SEVENTEEN

SOME MAJOR CITIES— OLD AND NEW CAPITALS

I am a nation full of quiet sleepy villages, lively towns, and bustling cities that hardly ever sleep. Most urban dwellers hail from rural areas, migrating to the cities and towns without severing their connections, which are like umbilical cords that tie them to the villages of their birth. Movement towards the cities is a natural phenomenon. People relocate from the villages to the towns and cities in search of greener pastures, better job opportunities, and exposure to the lure of modern living. There is often no permanent disconnect with the villages. Going back to the village on special occasions like Christmas, annual festivals, and holidays has become the normal habit of some urban dwellers with firm village roots.

LAGOS

Lagos, my erstwhile Federal Capital before the move to Abuja, is the quintessence of high living of life on the fast lane. It has been referred to as the crown jewel of my federation. Lagos is more populous and even more economically buoyant than several African countries. Lagos is my miniature representation as the microcosm in which nearly all of my ethnic groups are represented. It has been variously described as the 'center of excellence', 'the commercial capital', and the 'industrial hub'.

It is the zenith of grandeur and the nadir of squalor. One moment, the visitor is confronted with the state-of-the-art edifices and the architectural marvels that abound in Victoria Island, Victoria Garden City (VGC), and Lekki. A few minutes later, driving by the Lagoon or across it on any of the three bridges that span the Lagoon, the visitor is assailed by the sight of shanties and the dirty open sewers in the ghettoes of Isale-Eko, Mushin, and Ajegunle. The five-star hotels in Ikoyi and Victoria Island form the extremes of comparisons with the makeshift, open-air habitats readily available under the numerous bridges and flyovers on Lagos Island, the swampy backwoods of Ajegunle, the overpopulated Mushin, and the squalor of the Shomolu and Bariga neighbourhoods.

Some magnificent edifices adorn my major cities. The skyline of Lagos, viewed from various angles, will reveal a cloister of skyscrapers silhouetted against blue skies. The Independence Building, the NET Buildings, and the Investment House were all, at one time or another, torched—but still stand tall. The Fernandez Towers, the Igbinedion House, the Elephant House, the Western House, the Eleganza House, the Unity House, the UBA Headquarters, Kotangora House, the Niger House, and the towering buildings which house the major banks are some of the buildings that catch the eye. Cement and brick blocks, aluminum doors, glass windows, and fabulous glass structures and coverings are evident in the new edifices that are coming up, mostly in the Lagos Island City Center, Ikoyi, Victoria Island, Lekki, and Victoria Garden City.

Interspersed with these gigantic houses are vast cathedrals and big churches portraying a variety of spectacular architectural designs. The Holy Cross Cathedral and the Christ Church Cathedral are unique, reflecting the architecture of the colonialists who designed and supervised the erection of the churches. The semi-domelike appearance of the Methodist Church in Tinubu Square stands in bold relief amidst the old fortresslike Central bank structure and huge office complexes in the surroundings. The multimillion-naira Central Mosque built in the heart of Lagos is vast, with its silvery domes jutting up into the sky.

The Island Club in Lagos, which is nearly 100 years old, is my premier multiracial club. It was founded at the height of anti-colonial struggle and designed to be the usual meeting place of the leading contending, economic, political, diplomatic, and social forces and personalities. Among the founding members were

Adeyemo Alakija, Ernest Ikoli, Nnamdi Azikiwe, Louis Odumegwu Ojukwu, J. K. Randle, S. O. Gbadamosi, Arthur Prest, Louis Mbanefo, and Hamilton Biney, as well as a host of others. They were some of my distinguished and high-profile earth shakers and opinion moulders of their era. They were men whom the bombastic 'wordsmith' K. O. Mbadiwe would have called 'men of timber and calibre'.

The Yoruba Tennis Club is in the same vicinity. Indigenous Lagosians—who wanted to draw a clear distinction between colonialists and civil servant settlers on the one hand and thoroughbred Lagosians on the other—founded the club. It was basically a meeting point for the indigenous nationalist agitators during my pre-Independence struggle.

The Metropolitan Club on Victoria Island, Ikoyi Club 1938, Country Club, Ikeja, and Apapa Club are other major recreation clubs which enliven the city of Lagos. Affiliates of country clubs were found in my other major cities where membership club cards entitled the holders to share fellowship and socialize in any of the affiliated country clubs in the old regions. Three universities, a college of technology, a college of polytechnic, and colleges of education gave Lagos its own distinctive aura of an 'Acada' city. L. K. Jakande, the erstwhile 'action governor' of Lagos State, ensured that education was within the reach of all. It was not a secret that youths flocked to Lagos from the other states in search of free and accessible education.

In the middle of a network of roads, standing majestically like a gigantic amphitheatre, is the magnificent National Theatre, shaped like General Gowon's cap. Gowon had seen and admired a similar structure that looked like a general's cap when he visited Bulgaria in the 1970s. That was how the idea to borrow but adapt it to serve as a cultural monument in Lagos came about. This was the building that played host to some of the events on display by myriads of black people from Africa and the Diaspora during FESTAC '77. To commemorate the spectacular global fiesta, a whole new town, or 'FESTAC Town', was born.

FESTAC Town was conceptually a modern and well-laid-out town, full of many beautiful and modern buildings and modern amenities. It is a town on its own located on the outskirts of Lagos, and this is why it became a Mecca for tourists. Recently, dirt, smog, and dung—the scourge of many of the big cities—have taken over in FESTAC Town. Beautifully planned parks and many open spaces have been bought up or encroached upon and built up. Avoidable disorder has taken over and the dream of the town planners is fast receding into a nightmare.

Lagos boasts some famous building complexes which serve the people in a variety of ways. The big federal secretariat buildings at Ikoyi before the Capital's relocation to Abuja and the Lagos State secretariat at Alausa accommodated a vast number of civil servants from several ministries. The design of the federal secretariat is vigorous, and it was created to reflect the size of the civil service work force at the Federal level. The Lagos State Complex at Alausa encompasses the beautifully designed governor's 'round house' office, the State House of Assembly complex, and the State secretariat buildings.

The ultramodern and multipurpose Tafawa Balewa Square Shopping Arcade is complete with modern shops and office accommodations, a parade ground with terraces, and a trade fair pavilion. The site of the whole complex was formerly called Race Course, which served many useful purposes in the pre-Independence era. It was a parade ground for schools during Empire Day celebrations. It was used as a race course for horse racing. It also served as an athletics competition ground and a cricket pitch.

The National Stadium complex is situated at Surulere. The stadium itself has a seating capacity of 40,000. The complex contains the administrative buildings and gymnasiums, an Olympic size swimming pool, lawn tennis courts, practice pitches and a cavernous indoor sports hall. The National Sports Institute is also situated there, housing a school for coaches in the different sporting disciplines. The Trade Fair Complex is another marvelous piece of architectural design on the Lagos–Badagry Expressway. It has been built to serve the useful purpose of trade fairs and exhibitions, which attract participants and viewers from all over the world.

Lagos is an all-comers city. The receptive and accommodating ambiance of Lagos was once captured in the popular proverbial song recorded by the famous highlife music exponent Victor Olaiya, stating, 'The city of Lagos is liberally accommodating to both felons and vagabonds' (Eko gb'ole O gb'ole). Lagos is a busy and bustling city that grips one with a feeling of intense urgency. People are up and about almost all day as if to say, 'Life is tough but we are tougher'.

It is simultaneously my commercial nerve center and the administrative head-quarters of Lagos State government and is referred to as my commercial capital.

A conservative estimate of its population is about 20 million people, which makes Lagos the most populous city in Africa. It is much bigger even than most of the West African countries. Of my 36 states, Lagos State is one of my smallest in terms of land mass and size. It is arguably the most densely populated. Based on a United Nations study and the Lagos State Regional Master Plan, Lagos has a population growth rate of about 300,000 persons per annum and a population density of about 1,308 persons per square kilometre, Lagos State is presumed to be larger than each of 32 African countries. It is also projected to possibly hit about 24.5 million in population, which will make it one of the 10 most popu-lous cities in the world by the year 2020.

These explosive rates of growth have not only progressively complicated and exacerbated interrelated problems of human settlements and the environ-ment but have also greatly accelerated poverty. The demand for infrastructure, basic amenities, and housing will surely be on the increase. Issues of sanitation, waste management, crime, social conflict, governance, and management have to be seriously addressed. It is heartening that successive generations of politi-cians and city planners in my former Federal capital city are determined, in spite of all odds, to address these basic infrastructure problems.

Vehicular traffic jams are endemic in the city of Lagos. The city center is full of hustles and bustles of working activities by day and by night becomes socially alive at various merrymaking spots. Broad Street in Lagos, Marina Street by the Lagoon, Allen Avenue and Obafemi Awolowo Way in Ikeja, and the commercial streets in Apapa are some of the trendiest shopping centers and busiest busi-ness districts in Africa. When one adds the burgeoning business and social ac-tivities in Ikoyi and Victoria Island, then Lagos ranks among the liveliest and busiest cities in the world. The busy centers are beehives of various establish-ments where banks and office blocks compete for space with car marts, super-markets, airline organizations, business centers, saloons, boutiques, restau-rants, and night clubs.

Lagos is a city of contrasts. At places like Obalende and the much older low-density neighbourhoods like Yaba, Ebute-Metta, Mushin, and Shomolu/Bariga, modern architectural structures with long-span roofing in a variety of colours intersperse many buildings with rusty zinc roofs of houses that have known many seasons of corrosive heat, cold, and dust.

The triangular business district—made up of Opebi, Toyin Street, and Allen Avenue and dovetails into the ever-busy Obafemi Awolowo Road—is now enjoying the same popularity, if not more, than Broad Street and Marina on Lagos Island once had. The mere mention of the name 'Allen Avenue' invokes many notions and connotations to different people. 'Allen', as it is popularly called, has its own peculiar aura when considering popular streets and roads in all my cities and towns. Like a mustard seed, the avenue started modestly in the early 1970s with an innocuous residential and sedate setting at inception. The mustard seed is now a gigantic tree. Allen Avenue is a sprawling area with vast commercial potential.

Many banks are located on the Opebi/Toyin/Allen axis. The banks range from the older established ones to the new-generation banks and some other financial institutions. There are also a number of supermarkets, book shops, boutiques, car marts, big office complexes, and eateries all across the lengths of the three streets and Obafemi Awolowo Road. The entire business district is a potpourri of business activities. The Alade Market—where one can find goods and services, assorted cooking paraphernalia, and textiles—is also located off the popular Allen Avenue.

The Allen Avenue neighbourhood sometimes is associated with notoriety. Some perceive it as a haven for criminals. The notorious advance-fee fraudsters, otherwise known and euphemistically referred to, as '419-ers', are known to ply their antisocial activities there. Cocaine dealers and users, drug barons and their couriers, currency traffickers, foreign exchange dealers, money doublers, strip-tease joints, and commercial sex workers are known to make the place their rendezvous, particularly by night.

The Lagos suburb of Ajegunle is at once an enigma and a phenomenon. The place has a unique character. It is like an urban jungle and has acquired the unusual name of 'Jungle City'. It is an aberration of sorts, complete with its own exciting colour and cadence, its own evocative social drama, and its own enchanting fabulous reality. It encapsulates life in the subhuman conditions of existence, notably in the famous Boundary Market, where you can buy anything from a human skull to lion's fat and second-hand clothing smuggled from the neighboring Benin Republic or distant lands like China and South Korea.

In a sense, Ajegunle stands out like a sore thumb from the affluent neighborhoods of the government reservation area and the dockyard neighborhood boulevards of Apapa. It is a sprawling slum of about 3 million people, where houses are wedged together, and gutters and gullies serve as roads constantly ravaged by flood. Alongside innumerable beer parlours are open markets, stalls, shops, dingy restaurants, mosques, and churches. Ajegunle is another name for squalor and privation.

A visitor to Lagos who has not visited the fabulous Alaba International Market on the outskirts of Lagos has not yet 'seen it all'. It abounds with quaint furniture items and beautifully finished interior decoration materials and textiles. The place is an electronics shopper's delight—it is the quintessential electronics district. It reminds the experienced traveller of the famous Akhiabara electronics district of Tokyo, Japan. Times are changing; security problems and the desire to expand combine to compel the shop owners to prepare a modern and well-organized site at the Trade Fair Complex.

Lagos beaches are many and are beckoning. The Bar, Lekki, Ibeju, Maiyegun, and Badagry beaches are popular pleasure and relaxation spots. Interestingly, some of these beaches are taken over at night by the white-robed singing and clapping religious sects, worshipping there in the belief that their prayers will gain unhindered passage on the ocean waves and in the windy atmosphere to the throne of the Almighty God. This was more so on Bar Beach before the ocean began to encroach on the sandy beach, driving the revelers, priests, and worshippers away and threatening the very existence of the ultra-modern and highbrow environment of Victoria Island and the Lekki Peninsula. I am happy to observe that, in concert with the appropriate Federal and Lagos State government tourism sections, plans are ongoing to turn the imminent destructive doom of Bar Beach into an economic boom and prosperity. They apparently know how this can be achieved, as it has been done in some European countries.

ABUJA

Abuja, my new Federal Capital, is a symbol of change and modernity. It is the citadel of peace and the monumental melting pot of divergent tribes, creeds, and tongues. The city has justified its billing and has fulfilled the quest of the founding 'father' Murtala Mohammed for 'a virgin no-man's land', and I should like to add *where we should all be beginners, founders, and co-builders—not strangers or settlers*. At this juncture, I want to acknowledge the forward-looking and exploratory acumen of the intrepid team selected by Murtala Mohammed to conduct the search for the requisite type of 'virgin' land for a new capital. Akinola Aguda was the leader of the group, and Tai Solarin was a prominent member.

The Nicon Noga Hotel (now called Transcorp), the Sheraton Towers, the Agura Hotel, and the Meridian Hotel are some of the five-star hotels springing up in my new capital city. Like Manhattan in New York, Abuja is now being referred to as the 'concrete jungle of a city'. It has all the advantages of a preconceived and minutely preplanned city from inception to completion. The concept is quaintly referred to as the Abuja 'Master Plan'. It is generally agreed that when you are in Abuja, it is as if you are in a modern European city, well planned and well maintained. It is a fact that by its evidently vigorous activities, Julius Berger (the giant construction firm from Germany) has left its indelible mark on the fabulous buildings and the magnificent boulevards that abound in my new capital city of Abuja.

Abuja is fast becoming a city of peace that other warring African countries, torn apart by civil wars or internal squabbles, flock to in order to reach accord or negotiated reconciliation. The civil wars in the Sudan and the internecine debacle in Liberia found a forum for organized discussion and accord in Abuja. The Sierra Leone civil war used Abuja as the venue of dialogue and reconciliation. The shifting of my seat of government to Abuja is to the eternal glory of innovative and forward-looking Murtala Mohammed. It was his idea to relocate my Federal capital to a place where the chaos and confusion of Lagos should be forgotten. Abuja was established in order to afford a fresh beginning in which planning would be meticulous and execution would be prompt and exact. The buildings in the city centers and government secretariat complexes are all beautifully erected and very spacious.

Traffic lights and other public utilities are efficiently functional. Abuja is a model city and is better to see it in person than in imagination or by merely seeing it in pictures and in documentaries. The popular saying 'Seeing is believing' is appropriate with focus on Abuja. I am indeed very proud of my new capital city, which has become a shining example of what a modern and functional African capital should look like. The trip from the Nnamdi Azikiwe International Airport to the city is a manifestation of the warmth and excellence that awaits a new visitor to Abuja. It is a drive of about forty minutes through mountains and valleys, some artificial and others natural. Bright traffic lights herald the sophistication and modernity Abuja represents.

There are beautiful villas, state-of-the-art structures, and vast estates which give Abuja a distinctive aura. The new capital earn full marks for its particularly well-planned network of beautiful roads. Traffic lights are generally well obeyed. There are many road signs that offer guidance and advice to all road users. The attainment of this level of orderliness and strict adherence to laid-out plans and delineations are commendable. These feats are indubitably attributable to the indefatigable and uncompromising efforts of the much-celebrated and, later, much-maligned youthful and no-nonsense Federal Minister of the Federal Capital Territory, Nasir El-Rufai. No one, however highly placed, or any group, however deeply entrenched or high-profiled, was spared the inconvenience and embarrassment of demolition of their property once it was established that there had been any contravention of the original master plan of the capital city.

Several cities outside Lagos and Abuja, where the largest concentration of magnificent edifices are located, can also boast of their own brand of uniquely beautiful and historical buildings. All the new states and private universities are adorned with stately buildings and vast complexes that vary in style and design, from state to state and from campus to campus. The proliferation of states and the advent of state and local governments have made it imperative for state capitals to have modern State House complexes, big Secretariat buildings, stately Houses of Assembly, housing, and city halls befitting the status of state capitals.

Development also extends to local governments in the name of grass-roots development.

Building high walls and huge gates has been in vogue for quite a while. Threatened by intruders and criminals intent on doing harm and committing various crimes, my citizens concern themselves with their own safety. Such is the reality in Lagos in particular and in various cities and government reservation areas generally—that high walls and electrified gates not only serve to protect people against burglars, but also increasingly turn people into prisoners in their own homes. Indeed, the erection of walls and fanciful gates has been turned into an artistic and decorative aspect of construction. Fancy blocks and beautifully designed metalworks are usually prominent in the construction of defenses.

Some monuments and landmark buildings scattered all over different cities and towns are worthy of mention. The famous Lugard Hall, the Durbar Pavilion, the Trade Fair grounds, the Hamdalla Hotel, and the Durbar Hotel are all in Kaduna. The most distinguishing features of Kano are the domed minarets of the mosques that sprout up everywhere and the prismatic style of their ancient buildings. The National War Museum and Monument located in Umuahia houses varied and numerous collections of war artefacts and relics of the civil war. Sokoto, Ikenne, and Bauchi have a common monumental feature in the tombs and mausoleums built to honour my illustrious and legendary nation builders and leaders of thoughts—Usman Dan Fodio, Awolowo, and Tafawa Balewa, respectively.

CHAPTER EIGHTEEN

SOME MAJOR SPORTS, COMPETITIONS, AND SPORTS ADMINISTRATORS

ATHLETICS

I am a Nation of sports-loving people. My flag has been hoisted in victory several times both at home and abroad in distant sporting arenas around the globe. I made my Olympics debut at the Helsinki Olympic Games in 1952. Since then I had only missed an Olympic outing in 1976, owing to the politically motivated boycott of the Montreal games. This was because I did not want my athletes and other African athletes to share the same arena with the then-disliked apartheid practitioners and their home-bred athletes. My athletes had matched their skills and prowess against other nations' athletes at the quadrennial Olympic Games in Melbourne, Rome, Tokyo, Mexico, Munich, Moscow, Los Angeles, Seoul, Barcelona, Atlanta, and Sidney. It is remarkable that my athletes had featured in the various Olympic games spanning the years between 1952 and 2008 with the single exception of 1976.

In a similar vein, the Commonwealth Games afford my athletes the opportunity to mingle and compete with the athletes of other Commonwealth countries. Such competitions have taken my athletes to such places as Vancouver, Kingston, Edinburgh, Christchurch, Dublin, Cardiff, Toronto, Brisbane, Auckland,

Victoria, and Manchester. In order to foster continental fraternity and greater camaraderie among the youths of Africa, I was among the protagonists of the idea and ideals of the African Games. This is another quadrennial sporting series of events in which all African countries participate. I have had the honour and the joy of hosting this sporting fiesta in Lagos.

Each of the three aforementioned games—the Olympics, the Commonwealth Games, and the African Games—is an aggregation of a variety of sporting contests and events. These events include athletics, soccer, boxing, table tennis, judo, weight lifting, volley ball, hand ball, basketball, swimming, cycling, badminton, and greco-roman wrestling. Other events in which I do not participate include fencing, shooting, equestrian, gymnastics, and high-board diving. Newer events are lawn tennis, takwendo and synchronized swimming.

Opposite page:
1 Mary Onyeali was African female sprints champion, and she represented Nigeria at the Olympics and Commonwealth Games.

2 Green Eagles of Nigeria in 1980, winning the Nations cup for the first time.

3 The Nigerian football team that played in the U.K. in 1949, popularly referred to as **'The U.K. Tourists.'**

This page:
1 Teslim Balogun, Nigerian legendary footballer popularly known as Thunder Bolt.

22 Hogan 'Kid' Bassey was Nigeria's first World Boxing Champion as the World Featherweight Champion.

3 Dick Tiger was the World Middle and Light Heavyweight Boxing Champion.

As the results of my efforts at different Olympic stadiums in Tokyo, Los Angeles, Munich, Barcelona, Atlanta, and Sidney, I won a gold medal in women's long jump and another gold medal in soccer, silver medals in boxing, men's 4 X 400-meter relay race, and men's 4 X 100-meter relay race, and bronze medals in boxing, women's 4 x 400 meter relay race, and men's 4 X 400 relay race. My sportsmen and women are striving painstakingly and with all dedication and tenacity of purpose to capture more gold medals in future Olympic games. I have carved a niche for myself as a nation that parades succeeding generations of powerful sprinters and jumpers. In addition to the sprints and jumps in which my athletes excel, boxing, wrestling and weight lifting have been the events in which my athletes have shown great promise and capability. They have given good accounts of themselves, particularly at the African Games and the Commonwealth Games.

It was in Vancouver, during the 1954 Commonwealth Games that Ifeajuna won my first gold medal ever, at the high jump event. Ifeajuna had used the "Western Roll" style, taking off on the foot on which he had a solitary jumping shoe. The High jump event has since assumed new dimensions both in the take-off style and heights being jumped. The American jumper, Fosbury, turned his back on the bar after an angular approach and hurled himself face-up over the bar. Then he landed on his back on the padded landing pit, and a new style was born. This jumping style became known as the "Fosbury Flop." Using this technique, seemingly impossible heights have become attainable and my athletes are well adapted to the style.

More medals were to follow in the sprints, particularly in the 100 meters, relays, and the long and triple jumps, where S. O. Williams, Peter Esiri, K. A. B. Olowu, Paul Engo, S. O. Oladitan, Eddy Jeyifous, Charles Ehiezuelen, George Ogan, Ali, Ogbeide, Ajayi Agbebekun, and Eregbu excelled. I bemoan the fact that Charles Ehiezuelen was the leading triple jumper in the world before the boycotted Montreal Olympics. The prospect of my first possible gold medal was thus thwarted. My already selected Olympic football team had dazzled and stunned their opponents on the way to the boycotted games with occasional double-digit scores. The 1976 Olympics would have seen the likes of Odegbami and John Chukwu. But that was not to be, because of the principled boycott.

My sprinting potential at the international level came again to the fore with the emergence of, and rivalry between, A. K. Amu and Edward Omagbemi in the late 50s and early 60s. Before them, however, S. O Jolaoso, M.A. K. Ogun, Edward Ajado, Titus Erinle, and Aremu Arogundade had set high standards of performance and were medals prospects in the sprints. This dream nearly turned into real medals when I had both Olapade Adeniken and Davidson Ezinwa in the finals of the 100 meters at Barcelona in 1992. The latter also appeared once again in the finals of the Atlanta Olympics in 1996, although he still did not win one of the elusive sprints medals.

Innocent Egbunike took the athletics world by storm with his unique running gait when running the quarter mile at the Los Angeles Olympics and at Rome World Athletics. He ran a magnificent last leg in the 4 X 400 meters relay at the African Games in Nairobi, which elicited an unforgettable comment from the Kenyan President, Arap Moi, to the effect that "Innocent was not that innocent after all." This was because Egbunike overtook and outstripped the leading runners, including a Kenyan in that sensational last lap. Chidi Imoh nearly set the tracks ablaze with his blistering pace in the sprints, particularly at the African Games in Nairobi and the Olympic games in Barcelona. Sunday Bada gave the quarter mile his best shot at the 1996 Atlanta Games, to which the intimidating presence and the sensational and unforgettable performances of Michael Johnson brought glow and glamour. The latter rewrote the record books by winning the "double," the 200- and 400-meter races.

Among the female athletes, multi-talented Violet Odogwu was an all-rounder with spectacular performances in the hurdles, long jump, high jump,and sprints. She won a bronze and then silver medal at various games. Modupe Osikoya, endowed with lithe, long legs and strong body, was superb at the hurdles, long jump, and high jump. Fatima Yusuf was a revelation in Auckland as a gold medalist quarter miler. She was to repeat the feat with a record-shattering pace at the African Games in Harare in 1995. Fatima was in the finals of the 400 meters at the Atlanta Olympics, where she placed sixth.

Mary Onyeali was one of the foremost female sprinters in the world towards the end of the twentieth century. She ran the race of her life to anchor my gold winning 4 X 400-meter relay team at the 1994 Commonwealth Games in Canada. Onyeali was also at the starting blocks at the finals of the 100- and

200-meter sprint events at the Barcelona Olympics in 1992 and the Atlanta Olympics in 1996, where she finally won a bronze medal in the 200-meter race. She always delighted spectators with her almost-childlike, charismatic, and effusive show of joy after each of her consecutive strings of victories at various international athletics competitions. Faith Idehen, Beatrice Utondu (also a long jumper), and Charity Opara joined Onyeali in the medal-winning relay team. Young Mary Tombiri was a budding revelation at Victoria. She showed a lot of promise, poise, and class.

Falilat Ogunkoya and Kate Ihegulam sprang into world prominence at the Junior World Championships. Falilat was on the gold-winning team at the African Games in Nairobi. She took time off to get married and have a baby. Then she came back to the arena of competition and took the world by storm, having blossomed into superb form, recording times that baffled officials and was raring to sparkle at future meets. She did just that at the Harare 1995, and went on to repeat it in Atlanta in 1996 in a spectacular fashion, winning a bronze medal at the individual 400-meter race. She also anchored the relay team in the 4 X 400 meters with her brilliant and outstanding run, which earned the team a silver medal in that event.

My magic moment came at the 1996 Atlanta Olympic Games. The feeble tottering steps I took at Helsinki in 1952 became a giant stride into stardom and golden recognition. It could be recalled that I had tasted a 'teaser' in bronze, first in Tokyo in 1964, and then in Munich in 1972, both in boxing; I had graduated to silver medals at Los Angeles in 1984 in Boxing and Barcelona in 1992 in the 4 X 100-meter relay race. I finally achieved the elusive but spectacular gold medal at the 1996 Olympic games in Atlanta. It never rains but it pours: When gold finally came, it came in *two* rapturous bundles of joy. Chioma Ajunwa, a police inspector who had earlier been enmeshed in a controversial drug scandal and suspended by the World Athletics ruling body for four long years, came in from the cold and literally made mincemeat of an array of stars, including World and Olympic record holders in the long jump event. Her expected vindication did not come in the 100-meter dash, where she crashed out in the semi-final stages. It was the long jump where her spectacular first leap remained unbeatable and unbeaten throughout the series. My national anthem hit the airwaves and my flag was hoisted aloft, proclaiming my arrival at the golden stage of athletics. Because of her spectacular performance, Ajunwa was promoted to the rank of an assistant superintendent of police and copiously showered with financial rewards as she basked in public adulation.

My second gold medal also came in the Atlanta Olympics for soccer, during which my 'Dream Team' took the whole world by surprise. The team's artistry, doggedness, and never-say-die approach at all stages of the event became the nightmare of such world-acclaimed soccer maestros as Brazil and Argentina. Both were beaten at the semi-finals and finals, respectively. In both games my Dream Team came from behind to outclass and outshine first Brazil with a golden goal scored during the new "sudden death" (extra time) regulation; then Argentina, after they converted a disputable penalty award and within regulation time. My soccer-loving citizenry spread out the red carpet to receive the centennial Olympic team in Abuja and Lagos. Grateful Abacha government showered them with praises and gifts and seriously sought for a place to bask in the blinding sunshine that the heroes and heroines brought along with them to brighten and illuminate the prevalent and encircling gloomy political and economic atmosphere of that period in my history. Holidays were declared and parades were held.

As far as the teeming millions of overjoyed fans were concerned, and in their own visionary estimations, not only Chioma Ajunwa won a gold medal, but they saw 'in their own estimation, imagination, and adulation,' 11 gold medals dangling on the necks of skillful skipper Nwankwo Kanu, burly and strong Uche Okechukwu, agile and sensational goalkeeper Joseph Dosu, block-buster and swashbuckling Dan Amokachie, brilliant and dependable Celestine Babayaro, who celebrated each goal with excellently executed acrobatic back flips, Amuneke and Ikpeba, both fierce shooters of the ball, ball juggler and dribbling wizard, Austin "Jay Jay" Okocha, fleet-footed Babangida, bubbling Wilson Oruma, goal happy Teslim Fatusi, master passer of the ball Oliseh, and the Rock of Gibraltar of defenders, dreadlocked Taribo West, bulky Okparakwu, and Obafemi. They would remain the toast of the whole world for some time to come.

The triumphant accomplishments of my various teams at the African Games are a tremendous source of joy and fulfillment for me. My teams of highly competitive track and field athletes, skillful footballers, boxers, table tennis players, volleyball players, handball players, weight lifters, and wrestlers have always made me proud with their superlative performances. But for swimming, which alone accounts for a sizeable portion of the medals, and in which initially, in the absence of South Africa, the North African Arab countries excelled, I would have continually led on the medals table. As it had been for a long time, even when I hosted the games, I had almost always occupied the second position on the medals table, owing to lack of expertise and exposure on the part of my swimmers. Now with the emergence of South Africa into the sporting arena, I am either going to be consigned to the third position, or make deliberate and conscious efforts at improving my performances in the gold medal-"churning" events. I have to get my swimmers, boxers, wrestlers, and weight lifters adequately prepared to meet future challenges. I have tenaciously retained my grip of the bats, to capture almost all medals available in the table tennis event particularly at the African Games.

The significance of my tremendous achievements in track and field events can be better appreciated with a cursory excursion into the history of the development of sports over the years. My history of athletics is replete with colourful names and personalities. I have had several distinguished performers, outstanding performances of individual men and women, and dedicated administrators who have left their names indelibly on the sands of sports time. In the olden days, there was a dearth of international competitions. Those were the days of Empire Day celebrations that took place annually on the 24th of May. That was when all the primary schools in a town would compete in athletics—track and field events alone. Secondary schools were hardly involved, since there might be only one in an entire district or what is now a State or Senatorial District. With the emergence of a multiplicity of secondary schools, athletic competitions attained higher status and impetus. Inter-house sports competitions were used to discover athletes who would then represent the school in inter-school competitions.

The most popular inter-school athletic competitions in those days were between the established C.M.S. grammar schools or secondary schools in the old regions. The so-called AIONIAN Secondary Schools Athletic Competitions emanated from the anagram formed from the first letters of the participating secondary schools: Abeokuta Grammar School, Ibadan Grammar School, Ondo Boys High School, and Ijebu Ode Grammar School. Ilesha Grammar School, Olu-iwa

Grammar School, Oduduwa College, Ile-ife, Imade College Owo, and Manuwa Memorial Grammar School later joined the original four. In Lagos, there were annual athletic competitions between either two of the major secondary schools and, or between all the major secondary schools like King's College, Igbobi College, St. Gregory's College, C.M.S. Grammar School, Methodist Boys High School, Baptist Academy, and Eko Boys High School. Similar group competitions were entered into by secondary schools in the East and the North.

The local competitions were scaled up and enlarged in dimension to become known as the Greir Cup competitions. That was the stage reached when the best of the best of athletes from each of these secondary schools were pitted against one another on regional basis. The Hussey Shield Athletic Competitions became the peak of the whole exercise. There is no doubting the fact that some of the best athletes of those days emerged from these competitions. From the early 1950s, A. K. Amu was another schoolboy sensation who eventually became my national hurdles champion. He was from Edo Government College Benin. Samuel Akpabot excelled in athletics before he delved academically and fulltime into musicology as a university teacher and into part-time sports journalism. Sam Akpabot had a penchant for forecasting results of soccer tournaments. Ifeajuna honed his high jumping skill at Christ the King's College, Onitsha, before he entered the University of Ibadan, where he blossomed into world-class preeminence.

A. K. Amu was another schoolboy prodigy in the sprints and quarter mile at Kings College, Lagos, and later at the University College of Ibadan (UCI). He participated wearing my national colours in various local and international competitions for over a decade. Kunle Oyenuga leapt his way into my Olympic history books in long jump at the 1960 Games in Rome from his days at Kings College Lagos, as also did Bayo Oladapo, whose pint-size stature belied his unbelievable strides in the quarter mile. Paul Egom (Ashikawe) from Kings College, Sydney Asiodu from Igbobi College, Edward Akika from St. Finbars College, Chris Enahoro from Government College Ibadan, Charles Njoku and Victor Uwaifo from St. Gregory, Solomon Fadoju from Hussey College, Tunji Omowon from Ibadan Boys High School and then Ibadan Grammar School, Johnson Abaide from Christ's School Ado Ekiti, Arogundade from Olu Iwa Grammar School, Tim Fasanya, Oredein, Ojutalayo, Oredugba and Akinsuyi from Government College

Ibadan—all were discovered during their exploits and colourful performances at the Grier Cup and Hussey Shield Schools athletic competitions.

Lagos was the hub of all organized athletics competitions of that era. The major athletic clubs were in Lagos, and they included police athletics clubs, U.A.C. athletics clubs, Railway Athletics Club, Dyaks, Nigeria Ports Authority, P.W.D., and L.T.C. Athletics clubs. The big names of the 1950s and 1960s were the "flying policeman" Joseph Adeola, the legendary K. A. B. Olowu, "Flying Arrow" Arogundade, Oluwa, Ajado, Thomas Obi, from whose hand the relay baton nost unfortunately dropped in Melbourne, and Titus Erinle, David Ejoke, and Smart Akraka, who were all sprinters. Jaiye Abidoye was a promising miler, and before him there was the evergreen Oduguwa.

One bright afternoon in the mid-1950s, four sensational high jumpers in the persons of Majekodunmi, Odobo, Osagie and Guobadia put the smile on my face and enlivened my athletics annals by clearing the bar at 6 feet 6 inches. This was a fantastic height by the standards of the day. One cannot easily forget the near-impossible feat of Casmir Okoro, virtually limping on one of his legs, who won a gold medal at the All-Africa Games in Cairo with a leap of 7 feet 2 inches to set my new national record. These high jumpers came after Chijioke, Chigbolu, V. O Gabriel, and Policeman Igun. The latter also performed well as a triple Jumper. Baton exchange in relay races in those days was simply "face-me-and-hand-over" and not as complicated and technical as nowadays. Baton exchange in relay races has become so technical and decisive that it could make or break the chances of any team.

The women also gave a very good account of themselves, although not much has been documented and prattled about as in the cases of Schoolboys' competitions. Female athletic competitions had always been held side by side with the men's competitions. The names that readily come to mind regarding those early days of athletics include Clarice Ahanotu, Amelia Okoli, and Esther Ogbeni. The latter was the sprints champion. Emelia Edet was an all-rounder in track and field events; Jumoke Bodunrin and Ronke Akindele were both strong and powerful sprinters. Violet Odogwu also eminently fitted into the pioneering group. Other sprinters of note were Shade Payne, O. Onuwachekwa, Ufon Ukwo, Titi Adeleke, Titi Ogunde, Calister Ubah, Esther Emodi, and Gloria Ayanlaja. These female athletes laid the foundation and established the commendable tradition that blossomed into a harvest of medals at the Commonwealth Games and the All-African Games from the 1970s forward. My female athletes made me proud as they sprinted as gracefully as gazelles to win the bronze medals that dangled on their necks on the dais at the Barcelona Olympics.

It must be said that before the introduction and predominance of these global, Commonwealth and pan-African games, my sister nation, the then Gold Coast, now Ghana, was my keen rival in a variety of sporting competitions, particularly athletics, soccer, lawn tennis, table tennis, boxing and cricket. These were not competed for in single games as they are now. Such competitions were held separately at different times of the year. For example, if athletics took place within my soil last year, it would take place in Ghana this year. If Ghana hosted my soccer team this year, then I would play host to her soccer team next year. The same alternate interchange of dates and venues pertained in the other games with Ghana over the years. After a few years, Sierra Leone, Cameroun, and Gambia joined in the competitions, and the concept of true West African championships began to emerge.

SOCCER

My greatest pastime is soccer. The beautiful leather game is played and watched with passion by devoted and loyal enthusiasts and fans right across my cities, towns, and villages. It is the game that always makes my citizens exude patriotic fervour and unity in ecstasy. Soccer's language can be said to be my *lingua franca*, cutting across the barriers of tribalism, ethnicism, dialects, and religions. The all-consuming interest lavished on soccer is such that other sporting bodies under the controlling umbrella of the National Sports Commission (N.S.C.), or the Federal Ministry of Youths and Sports, are green with envy. They are never short of complaints of neglect and under-funding when compared with the fawning and over-pampering attention that is indulgently lavished on the game of soccer and the Nigeria Football Association (N.F.A.), which controlled the affairs of soccer.

From the halcyon days of Clubs' soccer in Lagos and other teams from cities and towns within my hinterland through the days of the exploits of the raw talents like Isaac Akioye, Olisa Chukwura, Isaku Shittu, John Dankaro, and Etim

Henshaw who travelled to play football (soccer) with bare feet in London as "U. K. Tourists" in 1949, to the annual Challenge Cup series, soccer has come a long way. First, the competition was called Governor's Cup. Then it became the Challenge Cup and was later renamed Football Association (FA) Cup. The same clubs which competed for the League series also competed against one another, first on zonal round robins and then on knock out basis in the final competitions. Town teams of yesteryears yielded to clubs. For that reason the old Ibadan Lions or Western Rovers were known at various times as WNDC or IICC or 3 sc. The old Kano team has resurfaced as Kano Pillars, and the old Kaduna team has resurrected as the Ranchers Bees of Kaduna. The fabled Jos team became Mighty Jets, and latterly Plateau Uni ted.

The inauguration of the Thermogine Football Cup competitions between the secondary schools in my old Western Region, and its counterparts—the Manuwa Cup and the Adebajo Cup, contests between secondary schools in Lagos—led to the formation of the Junior Academicals team, which consisted of the best footballers in these secondary schools. The Junior Academicals were to metamorphose into the Flying Eagles. As usual, Ghana, my "old friendly foe," offered exciting annual stiff competitions to both my senior National team (then known as the Red Devils) and the Junior Academicals, respectively.

Both of our National teams at the senior level met on 43 previous encounters between 1951 and the twilight of the twentieth century. The annual International Soccer tournaments were variously known by such names as Jalco Cup, Nkrumah Cup, Azikiwe Cup, and Lagos or Accra Festival Cup. Later on, we both raised our encounters to much higher levels through our involvements in the Olympics, African Nations, and World Cup elimination series. It should be emphasized that all the encounters at that time, were at the amateur level. Then I began to reach out and play against some other countries in Africa. That was after a British amateur football team "returned" the earlier visit of my 1949 "U. K. Tourists". They came in the 1950s to demonstrate their superior skills. They were quickly followed by two other professional club sides, Sheffield Wednesday and Blackpool United from England, towards the end of that decade.

The importance and relevance of modern football coaching attracted the interest of my football administrators. Hence, the introduction of foreign coaches started with the consecutive arrivals of Leslie Courtier, Jorge Penna, Otto Gloria,

Father Tiko, Alan Hawkes, Manfred Hoener, Clemens Westerhof, non-starter Carlos Albertos (who came and quickly left without reaching an agreement with my NFA), Bonfrere Jo, and Phillip Troussau. They all came one after the other, except for Bonfrere Jo, who was coach under Clemence Westerhof before he took over as chief coach. Some of my own home-based coaches also did their best under the circumstances in which they were given poorer remunerations, fewer incentives and less attractive conditions of service, compared with the facilities and remunerations accorded their foreign counterparts.

Coaches Sebastian Imasuen, Broderick 'Sabara,' and Fanny Amun gave creditable and encouraging performances when they coached my junior age-grade teams. The former coached and managed my under-16 World Cup team, the Golden Eaglets, which became the 1st football squad from Africa to win a FIFA-Organized tournament. That was the inaugural FIFA Cadet World Cup in China in 1985. Subsequent under-16 teams won the silver medal in Canada in 1987. Fanny Amun brought out the best from my well blended and polished under-20 team, which displayed terrific skill and promising talent in beating their Ghanaian opponents at the 1993 World Cup finals in Tokyo.

Fanny claimed to have "wobbled and fumbled" with my team on the way to winning a bronze medal in the African series, which formed the preliminaries to the ill-fated World Youth Cup "Nigeria '95," which never took place. This was because I had lost my hosting rights to Qatar, by courtesy of the Federation of International Football Association (FIFA). Coaches Hamilton, Udemezue, and Tunde Disu showed that they could stand on their own in modern coaching. They achieved good results in Moscow and Saudi Arabia where my under-20-years players, the "Flying Eagles," won the bronze and silver medals respectively.

The best outing and results I anticipated and never received was in Chile when an all-star team under Udemezue were summarily eliminated in the first round. Festus Onigbinde is a highly rated technical advisor and an accomplished coach who had also led my senior team, known as the "Super Eagles," to achieve Silver medal at the African Cup of Nations in Ivory Coast. Onigbinde has consistently and justifiably espoused the idea of employing indigenous coaches for the Super Eagles. FIFA recognized his potential by appointing him as a technical expert.

Chukwu has the enviable record of initially being the captain and later the coach of the Super Eagles. He was an accomplished tactician as the team captain, where he presided over "playing affairs" as "the Chairman," as he was fondly dubbed by the Press and his teammates. His dribbling runs and fierce 'banana' shots proved him as masterful and commanding. As a coach, he is a silent and skillful achiever. His "follow-the-leader" attitude towards the domineering Clemens Westerhof, before and during the 1994 World Cup series, spelt his doom as he was discarded for tamely "lapping orders" from Westerhof.

Ahmadu Shuaibu took over from Westerhof. The mediocre performances of the Super Eagles in Riyad in 1995 and the U. S. Gold Cup in 1995 would seem to have made the hiring of Brazilian Carlos Albertos as the technical adviser justifiable. The latter dithered and prevaricated over wages and was later dropped for the importunate Bonfrere Jo, who first spurned the offer but later chased it from Mali to Ecuador when the Minister, Jim Nwobodo, accompanied the Eagles to the African finals and then the world finals before Jo finally achieved the job. He had served his tutelage under Westerhof.

Nduka Ugbade as the captain tearfully clutched and kissed the World Cup at the maiden session of under-16 age-grade competitions in Beijing in 1985. That was when I sent out, loud and clear, the unmistakable signal to the World that I was ready to stake my claims on global tribute in soccer. My young lads played scintillating and exciting soccer to the delight of the whole world. Since then I have never looked back. I have now won twice, at the World Cup finals of under-17 and under-20 age grade soccer, the second time, as I earlier mentioned, being at Tokyo in 1993, under the bold and exciting captaincy of Wilson Oruma, who led the likes of Ojigwe, Kanu, and the Babayaro brothers. It is on record that Ugbade was involved in all the categories of age-grade World Cup finals right into the preliminaries of the senior edition of the U.S.A. 1994 World Cup. I won the second place silver medal in Canada. I lost narrowly to the eventual winner, Saudi Arabia, at the quarterfinal stages in Edinburgh. My under-20 age players have appeared in almost all the final stages since the inception of the competition in Tunisia in 1977. It was at the 1979 edition in Tokyo that the stocky, barrel-chested Diego Maradona made his spectacular debut. Unfortunately, my flying Eagles did not qualify for the Tokyo series.

It is my greatest pleasure and an unending source of happy reminiscences to mention the exploits of my under-20 team that came from behind at 0–4 to beat Russia in the "miracle of Daman" in Saudi Arabia 1989, when Tunde Disu was coach. It was a magnificent feat that saw the team go on to win its silver medal against Portugal in the final match. The miracle of Daman was the match in which the much-admired and celebrated 'left footer,' Christopher Ohenhen, scored twice with brilliantly taken free kicks from about 35 meters away from the goal posts. It was a magic moment in my soccer history.

There were a series of attempts resulting in non-qualifications, failures, and near-misses, including an "own goal" by Odinye when the team played against Tunisia on my own home ground in a decisive World Cup elimination series. But my ambition to fly my 'green-white-green' flag, at the quadrennial Global Fiesta finally came to fruition in Algiers in 1993. It was a cliffhanger of a match. My team, then known as the Green Eagles, needed a win or at least a draw to qualify. The Algerian team, called the Desert Warriors, who were playing at home in a virtually empty stadium and on a cold and dreary night, played only to protect their pride and national dignity. They had been eliminated earlier on, in the preceding round-robin matches against Ivory Coast at Abidjan and against my Green Eagles 4–1 at the National stadium in Lagos. What was an appearance of mere formality to Algeria was of great importance to me. My Green Eagles scored a goal in the first half through the stylish and fleet-footed Finidi George. The Desert Warriors were able to force a 1–1 draw at the final whistle.

That was how my Green Eagles secured a place for the first time ever at the World Cup finals. To participate at the World Cup finals has always been my dream and my target. My footballers went to the World Cup finals in Los Angeles in 1994 and put up a superlative display in their first appearance. It was a glorious debut. The Green Eagles turned out to be a revelation of the emerging African artistry, which presaged the colour and brilliance that African players would bring into the game in the new millennium.

First, they beat Bulgaria by a wide margin of 3–0. The same Bulgarian team was to reach the semi-finals of the series. In the next match, the Green Eagles lost by a score of 1–2 to the doped trickery of Diego Maradona, who led his Argentine National side. The Argentine forwards took a dive at the slightest contact with my Green Eagles. They quickly earned their goals through deftly taken free kicks when my inexperienced and bewildered players were still busy protesting to the referee while at the same time arranging their defense wall. It would be instructive to recall that the ace Argentine player, Maradona, was banned for 18 months by FIFA, the World Soccer ruling body, from playing in any of its organized matches. This was because he had tested positive for a banned performance-enhancing drug, which was evident in the match against my Super Eagles. A mere look at him on television as he sauntered into the pitch, flicking his head this way and that like a red-headed lizard, would convince any viewer that he was "under the influence" of certain unnatural motivators.

Greece was the next to taste defeat at the hands of the Green Eagles by 2 un-replied goals. Thereafter, my soccer heroes fell to the vastly superior and more experienced Italians. This showed forth when they frittered away a 1–0 lead, which they had enjoyed up to the 88th minute of play. Roberto Baggio, the European and World Player of the Year, dug deep into his repertoire of deft moves and accurate positioning, to not only score the equalizer, but gaining the subsequent penalty kick earned by the Italian side in the extra time of play. Again, the penalty kick awarded against my National Side was owing to the team's inexperience and loss of concentration when it mattered most. Sadly, my players became rather jittery and disoriented. It was remarkable that Italy went on to play Brazil in the finals and lost on penalty kicks after the regulation extra time.

Even though they did not reach the 'knock-out' stages of the final 8, my Green Eagles were voted as the second most thrilling team of the World tournament. Indeed, the Chinese Press adjudged "Jay Jay" Okocha, as the most skillful player, and the team basked in the sunshine that made it glow as it was ranked as number 5 of the 10 best teams in the world. The goalkeeper, Peter Rufai, also known as 'Dodo Mayana,' was a magnificent goalkeeper. In the absence of skipper Stephen Keshi, who was more on the reserve bench owing to injury, Rufai wore the skipper's armband. The defense was ably manned by the towering, indomitable Uche Okechukwu, robust and hard-tackling Eguavoen, stocky and durable Chidi Nwanu, bubbly and occasional-goal-making Ben Iroha, enterprising Emenalo, reliable Okafor. and skillful Friday Elaho. Together, they formed the backbone of a well-blended team that could take on any opposition throughout the world.

The team's mid-field players were impressive and spectacular. These included Oliseh, confident and reassuring with his pin-point accurate passes; the master dribbler and ball-juggling "Jay Jay" Okocha; the swashbuckling and fleet-footed Amokachie, who would cover with industrious aggression every blade of grass on the field of play, and Mutiu Adepoju, fabulous header of the ball, for which he was dubbed 'headmaster' by the radio football commentators. Up front, the team included the African Footballer of 1994, Emmanuel Amunike. He was speedy, and he packed ferocious shots in his left foot. His spectacular diving headers earned him kudos in both Tunisia and the U. S. A. in 1994.

The attacking line included Finidi George, whose dribbling runs down the right flank were entertaining and mesmerizing; Samson Siasia, who usually celebrated his goals by doing the dog's "walk and pee" crawling dance, just as Amokachie would do the hip-hop dance to the rapper's tune in ecstatic celebrations after dribbling the goalkeeper to score against Bulgaria. Last, but definitely not the least, is 'gangling' Rasheed Yekini ,who scored my first goal ever in a World Cup match and dramatically celebrated by using his clenched fists and pounding the opponents' goal net. He was literally announcing my arrival and the arrival of Africa as an emerging soccer force to be reckoned with.

It must be mentioned at this juncture that in appreciation and acknowledgement of the fantastic and "super" outing of my Green Eagles at their debut at the Los Angeles World Cup that they were met and greeted with jubilation and nationwide adulation. Out of sheer ecstasy and the general euphoric atmosphere that enveloped the team on arrival, accolades and felicitations were showered on the players and their handlers. The most memorable and enduring of all the celebrations of excellence was the new name bestowed on the team by Augustus Aikhomu, the former Military Vice President. He proclaimed that the team and indeed, the players, should thenceforth be known as the "Super Eagles," in recognition and appreciation of their superlative performances in Los Angeles. The name still sticks like glue to my National Team. It is apparent that it has come to stay.

I feel fulfilled for at last making my debut at the World Cup finals. It was a mission accomplished and a dream realized. The labours and exploits of my past football heroes of a bygone era now flit through my mind's eye. Hence, I will roll back the years and play back, with sweet reminiscences, the reels of these fabulous performances. The top-billed football stars will be the old fantastic footballers with flair and style, with speed and grace, with skill, elegance, and artistry. There was dynamism in their fierce shots, purposefulness in their headers, and sheer mesmerism in their dribbling. I will now attempt to lead a guided tour down memory lane, which culminated in my team's debut at the Los Angeles World Cup in 1994. Indeed, I have thereafter repeated my forays into other subsequent World Cup finals in France 1998 and the Japan/South Korea series in 2002.

I recall as if it were only yesterday the fierceness of the searing volleys, which were reputedly capable of literally "drilling" holes in the nets when delivered from the awesome legs of Skipper Etim Henshaw. I enthuse over the exploits of the great dribblers Friday Okoh and Onyeador, and I marvel at the devastating and accurate shots of "Golden Toe," Titus Okere. These were household names on all lips. They had a faithful band of fans and a followership that would journey from near and far to the Onikan Stadium in Lagos to watch these stars play.

The one that shone like a thousand stars was the inimitable maestro and tactician, Teslim Balogun, popularly known as "Thunderbolt". He had what it takes to be a complete and consummate footballer: He packed lethal power in both legs and headed the ball with unerring and uncanny accuracy to any angle of the goalposts or any targeted spot or well placed teammate. He always played in a manner to encourage his teammates, as well as remind his adoring fans that a match was not over until the referee's final whistle. He gave every match his total commitment. His body language was enough to send any defending opponent the wrong way. He was sheer poetry in motion. Balogun went abroad to parade his skills with the Peterborough Clubside in England and still came back home to play and convey his soccer wizardry, first as a player and later as a coach, to the senior teams and to the youths in Ibadan. An appreciative and adoring Lagos State government has immortalized his name by erecting a stadium complex at Surulere, named Teslim Balogun Stadium after their "home boy." A statue depicting his graceful and elegant dribbling poise also stands in front of the stadium.

It is only appropriate to deal with the role of the goalkeeper in isolation from the other players. This is because of their particularly important area of specialty in the game. The end result of any game depends on the number of goals conceded and the probable ones prevented by the goalkeepers. A good goalkeeper must have the agility of a cat and an automatic spontaneous reflex. I have been blessed with the performances of goalkeepers cast in this mold. Sam 'the Cat' Ibiam from Onitsha and Akioye from Ibadan were the goalkeepers of the "U.K. Tourists" of 1949. They later became known as the Red Devils. They dived with agility and parried shots with fabulous reflexes. Sam Ibiam kept goal for Onitsha and for my National team for many years.

Fair-complexioned "Gentleman" Carl O'dwyer was tall, handsome, and endowed with sharp reflexes and graceful movements within the posts. He was the goalkeeper of UAC Club in Lagos and performed a similar role in my national colours for many years. Unfortunately, he once had the misfortune of picking the ball repeatedly from inside his net, after conceding seven embarrassing goals to a Ghana team that had been goaded and motivated by a pervading spirit of nationalism and the propelling incentives showered on the players by the incomparable 'Osagyefo' Nkrumah, the Ghanaian Head of State.

One after the other, the goalkeepers appeared on my football scene and manned the goalposts. They dived, parried, punched, and caught the balls in manning the goalposts of my National side and their club sides. They caught fierce shots, successfully secured the goalposts, and dictated the tempo of the game with their well-aimed long kicks. The other goalkeepers of those days that quickly come to mind included Hart, Jaji, Olu Onagoruwa, Gasper, Andeh, Elumelu, Pedro, the Policeman Omiunu, Lateef Gomez, Rigogo, Ezekwe, Tunde Alatishe, and Joe Erico They were stalwarts in the art of goalkeeping, and they all performed well in their primes and always.

A new era of goalkeeping dawned in the last two decades of the twentieth century when the game began to assume highly technical standards. Gone was the "kick-and-follow" system, in which the attacking forwards waited for the long kicks of the goalkeepers, lurking within the periphery of the opponents' goal area. This ancient balloon of tricks has been punctured and deflated by the organized offside rules and tactics, which made nonsense of hastily cleared long kicks that allowed opponents to settle down. Goalkeepers now aid the build-up of attacks and moves with their throws and from dead-ball situations.

The advent of advanced coaching has corrected and ameliorated the system. A smart modern-day goalkeeper can initiate the intelligent build-up of attacks. He would either throw the ball accurately to a well positioned teammate or play a short kick to a player to initiate an attack. Everyone is positioned to be involved in the movement towards the opponents' goal area, making use of spaces with foraging attacks and ensuring that the defense is intact. The old clichés of "let us meet or find me within the opponents' 'Eighteen'" (goal area) has given way to "let's find or jink our way into the opponents' 'Eighteen'". The "shadow" is still very effective as a defense technique, when a known skillful and slippery attacking opponent is constantly shadowed and 'policed' by his opposite defensive number, who would stick to his quarry like a leech.

Goalkeepers who benefitted immensely under the new technical system included Lateef Gomez, Inua Rigogo, Joe Erico (popularly called 'Jongo Bonito', 'Giant cat' Emmanuel Okalla, Best Ogedegbe, and the younger Patrick Okalla. The giant size of Emmanuel Okalla was so intimidating as to affect the psyche and composure of an attacking forward approaching his goal area. His name and his goalkeeping prowess preceded him to any tournament venue, making him a household name in other African countries.

Peter 'Dodo Mayana' Rufai is also of the same genre as Emmanuel Okalla as a tall and lanky goalkeeping "cat". Peter Rufai was reputed to have stopped many penalty kicks against him especially when it mattered most. Two examples are the critical kick he stopped against the Algerian team in Maroc 1988 and the other one against Ivory Coast in Tunis 1994. They were both spectacular and decisive. Best Ogedegbe and Peter Fregene gave very good performances in their primes, even though they were shorter and stockier than the other two. The other goalkeepers of the new era included Aloysius Agwu, Agbonsivare, Peterside Ida, Ike Sorounmu, and Emmanuel Babayaro. Willy Opara had to cross over to a South African club side to sharpen his reflexes and regain his verve and composure after his dreadful performance in the Chile Junior World Cup.

Dejo Fayemi, the ebony black left footer with the sizzling left-foot shots was a regular member of my National team in the late 1950s to the 1960s. He was based in Ibadan, where he played with fabulous and skillful teammates in the team that comprised the fleet-footed right winger, Daniel Okwudili;

the blistering blockbuster Asuquo Ekpe, whose fierce shots were known to have actually broken or collapsed some goalposts when they were still being made from wooden planks or bamboo poles in some towns; Ayo Adeniji, the irrepressible and powerful 'Centre Half' who carried his dependability in defense to my National team of his day; "Wosan" Jide Johnson; and the one they loved to call "Kundi," who baffled opponents with his bounce and mobility. These football stars established in Ibadan a football playing style and tradition of great flair and mobility, which inspired other soccer greats like Gbadebo Falayi, "Josy Lad" Ladipo, Niyi Omowon, Niyi Akande, and the sensational left winger of the Green Eagles, Felix Owolabi, "Owo Blow."

But the greatest of them all from the famous Ibadan breed of footballers is the effervescent and superbly talented "Mathematical" Segun Odegbami. He possessed all the greatest attributes of a complete footballer. He had the speed and agility that facilitated his dribbling wizardry. He could disorganise and unsettle any defense formation with his dazzling speed, 'mathematically' accurate passes, and precision headers. His brawny yet elegant displays on the field of play yielded place to the brainy brilliance he was later to bring into play with his articulate and knowledgeable comments on television and as a sports analyst in the print and electronic media. Odegbami stepped up his talents to loftier heights by founding the International (Sports) Academy at his native Wasimi Orile in Ogun State. The Academy would also produce footballing talents that would register my National side in the annals of soccer greats of the world.

The Ibadan stable also produced Mutiu Adepoju, who was a young and brilliant mid-fielder who could cause havoc with his headers within 'the Eighteen.' He was also adept at releasing surprise shots anywhere around the periphery of the opponents' goal. Kunle Awesu brought comic relief into soccer when a frivolous and almost cynical smile seemed to play on his face as he dribbled an opponent. Then he would stylishly aim at goal or deftly release an accurate pass to a waiting teammate to 'deliver' a cheeky goal inside the opponents' net.

The football-playing gems that glittered from Ibadan have, in the highly talented Rasheed Yekini, a golden player worth his weight in gold. He could unleash the most ferocious of shots from the most impossible of angles to score the most exciting of goals. He moved variously from I.I.C.C. Ibadan to Abiola Babes in Abeokuta, Africa Sports in Ivory Coast, Vitoria Setubal in Portugal,

Olympiacos of Greece, and Gibbon of Spain. He left behind a record number of goals scored per season. He capped it all with the highest number of goals in the qualifying rounds on the way to my memorable debut at the World Cup in Los Angeles in 1994.

If the old Race Course (which is now completely taken over by the Tafawa Balewa Complex) was the hub of athletic competitions in those days, then the Onikan Stadium was the overwhelmingly popular rendezvous and Mecca of soccer. It hosted all my international matches, the Challenge or F.A. Cup finals, and the local league matches. Essentially, it was at the same Onikan Stadium in Lagos that all the great players of those days performed to the admiration of loyal and appreciative fans. From the earliest days of soccer, leading to the historical trip of the "1949 U.K. Tourists," Lagos was the showcase center of my soccer artistry.

Some great names flit through the mind as one again recalls with relish the exploits of fantastic players like 'one-way' Alabi Ntephe, who was so effective with his left foot as he hardly used his right; Bode 'Pan Lawal; the solid "back player" (Alayo eyin) Idi Omofeye, in whose memory a Yoruba song of that title was recorded; Peter 'Baby' Anieke; The Okoroji brothers; Dan Mazeli; dependable and very popular Baba Shittu; the Dankaro brothers; "world two" Tony Igwe, who was a combative and dependable stopper in defense; Sylvester Ogbomo; Victor Odua; Josiah Dombraye; Aloysius Atuegbu; Godwin Odinye; Sam Ojebode; Garuba Okoye; "Wonder" B. Hamilton; and Yakubu Mambo. These were some of the household names of accomplished and popular players that drew crowds of supporters and ardent lovers of soccer to the famous Onikan stadium.

One cannot forget the sheer delight and pleasure that radiated around these great football aces, particularly when they were on national assignments at the Onikan Stadium. It has also occurred to me that I would not only be unfair but would be doing a great injustice to the fragrant memories of my players who have died and would be committing grave and avoidable error of omission and spite on the ones that are still alive if I do not specially mention their names and some of the roles they played.

With a feeling of nostalgia, I continue to recall the dignified carriage of the "Master Dribbler" Albert Onyeawuna and the smart play of Onyeali and Uwalaka;

the immaculate and accomplished skipper Dan Anyiam, the dribbling wizardry of Friday Okoh, and the diminutive but fleet-footed and mesmerizing Cyril Aso-luka, who operated with distinction from the right flank; speedy Godwin Ironkwe, who earned his middle name appellation of 'Opel, as his speed was likened to that of a German car of that nsme; the dependable 'Rock of Gibraltar,' knock-kneed captain Duru, whose specialty was the sliding tackle; and the un-stoppable Noquapor, whom the great Nkrumah labelled as the "dangerous number 11" during one of his spectacular performances displayed before Nkrumah and the Ghanaian spectators at the Accra Stadium.

Another generation of great players in Lagos, included the fantastic trio of crowd pullers from the old E.C.N, Nnamoko, Oyiih, and Amakachi; Stationery Stores Ajagun and "Taylor" Haruna Ilerika both of who were the previous sensa-tional school-boy-footballers from the Zumrhatu secondary school in Lagos. They would dribble and run rings round their opponents, leaving them flat-footed with made-to-measure passes to waiting teammates, who would almost inevitably capitalise on them with such passes that had "G-O-A-L" figuratively written all over the ball.

Arguably one of my earliest and finest football exports and superb mid-field expert was Sylvanus Okpalla, who gave Mathias Obianaka many fine opportuni-ties to shine in the Rangers International attack. Johnny Egbuonu was another schoolboy sensation who dribbled his way to stardom and into the hearts of the well entertained Onikan Stadium football enthusiasts through the 'Academicals,' Rangers International Team, and later into my National team.

Thompson Usiyen was a playmaker any day. He could be relied on to pump in the goals when it mattered most. He had the balance and poise of a troupe dancer or a circus trapeze walker. Ehilegbu could, on a good day, which was al-most always, break through any tight defense to score the type of goal he scored against Ghana in Ivory Coast. Adoki Amasiemeka was most appropriately called "Chief Justice," not only because he was a football-playing lawyer who later be-came the Attorney General of his state, but also because he played with great authority, flair, and finality in his dribbling runs from the flanks before releasing telegraphic dispatch of passes that found the waiting heads of "deadly finishers" like Segun Odegbami's or Thompson Usiyen's to score great goals.

Bright Omokaro, Andrew Uwe, and Sunny Eboigbe were great defenders who played brilliant soccer at the highest levels of the game. A great comic relief was historically enacted on the field of play during Maroc 1989. It involved the surreptitious retaliatory exploits of the hard and robust tackler, Bright Omokaro. The Green Eagles had been reduced to 10 in number owing to the earlier expulsion of Bamidele via a red card. The ferocious but cleverly executed tackle by Omokaro got an Algerian player carried out on a stretcher. This brutal gimmick earned him the gratuitous nickname of "10-10", for helping his side to achieve a measure of parity in terms of the number of players present on the field of play by each team.

Two great players of blessed memory, whose names will remain indelible in the annals of football history and in the minds of my adoring and ardent football lovers, are Samuel Okwuaraji and Muda Lawal. The similarities of grace, style, combativeness, consistency, and athleticism between the two were as remarkable and conspicuous when they were alive and playing as they turned out to be in death. The only glaring difference in their physical outlook was that Okwuaraji wore dreadlocks. The two of them were reliable and accomplished mid-field players, spraying passes to well positioned attackers and falling back to assist beleaguered defenders. They scored great goals with either foot and were always lion-hearted in any daunting situation. Okwuaraji's first goal against Cameroun at Maroc1989 was a cannon left footer, unleashed in the third minute of play from the right flank, even though he operated more on the left. It was the fastest goal of the series and it completely disoriented the jittery Camerounian goalkeeper.

Okwuaraji's calculated moves, deft touches, and precise passes were his greatest assets. He was a fervent patriot who displayed admirable and selfless zeal by paying his own fares from Italy to get involved in preparations for international assignments in Lagos. He actually died on the field of play at the National Stadium in Surulere, when he slumped during an international encounter with Angola in 1989. A beautiful statue of Okwuaraji in national colours and in his characteristic gait graces the front of the National stadium at Surulere, Lagos. The statue evokes fond memories of a patriotic footballer who virtually laid down his life in the service of his grateful fatherland.

Muda Lawal could be described as a tireless workhorse on the field of play. He gave every match his all. He relished being involved in the thick of things on the field. He generally performed as a roving "trouble shooter" to nip looming problems in the bud and calm frayed nerves or tension by his decisive interventions. He became the first player in Africa to make a record five appearances in five different 'Cup of Nations' finals. He quit football in a blaze of glory and felicitations, when he was honoured with a befitting Testimonial Match. He did not turn his back completely in an outright fashion on football, as he became the I.I.C.C. coach in Ibadan. He was getting ready to attend an evening practice when he slumped and died in his house. A stadium complex has been named after him in Abeokuta, his place of birth.

Henry Nwosu played his way into soccer prominence from the age of 16, like the legendry Pele of Brazil, who appeared in his first World Cup finals against Sweden at a similar tender age. Though small in stature, Nwosu has a repertoire of soccer skills and tricks, which he always employed to befuddle opponents. He received my M.O.N. (Member of the Order of Nigeria) award in recognition of the performances of the Green Eagles that won the African Nations Cup in 1980, of which he was an outstanding member.

Stephen Keshi was a strong and resilient player who did me proud as the skipper of the National team for more than a decade. He combined intelligent soccer artistry with his "Generalissimo" duties as 'Skippo,' as his teammates and fans loved to call him. But because of his ability to read a game, mobilize, motivate, and generally inspire his teammates, he was endearingly referred to as "the Boss" by all and sundry. I recall that Keshi burst into tears of joy in the stadium in faraway Algiers when the final whistle was blown to confirm the qualification of my Green Eagles to participate under his captaincy and play, for the first time ever, in the World Cup finals, in Los Angeles. When his playing days were over, he took up coaching and eventually became the football coach of the Togolese team. He successfully coached the Togolese team to qualify for their first-ever World Cup finals in Germany 2006. Friday Ekpo showed some brilliance and panache in his soccer play, even though the irascible but great achiever, technical advisor Westerhof, who consistently refused to accord him a place in the scheme of things, often somehow misunderstood him.

It would be worthwhile to revisit the golden era of 'chairman' Chukwu, which dawned in the mid 1970s. That was when, like the phoenix, the Rangers International team of Enugu rose from the ashes of their Civil War to cart away the FA cup. This triggered the saga of a long, incessant, and fierce rivalry between the all-conquering Enugu Rangers and the fabulous I.I.C.C. of Ibadan. The two clubs carried their competitive zeal and rivalry into international competitions. Each of them won, one after the other, the much-coveted Continental Cup Winners Cup, renamed the Mandela Cup. The B.C.C. Lions of Gboko also won the Mandela Cup. This laudable feat was achieved under the inspirational guidance of coach Amadu Shuaib, who eventually emerged as the coach of my Super Eagles.

Other teams that proved their mettle at local and international levels included Iwuanyawu Internationale of Owerri, Bendel Insurance of Benin, and the vastly popular and very successful Eyinmba of Aba. Another great club that packed the stadiums wherever they played was the Stationery Stores of Lagos. The club was popularly known as Adebajo Babes in honour of the late industrious and enterprising founder, Israel Adebajo. It was also known as the Flaming Flamingos by the colour and logo of their jerseys.

I can now boast of two World Cup titles won by my Golden Eaglets. Silver and bronze medals have been won by my Flying Eagles in two World Cup outings. Three appearances at the World cup finals by my Super Eagles have adequately established my credentials as a formidable force in football. The icing on my cake is the consistently overwhelming superiority of my Ladies National team, the Falcons, in Africa. Both the Falcons and the Falconets have won virtually all their matches in Africa. In particular, the Falcons have represented me twice at the global level at the Female World Cup finals.

The only thing that bothers me now is the level or lack of awareness among the youths about my local league and local players. As my players flocked overseas, particularly to England and Europe, generally in search of greener pastures, so went the interest and attention of my youthful soccer fans, enthusiasts, and followers. Whereas they could reel out facts and figures relating to the players in the English Premier League, the Italian Seria A, the Spanish Primera La Liga, and the German Bundesliga, they could hardly recall the names of the local players and the names of the various clubs in my Nigerian Football League.

They glibly proclaim their membership of clubs like Arsenal, Manchester United, Chelsea, Real Madrid, Barcelona, and A C Milan.

The situation calls for a vibrant and dynamic NFA that could rekindle interest in football from the grassroot level and especially at the primary and secondary schools. Such an association should be less dependent on government for funding and teleguided administration. FIFA, the World Soccer Ruling Body, has continued to emphasise the non-interference of governments in football administration. Indeed, FIFA has prevailed on my Federal Government to abrogate the obnoxious Decree 101 that underlined its hold and control on soccer administration. Failure to do so may incur dire consequences, which could include my ban or expulsion from the body. Focus should be shifted to private-sector support and financing. Emphasis should also be placed on personnel who are of relevance to football in terms of training and experience.

However, the stage is set for me to showcase my tremendous potentials and the ability to stake my claims as one of the top 10 football nations in the world. It is only a matter of time, and my teams will attract world attention. At that point, I had made three appearances at the World Cup finals, including my significant and signal debut at Los Angeles in 1994; I had then won the African Cup of Nations twice since its inception; I have been a runner up on about three occasions and have also consistently attained the semifinal stages of almost all the African Cup of Nations series in which I participated its inception. Blessed with an array of talents with great potential and capable coaches, egged on by the roar of eager stadium spectators, cheering, praising, and blessing them, I know that the sky is the limit for my three categories of Eagles and the promising Falcons and Falconets in the nascent twenty-first century.

BOXING

Boxing gave me my first international exposure and global recognition in sports on th world stage. If the yardstick for measuring success in boxing, the noble art of self-defense, is the number of medals won in the amateur ranks or the number of championship belts won in the professional cadre, then my boxers have eminently acquitted themselves with distinction in boxing rings around the world. Garuba Idi and Ado Garuba climbed into the roped square and displayed their budding pugilistic prowess to win bronze medals at the 1956 Commonwealth Games. This celebrated achievement became the forerunner of great performances and more medals for me in the future. I had served notice on the world at large that young boxers from the largest black nation on earth are ready to showcase their boxing skills and finesse in the sport at any Boxing arena in the world.

My boxing had its birth at the Isale-Eko area of Lagos. The early stars were from that area. It had its roots in the old Royal Hotel, where the old masters like Billy Petrole held sway for years. It was left for William Faulkner, an expatriate Senior Welfare Officer, in collaboration with other expatriates D. J. Collister and Jack Fransworth plus Nap Peregrino of the Brazillian Quarters in Lagos to develop the sport at the amateur level. This brought boxing closer to the attention of the masses. They were thus laying the foundation for both amateur and professional boxing management in my milieu.

Nojim Maiyeguns became my first-ever winner of an Olympic bronze medal at the Tokyo Olympic Games of 1964. He had a brilliant and colourful boxing career in the amateur ranks before joining the professionals. He was popularly known as "Omo Oloja" (trader), probably because of his wide array of punching styles and moves, which dazzled and confused his opponents. When he turned professional, he began to operate from Vienna, where he had many successful encounters before his failing eyesight put a permanent stop to his illustrious career. An appreciative Lagos City Council named a major street after him in Obalende, Lagos.

My medal-winning feat was to be repeated at the Munich Olympic Games of 1972. That was where Isaac Ikhuoria also won a bronze medal. A well built and superbly fit athlete, Ikhuoria extended the benefit of his experience and valued service at the national level, to become a devoted and accomplished boxing coach. He also nurtured and honed the talents of the young boxing enthusiasts who abound in his home State, Bendel, now Edo State. The outcome of his coaching efforts became immediately apparent in the caliber and number of successes of the boxers emerging from that State at various organized boxing contests.

Konyeguachi gave spectacular boxing performances on his way to winning for me a silver medal in the featherweight category at the 1984 Los Angeles

Olympics. He also turned professional and began to fight out of Europe. He gave a very good account of himself in the paid ranks. It is worthy of mention that the American opponent, Meldrick Taylor, to whom he lost after they fought toe-to-toe for three gruelling rounds at the Olympics, later became the Featherweight Boxing Champion of the World. The Los Angeles games also revealed the talents of Jerry Okorodudu and Nwokolo, who narrowly missed achieving medals. The 1992 Olympics in Barcelona gave me satisfaction in the twin joy of superlative display of guts, skill, and patriotic zeal by both Richard Inzorite and Dakwori. They won silver medals in the heavyweight and super heavyweight boxing divisions, respectively.

Davidson Andeh and Jacklord, respectively, won accolades as gold and silver medalists at World Amateur boxing contests. The incomparable Davidson Andeh spectacularly won the lightweight division gold medal at the 1978 World Amateur Boxing Championships in Belgrade despite sustaining a broken finger on his right hand during the semi-final. He went ahead to out-box his Soviet Union opponent, Serik Konakbaev, in the finals. By and large, the exploits of my boxers at the Commonwealth Games and the African Games are really commendable. From light flyweight to heavyweight, they all performed skillfully and laudably, even where they did not win medals. Names that readily come to mind, apart from those great Olympic medalists, include Eddy Ndukwu, Peter Ossai, Joe Orewa, Fatai Ayinla, and Victor Enyika, who won many fights as an amateur bantamweight champion. When the latter turned professional, he soon became a budding contender for World championship until a freakish right hook from a previously unknown challenger stopped him and simultaneously put paid to his career and nearly to his life.

Wherever and whenever boxing is being discussed in my annals of sports, two names stand out like giant "Iroko" trees in the forest. I reached the zenith of world and international acclaim in boxing in 1956, when the legendary Hogan 'Kid' Bassey won the world featherweight title. He was a pint-sized pugilist and muscular bundle of kinetic energy as he unleashed a bewildering flurry of jabs, hooks, and crosses to overpower the hapless Cherif Hermia of France to claim the featherweight boxing championship of the world. It was a sweet and memorable victory, which brought limitless joy and was a source of great pride to my citizens and me. The victory was made the more memorable and very popular because the sports-loving Zik, the sage Awo, M. A. Ogun, and the well-known sports enthusiast J. M. Johnson were all spectators at ringside in Paris. They were on their way back from one of the Constitutional Conferences they had attended in London.

Hogan Bassey had earlier beaten Percy Lewis of Trinidad to win the British Empire and Commonwealth title. It must be said that he wore the boxing diadem with pride, distinction, and admirable dignity. He was a gentleman inside and outside the ring and a household name in Liverpool, his base of operation. He left when the ovation was loudest. He left when the American David Moore started denting his image as he sneaked some dangerous punches in on Bassey, executed fractionally after the bell. My sympathetic citizenry heartily welcomed "King" Bassey as he was offered the post of National Boxing Coach. He left a legacy of a disciplined and carefully guided crop of amateur boxers. By so doing, he had laid a solid foundation for the pugilistic careers of generations of boxers who would continue to win laurels for me at home and at international competitions. He later retired into full-time priestly duties in the church until he died.

Dick Tiger was the other giant "Iroko" tree that towered above all the others. He rose to pugilistic prominence in an era that bestowed on me the distinctive status of a nation that bred world champion boxers. Dick Tiger's given name was Richard Ihetu. He was the perfect embodiment of raw power, chanelled fury, and pugilistic finesse. Having reached the acme of his professional career locally, he took his campaign to England, where he carved a niche for himself after a series of fights. He won the Middleweight Boxing Championship of the British Commonwealth by beating Pat Macateer.

The Liberty Stadium in Ibadan was the venue of the World Middleweight championship return fight between Dick Tiger and Gene Fullmer in 1963. It was a brilliant display of ability in which Dick Tiger recorded a technical knockout of his American opponent in the eighth round. Having beaten all comers in the middleweight division, he aspired for greater glory and greener pastures by moving up to the light heavyweight ranks to carry on his all-conquering campaign. He wrested the title from the hands of Jose Torres of Puerto Rico. However, he succumbed to the superior boxing skills of Bob Foster in 1968. Thereafter, he returned home to pitch his tent with his Biafran kinsmen at the height of the Civil War. His death during this period was gravely mourned by all, friends and "foes" alike.

In the succeeding years, a new generation of boxers made courageous attempts to capture the world titles at various categories: Rafiu 'King' Joe was a very crafty and stylish boxer whose efforts to gain the featherweight title was thwarted by the Mexican boxing sensation called "Little Bird," Pajarito Moreno. Sugar Ray Adigun was a solid puncher who also had the capacity and ability to absorb solid blows from his opponents. This ability to absorb blows was uncharitably referred to as the cause of his flattened nose, which had been repeatedly targeted by his opponents' hard punches.

Obisia Nwakpa was another very good boxer. He had bright prospects of becoming the next featherweight boxing champion of the world until the South American Seoul Mambi beat him right inside the main bowl of my National Stadium at Surulere in a World title fight. In another World Featherweight Championship bout staged in the same venue, one of my great boxers, Dele Jonathan, beat Jim Watts of Scotland in 1975.

I had the pleasure and satisfaction of producing two new world champions when various versions of the boxing controlling bodies like WBA, WBC, and WBO emerged in the late 1980s and 1990s. Bash Ali, a very lively and entertaining boxer who fights on into his 50s was able to capture the WBO version of the world cruiserweight title. Ayanmele won the middleweight title also at the Main Bowl of the National Stadium. The latter lost the title when he was stripped of it, owing to his inability to defend the title within the stipulated period.

Lasisi arrived on the boxing scene and quickly earned the reputation of a deadly puncher. He would hit and so daze his opponents with such ferocious and rapier-like punches that they were soon made to feel dizzy and would begin to "see double." Many people thought that Lasisi "fortified" himself with Juju in order to be able to knock his opponents to a state of stupor. I believe that a well conditioned boxer, with trained and solid punches, will always triumph over his less-skilled opponents. This point was proven and driven home to his gullible fans when Lasisi was virtually turned into a punching bag by the trained and authoritative punches of Virgil Hill, in a lop-sided fight in which the latter nearly beat the daylights out of the once-dreaded Lasisi. He slid into temporary oblivion but emerged in 1995, in search of his glorious past and with a vow to win the world title at the earliest opportunity. But it became an unfulfilled dream as Lasisi slid back into obscurity.

I recall the whirlwind display of Hakim Anifowoshe during a world title bout that nearly turned into a nightmare in the hands of his opponent, called Victor Higuera. One of my former boxers, Anifowoshe, suffered a near-paralysis that cut short his meteoric career and ultimately killed him. 'King' Ipitan based in the USA was fast gaining a reputation as a bright heavyweight prospect as he continued to record victory after victory via the "knock out" route.

Recognition should be accorded to some of the other boxing greats of times past. They packed the boxing arenas from the Glover Memorial Hall in Lagos to Obisesan Hall in Ibadan and such other venues as the latter-day Sports Hall of the National Stadium in Lagos. These boxers included such names as Santos Martins, Sammy Idowu Langford, Jeff Sonny Dudu (who eventually became the Secretary of the Nigeria Boxing Board), Bola Lawal, known in the ring as Lulu Kid, Blackie Power. who later became a pastor as Reverend Ogunbiyi, Teddy Odus, my first boxer to be rated in the Commonwealth, Roy Jacobs, who matured into a popular boxing referee, Hurricane Badmus, Fatai Passo, Lat Darasin, nicknamed "the Apapa Assassin," Salau Gbadegesin, Moses Edeki, and the colourful and durable Lat Shonibare. Some other great boxers, old and new, amateur and professional, are Charles Nwokolo, Jerry Okorodudu, Albert Eromosele, Ike Ibeabuchi, and Henry Akinwande.

It is painful to recall the tragedy that befell the deaf and mute boxer, Love Muka, and Ray Amao. The name of the deaf and mute boxer on a promoter's programme of fights would always guarantee a packed and sold out boxing hall because of his daredevil and never-say-die style and attitude. He had to be literally dragged away from his overwhelmed victim or overwhelming tormentor to let him know that the bell had signaled the end of a round. When his fighting days were over, he became a drug addict and beggar and died later, without assistance from appropriate authorities. Ray Amao died after a successful and active career. He suffered from gangrene of the right foot and nearly had to have the foot amputated.

LAWN TENNIS AND TABLE TENNIS

Lawn tennis and table tennis are two games that are loved and played competitively, at local and international levels, by my sports-loving citizens and sportsmen and women. While some of the older government or mission schools were equipped with standard lawn tennis courts, almost all secondary schools found it much easier to make standard or makeshift tables, and then simply acquire table tennis equipment.

All the major cities have clubhouses, often called "Country Clubs." Almost all these clubhouses have various facilities for exercise and recreation. Invariably, such facilities would include lawn tennis courts and ping-pong tables. As usual in those days, Lagos was the venue of all the competitive aspects of the two games. In those days, again, my old "friendly foe" at the international level was the former Gold Coast, now Ghana. Only recently did I make my hosting debut at highly competitive international level in lawn tennis at the Nicon Noga Hilton (Trancorp) Hotel at Abuja. I also hosted an international table tennis tournament at the Port Harcourt Chokaris Competition. Table tennis acquired a new status, significance, and interest for me when it became a major event at the All-African Games, the Commonwealth Games and, indeed, the Olympic games.

The Lagos Lawn Tennis Association, based at Onikan in Lagos, was the headquarters of competitive lawn tennis. It was from there that my National champions and other qualifiers in the 'Singles' and 'Doubles' emerged. Before advancing competitively into continental tournaments by way of the African Games, certain prominent lawn tennis players had graced the tennis courts with their stylish tennis games. In the 1950s and 1960s, Walter Obianwu was for many years my National lawn tennis champion. In those days, any tournament played against the then Gold Coast (now Ghana) virtually assumed the status of a West African championship event. Hence, the winner of the international contest between my players and those from Gold Coast automatically became the West African champion—at least, in the people's estimation.

Thomas Obi engaged in a long and combative rivalry with Walter Obianwu. The latter gave a good account of himself with his dexterity and graceful movements, particularly in his general court maneuvers. His cross-court shots and powerful forehand drives were a delight to watch. Njoku Obi arrived from the

United States of America where he had been an undergraduate. He played his way to prominence by winning the National Championship title. He had a fierce booming service and was adept at the serve and volley set pieces.

The long and epic struggle for dominance between Thompson Onibokun and Lawrence Awopegba took the center stage after the exploits of Obianwu, Thomas Obi, and Njoku Obi. Such was the rivalry and competitive edge between Onibokun and Awopegba in the 1970s that fans and spectators pitched their tents behind either of the two, depending on what fascinated them in the difference of styles and tactics the players exhibited. Onibokun always came in from his base in Ibadan to display brilliant array of flashy forehand strokes, deceptive backhand cross-court shots. and slashing overhead smashes, which he usually leapt to deliver.

Awopegba, on the other hand, was based in Lagos and was an acclaimed master of the serve-and-volley game. He delivered irretrievable aces at his first services with his muscular right hand. When his services were infrequently returned, they came invariably as high lobs at which Awopegba sprang on his bouncy muscular legs to execute assured volleys. Awopegba's approach to the net was intimidating. He was an enthusiastic competitor who played with verve and grace. Both men intermittently reigned as champions. I like to adjudge with paternal impartiality that Onibokun was a shade better of the two due to his keener competitive edge and the fluidity of his court maneuvers, which was aided by his more lithe athleticism and the ability to answer the aggressive booming services of Awopegba.

Awopegba, Onibokun, and Yemisi Allan played lawn tennis at around the same period. It would therefore be difficult to write a comprehensive history of the game without giving them the prominence they all deserve. Allan had also played his way to the top and creditably wore the champion's mantle until David Imonitie and "The Duke," Nduka Odizor, appeared on the scene. In 1983, Odizor became the first, and hitherto my only player, to attain the "last 16" stage of the prestigious Wimbledon Lawn Tennis tournaments. He proceeded from there to become one of my regular Davis Cup players. He won medals along with David Imonitie at the African Games. Both of them went on to join the international lawn tennis circuit, where they earned fame and fortune for themselves.

Godwin Kienka and Ajayi turned out to be good players who stepped into the shoes of the duo of Odizor and Imonitie. Rotimi Akinloye won several medals at both local and international tournaments. He became a regular member of my Davis Cup team, where he played a very prominent role in my promotion to a high level in the international group competitions. He is also a very good lawn tennis coach and has groomed a crop of young players who will represent me in future competitions. Douglas Ikhide and Adenekan are some of the up-and-coming new players with a lot of promise.

In the female category, Rolake Olagbegi was the most popular player of her time. After her exit, there was a dearth of competent players. Later on, Godwin Kienka discovered and trained Clara Udofia to international preeminence. It is hoped that the Okalla sisters, who are budding young players, will grow up to be worthy international stars.

As it was with lawn tennis, so was it with table tennis in the various stages of development of the game in my sports program. The only difference is the greater mass appeal table tennis has over lawn tennis. The game gives joy and invigorating exercise to players. The general involvement of players defies gender, age, and height. The minimal space the game requires and the easily affordable cost of equipment for the game, are some of the requirements and advantages that make the game popular. It is remarkable that the equipment can be hastily put together in a makeshift fashion. Whereas the basically necessary and requisite items are the standard table and net, ping-pong balls, and bats, all these items except the balls can be improvised from anything similar. Consequently, a fairly large table can pass for the playing table. A wooden bar or a piece of rope or string attached to or placed on two 6-inch-high tin cans would easily serve as a net. A piece of plank or cardboard can be cut into the shape of a bat. This explains why the game is easily affordable and playable in every nook and household of cities, towns, and even villages.

For many years in the history of the game, Chinwuba was my National champion. Later on Demola "Fireman" Alli and the legendary Alagbala played the game of table tennis as the champions. They played with ferociously spun services and flashy smashes that made opponents scurry from side to side, not knowing how, when, and from which angle the next smash would come. They were greatly admired and imitated by younger players. Their footsteps were to be followed by Babatunde Obisanya and Muftau Oduntan. The two of them were great players who then became coaches.

Some of the other great players included Henry Jemoha, the Santos brothers, Solomon Bamgbade, and Kotun. They had all set the fast and furious paces that good players like Lucky Eboh and Atanda Musa were to follow. The keen rivalry between Atanda Musa, popularly called "Mansa" Musa and Yomi Bankole almost became personal and explosive in intensity. Bankole was popularly known as "the Hawk," owing to his histrionics and aggressiveness that at times smacked of bullying and intimidation. His style was, however, made to measure for Atanda Musa. The latter was always as cool as cucumber and his fiercely competitive nature was hidden under a veneer of restrained combativeness and dignified calm.

Fatai Adeyemo, Hassan Hakeem, and Sule Olaleye were some of the players who represented me creditably and won more medals at the All-African Games than players from other countries. The new and promising players are Peter Akinlabi, Aiyemojuba, Merotohun, and Segun Toriola. They have all taken part in some other global competitions including the Commonwealth Games and the Olympics. They are highly ranked as some of the best players in the world.

It is remarkable that as far back as 1961, the performances of my table tennis players were hailed at the world championships held in Peking. They participated in subsequent championships in Prague 1963, Llubane, Yugoslavia, in 1967, Munich 1969, and Nagoya, Japan, in 1971. In the various tournaments, my players gave good accounts of themselves by placing 37th, 18th, and 17th respectively. I hosted the 2nd Asian/African/Latin American Table Tennis Invitational Tournament in 1975. About 70 countries participated, and in attendance were some of the fiercest exponents of the game.

The ladies have also excelled themselves in table tennis, in which the pioneering efforts of Mabel (Imoukhuede) Segun could be seen as formidable and groundbreaking. Lawunmi Majekodunmi was another great player who was for many years my National champion. Kuburat Owolabi, Bose Kaffo, Funke Oshinaike, Bimbo Odumosu, Kehinde Okenla, and 'southpaw' Iyabo Amusu all represented me. Like their male counterparts, they performed brilliantly at various All-African Games and came back loaded with medals on each occasion.

SPORTS ADMINISTRATORS

I have been blessed over the years with the activities and performances of some great men and women who were very diligent and committed sports enthusiasts, administrators, patrons, benefactors, organizers, and promoters. They spent so much of their time, energy, and money in the interest of sports in all its ramifications. It is high time I seized the opportunity to recall and acknowledge their efforts. I wish to pour encomiums on them for the joy they brought to my heart and the pleasure and happiness they brought to sports lovers, sports enthusiasts, and the sportsmen and sportswomen who were the beneficiaries of their laudable efforts.

In trying to enumerate the series of athletic meetings of the earliest days, it would be worthwhile to trace the history of sports competitions of the 1940s and 1950s. As earlier mentioned, the Empire Day Sports Festival, held annually on May 24, was the most popular competition that involved government participation in terms of organization. That was the day in which the colonial governor took the salute in honour of His Majesty, the King of England, at the march past of participating primary schools. Those were the days in which some of the clubs that were fully functional were the Lagos Amateur Athletic Club (LAAC), the Police Athletic Club (PAC), the Zik's Athletic Club (ZAC), and several others, such as the Millers Athletic Club, which had a ready source of recruitment from the youth clubs. These organizers and promoters had to perform as role models by being available to the young sports enthusiasts for instructions and advice about other aspects of life apart from sports. These admirable men fulfilled all these functions with flair and distinction. They were as active within the arena as they were behind the scenes and at boardroom sessions.

Prominent sports personalities from the colonial era definitely deserve to have their names mentioned in these reminiscences. The name of Derby Allen was synonymous with the administration of football in those days. D. J. Collister was widely accepted as "the father of Nigerian Boxing." Jack Fransworth called the shots with authority and panache in boxing. They were all Britons. The incomparable zeal and impartiality in refereeing that the Irish missionary, Father Slattery, displayed on the field of play in football, earned him the sobriquet "Mr. Referee" in my soccer annals.

The dynamic roles of my patriots and sports-lovers should also be high-lighted for posterity. Zik was known to combine his anti-colonialist crusading zeal with an undying love for sports. He was a forefront athletics official and often took on the role of boxing referee. In this latter role he was once known to have uplifted, in Yoruba language, the spirit of a Lagos boxer who had been knocked down by a Ghanaian boxer, urging him to get up and fight. The boxer got up from the canvas to beat the count and then went on to win the fight. Zik's contributions to the development of sports are legendary. He was the first to create an aura of vastness about the existing "Sports Grounds" when he introduced the word "Stadium," which was then alien to my sports vocabulary.

J. K. Randle was a great sports lover who once introduced dog races. He encouraged swimming as a competitive sporting event. He actually led my athletics contingent to the Melbourne Olympics as the Chef de Mission. J. M. Johnson exuded such tremendous interest, enthusiasm, and influence in sports that he reached the zenith of sports administration when he was appointed my first ever Federal Minister of Labour and Sports. Alakija was also very popular in swimming. He was nicknamed "Eja nla" (the big fish). He encouraged and promoted swimming among the youths who adored him.

"S. O." Jolaoso was one of the true pioneers of sports administration in my sports annals. He was there and active when amateurism was enthroned. He had been a fine all-round athlete and had played football for awhile before he distinguished himself with his deft forehand in lawn tennis. He carved a niche for himself as a consummate sports organizer. He started as an official during the Empire Day Sports in Lagos. He soon became a popular sight in his red shirt at all the important athletics competitions for over three decades. He served through this period at the Lagos Annual Senior and Junior Athletics Championships, the Inter-Regional Athletic Competitions, the All-Nigeria Police Athletic Championships, and the Triangular Sports Meetings among the three leading athletics clubs of the day.

"S. O." was a foundation and life member of the Amateur Athletic Association of Nigeria (now AFN). He rose to the position of Chairman in 1957, after serving as the Honorary Secretary and Technical Officer. He was a founding member of the Nigeria Olympic Committee, a Vice President and Chairman of its Games Committee, and a Trustee. He was selected as a memeber of the official delegation to the first Olympic Games in which my athletes participated in Helsinki, Finland, in 1952. He thereafter attended almost every Olympic Games for the next twenty years in Tokyo, Mexico, and Munich as either the General Team Manager or Chef de Mission.

Abraham Ordia deservedly rose to the pinnacle of sports administration in Africa. Because he was one of the leading lights in the crusade against Apartheid, his actual initials of "A. A." soon became the trademark of his "Anti-Apartheid" stance all over Africa. He led several international boycotts against the abhorred apartheid system. Oyok Orok Oyok's name was practically synonymous with the history of my Sports Administration and that of Africa.

One of the notable philanthropists responsible for the development of sports is Molade Okoya-Thomas. Over the last three decades, he has continued to support the development of table tennis with the Asoju Oba Cup, which he named after his chieftaincy title. Tournaments that took place under this Cup title have produced a host of table tennis stars down the years. Okoya-Thomas makes himself available to render services as a member of various committees, at both State and National levels, for the upliftment of sports in one way or the other. His magnificient contribution came to glorious fruition in the completion and launching of the Teslimi Balogun Stadium at Suru-Lere, Lagos. He was a pillar of support for the Lagos State Government in the completion of the project.

Omeruah is a retired Army officer who made his mark in sports administration first as a Minister of Sports and later as an elected Chairman of the NFA. The debonair Air Force officer was known in sports circles as 'the man with the magic wand' because of his excellent performance as an administrator. It was to his credit and directly owing to his undisputable leadership qualities that I won the first FIFA-organized tournament of the Under-17 World Cup, in 1985. It was also during his tenure as the first democratically elected chairman of NFA in 1993 that the Super Eagles performed two outstanding feats: First, the side won for the first time on away ground at Tunisia, the African Cup of Nations in 1994. Then, they went ahead in the same year to perform well at their World Cup debut in Los Angeles, USA. Furthermore, the Eagles also won the Afro–Asia Cup for the first time. The enviable climax of Omeruah's tenure was the victory of my National Under-23 team at the 1996 Atlanta Olympics. That was where and when Africa's first Olympic football gold medal was won.

Fred Okpomu's meteoric rise in sports administration in the 1980s and 1990s made his name a household word in my world of soccer, both at the global level (FIFA) and at the entire African level (CAF). When the powers of the day began 'wasting' his talents, he was appropriately appointed the Advisor on Sports to M. K. O. Abiola. The latter, in his own sports-loving capacity, was known as the "Pillar of Sports in Africa." Other patriots became well known for their philanthropy in sporting ventures. Israel Adebajo founded the very popular Stationery Stores Football Club in Lagos. In doing so, he had bestowed a legacy of good leadership and fervent followership in the administration of football. Lekan Salami was more popular as a football administrator and avid supporter of the game in Ibadan than he was as a politician of note. The stadium located in the Adamasingba area of Ibadan was named after him.

Jerry Ikpeazu, Dankaro, and Baba Ali rendered very useful and noteworthy services to the cause of football. They diligently gave their time and offered useful advice based on their experience in football administration. I pride myself in M. K. O. Abiola as the anointed "Pillar of Sports in Africa." He deployed his vast wealth and *bon homo* attitude to great effectiveness in furthering the cause of soccer. His philanthropy to sports and other worthy causes was legendary. He was an enthusiast, a patriot, and a philanthropist rolled into one. His ebullient personality in the world of sports was celebrated not only among his compatriots but also in other countries in Africa. He founded the Abiola Babes Football Club, which featured in the Premier Division in my League Football.

SPORTS: WAY FORWARD

As a nation, I am poised to stake my claim to preeminence in sports at both the local and international levels. I have already established a reputation for myself as a nation that parades an array of sportsmen and women who have excelled in a variety of competitions and tournaments. I will ensure that I will no longer fail to qualify for the quadrennial World Cup Finals in soccer. I will maintain my regular presence at the African Cup of Nations finals. By securing regular appearances at subsequent Olympics, I will also confirm that my gold medal in soccer at the Olympics in Atlanta in 1996 was not a fluke. I will intensify my interest in the age-grade performances of the "Flying Eagles," the periodic

Olympic "Dream teams," the "Under-17" teams, the "Falcons," and the "Falconets." My true potential will blossom into all-conquering National teams in both male and female soccer.

It has become the vogue for many of my brightest talents, compelled by circumstances and the lure of money, to seek greener pastures in foreign lands. As a matter of fact, some of these bright talents have resorted to offering their services to other countries. Some are known to have lined up behind the flags of Portugal, England, Canada, and the United States of America. They moved to other countries and gave stellar performances for their adopted countries. I bemoan the loss, or concession by default, of medals and cups to the aforementioned countries through the outstanding performances of these (my) sporting talents. Although the phenomenon is observable across all professions, it is particularly obvious in professional sports.

I observe that these sports stars opt out to other lands because they see it as the only way to fulfill their naturally endowed potential. The reasons are not hard to seek. Here within my territory and at great inconvenience, they are often invariably forced to train under conditions that are inimical to progress, development, and attainment of expertise, all of which are available overseas. These conditions are characterized by the almost complete absence of requisite facilities, foreign exposure, equipment, diet, medical attention, and the kind of atmosphere they need to perform and excel. These conditions are also compounded by the lack of adequate administrative guidance, which makes it extremely difficult or near impossible for these promising sport stars to obtain adequate training grants. They are unable to go on vital overseas training tours or even arrive in good time for tournaments. These conditions have to be addressed and quickly redressed in order to arrest the embarrassment of seeing my sons and daughters carrying foreign flags at international tournaments and in distant lands.

I plan to embark on massive talent hunts in major sporting events in order to be able to "catch 'em young" and groom future athletes for the purpose of representing me in future competitions. I will call for, and encourage, private sector involvement in terms of financial sponsorship in various sporting activities. This is to actualise the release of sports and the administration of sports from the apron strings of government and its overzealous and interfering bureaucrats. I will be relying on my sports organizers and administrators to ensure that my dream to excel in all sporting competitions and tournaments should come to fruition. I know that, with such massive population and an abundance of talent, I will always excel in sports generally.

CPSIA information can be obtained at www.ICGtesting.com
Printed in the USA
LVOW03s0702150315

430572LV00001B/1/P